Acclaim for *Colorizing Restorative Justice*

Colorizing Restorative Justice is a much anticipated and mighty act of truth-telling! These stories arise from the lived experiences of a broad range of seasoned, loving restorative justice practitioners of color, mostly women, who fiercely unearth realities about the devastation caused by white practitioners who unthinkingly work without a racial or social justice consciousness. Required reading, *Colorizing* is a wake-up call for European-descended restorative justice practitioners. It is validating for Indigenous practitioners and practitioners of color and enlightening for anyone wishing to explore the intersections of indigeneity, racial justice, and restorative justice.

> — **Fania E. Davis**, African-descended, PhD, JD, author of *The Little Book of Race and Restorative Justice,* founding director of Restorative Justice for Oakland Youth (RJOY), and a leading national voice on the intersection of racial and restorative justice

This book in many ways represents a journey. The journey of the modern RJ movement, now decades old, sadly, as a collective, has for the most part missed, watered down with romanticism, and in many cases intentionally and sometimes unintentionally excluded the voices represented here. It's not that the voices—so profoundly expressed in this collection—were silent over the years. In many cases, they were shouted, then lost in the winds of oppressive patterns normalized. The older voices, still circulating and revolving in the wind and now joined with new ones, are collected here. It is my hope they land on ears willing to hear their wisdom that will enrich and perhaps even transform the RJ journey, even when the wisdom is uncomfortable.

> — **Harley Eagle**, Dakȟóta, Očhéthi Šakówiŋ Oyáte, member of the Wapȟáha Ská (Whitecap) Dakota First Nations Reserve, a consultant in, among other things, anti-racism and trauma-informed practice

In my over forty years as a teacher, researcher, lawyer, and social activist in the United States and Canada, I have read scores of books addressing issues of race and justice. This book stands out amongst all these works. It is unique in its penetrating exploration of the lived experience of people of color involved in restorative justice, coupled with an excellent analysis of the larger colonial structures that perpetrate inequality and racism. Consisting of twenty people of color as contributors, it is a well written and readable, well organized, and thoughtful critique of mainstream restorative philosophy and practice. Unlike many collections by multiple authors, it flows from section to section, providing an excellent analysis of the role of race in restorative justice.

The editor has been masterful in presenting the materials. His introduction provides an extensive overview of each section of the book and its chapters. His lengthy final chapter provides a penetrating structural analysis of the harms settlers have perpetrated and the need to recognize and address these harms by restorative justice.

In sum, this is a must read not only for those in restorative justice, but also for others, like myself, who address issues of race and justice.

— **Charles E. Reasons**, White Settler, PhD, JD, Law and Justice Professor at Central Washington University, author-activist who writes about social and legal problems in the US and Canada

Colorizing Restorative Justice

COVER IMAGE

Buffalo Hide Painting of a Black War Bonnet (1963)
Herman Red Elk, Iháŋkthuŋwaŋna/Očhéthi Šakówiŋ Oyáte*
Sioux Indian Museum
Image courtesy of the U.S. Department of the Interior, Indian Arts and Crafts Board, Sioux Indian Museum

The image on the cover resonates with *Colorizing Restorative Justice* through at least five themes: Indigenous, circle, action, authenticity, and emergence.

Indigenous. Restorative justice and restorative practices are rooted in Indigenous ways worldwide. The authors consistently acknowledge the Indigenous foundations of their work and draw strength and guidance from these roots.

Circle. Circles are an integral part of Indigenous life in community. Over the past few decades, they have become foundational—in a Westernized version—to restorative thought, philosophy, and work. The authors are clearly devoted to Circles, which is why they are passionate about bringing a critical race lens to Circle practices.

Action. The image is of an eagle-feathered headdress spread out. The headdress is a symbol that the wearer's actions mirror values that people honor and respect. These authors are warriors for racial justice, social justice, and decolonization in the restorative justice movement. Through self-reflection, they seek to align their actions with their values, which gives their warrioring moral and spiritual force.

Authenticity. Again and again, the authors call for authentic dialogues, especially about race and colonization, in the restorative justice movement. Herman Red Elk chose to paint on a buffalo hide to bring back a traditional art that was interrupted when White settlers almost exterminated the buffalo to destroy my People's food supply—an act of genocide. Authentic dialogue means going to silences and voicing realities.

Emergence. In Očhéthi Šakówiŋ (Lakȟóta, Dakȟóta, and Nakȟóta) thought and philosophy, this image also symbolizes emergence. By "voicing our realities," the authors are emerging as the restorative force that they have always been. Through the justice warrioring of People of Color and Indigenous Peoples and their accomplices, the restorative justice movement holds the promise of emerging as a transformational force, overturning centuries of oppression, colonizing, and white body supremacy. It is time we emerge as who we are.

*Lakota Language Consortium orthography.

COLORIZING RESTORATIVE JUSTICE

VOICING OUR REALITIES

Edward C Valandra
Waŋbli Wapȟáha Hokšíla
EDITOR

Foreword by Justice Robert G. Yazzie

Living Justice Press
St. Paul, Minnesota

Living Justice Press
St. Paul, Minnesota 55105

First edition

Library of Congress Cataloging-in-Publication Data

Names: Valandra, Edward Charles (Waŋbli Wapȟáha Hokšíla), 1955– editor. | Yazzie, Robert G., 1947– writer of foreword.
Title: Colorizing restorative justice : voicing our realities / Edward C Valandra, editor ; foreword by Justice Robert G. Yazzie.
Description: First edition. | St. Paul, Minnesota : Living Justice Press, 2020. | Includes bibliographical references and index. | Summary: "Twenty authors of color explore how race and colonization affect the practice and direction of restorative justice. These authors reveal how the restorative justice movement can benefit from embracing racial and social justice, including decolonization, as integral to its work and leadership"—Provided by publisher.
Identifiers: LCCN 2019022070 (print) | LCCN 2019981561 (ebook) | ISBN 9781937141233 (paperback) | ISBN 9781937141240 (pdf)
Subjects: LCSH: Restorative justice—United States. | Discrimination in criminal justice administration—United States. | Anti-racism—United States. | Race awareness—United States. | Race relations—United States. | Colonization—United States.
Classification: LCC HV8688 .C593 2020 (print) | LCC HV8688 (ebook) | DDC 320.97301/1—dc23
LC record available at https://lccn.loc.gov/2019022070
LC ebook record available at https://lccn.loc.gov/2019981561

ISBN-13: 978-1-937141-23-3
eBook ISBN: 978-1-937141-24-0

27 26 25 24 23 22 10 9 8 7 6 5 4 3 2

Cover design by David Spohn
Copyediting by Cathy Broberg
Interior design by Wendy Holdman
Printed by Sheridan Books, Ann Arbor, Michigan, on recycled paper
Printed in the United States

To

Wambli Wanblaka Valandra

Oyate Kin Ekta Kigla Win Tait

Their relationships are sacred.

Contents

Foreword

Living Justice Practice

Peacemaking is the people's process. It is the root of Indigenous knowledge and experiences. This process is becoming more and more a part of Indigenous governments and court systems. Peacemaking began with the first people, untouched by the world. Today these people have been hit with the force of the outside world. Chief Manuelito, one of the great Navajo leaders, reminded us that "wherever you go, don't ever come out of your traditional way of life, your prayers, your songs, your culture, and your language." In his mind, there was a clear notion that peacemaking is embedded in Navajo teachings.

Ideas and suggestions shared with the world are that peacemaking is an aspiration toward promoting peace and harmony. Indigenous Peoples have used the peacemaking circle to work out their issues in every respect from time immemorial. Almost all were forced to give up their traditional peacemaking practice, forgetting their core principles and values. Even then, Indigenous Peoples have retained their living justice practice; they only need to be reconnected.

The idea now is to have individuals from particular Indigenous nations, rooted in their own traditional value systems, teach peacemaking to everyone of all ages, all educational backgrounds, knowledge, and experience. Peacemaking has great potential to influence and guide today's Indigenous governments and court decisions, knowing these decisions are of resilience, stability, and consistency.

This publication will reach those individuals seeking to promote the growth of peacemaking among their people.

—Justice Robert G. Yazzie
April 8, 2019

Introduction

The twenty authors of color in this book raise unsettling issues about restorative justice and restorative practices (RJ/RP), situated as they are in white supremacist settler societies that sustain deep roots in European invasion and colonizing. The contradiction between restorative practices and the Western, white supremacist, settler societies in which we practice them is inherent. We People of Color and Indigenous Peoples have not created the contradiction. It is there. But we collectively experience this contradiction in ways Whites do not. We feel an urgency about addressing this contradiction that our White settler colleagues seem not to perceive or express. We also feel an urgency about critically informing communities of color and Indigenous communities that this contradiction, while not of our making or choosing, is one we negotiate in restorative justice.

Colorizing Restorative Justice centers this contradiction on the RJ/RP agenda going forward. The Black Lives Matter movement, Standing Rock's resistance (#NODAPL), the #MeToo movement, the LGBTQ community's struggle against persecution, and grassroots opposition to xenophobia (Build the Wall and the targeting of Muslims): these and many other non-mainstream challenges to white supremacy show that now is not a time for complacency with oppressive systems. Complacency—straining at individual missteps while swallowing institutional mega-harms—is complicity. The RJ movement's credibility and future are on the line. In *The Little Book of Race and Restorative Justice*, Fania Davis, African American activist, scholar, and RJ practitioner, acknowledges the problems associated with the contradiction and the harms that come from it:

> Restorative justice risks losing relevance if we, as practitioners, do not become more skillful at identifying, navigating, and transforming racial harm. Structural racism pervades all our institutions. . . . Given the nation's changing demographics and persistent, if not deepening, racial disparities, a restorative justice approach that ignores these inequities will be perceived as uninformed and uncaring, if not irrelevant and racist. Failing to acknowledge and take action to address racial injustice allows living legacies of slavery, genocide, and segregation to persist.[1]

Whereas one might think that the RJ movement would shine in championing racial and social justice, the movement has actually been silent, afraid, and conforming—complacent with institutional and structural harms. Rather than changing systems, RJ processes are called on to "patch up" the harms that racist and colonizing structures and institutions cause routinely. For example, a student of color who chafes at the racial microaggressions that White teachers and staff commit on a daily basis becomes "the problem," one that a restorative process is expected to "fix"—without naming the racial experience. So far, it would seem that restorative justice has not been "strong enough to co-opt the co-opters." Mara Schiff, White American, associate professor of criminology and criminal justice, clarifies her thoughts about RJ's co-optation:

> Is it possible for restorative justice to survive and transform such systems to produce socially just results, or is restorative justice more likely to get compromised and co-opted by the overwhelmingly dominant cultural ethos (and corresponding power structures) of the organizations it seeks to transform? Ultimately, is restorative justice strong enough to co-opt the co-opters?[2]

If RJ as a movement does not address racism and colonization, then, as Fania Davis warns, RJ/RP will itself function in racist and colonizing ways, because that is the default. It is how a society that has been organized institutionally, socially, economically, and politically around maintaining white supremacy and settler dominance—for centuries, indeed, since its inception—operates.

The demand for change is great, then, and *CRJ*'s authors do not shy away from it. For these reasons, their work warrants time and reflection. This book is a call to be pondered and digested slowly. It is not a book to be read quickly and then "put away."

As you read, I hope you will feel, as I have while editing these chapters, that the authors write *from* a place of love and *toward* a place with love. We clearly love Circles and doing the restorative work. We love the restorative approach, and we love the transformative potential that the restorative way of understanding and being opens for our lives, for our communities, and ultimately for the planet. We love the community that has formed around this book project. We love who we are, and we stand with dignity and integrity. And while our experiences of White settlers span the spectrum, we hold the possibility of being in better relations with those who, as a people, have perpetrated the greatest harms against us and our loved ones. We embrace the idea that these harms will stop and that White settlers, too, will be better for it. So, from a love deeper than most Whites can imagine, as authors of color we are taking the risk to share openly and honestly what we have experienced while working in restorative justice.

Part I: Where Are We? RJ/RP Challenges and Obligations

In part 1, the authors explore what restorative practitioners of color face in a field that is currently dominated by Whites and Western ways of thinking. Though People of Color are profoundly engaged in the restorative work and affected by how it is practiced, many if not most White practitioners have either opposed efforts to increase racial and social awareness as integral to the restorative work or remained silent. In *The Little Book of Race and Restorative Justice,* Fania Davis observes that the restorative justice movement has maintained silence about racial and social justice and decolonization and has kept these issues at a distance. Both professionally and on the receiving end, People of Color and Indigenous Peoples bear the price of this choice, which we had no role in making.

Sharon Goens-Bradley leads off the dialogue with an analysis of where restorative justice is and the challenges it faces from the perspective of a long-time practitioner of color. Like other contributors in this volume, Goens-Bradley references *White Fragility* by Robin DiAngelo, a White diversity trainer, in her call for Whites in restorative justice to act for racial and social justice. Goens-Bradley takes sharp aim at "white body supremacy," a term introduced by Resmaa Menakem, Black, author and leader in trauma research. White body supremacy manifests in the physical experiences of RJ: White Circle keepers (CK), White restorative justice coordinators (RJC), and White-dominated restorative justice or restorative practices organizations, such as non-governmental organizations (NGOs).

Goens-Bradley details the disparities in restorative practices that inevitably follow. She notes that restorative practices, while solid conceptually, are found wanting in practice along racial justice lines. Her critique challenges restorative practices, for example, to go beyond diverting Youth of Color and Indigenous Youth (YOCIY) from behaviors that a mainstream perspective deems harmful and to actively divert YOCIY from white body supremacy—the root harm that YOCIY suffer.

Like other critiques in this volume, Goens-Bradley's are experientially grounded. Goens-Bradley makes clear that her stories and observations are not about bashing Whites; rather, she wants Whites to recognize how they bring their white body supremacy into restorative practices.

Her call to White action, then, is this: Whites in restorative practices will continue to inflict harms on People of Color and Indigenous Peoples (POCIPs) as long as they refuse to "develop and apply a race-conscious lens."[3] She outlines the consequences of not having race-consciousness in their training arsenal. Whites will remain ill-equipped to have authentic relationships with POCIPs and YOCIY—a *sine qua non* in restorative work. Goens-Bradley is audacious in her call, given the response of many White RJ practitioners to a 2018 International Restorative Practices conference held in Minnesota that centered the perspectives of People of Color. Whites' fragility and their white body supremacy showed few signs of critical self-awareness.

For Whites who seek to answer her call, Goens-Bradley provides a race-conscious road map. The road map reads like an orienteering activity. First, she recommends that, to know the racial terrain they will venture, Whites must self-engage in developing at least seven cross-cultural competencies (along with ten other insightful questions) at the ground level and not in some sanitized or other mediated environment. Goens-Bradley warns Whites that their self-engagement will likely be fraught with degrees of difficulty—even before they take the necessary action step. Again, orienteering's degrees of difficulty in negotiating unknown territory come to mind.

Racial self-assessment is a prerequisite for White action. Goens-Bradley has witnessed failure all too often when Whites are unable or unwilling to own their personal white body supremacy. She reminds them not to rush but to take the time necessary to work on their whiteness; otherwise, avoidance and racial self-blindness holds centuries-long white body supremacy in place. Historicity discloses that racism, which includes colonization, continues to distort how Whites engage People of Color and Indigenous Peoples. Without self-assessment, Whites in RJ are no exception. The next two decades will reveal whether Whites working in restorative fields or with restorative approaches have heeded her call.

Barbara Sherrod turns her critical analysis on restorative justice's peculiar silence about collective harms. Her experiences in restorative practices disclose that RJ's more established advocates are less than enthusiastic about addressing harms on institutional, systemic, or structural levels. Perhaps these advocates, who perceive harms on an individualistic level, choose to focus on that level only, not on the collective level where white supremacy shapes institutional policies and practices. By so doing, though, they institutionalize a "restorative" practice of turning a blind eye to how White-dominated institutions tokenize or silence the People of Color and Indigenous Peoples working within them or for them.

To break this silence, Sherrod shifts her gaze toward the racial dynamics within schools, which leads her to address system-level harms. But her approach is one of caution, and for good reason. For Sherrod, restorative practices require honest self-reflection, which includes a person's emotional-spiritual realm. Sherrod's personal inventory, which she describes, serves as her compass when she does restorative justice or practices in White spaces. She emphasizes self-reflection, because not doing this causes harm. She relates stories about the racial relationships between children of color and White teachers. As the stories show, the latter's racial normalization, instilled from a society that normalizes white supremacy, hinders the White teachers from developing authentic relationships with youth, parents, and communities of color. For Sherrod, racial self-reflection, especially among White educators, is critical for creating a positive learning environment.

Sherrod also names the exhaustion she experiences when racial issues and Whites' fragility intersect in her restorative work. The racial violence that Whites visit upon children and People of Color requires "balancing the need to bluntly point out the violent comments or actions towards People of Color and the need to figure out *calling in*, so as not to push White people away from this work—the white fragility reaction."[4] Many of us who engage White people in our work know this exhaustion all too well. That is why Sherrod exhorts us to take up the idea of co-powering Circles. Co-powering means that one or two People of Color or Indigenous Peoples do not have to do the heavy lifting alone on behalf of their respective communities. Indeed, such collective visibility and solidarity decenters Whites and whiteness, so that real conversations can ensue.

Sherrod's inner compass knows that co-powering in Circles is but a beginning. Her first years in this field cleared her thinking about restorative practices. While youth can benefit from restorative practices, it is the adults who are in desperate need of them. Like other non-Western people(s), Sherrod takes an expansive view that, when it comes to naming or identifying harm, westernization is the culprit. By identifying Western thinking as the root of harm, Sherrod shatters the silence. Westernization pervades our adult consciousness and daily habits. Sherrod's criticisms of restorative practices are really aimed at modernity's assault on relationships. With Sherrod, *CRJ's* contributors anticipate a day when the word "justice" no longer generates the fear it does for us today and hence no longer silences the voices of tomorrow.

Christina Parker brings critical peacemaking Circles into the colorizing RJ/RP work. Like other Critical Studies, the critical study of peacemaking Circles concerns what qualitatively transpires within a Circle's space. Despite a person sitting physically in Circle, for example, an individual may experience being socialized out of it. People of Color and Indigenous Peoples know the "who's in, who's out" duality quite well. Parker reminds us of how the structures of mainstream institutions convey messages about power relations spatially and culturally. She makes clear that Circles contain a nuanced, social complexity that deserves our full attention and consideration; otherwise restorative practices end up perpetuating the very harms they seek to remedy.

Parker describes schools as contested sites where restorative practices or approaches and their Circles confront the Western educational model and tradition. Tension and disconnects are inevitable. On one hand, peacemaking

Circles are all about doing relationships inclusively, whereas schools are mostly organized one-dimensionally. They assume, Parker asserts, that one size fits all, "yet this approach ultimately reinforces exclusion and marginalization."[5] On the other hand, youth of color and Indigenous youth would benefit from an educational model that embraces their lived experiences and adapts school culture to reflect and make room for those experiences. At this intersection between transactional (rule-bound, exclusionary) and transformative (participatory, inclusive) relationships, Parker finds her mark. For peacemaking Circles to make their stamp, the conventional classroom—the ground zero of where faculty and children intimately interact—must be rethought. Otherwise our children of color and our Indigenous children will increasingly resist the classroom's defining and confining characteristic: Western authoritarianism.

White supremacy, of course, correlates with Western authoritarianism. How could it not? For example, Parker uses research that distinguishes between higher-order and lower-order dialogue. Higher-order dialogue teaches students to handle complex, controversial, and conflictual topics; lower-order dialogue is instructional, focusing students on learning the basics. The former dialogue takes place in higher socioeconomic status (hSES) community schools; the latter dialogue occurs within lower socioeconomic status (lSES) community schools. The hSES communities prepare their youth in ways that lSES communities cannot. According to Parker, hSES youth preparation features many forms of higher-order dialogues that develop students' skills for building teams, communicating, and being proactive about their own learning. Comparatively, lSES youth preparation distills to the lowest common denominator: raising low test scores. The lSES teachers forgo the luxury of higher-order dialogues because schools pressure them to raise low scores. Yet, higher-order dialogues are precisely what lSES communities and their schools need, and restorative practices and peacemaking Circles provide the means to hold them. Introducing restorative practices equips children with relationship-building skills, and peacemaking Circles offer a space where higher-order dialogue can lift up all students and encourage them to talk about what matters most in their lives.

However, Parker makes us appreciate that, while racially mixed Circles can invite higher-order dialogue, they can also prove risky spaces. On one side, White school administrators, teachers, and youth risk having People of Color or Indigenous Peoples inquire about their whiteness: their white supremacist society and institutions, white privilege, colonization, racism, etc. On the other side, youth and adults of color must figure out how to break through imposed silences about racial dynamics or challenge the white norms that are being universalized. We ask ourselves: How much vulnerability and emotional energy will I need to expend for Whites to let down their defenses enough to even begin a higher-order dialogue? Being in such spaces is exhausting and can easily leave POCIPs frustrated and distant—all the more so when it seems that our White colleagues have neither the capacity nor the will to hear us. Such is their privilege.

Despite the risks inherent in restorative practices or peacemaking Circles, Parker courageously ventures into a contested sphere to release restorative practices from Western hegemony's hold. She outlines various things we can all use in our anti-racism and decolonizing work. These things help us understand that relying on Western values, norms, and philosophy to deconstruct the West's oppressive systems will likely reinforce them. For example, what we study or implement in restorative practices and how we frame the harms that call for repair depend on how we select what we want to know or change (the variables). Make no mistake: selecting what to examine, practice, or repair are political questions, as the contributors and others are fully aware. Parker challenges POCIPs to reexamine our own reliance on Western thinking, especially when it comes to colorizing restorative practices and justice.

Erica Littlewolf, Michelle Armster, and Christianne Paras all take exception to restorative justice's claim that its roots derive from Indigenous ways. The "claim that restorative justice in its current iteration is honoring the traditions of Indigenous people is false," they write. "Instead, restorative justice is rooted in a Western, white supremacist, cisgender, male-dominated system."[6] In a word, colonization. Moreover, partnering with unjust systems or following their lead is not an Indigenous way—and never has been. At best, it is a coping strategy in the face of overwhelming oppression. Nonetheless, the claim of Indigenous origins becomes the bridge metaphor that the restorative justice movement uses to historically link restorative justice to traditional Indigenous ways or practices. This bridge metaphor, the authors contend, needs conceptual burning. Like other *CRJ* contributors, Littlewolf, Armster, and Paras assert that the homage restorative justice pays to Indigenous ways is perhaps honored more in the breach than in the observance. Not acknowledging these deep disconnects harms Indigenous People and People of Color, and it distorts the movement's self-assessment and hence self-narrative.

Leading off the chapter, Littlewolf brings to the dialogue her core reservation experience, a site of extreme settler colonialism. She raises the Discovery Doctrine as *the* document that continues to justify settlers' (both White and of color) illegal occupation of Indigenous Peoples' homelands and their continued genocide against us, particularly in the modern settler states of Canada, Australia, New Zealand, and the United States (CANZUS). Littlewolf also provides examples of how this doctrine manifests in restorative justice. For instance, restorative justice practitioners exclaim that they cannot be held accountable for what their ancestors have done to Indigenous Peoples, contrary to the centuries-old Corruption of Blood Principle.[7] For Indigenous Peoples, this principle does hold settlers accountable for what their ancestors have done, compounded by the fact that they remain the beneficiaries of Indigenous lands stolen through genocide. Littlewolf pushes restorative justice to the transformative edge with more examples that settlers likely find disquieting. Whether the movement's practitioners take the restorative plunge remains the question.

Armster urges practitioners in a genuine restorative direction as well. Like Littlewolf and others, she explains how multiple identities have formed her experiences and thus inform her restorative lens. As a conflict mediator and then as a restorative justice practitioner, she has witnessed how both fields react to non-mainstream identities. Armster challenges restorative justice's safe-harbor assumption—namely, that its practitioners are impartial, fair, egalitarian, open-minded, etc., and therefore that its processes must possess these qualities as well. However, her question—and one that other *CRJ* contributors also ask—distills to the core inquiry: From practitioner/professional to client, who really benefits from restorative justice?

Paras examines the role, station, status, and position that People of Color and Indigenous Peoples occupy in restorative justice: who in restorative justice determines our positionality? Paras recounts her first Circle in which the Circle participants talked about "race." She makes clear that even restorative justice can fall victim to tokenism or "the face of diversity." Structural tokenism is, of course, lethal: it saddles a Person of Color or an Indigenous person with a title (e.g., "Chief Diversity Officer") but with a low salary, little funding, and marginal power (e.g., advisory)—and then expects miracles. Paras peels away tokenism's layers to arrive at why organizations value practitioners of color as tokens: we provide them and their personnel a measure of satisfaction that they are doing their part in undoing centuries of racial harm.

Ironically, Paras's initial Circle launched her critical inquiry into how other participants experience either safety or harm within the same Circle. To distinguish safety from harm in what we consider a restorative process, Paras asks five questions that call out the westernized mindset in restorative justice. Until these questions are honestly addressed, restorative justice will continue to be suspect among People of Color and Indigenous Peoples.

Littlewolf, Armster, and Paras collectively raise the question: What is justice? Whose justice? Justice for whom? The US criminal and legal system, which has unapologetically buttressed white supremacy for centuries, looks to restorative justice as an adjunct diversion program. The affiliation between restorative justice and the criminal legal system has seen the former adopt some of the latter's norms, such as its binary nomenclature (e.g., victim-offender), acting only after a harm has occurred and, because of its adjunct status, being at the criminal legal system's call. The notion that the criminal-legal system is not about enforcing white supremacy and is instead about making sure that individuals receive their just deserts—which is still a long way from a restorative understanding—has little basis in reality. It is a fantasy, as *CRJ*'s authors contend.

For these women, restorative justice has to amp up its critical self-awareness, especially in regard to its complicity with oppressive, colonizing institutions. It has to co-partner with social justice when addressing and undoing harms that these systems, like the US criminal-legal system, churns out. Social justice is about achieving equity despite a society that condones inequities—socio-economic, socio-political, socio-health, and socio-educational disparities. Indeed, Littlewolf, Armster, and Paras deconstruct restorative justice's four assumptions that, intentionally or not, harm People of Color and Indigenous Peoples in the movement. Furthermore, they use a case study in which the above assumptions were outed during a one-day workshop about restorative approaches. Burning the bridge challenges restorative justice and its practitioners to reflect on, rethink, and restate its fundamental relationships with People of Color and Indigenous Peoples. What lies on the other side of the chasm that settlers' unjust society has not yet imagined?

Part II. Negotiating RJ/RP as Professionals of Color

In part 2, the authors reflect on how mostly White or White-led workplace environments impact their work as restorative professionals. People of Color regularly face these challenges, no matter what our work or profession. The academy, for example, is notorious for its blatant and subtle ways of marginalizing students and scholars of color. We face a chronic battle, no matter how "woke" we would like to think our field or profession might have become. As part of a mainstream white supremacist society, the restorative justice movement is no different. To be different, the intention to incorporate racial justice, social justice, and decolonizing justice into the restorative work must be set. So far, as the authors explain, this incorporation has not happened. Being woke about racial and social justice and decolonization requires a long process of waking, just as the process of waking to ways of responding to harms other than punishment has taken intention, time, and effort—and still we are working on it.

Sheryl Wilson poses a leading question for this book: How do People of Color (POC) survive in hyper-racialized White systems? She exhorts readers to be acutely conscious of all-White and White-dominated spaces; otherwise dismantling them is exceedingly difficult. As she explains, failing to name and dismantle such realities, which POC face daily, subjects POC to harm. Black Lives Matter, now internationally famous, shows that the most basic daily activities, like driving or walking, can have lethal consequences for us.

Like Wilson, professors Anne Bonds and Joshua Inwood, both White, map the workings of whiteness: "The concept of [white] privilege emphasizes the social condition of whiteness, rather than the institutions, practices, and processes that produce this condition in the first place."[8] This social condition, which ties power and structural advantage to whiteness, forms a social identity that takes over locations.[9] The restorative field is one such site of takeover. Ubiquitous as White identity is, not naming whiteness sustains its power and advantage. When Wilson calls out whiteness, she makes obvious the power and privilege that White people command over a "location," no matter how "woke" Whites may believe themselves to be.

Bonds and Inwood also recognize that whiteness has a spatial contingency to it: POC never know what will happen in White spaces. Will we be safe? Will we be respected? Will we be attacked, undermined, or gaslighted? Wilson illustrates how White spaces operate for her emotionally. She talks about how she feels when she enters them—an experience the contributors in this volume also know well. Wilson invokes Professor Elijah Anderson, African American sociologist, who observed White people's reactions when Black people enter *their* space. Whites try to make sense of the Black individual—"to figure out 'who that is,' or gain a sense of the nature of the person's business and whether they need to be concerned."[10]

However, Wilson flips the White gaze on itself when she expresses concern about the racial landscape of restorative spaces and the racial disconnects that the Whites who occupy them accept as a norm:

> While I felt the support of many of my White restorative justice counterparts and mentors, I found it difficult over the years to digest that . . . we [practitioners of color] still have been isolated, working in predominately White systems. This discussion is not new in many all-White/White-dominated fields where People of Color carve out a living daily. . . . When I work with White practitioners, it disturbs me that we are often serving diverse communities and yet we don't accurately resemble them.[11]

Wilson is fearless within these White spaces. Yet, in calling out whiteness, which other contributors do as well, she confronts white fragility.[12] Drawing on experiences from her restorative justice work, Wilson shows how white fragility—an oxymoron with a socio-strategic role—undermines what restorative justice and restorative practices need more than anything else: authentic conversations both in and out of Circles.

Fortunately, Wilson outlines a path to authentic, meaningful conversations in the restorative work. First, she makes clear that POC and Indigenous Peoples need accomplices more than allies. Wilson draws on Dr. Jalane Schmidt's differentiation of the two—a differentiation that, with some soul-searching, invites Whites to check their fragility. In the vernacular, whereas an ally is like a fair-weather friend, being an accomplice demands moral muscle and resolve from Whites who aspire to join the struggle for justice. In a Hallmark-card ideal scenario, White accomplices share jail cells with POC and Indigenous Peoples: they become co-conspirators, "someone with skin in the game, willing to take a risk."[13]

Finally, Wilson reaches out to the restorative justice and restorative practices communities to change, transform, and dismantle the all-White spaces that currently pervade the work. She lists eight things, including important practices like equity and inclusion, that those in the movement can do to promote this change. But above all, Wilson argues that the Circle—a contingent socio-space as well, since we never know what stories might be told or the Circle's outcome—holds the potential to revolutionize this difficult journey. If we follow Wilson's lead in holding to Circle values and calling out whiteness, how could it not?

Gaye Lang reveals through the events of her life the whitewater rapids that highly qualified Black educators, especially women, must negotiate in the US educational apartheid—and this inequity in a post–*Brown v. Board of Education of Topeka* era.

Lang recalls that, as a newly minted teacher in the early 1970s, her career choice was filled with professional uncertainty. She found herself a teacher at an inner-city Los Angeles school, and the community it served showed scars from urban racial conflict. However, in a telling recollection, Lang points out that the school's teachers and leaders were predominately Black educators who displayed collegiality, such as respect and mutual professional admiration. These values became her benchmark, as she and other teachers of color moved into suburban schools with predominately White teachers, staff, and leaders. It is not difficult to imagine that, in this racial environment, administrators' teacher observations felt more like racialized trials. For example, she observed early on that White people took offense over the reality that the highly qualified people who would be teaching their children and going on to become K–12 educational leaders were not White themselves. She shares her journey with us so that we can know this offense-response and how it persists today.

What becomes apparent from Lang's story is her incisive awareness of racial dynamics. This awareness gave her an advantage, especially when she had to negotiate the volatility and unpredictability of Whites' racial regimes. Lang also describes in excruciating detail the methods she had to employ to prove to her non-Black colleagues and to non-Black parents that she was indeed a highly qualified teacher, one that any school would have wanted except for the color of her skin.

When Lang moved from the classroom to administrative leadership, the racism and sexism did not abate. She relates how White stereotypes of Blacks determine job fitness and hence job placement. Black women educators who demonstrate strength and decisiveness are often assigned to schools that have both chronic academic and disciplinary problems. On one hand, Lang agrees that a shrinking violet would be ineffective in a school riddled with such problems. On the other hand, Lang also uncovers the racism and sexism underlying such pigeonholing. If we understand that "strength and decisiveness" are dog-whistle codes for Whites' perceptions of Black women as "overly aggressive," then we see racial stereotyping playing out. According to Lang, placing a Black woman who has been so labeled in a troubled school could potentially be career ending for her. Moreover, this pattern suggests that Whites—either because of an inability to relate to People of Color's experiences or because they just do not care—do not want to be bothered with youth of color and Indigenous youth.

Given her educational experiences with both racism and sexism, Lang advocates using Circles, a process associated with restorative justice and practices, to build relationships as well as to confront these two -isms. Lang relates an all-too-familiar story about doors not opening for her, even though she had obtained a doctorate and the requisite experience. She outlines how Circles could question this closed-door pattern, raise awareness of racial harm, and bring greater social justice to employment practices in education.

Finally, Lang names the elephant in the restorative justice community room. We may expect resistance to doing school differently, such as with restorative practices, but the restorative community has itself normalized racial behavior antithetical to RJ/RP values. Lang identifies what ails restorative practices: the Western world, in co-opting and institutionalizing Circles, has done so within the framework of white supremacy. Naming and challenging this paradigm has not yet been embraced as an essential part of RJ/RP work. When restorative practices and white supremacy intersect, as they inevitably do, things get messy. However, Lang is not afraid to wade into this mess, because she knows the transformative power that Circles hold. For all of us in restorative justice or restorative practices, we must embrace Lang's commitment to the Circle process; otherwise Circles become ringed empty spaces.

Rochelle Arms Almengor provides an illuminating narrative about her experience in restorative justice, one that stretches back at least twenty years. Almengor worked as a restorative justice coordinator (RJC) in a school with predominantly White teachers and administrators. Being an RJC, she countered the school culture that normalized harm to youth by shaming them. Despite the many school cultures that embrace punitive disciplinary measures, she nonetheless sees schools as sites where restorative practices can take root.

Moreover, not unlike her sisters of color contributing to this volume, Almengor has witnessed restorative justice becoming more mainstreamed (e.g., in K–12 schools). But she also points out, as others have, that organizational leadership remains problematic—out of reach—for women of color. Based on her own work experiences, she observes that the leadership in RJ/RP organizations does not reflect the communities they serve.

This racial disparity within the restorative work has led Almengor and others to question RJ/RP, citing personal case studies. Much like Lang, Almengor asserts the intersectional discriminatory power of race and gender. For her, the common excuses used to dismiss women of color—lack of ambition or preparation, etc.—are groundless and cannot justify the racial-gender hierarchy in leadership. *Colorizing Restorative Justice* shows that many women of color have skills and training equal to White practitioners. More than that, they have the experience *as People of Color* within communities of color that Whites do not have. Yet they do not have the opportunities and leadership positions that Whites do.

According to Almengor, systemic inequalities pose the real barriers to women of color advancing within the field. To make her point, she explores the experiences of Black female RJCs whose work addresses the intersectional -isms that plague schools. Many of these -isms mirror White societal attitudes, norms, and values concerning People of Color and Indigenous Peoples. In these case studies, RJCs of color reveal how the following areas of systemic inequalities conspire to marginalize women of color when they engage in restorative justice or practices:

- relationality and relatability (their empathy with YOCIY differs from Whites' racially objectifying and institutional responses to youth of color)
- workplace fit (institutional practices are incongruent with POCIPs' differing expectations and experiences)
- professional expertise (with respect to leadership, the restorative justice and practices fields do not value an RJC of color's life experiences)
- positionality (women of color are expected to practice restorative justice effectively from a subjugated, non-restorative space)

Almengor shows that Black and other women of color, not surprisingly, are willing to take calculated but exceptional risks to colorize restorative justice, despite Whites' expressions of fragility as they do so.

Desirée Anderson brings higher education into the fold of colorizing restorative justice. Much like K–12 educators, college and university administrators increasingly turn to restorative justice to address disciplinary matters. They gravitate toward this approach, according to Anderson, because relying primarily on legalism proves dissatisfying. Yet, as with legalism, educators continue to focus on specific incidents and the individuals involved, co-opting restorative practices away from the whole-school approach that is their hallmark.

While RJ can have positive results for individuals, Anderson contests this application on campuses. Her point is that higher education perceives restorative justice as an alternative approach to business-as-usual, rather than as an authentic community way of being. Reduced to reacting to misbehavior case by case, leaving policies and institutions unchanged, restorative justice is readily co-opted, i.e., exploited in ways neither intended nor foreseen.

Anderson's concerns are systemic. For example, Anderson notes that higher educational institutions embody a chain-of-command structure that reflects how White people understand the world around them. RJ is used to hold individuals accountable for harms but is not used to holding institutions and policies equally accountable. The chain-of-command structure stays in place. More poignantly, Anderson asserts that, although changes in racial demographics are increasing student diversity on campuses, whiteness is becoming increasingly centralized (as the norm) throughout mainstream colleges and universities. Higher education then defaults to denying that racism and bias are significant campus problems—a position that further protects whiteness as a norm.

Worse, Anderson fears that higher education may see restorative justice as an attractive way to address campus inequities. Yet restorative justice is not a diversity project. Restorative justice trainings do not currently incorporate training in racial biases, in the systemic nature of racial and social harms, or in decolonization. Therein lies co-optation's potential. The gaps in experience-based knowledge between groups remain unnamed. Participants must face not only the complexities of a harm but also the chasm of experiential awareness between Whites and POCIP and, for that matter, often among different POCIP as well. Once again, the call to make self-awareness of biases, including institutional and policy biases, an integral part of RJ work has not yet been accepted as good RJ practice.

Given these tensions, Anderson raises an interesting point about the sub-communities or recognized affinity groups that characterize higher educational institutions. These are structural clubs, organizations, or athletics. Because they are inherently fractured, i.e., exclusionary communities, they may militate against higher education's efforts to build community. A fractured social environment heightens concerns about how restorative approaches might be used in distorting ways—i.e., offered mainly to those whom the educational institution privileges.

For higher education to benefit from restorative justice more than superficially, Anderson states that these institutions must work at campus-wide ethos building. Vulnerability, compassion, empathy, and intentionality are a few characteristics that help shape the ethos of a restorative community, yet individualism (e.g., meritocracy and competition) and top-down structures (e.g., hierarchy, policies) stamp the ethos of higher education. These two models of ethos do not align.

The conflict of ethos that RJ practitioners in higher education face, then, is inherent: restorative ethos-building represents a major cultural shift for westernized educational institutions. The paradigm that has served White people's interests is becoming less relevant today, yet this reality makes its advocates more contentious. Although institutions of higher education often engage the struggle to address racism, colorism, sexism, ableism, and other -isms, they remain entrenched sites of white supremacy.

Mindful of this paradigm-level conflict, Anderson offers practical ideas to keep the restorative ethos—restorative justice's principles and community-building purpose—central. She poses three insightful questions that re-center us on what really matters when we do restorative justice work: unlearn ingrained socialization. This unlearning means having an honest, ongoing inner talk about who we really are and intentionally opening ourselves to unfamiliar experiences. Unlearning the ethos of white supremacy and interrupting how educational institutions pass it on to new generations calls for self-honesty, vulnerability, and openness to change—antidotes to co-optation.

Anita Wadhwa shares a compelling personal story—one she hesitated to make public for a year—that shows why restorative justice practitioners must confront race and racism internally. From Wadhwa, we learn that, in multiracial coalitions or collaborations, racial microaggressions occur—"even" in restorative justice. We also learn that, while restorative justice can build a "safe space" for genuine relationships to develop, we must not become complacent in these racially mixed spaces.

In her previous restorative justice work in schools, Wadhwa freely used racial and social justice frameworks. Within Circle, students and staff developed a critical consciousness that became a pathway for both healing and relationship-building among youth of color. However, her new school community's racial climate led Wadhwa to "hide the ball" (a phrase indicating the use of race neutrality or colorblindness), so as to make restorative justice palatable in both concept and practice. Moreover, Wadhwa had pitched restorative justice to the school's powers that be as a way to improve order within the school (read: "discipline"). Following restorative justice principles, Wadhwa employed a youth apprenticeship model, introducing a restorative justice leadership course and providing RJ training in Circles.

Despite the promising movement to institutionalize restorative justice in her school, Wadhwa observed that a White colleague began to distance herself from this important work. When Wadhwa approached her—an RJ colleague of three years—about this, she accused Wadhwa of racially politicizing restorative justice. As Wadhwa relates in her story, what became particularly painful to her was a White woman's dismissal of the gains that she and her two co-workers had made at the high school. For Wadhwa and others who know this story, her White colleague's accusation bore classic elements of white privilege and fragility.

How the White woman who had worked in RJ handled her discomfort with a colleague of color was not one of restorative justice's finer moments. Unable to truly own her white privilege, she resented how the restorative justice program's implementation was triggering her. She complained about how critical consciousness with respect to racial and social justice made her feel as a White person: "I know white privilege is real, but . . ."—the proverbial "but" that we have come to know so well from Whites. Wadhwa reflected, "Why couldn't she have come to me to talk about this [sooner] before getting, in her words, 'pissed' at me to the point of avoiding me?"[14]

More egregiously, when Wadhwa reminded her White colleague of the opportunities the program had provided her and expressed her feeling of being used, her White colleague retorted, "What do you want, reparations?" Reparations. At such racial junctures, the historicity of People of Color and Indigenous Peoples disrupts mainstream restorative justice/restorative practices. For the unreconstructed (a post-civil-war-era term), the specter of unremitted Black reparations distorts Black-White relations, just as the theft and illegal occupation of Indigenous Peoples' lands haunt today's Indigenous-settler relations. When Whites experience these momentous racial junctures, they often exhibit forms of cognitive dissonance or defensiveness—fragility.

Calling out the shortcomings or failures of the restorative justice establishment can force White colleagues and White-dominated institutions into positions of alienation from People of Color and Indigenous Peoples, as Wadhwa experienced. Other contributors to this volume have experienced similar alienation—and risk further alienation from White colleagues by writing chapters for this book. Despite this alienation, though, Wadhwa's story is spiritually restorative: naming what we experience as we struggle to colorize restorative justice is medicine for us and our communities.

Part III. POC Experiences of RJ/RP and Circle Work

What makes People of Color different from Whites in what we bring to the restorative work? Experience, community, and knowing structural oppression and colonization. No White person can fully know what it is like to be a Person of Color or an Indigenous person in a society steeped in white settler supremacy over centuries. No White settler experiences the multigenerational impact of catastrophic violence against us as peoples, violence that can erupt at any moment as we go about our daily lives. When relationships matter, as they do in restorative work, the solidarity of community born of lifelong experiences of racial and social harm makes mutual empathy around race a base-level bond. So, it is not a surprise that the restorative practitioners of color in this section bring a depth of experience with race in the restorative work that is as distinct as it is instructive. Experience matters. Whites in the restorative justice movement have yet to value how our experiences as People of Color and Indigenous Peoples equip us to engage the restorative work in ways that White experiences do not. We feel what is at stake in our bones and not only for our own communities and peoples. We carry critical messages for the restorative justice movement and its transformative role in our societies, yet when we raise our voices, we are too often met with marginalizing, patronizing, and tokenizing responses. These *CRJ* authors will have none of this.

Gilbert Salazar examines, in a refreshingly artistic style, how personal vulnerability provides an antidote to white fragility. POC and Indigenous Peoples are well aware, as Salazar illustrates in his essay, that the process of Circles or other training spaces "sparks either discomfort or activation from participants, including what is now referred to as white fragility."[15] Salazar employs a short play, *Sippin'*, to highlight how POC experience white fragility in activated mode. The play raises many questions about mixed-race dynamics, but two stand out for me: How can Circle, with its elements of container and witnessing, rupture white fragility's paradigms?[16] How can vulnerability and storytelling give us tools that can elicit accountability—honest self-reflection—among and within RJ and RP practitioners? This last question is critical.

Salazar's play exemplifies how racial realities, when introduced even in small doses, can quickly become toxic in a mixed-race space. For instance, in *Sippin'*, calling out whiteness brings feelings of discomfort or of being unsafe all around. Yet Salazar asks people to lean into, rather than withdraw from, these unsettled moments. Even though leaning into these moments does not come without hazard, doing so can lead to restorative moments—or not, depending on the group.

Just how these moments become restorative is Salazar's challenge to us. For one, Salazar offers a framework, the Privileged Identity Exploration (PIE) model. Like other People of Color and Indigenous Peoples, Salazar realizes that any racial or decolonizing exercise that results in awakening (by articulating the unstated) can be both tricky and sticky, especially when White people are in the Circle. For example, Salazar uses PIE to deconstruct Whites' behavior when they exhibit white fragility and notes how this behavior interrupts much-needed talks around issues of race, racism, whiteness, white privilege, and white supremacy.

Salazar recognizes such White behavior for what it represents in these spaces: a defensive posturing. However, such posturing can also lay a foundation for vulnerability. Within this complex space, Salazar shines. He construes white fragility as a practice in vulnerability, which, when named, can lead to healing.

For example, Salazar relates a White woman's story about her time among the Water Protectors at Standing Rock. From her story, Salazar realized that restorative justice can do for White people what the Water Protectors were doing: disarming their white fragility. His practice of Circles reveals Whites' potential to embrace their vulnerability, which, if they choose, can open them to their healing journey. The restorative conversations witnessed within Circles are, for Salazar, a space "where others may know who we are." For many Whites, though, this experience can be frightening.

Shameeka Mattis reminds us that, as inviting as restorative Circles appear, they remain emotionally contested spaces racially. Mattis, who identifies as a Black queer woman, expresses humility and appreciates the value of doing restorative practice work. Not surprisingly, these two attributes call her to be accountable, i.e., self-reflective, while engaging in restorative practices, particularly among communities of color. She embraces restorative practices as a way of life—in her words, "walking the talk."

People of Color and Indigenous Peoples within settler states have our collective and individual experiences with Whites, and these experiences shape how we think about Circles and thus approach them, especially when POCIPs and Whites co-participate. Mindful that communities of color and Indigenous communities must continuously negotiate and monitor our social behaviors in a society that maintains structural oppression (which includes being profiled and surveilled), Mattis is keenly aware of positionality and how it can either empower or disempower restorative practices and Circles. As with so many other contributors, her candor about POC Circles' inner and outer dynamics is refreshing medicine.

For instance, is it not true that, as POCIPs, we feel safer in Circles in which the participants reflect us? Are we not freer to experience meaningful healing and reconciliation among us when we are free of the worrisome, wearisome burden of triggering Whites' fragility, often just by who we are? As a Circle facilitator, Mattis answers this question in the affirmative. In safe communal spaces, she asks four self-reflective questions: two are self-determining in the face of racism; one is about combatting oppression; and the other names the ubiquity of whiteness.

Mattis considers other structural spaces she has worked in—ones we are all familiar with: the court system and the hierarchy of internalized oppression. We recognize courts as spaces well known for terrorizing POCIPs. As for internalized oppression, each community of color and Indigenous community has had to absorb a myriad of Whites' oppressions, only to become oppressors within our respective communities: e.g., oppression Olympics, gatekeeping, model minority, inferiority complexes, or inherent marginalization.

Mattis is acutely aware not only of how these spaces operate within and without POCIP's communities, but also of how they can be manipulated to divide and rule us. To undo the harm oppressive spaces inflict on POCIP, Mattis consciously addresses her own control issues, something we can all relate to. But relinquishing control is only part of undoing harm; Mattis reminds us that genuine listening—intentional listening—is at restorative practices' core. I recall my grandfather saying to me that, when spoken, our Lakȟóta language literally paints a picture in our minds. Attentive listening, being a skilled listener, is difficult, however, when the most highly valued norm is literacy. That is why Mattis raises the other attribute of listening: silence. Silence is not just about being quiet; it is also about being attuned to silence's other meanings and messages. Among my people, for example, silence often means "no"; one cannot assume it indicates assent.

By acknowledging the social dynamics in Circle, such as colorism, Mattis invites all participants to become aware of each other's awareness: our value systems are on display. To be vulnerable in this humble way is restorative practice's strength. Mattis's commitment to being in her rightful place resonates with *CRJ*, since colorizing restorative justice is about voicing our realities. Mattis's voice reminds us that we are prisoners to neither racial oppression nor colonization. We can be who we are meant to be, and our restorative story begins with recovering what is ours: being in our rightful place.

Abdul-Malik Muhammad sees the restorative work of addressing and repairing harms as going beyond the interpersonal. Any time a non-mainstream movement touches the lives of People of Color, it is by definition radical: whatever the focus, it also exposes white supremacy. It is not surprising, then, that Muhammad engages restorative justice and practices not for transactional outcomes only but for radically transforming systems. Muhammad focuses on school-age youth of color and Indigenous youth to stem and turn the tide of structural violence—the school-to-prison pipeline.

And though restorative justice and practices depend on relationships and trust, Muhammad exposes a recurring blind spot in the movement: a lack of awareness that resorting to institutional authority (power over), no matter how well meaning, disempowers adolescent males of color. The use of power-over tactics undermines trust and hence relationships. By contrast, in the African Centered School movement, as Muhammad explains, the teacher-student relationship is a vibrant exchange of mutual learning and inspiration. Culture shapes the learning experience for adults and youth, and "the communal circle in traditional Afrikan societies" provides the "interactive and reciprocal act of communication" that makes learning dynamic, joyful, creative, liberating, and indeed spiritual for all involved.[17]

In standard, Western K–12 education, however, children of color and Indigenous children do not experience their own culture-based learning, either in method or in content. Instead, studies show that these youth often feel alienated. Many factors contribute to their alienation: their teachers do not look like them; curricula do not reflect their experiences, culture, or history; the ways of educating are fear, shame, and control-based; school policies result in disciplinary disparities between them and White children; and so on. For Muhammad, culture, the journey from boyhood to manhood, hope, bias, equity, and liberation are integral components to learning, and the restorative practices movement must consider them whenever practitioners interact with school-age boys and young men.

Muhammad applies the four-quadrant Social Discipline Window (SDW) framework to help us rethink our own socialization around authority (control) and nurturing (support): How does our way of balancing these two affect our relationships with our children?[18] Depending on the quadrant, Muhammad interrogates the dangers of either institutional dependency or community enabling—or both. In all but the "with" quadrant, youth are likely to stay disconnected, because traditional, top-down discipline remains the default.

Muhammad goes on to show how a restorative approach "listens" to behavior when words fall short. He cites Dr. Watlington's observation about the emotional and behavioral dimensions of our vocabulary. When we lack the words or are discouraged from voicing our feelings, our behavioral vocabulary takes over to express our stifled emotions. Likewise, when institutional policies and norms suppress youths' healthy expression of their emotions, their behavioral expressions do the communicating, and their behaviors mirror the institution's dysfunction.

The Cipher, which Muhammad introduces beautifully, offers youth ways to express emotions through both words and behavior. The Cipher is a non-standard, organic Circle process that richly combines both emotional and behavioral vocabularies as a form of healthy, community expression. To the uninitiated, the Cipher may appear "unruly" when compared with more staid versions of Circles. Organic Circles may adopt non-mainstream protocols, and their rhythms may not fall into any recognizable pattern, and yet these "Circles"—in this case, Ciphers—can be powerfully restorative.

This cultural awareness is Muhammad's point and restorative practitioners' challenge. Muhammad admonishes us that questioning our own biases is not enough to support youths' transformative change. Only when oppression—be it structural, institutional, or personal, social, racial, political, cultural, or economic—is outed can the damage it perpetuates be named and transformation follow. Only then will restorative justice effect genuine equity and authentic liberation.

Leon Dundas examines the nature of colorizing the restorative justice movement, bringing at least twenty-five years of restorative justice experience to the discussion. Dundas defines CRJ as power-sharing, i.e., a dialogue-based approach that centers the decision-making process around those who have been excluded or marginalized.

With this working definition, Dundas treats us to models and ways of thinking that rightly guide restorative justice away from national or state institutionalization and back to local communities, where its transformative potential is greatest. For Dundas and other *CRJ* contributors, the question raised is one of scale and relationships: Is restorative justice best suited to local communities where relationships are more intimate and less clinical? Dundas and others express this concern as restorative justice moves into the mainstream through provincial or state agencies, through NGOs organized across provincial or state regions, or even through national policies and programs. Moreover, because Dundas's restorative experience is wide, he connects restorative justice internationally, reminding us that structural violence, inequity, and exclusion are common to communities of color and Indigenous Peoples globally.

With his critical eye toward these developments in restorative justice, Dundas identifies two tiers of practitioners: RJPoids and RJPoints. RJPoids are individuals from the dominant social group who direct restorative justice and set its course: researchers, consultants, policy makers, managers, grant writers, and trainers. The latter are individuals who actualize restorative justice on the ground. RJPoints are the unsung community members who do restorative justice because it is the right thing to do for those harmed by either structural or individual action. Despite differing orientations, RJPoids and RJPoints share the world stage of race, racism, and colonization—evident in the colorizing restorative justice dialogue.

Dundas takes critical aim at restorative justice's institutionalization. Many People of Color and Indigenous Peoples embrace the restorative work and want to practice it, he observes, but they run into institutional barriers. For example, standards, accreditation, and ownership function as a form of gatekeeping within the restorative movement. Dundas is clearly in the camp that resists giving formal institutions the last word on restorative justice. His view suggests that other, organic restorative practices and models need their own space to grow from grassroots communities without institutions determining how much space or what kind of space they should be afforded.

Dundas aptly calls this contested space between the RJPoids and the RJPoints political. Since restorative justice concerns itself with addressing harms and undoing them, Dundas reminds us that racism and colonization are systemic harms and that undoing them requires a restorative justice movement that is morally strong. Undoing these harms confronts the political dimension of dominance and the disproportional power that People of Color and Indigenous Peoples experience in so-called democratic modern states. The call to confront the political in restorative justice is clear, and yet doing so is precisely what RJPoids avoid, as many have become system players with RJ/RP's institutionalization.

Dundas lays the self-reflection challenge at restorative justice's doorstep—and why not? He poses a question that makes RJ people pause: "What do we aim *not* to restore?" This question is profound, cutting to the core of restorative justice. Restorative approaches emphasize the critical role of relationships, and Dundas argues that, for society-wide transformation to occur, we must make a fundamental shift in consciousness or paradigm that starts with self-reflection. Self-reflection, personally and as a movement, reveals how structural benefits continue to accrue from outstanding harms: the theft of other people's labor (Indigenous African Peoples and their descendants in the US) and the theft of other people's land (Indigenous Peoples in settler states). Self-reflection also reveals the institutionalized theft of other people's potential based on how those with privilege have assigned or defined one's social station by categories that we cannot or should not be pressured to change: race, sex or gender, religion, class, language, and so forth.

Elizabeth Cook-Lynn, Húŋkpathi Dakȟóta and co-founder of Native/Indigenous Studies, counseled those choosing to study Native/Indigenous Studies that, because of colonization and genocide, they cannot remain neutral in the field. Dundas brings that same counsel to restorative justice practitioners, whether frontline or system embedded: given how racism and colonization permeate every facet of our lives, we, too, cannot remain neutral in restorative justice.

Part IV. Restorative Lessons from within the Community

The power of restorative processes hinges on relationships, and relationships build community. Conversely, being in community, which restorative practices create spaces for, nurtures relationships and deepens them. As People of Color and Indigenous Peoples, we are communally minded, because our communities have been the means for our respective survivals since time immemorial and most certainly in the rough waters of white settler supremacy over the past five centuries. This acknowledgment of our survivability is not to say that our communities are free of dysfunction. Given the trauma we have had to endure over generations, post-traumatic stress disorder (PTSD) patterns are ingrained and internalized. Dr. Joy DeGruy, Black, author and consultant on race, culture, and education, names these patterns in African American families and communities as the "post traumatic slave syndrome."[19] As the authors in part 4 discuss, communities are foundational to our identities, our healing, our safety, and our well-being. For a restorative philosophy and practice to work for us, we must operate from within and through our communities. Being restorative means being community-minded and community-committed. The trick is realizing that this calls us to think and act differently from Western ways. Consequently, we have some healing and re-learning to do.

Victor Jose Santana begins his essay in a familiarly restorative, Circle way: he tells us his personal story and how his journey became foundational to both his work and his life. We can relate to his story. As People of Color and Indigenous Peoples, we continue to experience the brunt of Whites' (and our own lateral) oppression, so when restorative justice or practices finds us or we sit in Circle, our passion for justice is discernible.

Though we bear the weight of white supremacy collectively, we are far from being a monolithic dark-skinned minority, as convenient racial labels would suggest (e.g., "People of Color," "American Indians or Native Americans"). Santana acknowledges that sharing our different oppressions deepens our mutual understanding. However, it is not our common oppression per se that binds us, but rather how, in spite of our oppression, we nurture our relationships with one another.

Santana shares a lesson with us about building trust. During a Circle, he mistook the word "belief" for "relief," and it led to the Circle's abrupt end. Many of the participants who were initially triggered had suffered religious persecution: if Circles were another belief, they wanted no part of them. A more meaningful second Circle could be convened only after the misunderstanding had been corrected. From Santana, we realize more than ever that, when engaging communities of color or Indigenous communities, trust and relationship-building during the Circle process requires a greater mindfulness and attention to detail.

Fortunately, Santana shares his detailed approach or methodology for engaging communities, whatever the issues or challenges a community may face. While each of the methodology's four facets are important for trust and relationship-building, the introduction is the most critical, because it establishes a respectful entry point into a community. Santana reminds us that community introduction is more than physically coming into a community with good intentions. His methodology involves pre-work that, among other things, addresses who might be the most appropriate people to lead the restorative justice work using Circle processes.

Santana is concerned about restorative justice's increasing popularity within the mainstream, because this popularity may lead to deviations from restorative justice's original purpose—namely, to do justice in more inclusive and transformative ways. For example, *CRJ* contributors, including Santana, note that professionalizing the field has sustained racial inequities between frontline practitioners of color and restorative justice programs that accept mainstream hiring norms, such as credentialing. Indeed, Santana notes a difference between using Circles to address a racial incident and using Circles to address systemic racism within groups or organizations. For the latter Circle, we return to the disparity problem: restorative groups and organizations seldom reflect the communities they serve. For many who do restorative justice work, identity signifiers—"tell us your story" or "who are you?"—become relevant: self-reflection is an integral part of letting community members know who you are.

Despite concerns about professionalizing restorative justice, at a grassroots or community level, implementing restorative justice within an organization or group deserves consideration. As policy, restorative justice creates spaces for people to engage in relationship-building in ways that top-down or transactional procedures do not (think of formal grievance policies). Of course, homegrown organizations that adopt restorative justice as their policy are much less rigid than state-level institutions. Santana reveals how restorative justice, as it becomes part of a state's criminal or juvenile justice system, overlooks restorative justice practitioners' vital role. Santana emphasizes a tenet of restorative justice that can easily be forgotten: justice is not a one-size-fits-all process but must be adapted to the needs of those involved.

Finally, Santana experiences restorative justice and Circles as having a spirit and culture of care. Circles are spaces created from people's willingness to be vulnerable, to acknowledge triggers, and to own limitations. These are hallmarks of self-awareness and humility. Here we can agree with Santana that restorative justice can be both healing and harmful: which outcome emerges truly depends on the sense of self and self-awareness of those involved.

Belinda Dulin begins her story with a 2009 American Civil Liberties Union's (ACLU) report that put numbers to the school-to-prison pipeline in Michigan. The report affirms what communities of color and Indigenous communities know from experience: our children receive more severe disciplinary sanctions from school personnel than White children do for the same infractions. Because of this racially targeted disciplining, who can blame our children if they choose to withdraw emotionally from or rebel against the very personnel who, though entrusted with their education, nonetheless objectify and dehumanize them?

The ACLU report points to restorative practices as a way to disrupt this pipeline. Yet, after almost a decade of start-stop interventions and endless policy discussions without any real effect, Dulin, like so many other restorative practice practitioners of color, asks herself the critical question: Who is missing from the table when restorative practices are being discussed, designed, and implemented? When it comes to school discipline and its impact on our children of color, Dulin invites restorative practitioners to expand their bandwidth and intentionally include children, parents, and communities of color in all phases of restorative practices.

However, Dulin is not Pollyannaish about her invitation. Dulin and other *CRJ* contributors understand that having a restorative program in a school may not provide the hoped-for results: less conflict, fewer in-school suspensions, lower rates of dropouts and expulsions, and, above all, a more racially just school culture. Dulin asserts that, because restorative programs target the transformation of youth of color or Indigenous youth, they are done on the cheap. Scarce budgets; low commitment to restorative practices; inadequate training in restorative practices; restorative practitioners who parachute in and then leave; institutional rules and regulations that circumscribe restorative practices; and insufficient time to incorporate restorative practices: doing RJ on the cheap leaves a school's culture unchanged, which means patterns of discriminatory disciplining continue uninterrupted.

The traditional, mainstream view is that education is a public good, but who is included in that public? Who "deserves" that good? Communities of color and Indigenous communities know that school norms, including what is taught in schools, do not reflect the "public" we experience in our communities. As with disciplinary practices, schools formally structure parent and community engagement. For communities of color and Indigenous communities, such choreographed engagement reinforces the school's power structure and is not welcoming to our people. Dulin recognizes that for restorative practices, particularly Circles, to take root in a school, we must address the distinction between public (as in formal or clinical) and community (as in intimate or authentic). Because restorative practices bring community into a school, schools mistakenly conclude that restorative practices can thrive on the cheap—as marginalized programs to deal with marginalized people. The outcomes mirror the input: restorative practices either do not reach their potential or outright fail.

By contrast, authentically incorporating restorative practices into a school means engaging community members as co-partners—and for all the reasons Dulin sees as critical in halting the school-to-prison pipeline. It means weaving a seamless web between what the community can offer to the school and vice versa, so that parents and communities do not feel alienated from our children's educational experiences. For practitioners of color, Dulin offers suggestions about how to include the most vulnerable people in a school: our children. We appreciate Dulin's suggestions. Not only do they provide a road map for involving community members, but they also affirm that we are doing the right thing, despite the ingrained punitive thinking that justifies push-out.

Appealing to both educators and restorative practitioners of color, Dulin reminds us that our role in stopping a school's pipeline to prison is critical. Despite her personal successes, though, Dulin raises the systemic issue: schools need more and more practitioners of color, hence her invitation to join her in Circle. *CRJ*'s contributors are pleased to show up there.

Janice Jerome explains how working in restorative justice helped her embrace a difficult past—an embrace that has become a source of agency for her. Not unlike other People of Color and Indigenous Peoples who may have internalized shame about a childhood community, Jerome carried shame about her hometown for decades. Jerome's formative years had aspects to it that many People of Color and Indigenous Peoples recognize: kinship and extended families who defined neighborhoods, participated in child-rearing, and helped to shape her identity. Yet, Jerome's childhood also reveals how the structural violence that communities of color and Indigenous communities face can be internalized and then projected outward toward members of the community, including one's own family.

Sharing deeply personal memories, Jerome calls our attention to an unsettling reality—namely, that the violence our communities face from without finds its way into our families as well as our bodies. Jerome reveals how trauma from witnessing violence led to her ill health, which became a further source of shame. Research has now corroborated this impact of chronic trauma on health. Especially as children, we internalize strong emotions, like shame, from trauma, domestic violence, or other forms of oppression, and these emotions affect our bodies, behavior, and well-being.

Working-class Black folk founded her childhood hometown, Pitsburgh, in the late nineteenth century. For many years, it was a prosperous, safe, and stable community. However, her family's move to East Atlanta separated her from her original community, which over time became impoverished and increasingly violent. Jerome experienced both family shame and community shame about Pitsburgh, and the two conflated to such a degree that she severed any association with her hometown. She feared her classmates, friends, and coworkers would think less of her if they knew her origins. At one time, Indigenous Peoples could also relate to Jerome's fear of being from a community—in our cases reservations—viewed as an unfit place to live. With the settlers' 1950s and 1960s Relocation Program, many Native families migrated to urban centers to escape "poverty." Similarly, East Atlanta provided Jerome an identity escape hatch—temporarily at least.

When Jerome began restorative justice work as a practitioner in the early 2000s, her job included mediation and diversion in programs involving youth of color, who came from low-income families and high-crime communities. She could relate with them, yet her deep shame kept her from sharing her story.

Eventually, Jerome created her own organization that employed restorative justice. In doing so, she inched closer to embracing her origins and identity. Though she posed questions to others about their personal story or journey, Jerome would not fully divulge her own. Finally, she accepted an invitation to pilot healing Circles in three communities, one of which was Pitsburgh. This pilot program addressed trauma-related issues, and Jerome could speak to these issues using restorative approaches. Her return to the place of the original trauma and violence triggered her emotionally and unlocked the shame—as well as the secret that kept it there. The Circle process and her commitment to the restorative work brought her full circle.

Jerome's journey is a deeply personal story, of course, one that Circle participants recognize immediately because it comes from her soul. Jerome reveals how important self-reflection is in restorative justice: peacemaking begins within. Turning a critical, self-reflective lens inward, as she did, we can embrace humility, and the self-awareness that follows checks our self in ways that transform us and instill a much deeper self-acceptance. We can celebrate with Jerome, recognizing that restorative justice's call reaches deep within and heals from the inside out; its transformative power touches us all.

Johonna McCants-Turner raises the question: What does safety really mean in the lives of People of Color and Indigenous Peoples? She explores the factors that constitute safety and how restorative justice must do a better job at creating safe spaces, especially for marginalized peoples. McCants-Turner's journey brings the restorative justice and restorative practices worlds into contact with the worlds of transformative justice and community accountability. While these worlds share some common ideals, such as repairing harm, their approaches differ. Transformative justice embraces a commitment to community at the grassroots level, while restorative justice mostly mediates between communities and state or other institutions.

McCants-Turner draws our attention to the reality that, whenever a state's apparatus—be it law enforcement, social services, immigration, or schools—intervenes in our daily lives, we experience this intrusion as a source of danger, even though in theory those intervening are trying to help, serve, or protect us. How many of us can relate a story about the danger we sense when we see a White police officer, or the hopelessness we feel when we learn that a White judge or a co-opted judge of color will preside over matters better left to a community to resolve? McCants-Turner's story personalizes these dangers in ways familiar to our communities. Because we exercise little to no control over state power and because states have a history of targeting our communities with countless forms of violence, our safety will not come from external, state sources; rather, it must come from within our own communities.

Prior to the establishing of the US, we secured safety from within our community. Communities of color and Indigenous communities organically created non-institutional ways of doing justice that settled disruptive behavior among community members, so that community harmony and stability would continue. But for many non-White communities, our post-US experiences with westernized states have been filled with violence, especially for women, youth, and LBGTQ of color.

In order to mitigate the racial injustices inherent in mainstream legal, judicial, and enforcement systems, McCants-Turner describes how community collectives are providing strong alternatives. Because safety is core to the well-being of People of Color and Indigenous Peoples, and because the state is not reliable for ensuring our safety and may well do us harm, both transformative justice and community accountability place safety in the hands of community people. Absence of violence, which safety certainly requires, does not characterize the state's relationship with non-White communities.

Where is mainstream restorative justice in this struggle for safety that we face? Many restorative justice practitioners find places to do restorative work within a range of state structures, not only with the criminal and civil legal systems. Embedded within these institutions, restorative practitioners feel pressure to keep their critiques and critical analyses to themselves, since speaking out could cost them their jobs and funding or their professional or community networks. Institutions have a way of eliciting self-censure and silence—a main way being the paycheck. Yet without a critical social or racial justice lens, how can restorative justice achieve more than little pockets of justice—justice only up to a point? For us, this silence means violence against us. McCants-Turner's analysis and experience indicate that this is the critical point: Will restorative justice as a movement be satisfied with the role of being the state's institutional poster child or, to use another metaphor, the velvet glove (for a few) on an iron fist (for the many)?

McCants-Turner shows that the state and its institutions are not our only option. For her and others, social and racial justice can unite restorative justice with transformative justice. Safety from harm is possible, but we have to take responsibility for securing it and that means breaking through the silences. She names at least four things that community members can practice to create a safe community—practices that help us internalize community accountability. To be sure, what McCants-Turner envisions is not a "McGruff the Crime Dog" type program. Rather, she describes a deep community strategy that understands domination's dynamics and from that understanding develops self-determining community actions. Safety becomes a reality, she tells us, when the relational intimacy we create in our communities—the intimacy born of voicing our realities, hearing each other's stories, and showing up for each other in support—forms our path to justice.

Part V. A Call to Settlers in RJ

Alice Walker, African American, novelist, poet, and activist, writes, "Healing begins where the wound was made."[20] Restorative justice is about healing, but how can this healing happen or be real until we who are in the RJ movement attend to healing "where the wound was made"? The unhealed wound? The world knows, as we all do, that the US was birthed with genocide and slavery, and that the legacies of these massive harms remain in force today. Every place the foot of a person whose people are not indigenous to this hemisphere lands is a place of fraud, theft, and murder. And the wealth that White settlers have extracted from this land, both personally and institutionally, has been gained through enslavement and then concentrated in White hands through theft, injustice, terrorism, violence, murder, and exclusion.

As long as the restorative justice movement confines its focus to harms done by individuals today, the work will prove superficial in effect. If RJ remains silent about these twin wounds, its ability to transform society will remain compromised. The mindset that believes in doing harm to gain benefits will continue unchallenged. Even the transformative impact on individuals will be limited, imbalanced, and unsatisfactory, because the far greater harms that do far greater structural damage hang all around us. The restorative effect will stop with "just us," violating the core RJ principle of inclusion. Moreover, unrepaired harms make us all complicit in their perpetuation. Part 5 colorizes restorative justice by taking us back to "where the wound was made." Repairing these harms heals trauma on all sides, so that our children can learn the ways of self-transformation—personally and as peoples.

In my own chapter, I, **Edward Valandra, Waŋbli Wapȟáha Hokšíla,** voice what has been on my mind since I first heard about the restorative justice movement seventeen years ago: How can settlers in RJ, while citing RJ/RP's Indigenous roots and committing themselves to repairing harms, live on land stolen from Indigenous Peoples through genocide and *not* act to undo this catastrophic harm? How can settlers in RJ credibly hold children accountable for stealing others' property or personal belongings and not hold themselves accountable for the mass fraud and crimes that their settlement in North America involves—crimes from which settlers benefit and Indigenous Peoples suffer every day? These questions go to the core of RJ's integrity as a movement. Justice Yazzie, a Diné citizen, says, "You cannot get to a good place in a bad way." By calling these questions out of silence, unsettling as they are, I aim to heighten critical awareness of how White fantasies keep harms against

Indigenous Nations off settlers' radar and prevent settlers in RJ from "walking the restorative talk."

I open my chapter by naming the ongoing structural harm that is settler colonialism. Why is settler colonialism a harm? Because it requires structural genocide. For colonizers to take over an Indigenous Peoples' land base, we who have been rooted in our homelands for millennia before White European invasion must go. Settler colonialism operates on the "logic of elimination." Any vestige of Native permanence must be obliterated. The Whites' brutal ethnic cleansing of the Cherokee is a prime case study. The Cherokee turned themselves into model "civilized" neighbors in every way, from their agricultural bounty to their high literacy to their forms of government. Yet their very successes enraged White settlers. The Cherokee's permanence triggered White settler society to go on a thieving, murderous rampage that destroyed all that the Cherokee Nation had achieved. One in four Cherokee citizens perished on the Trail of Tears, a forced march that drove them from their ancestral homeland to Indian Territory.

Various methods effect Native Peoples' elimination, from killing our families to destroying our food supplies, from forcibly removing Native nations from our land bases to destroying our family structures, cultures, languages, economies, educational systems, and ways of life. Moreover, the logic of elimination operates structurally and institutionally. I cite many decolonization scholars, some of whom are White, who affirm that settler colonialism is "a structure, not an event."[21] "This structure secures settler 'permanence' by disappearing Indigenous populations."[22] The harms that settlers in RJ must undo—an ongoing aggregate that I call "The First Harm"—began in the past but do not end there: colonial structures perpetrate genocidal harm against Indigenous Peoples every day, robbing our generations and those not yet born of their rightful legacies, patrimonies, and futures.

For settlers in RJ to undo The First Harm, I contend that Whites in particular must develop a critical awareness about race, whiteness, and fantasies of white entitlement, such as the infamous Doctrine of Discovery. The historical record shows how these fictitious constructs perpetrate catastrophic racial and political harms: harms against us as a racial group and against our nations as political threats to US (colonizer) domination of our land and resources. Yet, while championing restorative responses to one-on-one harms, RJ/RP has not engendered a critical consciousness about race and colonization among its White practitioners equal to repairing the mass harms in White US history.

So, what can be done? I engage "The Talk" with settlers "about this dilemma your ancestors created for you and which you sustain."[23] I start The Talk by exploring White notions of community: What binds people in relationship? German-Jewish philosopher Hannah Arendt observed that the world of things that we have in common, like a table that we sit around, gathers us together. But what happens when fantasies—things that simply are not true—take hold of our minds? Then we cannot see the world of things—it disappears—and "the world between us loses its power to gather us together."[24] Settler colonialism, white supremacy, white entitlement, and your Discovery Doctrine, which encompasses other human-rights-violating settler doctrines, statutes, case laws, and policies: these are the fantasies that obscure the world between us and have made authentic coexistence impossible. Even naming these constructs as fantasies can trigger White settlers' vociferous anger, visceral rage, and physical violence: "Given how little it takes to trigger settlers' anger and defensiveness, it is not clear to me how you will dismantle your settler structures enough to be able to dialogue about The First Harm, much less to undo it."[25]

Still, for those willing to walk the restorative talk all the way to undoing The First Harm, I turn to Circle dialogue as the place to start. Honest, authentic dialogue, as may be possible in Circles, offers a means for peeling off fantasies, so that the world we share stays central and regains its power not only to draw us together but also to transform us as it does. Then, what once seemed impossible—repairing The First Harm on which every facet of US life is built—may become possible.

Summary

Clearly, siloing RJ from racial and social justice issues, including de/colonization—as if RJ/RP could be effective, much less fulfill its promise and potential, in a "colorblind," injustice-blind bubble—is not an option as far as the contributors in this book are concerned, and we hope those who read our work feel the same. Not only is such a stance contrary to RJ philosophy, values, and principles, but it also does great harm. The "RJ in a bubble" approach harms the youth and adults RJ/RP serves; it harms colleagues of color and Indigenous colleagues; it excludes communities of color and Indigenous communities as equal partners; and it undermines the integrity and evolution of the movement and prevents it from being truly revolutionary. The accountability that everyone calls for and that proves so transformative—being mindful of our shared roles in harms—seldom reaches beyond the individual level to the institutional, much less to the collective accountability that is the game changer for peoples.

We have work to do, and these authors help us get started.

As a final note, I struggle with the accepted Western norm of keeping the racial position and experience of authors invisible in the name of colorblindness and racial neutrality. For example, the academic and mainstream practice is not to name the race or ethnicity or Indigenous nation or other non-mainstream identifiers of anyone in written literature, except to highlight the unconventional, i.e., American Indian, Black, or Hispanic senator or mayor, Black US president, Black governor, etc. Rarely do we read in print about a *White* senator or mayor, *White* US president, *White* governor, etc. Moreover, in their bios, academics, including academics of color, seldom name how they self-identify racially or ethnically or, if Indigenous, with their Native nation. Therefore, we in this work—aware as we are that colorblindness is not the answer to repairing racial harms—must make clear our own racial and national positionality. This practice will make it easier for authors to name the racial and national positionality of those we quote as we go forward.

NOTES

1. Fania Davis, *The Little Book of Race and Restorative Justice: Black Lives, Healing, and US Social Transformation* (New York: Good Books, 2019), 37–38.
2. Mara Schiff, "Institutionalizing Restorative Justice: Paradoxes of Power, Restoration, and Rights," in *Reconstructing Restorative Justice Philosophy* (Furnham, UK: Ashgate Publishing, 2013), 163.
3. Sharon Goens-Bradley, "Breaking Racism's Insidious Grip on Restorative Practices: A Call for White Action," in *Colorizing Restorative Justice: Voicing Our Realities,* ed. Edward C Valandra (St. Paul, MN: Living Justice Press, 2020), 38.
4. Barbara Sherrod, "Your Silence Will Not Protect You," in *Colorizing Restorative Justice,* 57.
5. Christina Parker, "Who's In and Who's Out? Problematizing Peacemaking Circles in Diverse Classrooms," in *Colorizing Restorative Justice,* 67.
6. Erica Littlewolf, Michelle Armster, and Christianne Paras, with Lorraine Stutzman Amstutz, "Burn the Bridge," in *Colorizing Restorative Justice,* 87.
7. The Corruption of Blood Principle is defined as "the effect of an attainder which bars a person from inheriting, retaining, or transmitting any estate, rank, or title" (*Merriam-Webster*). "An attainder was the harsh consequence of conviction for treason or a felony. It resulted in the forfeiture of the convicted person's property. It also involved corruption of blood, which barred the person from inheriting, retaining, or passing title, rank, or property" (*Merriam-Webster*).
8. Anne Bonds and Joshua Inwood, "Beyond White Privilege: Geographies of White Supremacy and Settler Colonialism," *Progress in Human Geography* 40, no. 6 (2006): 716.
9. Ibid., 717.
10. Sheryl Wilson, "Calling Out Whiteness," in *Colorizing Restorative Justice,* 104.
11. Ibid., 103.
12. Robin DiAngelo, *White Fragility: Why It's So Hard for White People to Talk about Racism* (Boston: Beacon Press, 2018).
13. Wilson quotes Schmidt in "Calling Out Whiteness," 107.
14. Anita Wadhwa, "'What Do You Want, Reparations?' Racial Microaggressions and Restorative Justice," in *Colorizing Restorative Justice,* 163.
15. Gilbert Salazar, "Passing the Cup of Vulnerability: Offering Vulnerability as

a Challenge to White Fragility through the Elements of Circle," in *Colorizing Restorative Justice,* 173.

16. On the notion of Circles as containers, see Kay Pranis, *The Little Book of Circle Processes: A New/Old Approach to Peacemaking, The Little Books of Justice & Peacebuilding* (Intercourse, PA: Good Books, 2005), 9.
17. Malik Muhammad, "The Cipher, Circle, and Restorative Practices with Black and Brown Boys," in *Colorizing Restorative Justice,* 213.
18. See also Ted Wachtel, "Restorative Justice in Everyday Life: Beyond the Formal Ritual," *Reclaiming Children and Youth* 12, no. 2 (Summer 2003): 83–87.
19. See Joy DeGruy, *Post Traumatic Slave Syndrome: America's Legacy of Enduring Injury and Healing* (Portland, OR: Joy DeGruy Publications, 2005).
20. Alice Walker, *The Way Forward Is with a Broken Heart* (New York: Ballantine Books, 2001).
21. Edward Valandra, Waŋbli Wapȟáha Hokšíla, "Undoing The First Harm: Settlers in Restorative Justice," in *Colorizing Restorative Justice,* 328, 337.
22. Ibid., 328
23. Valandra, "Undoing The First Harm," 349.
24. Ibid., 352.
25. Ibid., 353.

PART I

Where Are We? RJ/RP Challenges and Obligations

In part 1, the authors explore what restorative practitioners of color face in a field that is currently dominated by Whites and Western ways of thinking. Though People of Color are profoundly engaged in the restorative work and affected by how it is practiced, many if not most White practitioners have opposed efforts to increase racial and social awareness as integral to the restorative work. In *The Little Book of Race and Restorative Justice,* Fania Davis observes that the restorative justice movement has maintained silence about racial and social justice and decolonization and has kept these issues at a distance. Both professionally and on the receiving end, People of Color and Indigenous Peoples bear the price of this choice, which we had no role in making.

CHAPTER 1

Breaking Racism's Insidious Grip on Restorative Practices: A Call for White Action

Sharon Goens-Bradley

Introduction

Let's begin with a difficult and unavoidable truth: white body supremacy is alive and well. It is pervasive, insidious, and lethal. Much like settler colonialism's ability to change, white body supremacy morphs to take new forms in each generation.[1] Even now, it is playing out in our systems, such as our educational, medical, and legal systems. And, to the extent White people either fail to see or willingly ignore the subtle ways in which they participate in white body supremacy, they continue to bring it (and therefore systemic racism) to everything they do, including restorative practices (RP) work.

What is white body supremacy? In *What Does It Mean to Be White?* Robin DiAngelo, a White woman with a PhD in multicultural education and decades of experience as a diversity trainer, describes it this way:

> The all-encompassing centrality and assumed superiority of people defined and perceived as white, and the practices based on this assumption. . . . White supremacy does not refer to individual white people per se and their individual intentions, but to a political-economic social system of domination. This system is based on the historical and current accumulation of structural power that privileges, centralizes, and elevates white people as a group. . . . I do not use it to refer to extreme hate groups. I use the term to capture the pervasiveness, magnitude, and normalcy of white dominance and assumed superiority.[2]

So, while RP diverts many youth of color and Indigenous youth (YOCIY) from life-harming suspensions, expulsions, arrests, and convictions, *RP has yet to divert them from the underlying dynamic of white body supremacy and will continue to fail them in this way until White Circle keepers (CKs) proactively develop and apply a race-conscious lens.* Until then, White CKs can't help but actively reinforce the toxic and fundamentally oppressive meta-messages that poison the hearts and minds of our YOCIY: because of who you are racially, you are morally and intellectually inferior, you must rely on the charity of others, your choices are limited, your lived experiences are irrelevant to the larger society (except to the extent they fit in to benefit white body supremacy), and you must conform to white expectations and needs; otherwise nonconformity results in being rejected and/or punished. As white body supremacy plays out in RP, it tragically nullifies RP's revolutionary core goals of upholding the value of every person, building relationships within community, and repairing harms. By way of example, consider the following story:

> *Julie, a White Circle keeper, loved facilitating Circles in the schools. Like many White people, she lived in a predominantly White world but, more than most, was deeply aware of the greater diversity in the larger community. Being around the kids of color enriched her life in ways she often shared with others, and she felt lucky to have a job in which she learned about kids with different life experiences from hers. But when asked, as a White woman, what she was specifically able to offer kids of color or how she was using her privilege to advocate for those children, she was speechless.*

This anecdote shows how a White CK lacks a race-conscious lens through which to understand her experiences and her work. She doesn't see the ongoing, actively enforced racial hierarchy in the US and how one's lived experience is largely dominated by this racial hierarchy. She doesn't see herself as a *racial* being with experiences that are specific to being White. She doesn't even know she doesn't know this—and that the youth she is serving, *because of their race,* have such different experiences from her own. She sees her work through the frame of how the YOCIY enrich *her* life (a White-centric view), and she *assumes* that a White, middle-aged, middle-class woman by her very engagement is able to benefit others. To the extent that the life experiences of those she is purporting to serve are different from hers, she assumes that her involvement is bringing them into a better frame; their involvement is rendered irrelevant to the work (except to the limited extent that it helps *her* to hear their stories or pick up some youthful slang, so that she can "relate" to the kids). If her RP work is paid, she may feel grateful to have "meaningful and rewarding" work.

As a result, the YOCIY must subordinate their own experiences to Julie's worldview if they are to participate in a Circle. As we'll explore further below, they'll have to use words, speech patterns, and body language with which Julie is comfortable (vs. the service professional accommodating to *their* preferences); they'll need to shrug off the numerous microaggressions that she'll inadvertently commit (vs. experiencing a safe space); and they'll need to avoid topics of race to protect her need to be comfortable (vs. being deeply heard in Circle). And, perhaps most insidious, in all this, the YOCIY will have had imposed on them yet another White "role model" who promotes White culture and bodies as the ideal against which all others are inferior.

In short, Julie's behavior embodies racism and brings it to the RP paradigm. She is acting out internalized white superiority, replicating the generations-old patterns of colonialism (exerting power over others), and modeling appropriation ("It's okay for me to benefit from our relationship whether or not I can benefit you"). All of this actively undermines the sense of self and the emotional growth we're committed to providing our YOCIY. Transformative growth requires a level of emotional trust and safety, including being seen and respected for who you are. There is no safety for YOCIY around White adults whose upbringing lacked a race-conscious lens, which renders them unable to step out of the white body supremacy framework on which US culture is built.[3]

There is no safety for YOCIY around White adults whose upbringing lacked a race-conscious lens.

In this chapter, I will describe the race-conscious lens more fully and why it's important to deconstruct white body supremacy. I'll give more examples of the violence perpetrated against and harming YOCIY when White CKs lack a critical race-conscious lens. Finally, I'll offer specific suggestions for building a better future where race is not a card one politicizes. If White CKs are to realize RJ's overarching goals, they must develop a proactive, race-conscious lens when serving YOCIY.

As a CK (and mother) of color, I write this chapter with both anger and hope. Anger that white body supremacy continues to poison our youth, even in our well-intentioned and countercultural RP forum. And hope that my White colleagues—who numerically dominate the "professional" (i.e., remunerated) RJ field, particularly in Minnesota—will accept my personal invitation to engage in the deeply transformative, albeit uncomfortable, personal work to understand white body supremacy within themselves. The invitation's purpose is clear: so you don't join countless others in acting out white body supremacy and causing harm to our precious youth.

Operating without a Race-Conscious Lens

Without a race-conscious lens, White people often miss the ongoing, handicapping racial impact of the following undisputable facts: the United States of

America was built on the subrogation of the needs and values of Black, Brown, and Red bodies to those of White bodies, i.e., white supremacy. Even before its founding, people in White bodies stole the land and the labor of Black, Brown, and Red bodies—and just as importantly, they acted on reinforced beliefs that their theft was acceptable and justified. Our history shows, White propertied men (and their lived experiences) have always comprised the US centers of power, such as national and state governments, and continue to do so. This institutional composition has legalized and enforced an inherent, self-serving racism in countless policies and laws. The Naturalization Act (1790), Indian Removal Act (1830), and Fugitive Slave Law (1850) are just a few explicit examples of how statutorily White immigrant preference, slavery, and the theft of Indigenous land were codified and supported through force, intimidation, and egregious violence, which includes whippings, shootings, lynchings, rapes, and murder. Eighty years of Jim Crow, followed by contemporary iterations of mass incarceration, job discrimination, school segregation, and state-sanctioned violence against Black, Brown, and Red bodies brutally continues to enforce subliminal, as well as explicit, messages about White bodies possessing greater inherent value over Black, Brown, and Red ones. No US-born and raised citizens can escape the unconscious absorption of these ubiquitous, toxic messages or the systemic way in which this country shifts financial, cultural, and psychic resources to Whites from POCIP (People of Color and Indigenous Peoples). Few White American citizens, even those who consider themselves to be firmly anti-racist, hold themselves accountable to this stark reality. Accountability would include taking the time to become knowledgeable about their history, taking responsibility for the ways in which it has privileged them and disenfranchised others, and making conscious and strategic efforts to make amends. In other words, to be accountable, White American citizens must own their history and what it encompasses.

To be accountable, White American citizens must own their history and what it encompasses.

To have a race-conscious lens means to see how one's lived experience in the US is largely dominated by onc's racial place in the above system. People of Color typically have an easier time than Whites developing a race-conscious lens; the lack of inclusion in resource distribution, in values definition, in perspectives acknowledgment, etc. is easier to see from the outside than the inside, especially in our segregated societies. Just as men are often blind to the ways in which the system of patriarchy gives them preferential treatment in our society (the job market, political realm, and educational sphere, to name just a few), so are White people less able to see themselves as structurally *benefiting* as individuals *because they are part of a specific racial group or, in short, are a racial being.*

Consider this race-conscious analysis of why more People of Color are not in positions of "authority," including as CKs:

- In US (white) culture, power is understood and held hierarchically.
- In hierarchy, access to the top (and resources) must be limited.
- The recognition of "competence" and the capacity to earn higher incomes are typically limited to those with advanced degrees.
- Formal education, especially foundational education, focuses almost exclusively on the lived experiences of White bodies and distorts and minimizes the oppression and the roles of POCIP.
- Degrees are typically limited to those who are able to pay ever-increasing tuition.
- Jobs are typically limited to those with "experience."
- The recognition of "experience" is typically limited to that obtained through participating in a specific structure, as opposed to "life" experience, for which one is either unpaid or low-paid.
- Specific to Circle keeping: despite having a history that is thousands of years old, Circle keeping has been codified as a practice that can be monetarily compensated, thus making it attractive to all those who value and operate out of the aforementioned points. CKs of color, who prioritize helping their communities—often working voluntarily for free or because of deep and/or grounded community relationships—are not heralded with the same acclaim, respect, or credibility as White practitioners.

Thus, when one sees the impact on one's life of being one "race" vs. another, one can see the systems-wide advantages that support White people in being disproportionately represented among positions of influence, including as directors of the nonprofits that are paid to do mediation and RP work. Without such a race lens, if one assumes that people of all races have had equal access to resources and that we are living in a post-racial society, then one concludes, consciously or unconsciously, that the disproportionate representation of White people holding influential positions must be due to their white body superiority.

Without the benefit of a race-conscious lens, nonprofit leaders who are White miss how race plays out in the power structures of their organizations.

Furthermore, without the benefit of a race-conscious lens, nonprofit leaders who are White miss how race plays out in the power structures of their organizations. Unlike POCIP, they probably don't routinely talk to their (White) friends about racism, race equity, or white privilege in a substantive way. Without routine critical analysis, they have scarce defense against their racial socialization and against the onslaught of negative images and stereotypes of Black and Brown and Red people. While they would vigorously defend themselves against any charge of racism, and while they genuinely wish to be of service, fundamentally, their beliefs about the leadership, wisdom, and abilities of POCIP are likely to be similar to those they'd consider explicitly racist, as the White nationalist.

Below, I'll show some ways in which the lack of a race-conscious lens plays out in Circles and harms our YOCIY.

Collapsing around Race

Two White CKs, deeply committed to giving youth some resources to cope with the pervasive poverty surrounding them, were about ten minutes into the Circle when an African American teenager passionately vocalized her support of Black Lives Matter. The CKs, both visibly shaken, could not retain the ability to stay in the spiritual space necessary to support the group as it grappled with conflicting beliefs and ideas. They stepped out of their roles to express disagreement with the young person and dismay in general. They wondered aloud why all lives didn't matter and why their lives needed to be upended by "unproductive" protests. Witnessing this negation, the teen, whose life experiences were dominated by first- and second-hand examples of Black lives being routinely destroyed by the criminal "justice" system, completely shut down and refused to participate in the Circle, which further distressed one of the White CKs. The Circle ended prematurely, lending little support to the youth the keepers purported to serve.

DiAngelo created the term "white fragility" to describe the inability of White people to handle the emotional stress they feel around frank conversations about race and racism. While Whites don't often have to encounter this racial stress, when they do, they weaponize their behavior by "withdrawal, defending, crying, arguing, minimizing, ignoring, and in other ways pushing back to regain [their] racial position and equilibrium."[4]

As a result, despite being in Circles, White CKs often react defensively to remarks about race. For example, they change the subject; they make issues explicitly about race broader and more neutral ("Yes, we've all had trauma and have experienced times when we felt discriminated against . . ."); or they try to join with YOCIY in acknowledging racist systems without openly acknowledging their own (White) advantages in that system.

And how does white fragility impact YOCIY? Understandably, YOCIY want the defensive reactions to stop. I have seen them try to **placate and protect** White CKs in an attempt to bring them back to equilibrium. Unfortunately, this serves to reinforce the White status quo at a brutally oppressive psychic cost to the YOCIY. I've also seen YOCIY respond with anger, shutting down, or even demanding that a White CK talk about their own (White) internalized racism. The latter strategy typically activates even more defensiveness from White CKs, which often leads them to use their power to end the Circle or simply dominate the conversation. The Circle process is derailed, and participants leave with varying levels of frustration, rage, guilt, shame, or reinforced perceptions around racial stereotypes.

Perpetrating Microaggressions

> *Even though she knew many of the youth in the school, the Circle keeper did not make an attempt to learn the names of the youth in her Circle and how to pronounce their names correctly. Without asking their permission, she told them she was giving them all nicknames so that she could better remember them.*

If you can't define microaggressions, you're White, and if you grew up in the US, it is all but certain you're committing them.

In 1970, Harvard University professor Chester M. Pierce identified microaggressions as "brief, everyday exchanges that send denigrating messages to certain individuals because of their group membership."[5] More recently, they have been understood as being more normalized than previously thought. Moreover, Roberto Montenegro, a chief fellow in child and adolescent psychiatry at Seattle Children's Hospital, studies the biological effects of microaggressions and says this about microaggressions:

If you can't define microaggressions, you're White, and if you grew up in the US, it is all but certain you're committing them.

> It isn't about having your feelings hurt. It's about how being repeatedly dismissed and alienated and insulted and invalidated reinforces the differences in power and privilege, and how this perpetuates racism and discrimination.

Below are some specific examples of microaggressions, all of which serve to protect the White CK's comfort and familiarity, while diminishing the value of the qualitative experiences of YOCIY and their very being:

- "Where are you *really* from?" (This insinuates that they are not really American.)

- "You are SO articulate!" (This signals surprise that a YOCIY has vocalized an astute observation or remark, thereby revealing an assumption that YOCIY are not astute.)
- Mistaking a teacher for a student. (This shows an expectation that POCIP aren't professionals.)
- Making statements like, "I don't see color. I believe we are all equal. I don't care if you're black, white, or purple with pink polka dots!" (In addition to being illogical, this completely misses the well-documented lived experiences of POCIP that we are not, actually, all treated equally.)
- "My child/spouse/friend is Black/Latinx/Indigenous, so I know what it's like . . ." (This suggests that being close to a POCIP means you fully understand racism, which of course is untrue, as shown by the failure of Whites to educate themselves about racism through their associations with slaves and domestic workers.)
- Micromanaging, judging, or attempting to control the ways in which the POCIP CKs connect with YOCIY. (This shows a subtle but strong judgment that the POCIP CK is not as competent or as equal in status to their White counterpart.)
- "When I worked with YOCIY, they told me that they didn't realize I was White!" Seeking affirmation from (or trying to prove to) a POCIP that you're different from other White people. (This is an attempt, often aggressive, to ask a POCIP to make you feel comfortable and "woke.")
- Generalizing POCIP experiences of racism with blanket statements like "Well, we've all experienced trauma, felt like we didn't belong, had hard things happen to us." (This negates the specific experience of race/racism for the POCIP.)
- Accusing POCIP of "attacking" them and/or "playing the race card" when historical race-related wrongs are centered in a presentation, training, or conversation.
- Utilizing tears and victim statements to derail or distract the group from the aforementioned presentation, training, or conversation.

It isn't about having your feelings hurt. It's about how being repeatedly dismissed and alienated and insulted and invalidated reinforces the differences in power and privilege, and how this perpetuates racism and discrimination.
—Roberto Montenegro

In short, like white fragility, microaggressions in a Circle shatter youths' sense of trust and safety. Learning how *not* to perpetrate microaggressions on YOCIY (or POCIP) is essential for any CK wishing to promote genuine healing and community.

Landing in White Superiority

A young White director of a nonprofit was recently asked to increase a restorative presence in schools in his neighborhood. He was very personable, enthusiastic, and idealistic. Although he lacked knowledge about this community and had never worked with youth or had any or in-depth training in facilitating restorative practices, he was confident he'd be successful. His plan? Hire a POCIP to execute the plan (under his supervision).

This scenario exemplifies the power and invisibility of white body superiority and its attendant culture embedded in the very structure of US nonprofit organizations, including RP programs.[6] How does it come to pass (and why aren't we more surprised?) that a young White person is given the top role, including decision-making, while the POCIP they will hire—who know the community and will provide key insights and authentic engagement—are given the lower role and lower pay?[7] How is it that this White man has the confidence to "lead" the efforts, while relying unequivocally on a POCIP to provide "technical" help? The importance of seeing this structural issue—and the white body superiority on which it is built—cannot be overstated.

Below are some additional white supremacy dynamics I've seen or heard in RP contexts.

My family had immigrated to the US from an African nation. I was asked to be a co-keeper to help address some harms that had happened in my community. But when I attempted to engage with my people in ways more culturally comfortable for them, I was told to stop, that I was not following procedure and going "off-track."

POCIP Circle keeper

When engaging in a decision-making group that funds opportunities for RP initiatives, I witnessed preference continually given to those who prepared their applications utilizing a Eurocentric frame, using language and paradigms that exemplified a college education but did not demonstrate any knowledge of the communities they'd be working within. Those who applied (usually POCIP) with deep roots in communities of color, who embraced RP as a way of life, and who could often do the work with more fidelity than their White counterparts were seen as "not professional enough."

As reported by a POCIP CK

We don't have time to engage in long-term anti-racism training; we can't afford it, and it would divert us from serving our youth.

White nonprofit leader

White Superiority in Nonprofit Cultural Norms

Minnesota's mission-driven, nonprofit leaders and the volunteers who work for their organizations are overwhelmingly White and lack a race-conscious lens.[8] As a result, the larger white body supremacy culture influences how the White people behave and how the organizations function. These cultural influences promote organizational cultures, norms, and values that exclude the lived experiences of POCIP. For example:

- Policies and procedures value reason (over emotion), individualism (over the collective), productivity (over relationships), hierarchy (over community), White-based credentials (over lived experience), and statistics or data (over stories).
- POCIP who operate from a relational, cultural framework are often seen or deemed as unprofessional, inferior, or outliers.
- Most nonprofit staff are *not* supported in creating relationships with those they work with (their supervisors tell them there is no time for that). Nonprofit organizations tend to view such relationships as tainting their RJ "direct services" model.
- The nonprofit model itself is grounded in systemic racism. Funding generally comes from people or businesses that have accumulated wealth at the expense of others (often POCIP) but then, savagely, feel obliged to help the "less fortunate." In any event, to those working to address the systemic reasons that perpetuate poverty overall or that target POCIP. To some extent, given that the needs of those in poverty always outstrip the resources of nonprofits, nonprofits use systems to determine a hierarchy of need. These systems are filtered through the lens of cross-cultural incompetence.

Despite being in Circles, White CKs often react defensively to remarks about race.

These dynamics extend to White CKs as well.

Our organization relies on a volunteer model to do our work, and we would be out of business if we had to pay for something that people should want to do for free. Most of our volunteers are middle-aged, middle-class White women who really want to give back to the community.[9] *We do try to get volunteers from communities of color, but they are very hard to find. I don't understand why more of them don't want to help their own people.*

White nonprofit director

This thinking, common to many nonprofits, is fallacious and frankly racist, since it victimizes communities of color:

- It is internally inconsistent. Do we think White people should not be paid for helping White people? In all the ways we have tied money to effort, why do we suddenly expect free labor when promoting the welfare of POCIP?
- Many POCIP *do* volunteer (that is, expend effort without being paid) but are typically more focused on connecting through *existing community,* such as in one's church, neighborhood, or family vs. being connected to unpaid labor through third-party (and often White-dominated) nonprofits.
- Finally, in a field dominated by women, the structure of utilizing volunteer labor to do substantive community work speaks in and of itself to structural sexism. Again, the concept that this service-oriented work is not deemed worthy of payment is problematic and creates dynamics that replicate a colonial and sexist frame.

All the above are various ways in which the RJ field in particular (and nonprofits in general) has as yet not escaped the white body supremacy and systemic racism and sexism that permeates our US society. However, I am hopeful that RJ can break out of this restrictive paradigm; below are my suggestions to get us started.

The Call to Action

First, Assess

To engage in RJ work, all CKs must cultivate cross-cultural competence relating to the communities with whom they routinely engage. This cross-cultural competency includes, at a minimum, the following:

- Learning about their own and others' social identities, especially around race, culture, religious beliefs, and lived experiences
- Identifying their own unconscious biases and learning specific strategies and supports for interrupting them in real time
- Learning how to build cross-cultural relationships and how to engage in respectful (even if uncomfortable) cross-cultural conflict
- Building the capacity to hear and respond to honest feedback related to race, racism, and racial privilege without personalizing the feedback
- Learning about the systemic privilege and power attached to specific identities in the US and learning strategies for evening the playing field within specific individual and group interactions
- Engaging in ongoing individual and group work to understand all the ways in which racism manifests internally, personally, and systemically[10] (for those CKs who are White, this includes learning to speak and listen with greater humility and accountability)
- Learning how to engage cross-culturally with empathy and, specifically, looking at issues through others' worldviews

It can be exceptionally difficult for White CKs to step out of dominant cultural narratives to realistically assess how YOCIY experience them as a White person. Here are some questions to support White CKs with that self-assessment:

1. If I am working in communities of color or Indigenous communities, what are my motivations for being here? What value do I add to the community and to the effort to upend structural racism?
2. How do I remain accountable and respond to feedback I've been given by POCIP (or even White people) around my own racism?[11]
3. What kind of meaningful relationships do I have with People of Color or Indigenous Peoples who are not subordinate to me in any way?
4. What are some examples of microaggressions that POCIP and YOCIY routinely encounter? What strategies can I use to "run interference" for them when these microaggressions occur? For example, when I hear racist comments made by other White people in my presence, can I publicly challenge them, rather than leaving it to the POCIP?

When I hear racist comments made by other White people in my presence, can I publicly challenge them, rather than leaving it to the POCIP?

---

5. What are some systemic (both historical and current) reasons why POCIP statistically have fewer net assets than White people? What is my role in this system? What is my role in changing it?
6. What are examples of historical trauma, trans-generational trauma, and collective trauma that may impact the YOCIY that I routinely serve? What are ways in which I can reduce the likelihood of re-traumatization of YOCIY in my nonprofit and/or Circle?
7. What are ways in which I can proactively engage in trauma-informed and racial equity practices?
8. What are my strategies for ensuring that nonprofit leaders and CKs reflect the makeup of the communities they are serving?
9. What are ways in which I will work to support greater inclusion, affirmation, and comfort of YOCIY and POCIP, especially through questioning and changing normative dominant cultural practices?
10. If I influence hiring decisions, how can I find and select candidates who will authentically engage and ally with communities of color?

Before moving to the "action" step, I strongly encourage you to *take the time* needed to assess your own cultural competence and then learn how to become more racially and culturally competent. Because such a personal inventory is emotionally and spiritually difficult, many White people have a hard time staying with this step and, quite understandably, wish to move immediately on to the action step. This desire to avoid self-assessment may come both from a deep wish to promote equity and from a deep discomfort (shame?) with what has prevailed over the centuries due to ignorance, apathy, and/or resistance from White people. This White avoidance of self contributes to the level of inequity between White and other communities. Regardless of its source, the efficacy and sustainability of one's efforts depend on deeply engaging in this work. And, even when one is at the point of sufficient competence to move to the action step, the above work must continue and for several reasons: to defend against the constant onslaught of the white body supremacy frame; to better hone one's skills; to genuinely sidestep its perpetuation; and to be fully present with those we are serving.

Then . . . Act

After a critical level of self-assessment and learning, White CKs need to act. While it's true that one needs to do a certain level of initial and continual work around assessment and learning before taking action, I've also witnessed

White people getting stuck in the fear of making mistakes and hence failing to move on and take any action at all. Part of overcoming the white supremacy frame involves rejecting the need for getting-it-right perfection. The other part requires embracing a stance of humility and engagement, while engaging in the important work (consistent with our RP commitments) of promoting genuine equity and community.

Because structural racism was created by White men to benefit themselves and (to a lesser but nonetheless privileged degree) White women,[12] and because the legacy lives on and benefits all White people to some degree, White people must own it. The responsibility to end structural racism rests with them. Forms that this responsibility could take for RP organizations, such as nonprofits, include the following:

- Putting in place hiring guidelines that prioritize hiring staff who can demonstrate that they operate from an anti-racist/anti-oppression lens and who can verify that they have authentic connections to the communities with which the organization works
- Providing anti-racism trainings for all staff *and* volunteers that include recognizing structural racism and the ways in which White staff individually and collectively benefit from or are impacted by these structures
- Mandating the above-mentioned training as part of the orientation process
- Providing opportunities for all staff and volunteers to continually grow and learn in a supportive and non-judgmental environment
- Establishing accountability procedures and partners: POCIP who act in a *paid* advisory capacity give feedback about the organization's initiatives and implementations
- Analyzing and challenging current structures that privilege White ways of being and working
- Developing and prioritizing decolonized ways of engagement both internally and externally. For example, dispensing with agendas and jargon, such as "evidence-based practices" and "getting people on board," and focusing instead on true, i.e., meaningful relationship-building as modeled by the community one is in.

Please note that if some of the above language is confusing or off-putting, it will make more sense after one has engaged in deep anti-racism learning.

Back to Julie

Many may feel that in its current state, RP is "good enough" at providing affirming, non-punitive environments for YOCIY. And, yes, many YOCIY have benefited from these services and have had positive, life-changing experiences, especially when these practices have diverted them from suspensions, convictions, or incarceration. But we are falling so far short of our stated RP goals. RP could be truly revolutionary, creating an experience that leaves all who participate feeling fully validated with their full humanity intact.

RP could be truly revolutionary, creating an experience that leaves all who participate feeling fully validated with their full humanity intact.

So, I call on my White CK colleagues to do more—to take a serious look at the ways in which they participate in the perpetuation of harmful practices through passive (but willful) ignorance and unwillingness to change. For Julie, this doing more means realizing that *good intentions without knowledge will harm the students she genuinely wants to support.* She must make time and effort to understand (deeply) the history, traumas, strengths, and challenges of the YOCIY she is serving. She must both know that and understand how, as a White person, she has passively reaped benefits that have been systemically and insidiously denied YOCIY. She must ask herself critical questions, such as, "How can I ensure that, despite my being White, I am genuinely assisting those in my Circle, empowering them independent of their relationship to me? Am I the best person to be doing this work? Would it benefit these YOCIY if someone else worked with them?" To be sure, these are difficult, yet critical, questions to ask and answer. For one, they take into consideration not only one's own identity and therefore well-being, but also the well-being of the larger community.

But because I see increasing numbers of White people making a demonstrated effort to confront racism, the time has come in which White leaders overall, including White CKs, will have little choice but to engage at this level. CKs have the added advantage of the motivation that brought them to RP originally: to uphold the value of every person, to build relationships and community, and to address and repair harms as a result of wrongdoing. Whatever the source of their strength and determination, the result of their work will be greater accountability and humility in our RP practitioners, and genuine, life-changing, deeply anti-racist empowerment of *all* the youth in our Circles, including YOCIY.

DISCUSSION QUESTIONS

1. What would it mean to have an "accountability partner(s)"? Which people in your life could fill this role? If no one, how might you go about finding someone to help you?
2. What ARE your motivations for working in communities of color, and what are the ways in which white supremacy culture negatively impacts these motivations? Please find an accountability partner to discuss this with.
3. If you work or volunteer for an organization, how do you observe white organizational culture playing out? How does this culture benefit you (if you are White) or become a barrier to your success (if you are not)?

ACTIVITIES

1. Use the questions in this chapter to assist you with writing a personal inventory of the times you have caused harm to POCIP. Share your writings with an accountability partner.
2. Make a list of ways in which you can repair a harm you've caused and begin to make restoration/amends/reparations to those communities/people.
3. Read Tema Okun/Kenneth Jones article "White Supremacy Culture," www.cwsworkshop.org/PARC_site_B/dr-culture.html.

RESOURCES

DiAngelo, Robin. Interview on "White Liberals Protecting Racism." https://www.youtube.com/watch?v=pGM6SVwcvmo.

Menakem, Resmaa. *My Grandmother's Hands: Racialized Trauma and the Pathway to Mending Our Hearts and Bodies.* Las Vegas, NV: Central Recovery Press, 2017.

People's Institute for Survival and Beyond (www.pisab.org). This organization offers workshops on undoing racism.

NOTES

1. As Jonathan Kahn recently stated:

> Good old-fashioned racism embedded in our laws and structures doesn't look the same from era to era. It is always hard to identify racism in real time because no one thinks they're a racist. In the aftermath of the Civil War, we could say, "Look, no more slavery!" But we didn't see that Jim Crow was racist. Indeed *Plessy v. Ferguson* was widely considered a good decision at the time, not racist at all. Now, we can say, "Look, no more Jim Crow!" But we still have racially gerrymandered districts, the

enduring legacy of housing discrimination, persistent health disparities, and racially problematic practices throughout the justice system. Racism changes from era to era; the hard thing to do is identify it in our own era and call out racist actions, attitudes and policies for what they really are.

Jonathan Kahn is the James E. Kelley Professor of Law at Mitchell Hamline School of Law and author of *Race on the Brain: What Implicit Bias Gets Wrong about the Struggle for Racial Justice* (New York: Columbia University Press, 2017).

2. Robin DiAngelo, *What Does It Mean to Be White? Developing White Racial Literacy* (Bern, Switzerland, and New York: Peter Lang, 2012).
3. While this chapter focuses on the welfare of youth, it also demonstrates the difficulties of creating trusting and safe relationships between POCIP and White people who have not proactively developed a race-conscious lens.
4. Robin DiAngelo, *White Fragility: Why It's So Hard to Talk to White People about Racism* (Boston, MA: Beacon Press, 2018). DiAngelo offers the following examples of situations that cause racial stress for White people:

   - Suggesting that a White person's viewpoint comes from a racialized frame of reference (challenge to objectivity)
   - People of Color talking directly about their own racial perspectives (challenge to White taboos on talking openly about race)
   - People of Color choosing not to protect the racial feelings of White people in regards to race (challenge to White racial expectations and need/entitlement to racial comfort)
   - People of Color not being willing to tell their stories or answer questions about their racial experiences (challenge to the expectation that People of Color will serve us)
   - A fellow White not providing agreement with one's racial perspective (challenge to White solidarity)
   - Receiving feedback that one's behavior had a racist impact (challenge to White racial innocence)
   - Suggesting that group membership is significant (challenge to individualism)
   - Acknowledging that access is unequal between racial groups (challenge to meritocracy)
   - Being presented with a Person of Color in a position of leadership (challenge to White authority)
   - Being presented with information about other racial groups through, for example, movies in which People of Color drive the action but are not in stereotypical roles, or multicultural education (challenge to White centrality) (pp. 103–4)

5. See also Derald Wing Sue, *Microaggressions in Everyday Life: Race, Gender, and Sexual Orientation* (Hoboken, NJ: Wiley, 2010).
6. White culture has been defined as the dominant, unquestioned standards of behavior and ways of functioning embodied by the vast majority of institutions in the United States. Among other things, it defines what is "normal," "high-performing,"

"successful," "professional," "effective," "good," "sustainable," "respectful," "timely," "knowable," "appropriate," "relevant," "important," "leadership," "acceptable conflict," "an acceptable tone of voice," and "accountability."

7. An even more extreme example of this dynamic is that more and more White nonprofit staff are asking their stakeholders of color to meet with them (unpaid) to provide tips for improving services to them.
8. Minnesota Compass (mncompass.org) Volunteerism is tracked for organizations that usually do not include the more informal and regular ways in which POCIP help their communities, neighbors, families, and religious institutions.
9. See above for the systemic reasons why more volunteers are White.
10. Some argue persuasively that we all carry racial trauma, and we will continue to act out in ways that are destructive until and unless we engage in trauma work to heal. While White people have very different trauma from POC and Indigenous Peoples, the trauma is still real, and, if Whites are ever to undo racism (which only they have the power to do), their trauma must be proactively addressed.
11. Overall, if a response is disproportionate to a situation, some kind of unresolved trauma may be involved. The fact that so many White people are unable to respond to even gentle correction around race without huge emotional responses may be due to unresolved White trauma around race. It is essential here to note that White trauma around race is very different from the trauma around race experienced by POCIP. Resmaa Menakem has written an excellent book regarding racial trauma (that experienced by Whites and that experienced by African Americans) called *My Grandmother's Hands: Racialized Trauma and the Pathway to Mending Our Hearts and Bodies* (Las Vegas, NV: Central Recovery Press, 2017).
12. See Joseph Feagin, *The White Racial Frame* (London and New York: Routledge, 2013).

Chapter 2

Your Silence Will Not Protect You

Barbara Sherrod

Your silence will not protect you.
—Audre Lorde, *The Cancer Journals*

"*How come there's only seven of us sitting at the table?*" It's a question I ask myself at every school commission and school climate meeting. I am not the only Black woman at the table (always less than ten of us); however, I can count on all my fingers and toes the times when we have been the only Black "practitioners" at the table. White lawmakers, attorneys, politicians, and executive directors are usually the ones at the table talking about restorative practices—forgoing the "With" part. In my last two years as a researcher and restorative practices specialist, I have witnessed those in power advocating for restorative practices while dismissing the restorative idea that the harm done on institutional levels must first be acknowledged, that institutions must hold themselves accountable, and that restoration must take place before we can move forward.

The intent to advocate for restorative practices is nice. However, I must point out that, even those "for" restorative practices remain less than confident about using its values as tools on a systemic level—a hallmark that shows true commitment in this work. Acknowledgment and accountability would honor restorative practices' Indigenous North American and Indigenous African roots, while at the same time making sure that Black and Brown children understand that their connection, communication, and community within the restorative work are innate. These Indigenous values are traits our communities cannot forgo, even if restorative practices have been repackaged and marketed as a promising new way to "*control yo bad-ass kids!*" Restorative practices require ongoing, internal inventory checks first to see where you are emotionally and spiritually—then to ask, how will this self-check show up in our practice?

It shows up, of course, in the way we socially interact. As a Black woman, I am cautious about interacting with non–People of Color in this work. I have to protect not only my physical self but also my intellectual property. Daily I ask, "*How can I honor this work, bring its true intention forward, and keep it alive without having to sacrifice myself or struggle based on the nonprofit culture or society that expects me to work for little to nothing?*" The few Black practitioners I know share my sentiments. In our work, we are required to interact with non–People of Color. I find that many of them are disconnected from themselves and specifically from People of Color. Restorative practices require that we prioritize relationships and transparency internally. To do this, we must relinquish the power that adults hold over children (e.g., children as minors do not possess all the rights adults enjoy), yet many are not capable of this. Becoming transparent in order to build authentic and fulfilling relationships is the end goal: to create a space and, within that space, a place for all children, especially Black and Brown, to thrive holistically and feel they belong.

Imagine, then, asking White women to relinquish power not just to children, but to Black children. Imagine telling them that their degree in child development or elementary education is well earned; however, what really matters is their interaction with and perception of Black families and families of color. Imagine the awkward but necessary conversation of having to tell White teachers that, while their intentions may be well received, their microaggressions and subtle racism (enforcing zero-tolerance, classroom extractions for "defiance," and ignorance of or blindness to their own biases) create a hostile school environment in which Black children do not feel safe to learn or to simply be in. Sometimes, the conversation goes well for me, since I have "specialist" in my title. But the message doesn't always smooth over well with White educators who have been teaching longer than I have in my career—when their professional experience trumps my lived experience as a Black child, teenager, and woman. Their experience in the classroom negates my experience of being exposed to institutional racism at the hands of a teacher "preparing" me for the real world.

Credibility is useful and essential in some practice-based professions. Restorative practices, in response to their increased popularity in the education and justice fields, have become associated with, or co-opted by, the legal field, although they can be identified as social pedagogies. Restorative practices have been around for centuries, but Western modernity has reduced them to nothing more than an alternative to a punitive system. America runs on punitive the same way it runs on Dunkin'.

Restorative practices have been around for centuries, but Western modernity has reduced them to nothing more than an alternative to a punitive system.

To completely shift larger institutions would mean that we must dismantle systems that continually oppress and act violently toward People of Color.

In my responsive Circles for Black and Brown girls, I hear the same comments from students as young as eight who point out the biases and anti-Blackness that their non-Black teachers present: "She only tells us not to touch her books." "The White girls can take a long time in the bathroom, but we cannot." "When Black boys get upset and cry, she sends them out, but when the White students do it, she comforts them." "Some of our teachers don't pay us much attention because they think the White students are smarter and it shows." How do we as Black practitioners, knowing all of this information, find ourselves obligated to put our children in Circles with the White people who behave these ways? These same White people have access to resources that not only inform them of common biases and anti-Black/Brown culture but also provide ways to become aware, yet they choose not to engage in self-work on race: discussing race is "impolite" or simply not on their radars. As a Black woman in this field, I am exhausted with balancing the need to bluntly point out the violent comments or actions toward People of Color and the need to figure out *calling in*, so as not to push White people away from this work—the white fragility reaction.

White fragility's intersection with race is where oppression shows up in restorative work. The urgent remedy is to co-power Black and Brown people to show up in Circles, schools, communities, and other spaces where White people have a majority say and to begin to take up these predominately White preserves—physically, mentally, and emotionally. Organizations and schools committed to restorative work often say that one of their largest challenges in implementation is getting parents to show up, especially in schools that serve mostly Black and Brown children. These schools are run by and often filled with White teachers. White staffs ignore that, for many People of Color, public institutions (e.g., courts, prisons, military) play an important role in white supremacy; the impact of that is a mistrust that has been passed down from generation to generation.

White fragility's intersection with race is where oppression shows up in restorative work.

For any Person of Color working with larger institutions that are centered in whiteness, speaking out is risky. Calling for the larger community to hold itself accountable—questioning and ultimately dismantling its centered whiteness—can cause institutions not only to push back but also to tank restorative approaches altogether. This White reaction exposes marginalized communities at risk to even more systemic violence and oppression. For those of us skilled in this work, we must do a tricky dance: we must figure out when to push for race and equity, when to speak about biases, when to call outsiders into this work, and when to hold space—meaning when to keep those who could disrupt the culture shift outside the community.

Despite the risks to relationships that can lead to more restorative practice work, to more inclusion, I remain vocal. I've had older Black women say to me, "I am frightened for you, because saying what you say can get you shut out of many spaces in this state and in this work." Confirmation for me that this work has been stolen from its spiritual roots lies in this: the true heirs of restorative approaches too often believe that it is no longer a divine right to call things for what they are. Tokenism has become so ingrained in this culture. The justification is that it does no one "any good" to call attention to non-Black/Brown folks who hardly grasp the theory, make no effort to apply it with fidelity to their own dirty baggage, and yet receive pats on the back for "saving" our communities.

I've had older Black women say to me, "I am frightened for you, because saying what you say can get you shut out of many spaces in this state and in this work."

On the flip side, when I speak at the table after asking myself, in the tune of Audre Lorde, "What are the tyrannies you swallow day by day and attempt to make your own, until you will sicken and die of them, still in silence?" other Black women smile and wink at me, as White people gulp for air and then follow up with support. Sooner rather than later, these Black women use their power to bring us all to the table. Their response affirms for me that my truth-seeking words are always appropriate. When we are in the room at this point, code-switching and the White gaze are not the priority, but self-preservation is—*Ubuntu*. Bringing one another to the table and lifting our voices is what we do—and must do—because, as one of my colleagues says, "It's what *they* always do, so why not?"

An example of how White people engaged in this work practice silencing around race is found in their unwillingness to go deeper with Circle conversations that involve parents, staff, and youth of color. They show an observable, though rarely expressed, fear of being called out for their own transgressions. Even in the name of moving forward restoratively, they allow their white fragility to take priority over our well-being as a Black or Brown person. While the same can be said about People of Color in this work, I still see more reluctance coming from White participants than from Black. When White people are engaged in this work, they use the Circles and tools to focus on "isolated incidents"; they avoid stepping back and observing the entire interaction to get to the root of relationships. This White positioning alone can deter communities from adopting a culture rooted in restorative values.

When restorative justice practitioners implement restorative practices in any capacity, it is important that we remain mindful of race. Even at the elementary school level, it is important to know that, in restorative culture, we honor and acknowledge everyone's differences. This acknowledging can be a challenge if you "don't see color" or believe that you are treating all your children "the same regardless of race." To truly see transformation, we need to understand the importance of seeing color and treating children in a way that reflects where they are in that moment. Refusing to acknowledge or honor who people are in Circles causes a lasting harm, i.e., it reinforces historic harm in the present. A harm rooted in anti-Black-and-Brown rhetoric or behavior leads children of color to believe that their root identity has no place in the Circle or in restorative communities.

Refusing to acknowledge or honor who people are in Circles causes a lasting harm, i.e., it reinforces historic harm in the present.

So, what is the main identity that we see now in restorative practices and restorative justice? The answer will not shock many: this field is now oversaturated with White men and women. With no real connection to this work, they have an agenda to reform justice that supersedes forming authentic relationships, yet it is authentic relationships that maintain fidelity with transformation. The idea that restorative practices and restorative justice will reform the justice system is a long-term goal, as Whites transition from being a majority racial group to a pluralistic, non-majority racial group. Believing the reform agenda for restorative justice shows a lack of understanding: it is not justice reform but the connectedness between community members and restorative responses to conflict that influence healthier relationships and decrease the likelihood of recidivism. I cringe as I hear people in this work run around throwing "restorative *justice*"—emphasis on *justice*—in the face of Black people, especially Black children, in a world that is post Michael Brown, Sandra Bland, Tamir Rice, and Freddie Gray. Using terms like "offender" when speaking of harm done, while claiming to build community, reminds us that schools mirror prisons. As in prisons, People of Color make up a majority of the public schools' population.

Focusing solely on transforming a justice system to be "fair" takes the easy way out. The focus on "fairness" does not encourage steps to dismantle a justice system that thrives on inflicting pain on People of Color in the first place.

This belief that we can use restorative approaches within a "justice" system that has its roots in white supremacy alone lies at the heart of how restorative practices and restorative justice have been colonized. What seems motivated by good intentions—diversion programs and teen courts, training in restorative practices, and implementing them—can, in fact, be harmful. Children of color begin to associate restorative processes with the justice system or with a response to conflicts in their communities. Whereas these applications are only a part of the process, they experience them only when harm has occurred and rarely before. Restorative practices offer a process that gives children and their village a space that ensures freedom, yet in some spaces, a Circle with correctional officers positions them on the outside looking in. When restorative practices and restorative justice are taken from the hands of People of Color and placed into the hands of Whites engaged in this work, they reinforce what centralized whiteness has always said: our bodies do not belong to us; our voices cannot be heard over theirs; and until they say when, our stories are not real.

Children of color begin to associate restorative processes with the justice system or with a response to conflicts in their communities.

I am exhausted. Why speak up if I will be glazed over? My body and soul are tired, as were our slave ancestors, and I just want to rest like they wanted to rest. But Black women's legacy shows we cannot—will not—rest; we keep going because our children and our children's children depend on us.

When I first came into this work, I believed it was easy: we sit in Circle and talk, we get to know one another, relationships grow stronger, and children behave better. I quickly learned it is not that simple. I learned that the foundational work of restorative practices is for adults: focusing on strengthening adult relationships where the core is communication and empathy, and then passing that way of life on to the children. Using restorative approaches increases adult buy-in, but it also requires self-check, so that all in this work can see where biases lie hidden and then can figure out if these biases are essential or detrimental to implementation and culture shift.

What do we need to keep restorative practices alive? To not be co-opted? To remain committed to its center? We need a level of acknowledgment that sees the daily reality that People of Color experience. It is not enough that school systems and institutions interested in restorative culture simply throw adults and children into Circles focused on relationships. There has to be space held—and places held within that space—where stakeholders can come forward and share where they have been harmed or have done harm in that community. Every Indigenous North American and Indigenous African connection to restorative values must be recognized at the expense of Western values. We must go deeper than acknowledging the Maori culture. What do the people of the First Nations believe? What can we learn from South Africa's Truth and Reconciliation Council? What do we know about the values of the Nguni people, and, if possible, how can we apply them to minimize Western culture's harm to humanity and to the natural world?

The second step concerns accountability. How do we hold ourselves accountable to community, and what is it that we are being held to? This step is most important for People of Color, especially Black people. In my four years of working in schools, the narrative I challenge constantly is "These parents don't care." What makes you think these parents who have been pushed around by the school system don't care? In order to experience high parent engagement, especially with Black and Brown parents, school staff must provide opportunities. For example, Circles are a viable way for parents to come together with school staff to share their respective loves and wishes about the school as well as their concerns. Institutions cannot ignore People of Color who are community members. The former must acknowledge the latter as having an equal, if not greater, stake in the community compared to politicians, business owners, school staff, and other non-grassroots interests.

Schools and communities that come together for intergenerational conversations around class, race, gender, and community well-being define transformative change. Discussions evoke members to change the accepted narrative and, ultimately, the biases about and amongst one another. People of Color in Baltimore use restorative tools to address systemic racism. Our transformed awareness led to our 2015 uprising: not only our elders but also our youth all over the city and county of Baltimore demanded change. We who are at racism's and settler colonialism's receiving end understand the urgency to teach our children the conditions that cultivate harm and violence—how intentional, systemic underfunding and neglect adversely impact our communities. Conversely, restorative practices and restorative justice cultivate an equitable society, one that no longer cringes at hearing the word "justice."

DISCUSSION QUESTIONS

1. After reading this chapter, how has your own understanding of your personal identity changed, especially in relation to your involvement in restorative practices?
2. According to Sherrod, why is "colorblindness" problematic when engaging in restorative practices?
3. After reading this chapter, what do you, as a White practitioner, believe is your obligation within this work?
4. How do we, as restorative practitioners, work to address the structural inequalities inherent in the criminal legal system? Can this work be done exclusively in Circle? Why or why not?

ACTIVITIES

1. "Your Silence Will Not Protect You"

PURPOSE For participants to understand and explore the complexities around speaking out in uncomfortable situations.

MATERIALS Talking piece, Circle values and guidelines.

PREPARATION Arrange everyone in a circle on the floor or meeting space.

OPENING "My silences had not protected me. Your silence will not protect you. But for every real word spoken, for every attempt I had ever made to speak those truths for which I am still seeking, I had made contact with other women while we examined the words to fit a world in which we all believed, bridging our differences."

—Audre Lorde, "The Transformation of Silence into Language and Action," a speech given December 28, 1977.

MINDFULNESS MOMENT (Optional) Eyes closed or soft gaze. Three deep breaths—inhale through nose, exhale via mouth.

VALUES ROUND What value do you need to show up as your best self in a difficult conversation?

CHECK-IN ROUND "How are you doing?" "Is there anything on your mind you would like to share with your group?"

MAIN ACTIVITY Transforming Silence into Action

Read "Your silence will not protect you." For Circle participants to better understand the complexities of this work, encourage them to think about the ways that society, when rooted in white supremacy, can silence others.

ROUND What comes to mind when you hear, "Your silence will not protect you"?

ROUND Can you remember a time when you have been silenced or when you have silenced someone else?

ROUND What social identities were silenced? How?

ROUND What would you say to them if given another chance?

CLOSING "For we have been socialized to respect fear more than our own needs for language and definition, and while we wait in silence for that final luxury of fearlessness, the weight of that silence will choke us."

—Audre Lorde, "The Transformation of Silence into Language and Action."

***Thank Everyone for participating in the Circle today!**

2. **"For Black Women Only"**

   PURPOSE This Circle prompt is created to be facilitated and used for Black women only. The purpose of this Circle is to provide space and support for Black women in restorative practice/justice and racial justice work.

   MATERIALS Talking piece, Circle values and guidelines.

   PREPARATION Arrange everyone in a circle on the floor or meeting space.

   OPENING "Caring for myself is not self-indulgence, it is self-preservation, and that is an act of political warfare."

   —Audre Lorde, **A Burst of Light**

   MINDFULNESS MOMENT (Free-Write) Make a list of who you are, internal and external.

   VALUES ROUND What virtue can you call on to continue to practice self-care, push for Black liberation, and promote the advancement of this work?

   CHECK-IN ROUND "How are you doing?" "Is there anything on your mind you would like to share with your group?"

   MAIN ACTIVITY Building Support among Black Women Discussing as members of an affinity group, how does your identity show up in this work? What connections have you made between yourself and Sherrod based on her experiences in the work? To provide support, take this opportunity to draw connections with one another and to develop a support plan to continue in this work, while preserving one's self.

   ROUND What connections, if any, did you make between yourself and Sherrod?

   ROUND What emotions do you experience when you are faced with a situation in this work that causes internal conflict on how to respond?

   ROUND When it comes to Black women, why is self-preservation perceived as political warfare?

   ROUND How do you practice self-preservation, especially in tough times with your work?

   ROUND What virtue can you call on to continue to practice self-care, push for Black liberation, and promote the advancement of this work?

   ROUND How do you provide support for other Black Women exclusively?

CLOSING "We are African women and we know, in our blood's telling, the tenderness with which our foremothers held each other."
—Audre Lorde, *Eye to Eye: Black Women, Hatred, and Anger*

***Thank Everyone for participating in the Circle!**

3. **The Audre Lorde Questionnaire to Oneself**

   Adapted by Divya Victor from Audre Lorde's *The Cancer Journals.*

   1. What are the words you do not have yet? [Or, "For what do you not have words, yet?"]
   2. What do you need to say? [List as many things as necessary.]
   3. What are the tyrannies you swallow day by day and attempt to make your own, until you will sicken and die of them, still in silence? [List as many as necessary today. Then write a new list tomorrow. And the day after.]
   4. If we have been socialized to respect fear more than our own need for language, ask yourself: "What's the worst that could happen to me if I tell this truth?" [So, answer this today. And every day.]

RESOURCES

Lorde, Audre. *A Burst of Light: And Other Essays.* Mineola, NY: Ixia Press (an imprint of Dover Books), 2017.

Lorde, Audre. *The Cancer Journals.* San Francisco, CA: Aunt Lute Books, 1980.

Lorde, Audre. *Sister Outsider.* New York: Crown Publishing Group, 1987.

Victor, Divya. "The Audre Lorde Questionnaire to Oneself." Adapted from "The Transformation of Silence into Language and Action," collected in *The Cancer Journals.* This resource was created by Divya Victor for students of her creative writing courses at Nanyang Technological University in January 2016. https://divyavictor.com/the-audre-lorde-questionnaire-to-oneself/.

Chapter 3

Who's In and Who's Out? Problematizing Peacemaking Circles in Diverse Classrooms

Christina Parker

In schools, restorative practices address children's needs to repair individual harm and build a safe and healthy school community. Because these practices are based on relationships of trust, they help create strong connections between teachers, families, and children. They also help build strong learning communities that promote curricular-wide, peace-building, and social-justice education. Restorative practices involve reflecting critically on curriculum content and pedagogy to promote an inclusive, just, and equitable learning environment for all children. The peacemaking Circle is one such restorative tool at our disposal. Limiting Circle processes solely to addressing conflicts after they occur misses entirely the opportunity to use them for developing communal relationships and proactive dialogue. Circles not only integrate social justice as classroom practices but also work toward building community through dialogue.

Integrating restorative practices in schools involves creating spaces for dialogue—both for post-incident conflicts and for developing proactive strategies for peace-building.[1] Yet opening spaces for dialogue and dissent is, almost without exception, a challenging process that requires skilled facilitators, a strong community, and good relationships among participants. Participants' identities are likely to be diverse and multifaceted, making the process even more complex, particularly if we consider how power and privilege transcend dialogues, even restorative ones.

Peacemaking Circles can be used to facilitate classroom and school-based dialogue that encourages relational connection, communication skills, and peace-building, which include equitable views on power. The Circle process facilitates dialogue, deepens relationships, and upholds strong values that support a safe and inclusive classroom community. What is more, when done correctly, the process allows children to actually feel included. And when young people feel included, they are much more inclined to actively engage in ways that lead to further social and academic success.

However, some voices may still remain marginal, even when inclusive peace-building dialogue is carefully integrated and implemented. This marginalization is challenging to overcome: we operate within the confines of structural institutions of control and power, of which schools are clear institutional sites. In this chapter, I critically reflect on "who's in and who's out" in restorative justice practices: How do the ideals and concepts of justice-oriented education manipulate post-conflict responses? And how can proactive tools support restorative approaches to discipline and conflict? These questions cut to the core of restorative practice's frameworks and application—as well as to the relations between Whites and People of Color (and between Whites and Indigenous Peoples) where disparities in class, race, gender, political, and social power are evident.

In what follows, I reflect on peacemaking Circles as a process for building relationships and connections by facilitating proactive and inclusive dialogue about conflicts. I critically explore how some bodies are included in Circle processes while others are excluded. I also consider the role of teachers' backgrounds, biases, and levels of expertise in facilitating Circles that engage conflicts, particularly with marginalized youth. Finally, I discuss the limits of conducting research on restorative practices and peacemaking Circles using a Eurocentric lens.

As a woman of color who has been teaching and researching peace-building practices in diverse K–12 classroom contexts for more than twelve years, I have become increasingly aware of how my own research positionality—how my race, gender, and status intersect with power and privilege—allows me to witness the intricacies of inclusion and exclusion in pedagogical processes, especially those that are designed to engage diverse learners. In my own schooling experience, I have also encountered a variety of school-based conflicts.

Thus, my lived, personal experience informs my professional experience. My perspective as a researcher, teacher, and teacher-educator shapes how I see and interpret inclusion and exclusion in classrooms. On one hand, children/youth from varying ethno-cultural backgrounds, gender identities, migration statuses, socioeconomic positions, and language capabilities, for instance, are often hidden and structurally excluded in ways that their teachers are unable to recognize. On the other hand, I have witnessed restorative interventions in schools that created changes in how they build and sustain classroom communities. In what follows, I share insights that I have drawn from these diverse students' and teachers' experiences with participating in peacemaking Circles.

Most of the research on restorative practices, conflict resolution education, and peacemaking in schools ignores children's diversities and prescribes a one-size-fits-all approach, yet this approach ultimately reinforces exclusion and marginalization. To facilitate inclusive and fair practices, we need further critical inquiry into how to increase the use and effectiveness of peacemaking strategies, particularly when working with youth of color. I believe that proactive restorative practices can work to reintegrate and reconnect with young People of Color. They can direct those who are marginalized away from the school-to-prison pipeline and build a strong pathway for youth success and community engagement.

Most of the research on restorative practices, conflict resolution education, and peacemaking in schools ignores children's diversities and prescribes a one-size-fits-all approach, yet this approach ultimately reinforces exclusion and marginalization.

Youths' varying experiences and positions of marginality influence educators' choices when they facilitate proactive restorative practices. Researchers and practitioners need to consider how to attend inclusively to cultural and ethnic diversity. While some researchers and practitioners have explored how young people experience peacemaking and conflict-education programs, few have reflected critically on how diverse and marginalized youth of color experience particular restorative and dialogic pedagogies. Such critical exploration and reflection are necessary—and perhaps should be mandatory—to address the structural dimensions of social injustices and thus to create spaces for conflict transformation. This call for exploration and reflection raises critical questions around how restorative and peacemaking practices impact young People of Color, who are diverse between and among themselves. It also raises questions around what can be done to better prepare educators to facilitate these young people's inclusion.

Engaging Circle Praxis to Facilitate Inclusion

Now, more than ever, young people's voices challenging injustice and inequity need to be heard. Without their voices, we cannot sustain a democratic platform for dialogue. In order to go above and beyond the status quo, teachers need to engage in bottom-up dialogic pedagogies. These pedagogies not only critically engage quieter and marginalized voices, but they also encourage all students to question "who's in and who's out" in their relational spheres. Educators who engage restorative approaches, such as the Indigenous-based Circle process, more successfully promote students' learning and inclusion. Pedagogically, consistently exposing students to alternative methods that promote inclusion creates a transformative space. While some students might still choose not to engage, they are nonetheless given an opportunity to do so.

Restorative practices, such as the Circle process, draw from Indigenous ways of learning and being together, of knowing and communicating. In many ways, the Circle process challenges normative discussions—that is, White, upper-class ways of communicating—so that quieter and marginalized voices may be given greater valence and opportunity to participate. Teaching youth to discuss and deliberate on what is "normal" runs the risk of reproducing dominant systems of oppression and exclusion. But dialogue based on a Circle process aims to transform and revolutionize thinking, communicating, and, ultimately, relationships.

Practicing Circle-related skills in the classroom is critical in today's sociopolitical and transnational landscape. Standardized testing largely forces educators to confine themselves to the authoritarian classroom of previous centuries: children are seated in rows, facing a master who fills them with knowledge.[2] In this classroom setting, the children who thrive are predominantly male and White—exclusion is paramount and built into the schooling's structure. By continuing with this path, educators implicitly restrict themselves to the ethos of early educational institutions that were geared toward a very different way of life in a very different society. Such authoritarian, Eurocentric teaching methods limit youth from developing the ability for engaging today's social and economic landscape, especially with its gifts of transnationalism and diversity.

Authoritarian educators inevitably render dialogue obsolete; they promote exclusion and reward by conforming to a defined norm that they find familiar and comfortable. Such educators identify with authoritative structures, which—albeit ironically—typically run parallel to restorative practices. This approach is known to disproportionately impact racialized students.[3] For instance, restorative practices may be implemented in a school where police officers exercise their authority to arrest subjectively—punishing for "defiance" being a prime example. Student resource officers (SROs) monitor school-age children for "disruptive" behavior, and administrators can choose either to suspend or expel students in conjunction with or instead of attempting a restorative approach.[4]

When race cannot be discussed openly in Circle dialogues, though Circle practice aims to include all voices, the possibility for marginalization still exists. Any restorative dialogue requires thoughtful consideration of historical oppressions and how certain cultural groups, values, and beliefs are marginalized. Yet even in these dialogues, the dominant cultural group's worldview remains the default.

When societal structures perpetuate a culture of silence around issues of race, marginalized and oppressed people are also further silenced. In turn, this persistent silence constrains possibilities for building relationships and connecting through dialogue.[5] When race cannot be discussed openly in Circle dialogues, though Circle practice aims to include all voices, the possibility for marginalization still exists. Any restorative dialogue requires thoughtful consideration of historical oppressions and how certain cultural groups, values, and beliefs are marginalized. Yet even in these dialogues, the dominant cultural group's worldview remains the default. In societal contexts where power, privilege, and oppression reign supreme, any form of dialogue becomes indoctrination.[6] With inequitable power, subaltern groups are socially, culturally, or economically dispossessed and cannot speak because the colonial oppressor is unable to hear. As a result, the oppressor is also unable to understand knowledge and perspectives other than through the lens of their own Western consciousness and values.[7]

Pedagogical Value of Conflict for Marginalized Students

My work in K–12 schools shows the pedagogical value of conflict. Given the right opportunity and space for dialogue about conflicts, all youth engage more and experience greater participation. Restorative classroom-based discussions and activities allow youth to safely and critically reflect on social and interpersonal conflicts. Hence, equipping teachers with restorative ways to engage their students supports diverse students' inclusion. Peers can then build healthier and more satisfying relationships both among each other and with their teacher(s). Such sustainable, long-term practices reduce in-school and out-of-school suspensions and school-based violence.

However, restorative practices fall short of this potential if they are used alongside authoritarian practices. Restorative principles are circumvented when educators have to implement restorative practices—proactive community-building and post-incident problem-solving—within a non-restorative framework. Among other things, that framework pressures them to teach for and toward standardized testing models and to use punitive discipline measures. Here, the structure of traditional classroom seating and traditional school culture predominate, as do implicit rewards for students' silence and compliance with behaviors that, though not necessarily culturally or socially taught, are still expected. In this context, youth of color and other marginalized youth are more likely to disengage from restorative dialogue and interventions than youth whose culture is predominately valued. When students in a minority position have one or more additional risk factors—e.g., socioeconomic status, race, language, gender, sexual identity, immigration status, religion, developmental characteristics, and environmental and psychological factors—their marginalized positions influence not only how they choose to participate in a restorative classroom dialogue but also how their teacher might facilitate that dialogue. For instance, discussing issues such as systemic racism in policing, religious perspectives on whether or not life begins at conception, or President Trump's immigration ban can lead to conflict if a minority or dominant student overtly expresses an idea that appears different from what his or her peers believe. Ultimately, though, the very conversations that we are tempted to ignore or avoid because of their potentials for conflict can be the most powerful, if facilitated effectively.

Ultimately, though, the very conversations that we are tempted to ignore or avoid because of their potentials for conflict can be the most powerful, if facilitated effectively.

Implementing Circles in a class where youth have strong relationships with each other and with their teacher is useful for discussing topics related to classroom norms and guidelines, for celebrating successes, for sharing appreciations, such as admiring qualities in each other, and for sharing goals or things they are proud of. In such Circles, relationships deepen as the youth collectively move forward, holding each other accountable. However, even where relationships between students and the teacher are strong, teachers may avoid conversations that could generate conflict. For instance, teachers may open up a space for youth to discuss gun violence but shy away from exploring its complexities. For example, they may fail to critically reflect on how gun violence is racialized, thus perpetuating the marginalization of racialized youth in dialogue. Furthermore, if teachers are unprepared or fearful of inviting dialogue that they deem overly controversial, they might hold back on supporting and including perspectives from diverse, marginalized youth.

Critical approaches to restorative practices include—but are not limited to—paying attention to culture, diversity, and equity. However, including cultural diversity and equity is not a linear approach, nor is it based on a one-size-fits-all model. When we integrate restorative practices and peacemaking Circles proactively in the classroom, the content and pedagogy need to be culturally inclusive and accessible to all youth. Engaging with conflict critically and proactively involves considering which of our children are included and which are excluded. While some teachers develop close relationships with youth, they may still remain reticent about drawing on the diverse and divergent perspectives that the students bring to the classroom.

Many educators lack confidence in facilitating conflict. They may avoid engaging their students in dialogue about conflict and social issues, fearing that the conflict might escalate and they could lose control of the classroom. Educators may also fear that risk-averse administrators might retaliate politically if parents complain about conflict in their classroom. But engaging youth in challenging dialogue about controversial or conflictual topics in the classroom allows the students to meaningfully connect with their classmates, their cultures, their community, and their society.[8] In order to develop confidence and competence in negotiating complex topics, both teachers and youth need practice in engaging in non-polarizing dissent and dialogue among peers.[9] Such classroom dialogue challenges the notion of youth as passive or immature learners and instead encourages them to examine and deconstruct challenging ideas—to develop critical consciousness.

Studies in critical race theory, critical multiculturalism, and critical peacebuilding education show that higher-order dialogue in classrooms mostly takes place in higher socioeconomic status (hSES) communities. Teachers (mis)perceive the ability of lower socioeconomic status (lSES) students and youth of color to handle conflictual dialogue. This misperception may stem from the fact that Whites account for a significant majority of public school teachers, while youth of color account for a significant majority of students in many public schools and half of all public school students nationwide. Whites may anticipate that, during such dialogues, youth of color may shine the spotlight on them and ask about their white supremacy. Moreover, White teachers are expected to focus on delivering content-driven curriculum, particularly in those same lSES communities that are struggling with low test scores, and therefore believe they cannot devote instructional time to higher-order dialogue.

Whites may anticipate that, during such dialogues, youth of color may shine the spotlight on them and ask about their white supremacy.

Given these environmental constraints, most educators in lSES communities default to a narrow, authoritarian approach with little space for relationship building and minimal engagement with conflict. Furthermore, this default exposes our youth of color (a vulnerable target group) in lSES communities to being tracked and classed in streams identified for slower learners, who in turn are given fewer opportunities for academic enrichment.[10] In stark contrast, hSES communities seemingly create greater spaces for relationship building. Given their larger pool of resources, learners, parents, and the community are vested in preparing mainstream youth—those privileged by race and class—to be effective and contributing members of society. Such preparation may involve learning team-building skills, communication skills, and having exposure to advanced perspectives on proactive learning through conflict and divergence.

In today's knowledge-driven economy, delivering scripted, content knowledge to youth will neither enhance their learning nor equip them with the tools and skill sets needed for success. The US Departments of Education and Justice have recommended that school-age youth should not only be held accountable for conduct, but should also have opportunities to learn from disciplinary incidents, if only so that they build social and emotional skills.[11] According to a team of educators, psychologists, and social scientists, during proactive peace-building, restorative interventions can "enhance and teach a range of individual skills" that help children learn how to grapple with conflict under safe conditions.[12] While such learning and skill-building can occur in post-incident handling of conflicts, equipping our young people with these skills ahead of time—e.g., by participating in a Circle process—is more useful.

Coaching and training the entire school staff—including custodial staff, support staff, administrators, and teachers—yield a far greater structural impact for youth and the school community . . .

For instance, in my own practice as a Circle practitioner, I worked with a Black young woman who assaulted another Black young woman. Neither had prior experience with the Circle process. The person who was assaulted refused to participate, and the one who did the assault needed a significant number of preparatory, community-building Circles before she could willingly open up about her participation in and responsibility for causing a violent incident. Such youth might be better equipped to accept responsibility and engage in trust-building and forgiveness after a violent incident if they are regularly exposed to restorative and peace-building practices at school and in their communities.

Still, communities with limited resources and limited amounts of time face many challenges when implementing restorative practices. For one, they must shift away from authoritarian teaching and punitive approaches to schooling and discipline: these pose structural challenges. Moreover, training targets only the leaders or administrators, who move on after the funding runs out. Coaching and training the entire school staff—including custodial staff, support staff, administrators, and teachers—yield a far greater structural impact for youth and the school community, and yet this is not the school-wide and ongoing training that many lSES schools receive.

Inclusion and Exclusion in Circles

One upper elementary teacher (a White woman) I mentored and coached in implementing Circles commented that she felt the Circle process was beneficial for her transient student population, including the several students in the class who were refugees—many had arrived or left throughout the school year. For instance, one student who was a refugee did not understand much English and was understandably silent the first month in his new classroom. He spoke for the first time in front of his peers when they were in Circle. After he shared, all his peers spontaneously clapped to acknowledge him. The opportunity to speak in well-facilitated Circle dialogues seemed to lead, over time, to more students participating orally, while also nurturing healthy peer relationships. This teacher's Circle implementation illustrated how, when done effectively, Circles increase the opportunities for youth to participate in class. Furthermore, when an interpersonal conflict arose later that year, the youth took the initiative and requested that they all come together in Circle to discuss the issue.

In an eighth-grade classroom comprised entirely of youth of color, another White, female teacher introduced Circles to her students. Although she had twenty years of teaching experience, restorative practices were new to her. While she was enthusiastic about implementing what she had learned in her restorative practices training (which she had attended voluntarily), her school principal was not supportive of Circles. Despite this nonsupport, she began holding weekly Circles. As a part of bringing Circles into her classroom, the teacher tried to find ways to encourage her students to overcome their fear of speaking in front of peers. To prepare for talking in Circles, she assigned writing tasks, such as journaling. The writing tasks and topics varied in level of difficulty and depth. She began with individual reflective writing that typically previewed icebreakers for the Circle, such as "Name something you wonder about" or "Write ten things that would be in your witch's brew." While these prompts often helped most of the youths identify something they could say in Circle, it did not always seem to significantly alter the quality of their responses. During one Circle when youth talked about the ingredients in their witch's brew, this teacher expressed some surprise at how uncreative the ingredients were. Some of the students suggested water, pumpkin, spices, and roses.

One particular ingredient was an Afro (a hairstyle), which a boy who was East Asian listed and seemingly directed, perhaps disrespectfully, to one of his Black classmates who grew an Afro. The teacher chose to confront the inappropriateness of this so-called ingredient and suspended the talking piece to do so. She directly asked the East Asian student if he thought his response would be offensive to some people. This student quickly replied, "No, it's just funny." The boy with the Afro remained silent and looked away. The teacher reiterated that some students could find that suggesting an Afro for a witch's brew ingredient was mean, but did not discuss this further. She then reopened the Circle.

Youth relational dynamics complicated how the dialogue ensued in this

---

In some cases, the Circles provided a platform to target others, while at other times, they opened up space to name and challenge harmful behavior.

Circle. The Black student with the Afro was often a target of mean so-called jokes concerning his hairstyle and body weight. While this student remained quiet at times, he also took on the role of bully himself, returning aggression with aggression. As are a disproportionate number of students of African heritage,[13] he was suspended many times throughout the school year. This teacher often verbally reprimanded him in front of his peers for speaking out of turn and for being rude to her and his classmates. Clearly, the complexity of peer-to-peer and teacher-to-youth relationships in this classroom impacted how students engaged each other during Circles. In some cases, the Circles provided a platform to target others, while at other times, they opened up space to name and challenge harmful behavior.[14]

Teachers' Biases and Perspectives Shape the Process

In my work of training, mentoring, and coaching teachers to implement peacemaking Circles, I often find myself caught in a third space—a space that is open for dialogue, critical reflection, and examining deep injustices. I often ask myself how best to coach teachers to see inequities, even when they believe they are implementing restorative practices. Exclusion still permeates many restorative peacemaking Circles, particularly when a minority—i.e., those who lack power and privilege—is ignored or silenced by those who have more power, e.g., racially dominant students, teachers, and/or administrators. Those of the racially dominant group have more space to control the Circle process. Teachers I have worked with contend that the ethnicity of their students does not influence their restorative justice practices. Yet, when observing their interactions with youth, it is easy to see how quickly youth of color are targeted. They may be called upon sooner and with more intensity than their White peers, if, for instance, they are talking out of turn, come in late, or have incomplete work. Such microaggressions are not documented in most restorative practices research, and questions of "Who?" and "Why?" become pertinent.

Those of the racially dominant group have more space to control the Circle process.

The discomforting reality is that teachers in any school are neither value neutral nor colorblind. They carry their own implicit and explicit biases. These biases shape how and when they respond to conflict. While training, mentorship, and coaching can help teachers identify how biases influence their choices, many deeply embedded, unconscious biases remain present in any restorative justice practice, regardless of a facilitator's ethnic background.

Ultimately, the ethnic, cultural, and gender identities—to name just a few—of elementary students and teachers influence how schools approach conflictual issues.[15] Most K–12 educators have had little opportunity to gain confidence or skills for handling complex social, political, and moral subject matters, either during their own student years or in typical professional development education.[16] Furthermore, many youth and educators do not feel confident or prepared to address conflicts in their classrooms, particularly when conflicts are connected to race, culture, gender, religion, politics, wealth, and other contentious issues. In practice, then, only some restorative practices initiatives challenge social relations that are visibly inequitable.[17]

Most of the public school teachers I have worked with in diverse and marginalized communities are slow to examine the cultural relevance, equity consequences, and effectiveness of selected peacemaking and restorative community-building tools. These alternatives to exclusionary punishment are designed to de-escalate conflict and repair relationships before and after instances of harm in schools. Yet, many dominant-society educators do not understand how school culture sustains dominant norms and values. For instance, one school administrator in a low-income community with many racialized youths told me: "We don't have that many disputes or issues at our school to talk about. . . . [Restorative] practices are really only meant for students to vent and air their [dirty] laundry, and this is not needed at school. It builds on the negativity. . . . I'm not going to support that." This school administrator's statement misconstrues what restorative practices actually do in a school.

Most of the public school teachers I have worked with in diverse and marginalized communities are slow to examine the cultural relevance, equity consequences, and effectiveness of selected peacemaking and restorative community-building tools.

Even in "supportive contexts," teachers and administrators often fall short when it comes to actually implementing restorative processes. When conflicts arise—whether bullying, gender-based violence, or ongoing interpersonal conflicts between youth—most educators are too influenced by the traditional school culture, i.e., a punitive system, to engage wholeheartedly with a restorative process that necessitates change, equity, and inclusion.[18] At another school that had strong administrative support and used Circles consistently, many critical incidents were handled in ways that led to further exclusions. For instance, to address a case of online bullying, the administrator led a Circle with the entire cohort of seventh-grade students. However, most of Circle's participants refused to accept responsibility for their actions and instead stated that their actions were not only justified but also completely appropriate.

At another school, I worked with a teacher who consistently implemented community-building Circles, yet she never addressed a violent incident that had taken place between two boys in the class. During the class Circles, the two estranged students both sat slouched with their eyes cast downward and participated minimally.

In one of these Circles, another boy in the class chose to sit outside of the Circle. While initially the teacher made efforts to invite him in, he consistently protested. Eventually, she just ignored his presence, essentially abandoning her commitment to him, as she waited for him to be removed from the school. She believed his removal was about to happen, given that he was constantly involved with the police and was possibly involved in gang activity. However, during a later Circle, as youth talked about what they had heard in the news about ISIS and chemical weapons, this young man felt compelled to share a story. He had witnessed firsthand in Syria how chemical weapons affected people. Critically for him, the Circle's topic paved a way for his re-entry into the classroom community.

His sharing and inclusion spurred a whole-class discussion where various youth contributed to dialogue on the possibilities of World War III, a discussion which the teacher encouraged and expertly facilitated with the use of the talking piece. At the end of the Circle, she commended the youth for their engagement, saying, "I didn't plan for that; it turned out to be quite deep." In this moment, both the teacher and youth took a risk to dive deeper into dialogue—scaffolded, of course, by the peacemaking Circle format—sharing aspects of their identities, asking questions, and challenging the content.

While this young man participated in this siloed event, he continued to sit outside during future Circles. While I encouraged the teacher to still pass the talking piece to him, she resisted and subsequently told me that she should meet his self-exclusion with further exclusion—in effect doubling down. Despite a glimpse of connection, he was still out of the Circle. This teacher's classroom illustrates how prior complicated relationships impact Circle processes. It also shows how some "well-meaning" restorative teachers are still ethically okay with excluding so-called behavioral or challenging youth. Clearly, restorative practices are not only about implementing particular tools or strategies; they are also about an ethos that relies on mutual respect, listening, and the commitment to confront and speak one's truth, no matter how decentering that truth is.

Additionally, restorative practices involve guiding youth through advanced academic exercises that build their capacities for critical thought and engagement. Many skilled teachers teach about conflict by acknowledging contentious perspectives and describing multiple narratives; they pause at points of contention to deliberate, dialogue, and resolve moments when views diverge. These educators take comfort in the power of integrating restorative practices within classroom dialogue. Restorative practices focus on relationship

Restorative practices focus on relationship building and healing; they generate trust and comfort by embodying a risky pedagogy; and they dismantle systems of oppression and control by critically reflecting on multiple viewpoints.

building and healing; they generate trust and comfort by embodying a risky pedagogy; and they dismantle systems of oppression and control by critically reflecting on multiple viewpoints.

Still, many well-intentioned teachers use restorative practices for proactive community building but not for preventing conflict or for post-conflict incidents. Others, including many in lSES communities, attempt to engage restorative practices at the proactive or post-incident level but struggle against the ingrained structural and institutional constraints. These constraints intentionally feed into a deficit-oriented landscape that diminishes opportunities for growth and for deeper social and academic development.

I mentored and coached one teacher who spoke to the challenges she encountered when she attempted to reframe the language typically used with her diverse group of students during post-incident conversations. She attempted to move beyond the role of disciplinarian, which focused on blaming-and-shaming "Why?" questions, and instead asked the restorative questions that invite each young person to voice his or her own perspectives and concerns:

> I know it's not really valuable to ask a child why they did something, but how many times do I do it, and do I hear others doing it and hear myself doing it? And I try really hard to refrain from that, and instead try to use, "What were you thinking when that happened?" Just kind of rephrasing the question to validate even the [one who triggered] the problem . . . helped me to stop asking why and to look at the bigger situation of how we are going to solve this.

Traditionally assumed to be disciplinarians and curriculum deliverers, teachers may find it difficult to embody and implement restorative practices, even after they have been thoroughly trained.[19] After attempting restorative practices, teachers tend to revert to habitual and therefore expected ways of handling conflict through top-down, judgmental discipline, including tactics such as sending student to the office and controlling classroom dialogue. When teachers engage with conflict in these habitual ways, they find that this pedagogical style hinders them from consistently engaging in restorative language. It also reduces their readiness to carefully critique the underlying cultural and social implications of their choices, particularly with marginalized youth.

Paying Attention to the Silence

Although conflictual issues exist in all classrooms, they are most often silenced. Social prejudice may also contribute to this silencing, marginalizing or excluding youth during peacemaking Circles, especially when a dialogue touches upon or implies linkages to their core cultural identities. My ethnographic research found that while participating in a talking Circle, quieter youth, who at first passed the talking piece without speaking, after a few rounds expressed delight when they spoke. These young people helped me to see how their silence was sometimes a unique form of participation.[20] In addition, pedagogies that honor silence can open up a space to question or respond in honored silence. This pedagogy can allow teachers to know whether students' silence is a result of them taking a political stand or reflects a choice to remain quiet.[21] When I meet with youth individually or in small groups, I often ask how they feel when they participate in classroom discussions versus Circle processes. Youth consistently confirmed to me that not all voices and perspectives are aired in the classroom(s); some perspectives they only expressed to themselves internally—in their own "silenced dialogue."[22]

For instance, in one school, I worked with Muslim youth who shared that they feared peer reprisal if they voiced dissenting perspectives. One girl in the fourth grade, who had a racialized female teacher, pointed out that, because only six Muslims were enrolled in her class of twenty-three, much of the classroom dialogue didn't connect to her identity and focused on "other [cultures] and religions . . . like Catholics." When I asked her what she did in those circumstances, she replied, in an uncharacteristically quiet voice, "I just be quiet." A group of seventh-grade students, who had a racialized male teacher, described what they called an "internal Muslim-Muslim" dialogue: they held it in their heads when material they didn't agree with was discussed. Their silence at these times reflected a choice not to attract attention to their identities, particularly when they felt emotionally disconnected or not personally identified with perspectives that arose in classroom dialogue.[23] Thus, youth silence can at times indicate their perceived sense of exclusion, and at other times, perhaps, agreement with their peers and/or the teacher.

Their silence at these times reflected a choice not to attract attention to their identities . . .

Youth may be reserved for various reasons. One Black young woman, who had a White female teacher, reflected: "People are also judging you, especially at this age [adolescence], and I don't like participating."[24] Another Black young woman in the same class noted: "I don't share because I don't feel comfortable." At the same time, many other racialized youths in this same class participated actively and repeatedly remarked on the value of the Circle experience in broadening their awareness, connecting with their peers, and learning more about topics varying in scope. For instance, one East Asian young woman in the class, who typically remained quiet during classroom discussions but participated actively during Circles and activities focused on restorative practices, stated, "In Circles, you could see everyone's point of view and try to resolve it."[25]

Even Circles set up with the right space, the right principles, and the "right" values nonetheless carry the potential to silence some youth who may not feel adequately prepared or ready to verbally engage in Circle dialogue. The minority youths' non-vocal participation does not necessarily reflect their knowledge level, nor does it gauge their capacity to engage in dialogue. Racialized youth are inherently aware of the un/conscious biases and dialogue that perpetuate stereotypes and discrimination. However, they often lack the necessary critical tools and/or capacity to speak up, particularly when they are confronted with systems of White control and power. In this way, racialized voices are silenced in classrooms and schools: they feel forced to self-censor whenever their beliefs or perspectives do not square with the dominant-narrative discourse.[26] However, I have found that many female and racialized youth have participated more frequently and confidently in Circles when they experienced peer support or teacher encouragement to share their perspectives.

The reality is that when teachers assume that all individuals agree, the dominant voices tend to be empowered. Power and privilege act to silence divergent and alternative perspectives, with the result that these perspectives remain unexamined. This allows dominant systems to maintain and reproduce oppressive structures. When the voices of marginalized or racialized youth break through the silence and are heard, dominant society's tactics are revealed. Thus, teachers need to prepare all their students—both the more confident, dominant students and the quieter, less dominant ones—to engage with (and own) the conflict; Circle processes provide powerful pedagogical opportunities to do just that.

In this way, racialized voices are silenced in classrooms and schools: they feel forced to self-censor whenever their beliefs or perspectives do not square with the dominant-narrative discourse.[26] However, I have found that many female and racialized youth have participated more frequently and confidently in Circles when they experienced peer support or teacher encouragement to share their perspectives.

Moving Forward with Critical and Culturally Responsive Research with Communities of Color and Indigenous Peoples

In challenging racist patriarchy, Audre Lorde eloquently articulated, "The master's tools will never dismantle the master's house. They may allow us temporarily to beat him at his own game, but they will never enable us to bring about genuine change."[27] Her powerful words invite both researchers and practitioners to question how we use particular tools and strategies when we challenge oppression, both from within and from without. If we rely on the Western-based research methodologies that researchers use to study, critique, dismantle, and promote restorative justice practices in schools, then many deep-seated issues arise. Because we end up using Western constructs to deconstruct Western constructs, we are much more likely to reproduce the very same hegemonic structures that sustain both our oppression and marginalization. Some research and evaluative studies, for example, may have been conducted with the intention to expose and ultimately dismantle inequitable systems, yet the studies nonetheless end up reinforcing the status quo—as we unfortunately see. Despite all that we know now about the life-damaging consequences of school exclusion and marginalizing racialized youth, little has actually changed in the praxis, however much of the focus may be on providing quality, competitive, and equitable schooling for marginalized youth.[28] Clearly, the realities surrounding the school-to-prison pipeline, Black Lives Matter, and the Standing Rock Water Protectors show that research and evaluative studies need to do more to challenge inequality—more than voicing deep concern about systemic injustices.

Because we end up using Western constructs to deconstruct Western constructs, we are much more likely to reproduce the very same hegemonic structures that sustain both our oppression and marginalization.

A good start on vetting restorative processes that perpetuate injustice is to critically examine our research and evaluation procedures. This kind of vetting needs to be at the forefront of any study on restorative processes. We need to engage in a critique: How do we design and conduct research? Who is designing and conducting the research? And why is this particular research necessary? Many layers of stakeholders—such as community-based organizations, schools, and government agencies—rely on research that show restorative justice's effectiveness. Indeed, we now have a plethora of studies that document through rigorous quantitative data how restorative practices reduce suspension and expulsion rates, particularly with marginalized youth. I am not advocating that we ignore these quantitative and qualitative studies, which are vast and deep. However, I do suggest that we stop and think critically about this body of research, which has been designed and conducted through a Eurocentric lens.

For example, studies that group all youth together, without considering diversities such as gender, race, ethnicity, and social and economic status, raise red flags. Any restorative justice practitioner, teacher, or researcher who is a critical thinker knows that the one-size-fits-all method is not consistent with restorative practice philosophy. How communities of color experience restorative justice practices is critical to creating, designing, and engaging in attentive research—research that will actually prove helpful to communities of color. Consistent attention to *who is in* and *who is out* of the Circle involves gathering data on youth beyond their race to include various aspects of their social identities. We need to draw upon Indigenous methods of critical, decolonizing thinking to invite robust inquiry into the research process, from start to finish. Researchers also need to consider transparency: How does their own (powerful) positionality shape their subjective perspectives, which in turn guide their research?

A one-size-fits-all research model, which focuses on building frameworks for restorative justice approaches or practices, ultimately contributes to further excluding marginalized youth. Eurocentric research has arguably legitimized policing in schools, and it perpetuates punitive procedures for resolving conflicts. Youth who typically carry marginalized identities and histories often face aggressively harsh disciplinary responses from adults charged with their care and education.

We need critical theory and research that interrupts these patterns. With greater critical awareness, researchers, evaluators, administrators, teachers, and school-age youth can draw on social and institutional supports to develop scholarly knowledge. This knowledge must also be accessible and relevant to community members. Heightening our awareness of how restorative processes can marginalize youth of color will contribute to restorative education. A close fit between restorative education values and the fairness of restorative processes will help the movement fulfill its potential for building an equitable, just, and vibrant democracy.

We need to draw upon Indigenous methods of critical, decolonizing thinking to invite robust inquiry into the research process, from start to finish. Researchers also need to consider transparency: How does their own (powerful) positionality shape their subjective perspectives, which in turn guide their research?

Deep Implementation in, out, and beyond the Circle

Schooling for collaborative, engaged citizens involves educating with a Circle-minded approach—with conscious attention to who's in and who's out of the Circle. Education needs to focus on constructing inclusive Circles that build on youths' continuous learning journeys. Because Circles instill inclusivity, they build a foundation of peace that does not shy away from conflicts and other dialogues with conflict potential. Indeed, implementing Circles specifically focused on conflicts—both interpersonal and on a broader scale—is essential for democratic education. As counterintuitive as it may seem, such robust dialogue practices are integral to creating restorative, peaceful classrooms. Paying critical attention to who is participating becomes essential for all aspects of restorative practices. This awareness of participation also includes critical attention to the researchers who design and conduct studies on restorative practices and the evaluators who assess the impact of those practices. The latter must ask insightful questions, such as, Who is affected by the research and how?

Overall, many factors contribute to implementing restorative practices and peacemaking Circles in diverse classrooms. Here are some of the factors that affect the critical and inclusive core of restorative practices.

1. *Teachers' background and identity are contributing factors to how they choose to respond to conflict.* Teachers' own racial, ethnic, and class backgrounds, professional and personal experiences, and personal value systems impact the choices they make. These personal factors influence how teachers react to conflict, which in turn frames their ability to embrace the constructive, positive potential of conflict dialogues.
2. *Enabling teachers to engage conflict involves training them to facilitate restorative practices.* Empowering teachers through training creates opportunity-rich environments for all youth. This training includes feedback on how they implement Circles and dialogue; ongoing coaching for their practice to identify best practices that promote inclusion; and using Circles to debrief their experiences with feedback from third-party observers and youth. The teachers' school environment also affects their ability to promote inclusive restorative practices. They may be functioning as lone-wolf teachers, or they may be working with a supportive educational leader (e.g., principal), who is confident in managing the systemic and institutionalized oppressions that permeate schools.

3. *The classroom setup and environment impact the inclusion or exclusion of learners.* Space to move desks and chairs to encourage small groups, shifts to Circle setup, and space for learners and teachers to freely move around the classroom: these physical factors contribute to making inclusive processes a natural and everyday response.
4. *Youths' diversity of identity and experiences affects how they connect to the curriculum, and teachers have different abilities to leverage these differences effectively.* Experiential learning is another important factor that contributes to implementing restorative practices inclusively. However, the diverse makeup of students also impacts classroom environments. Whether the class is homogenous or heterogeneous will affect how the group experiences and interprets various topics and issues. Skilled teachers capitalize on these different perspectives and are mindful of bringing in alternative perspectives from varying sources, such as through guest speakers, case studies, or media.
5. *Research through participatory Indigenous methods is necessary to gather a fuller understanding of how marginalized youth experience restorative practices.* How do privileged scholars position and frame restorative practices? In considering this question, is an exercise in participatory Indigenous methods worth the effort? Are other needs carefully and critically reflected upon? When researchers subsume a savior mentality, for example, the researchers' perspective and their study become all the more questionable. They may be unable to consider how their privilege contributes to further excluding and essentializing the very marginalized groups they seek to study.

In short, Circles provide unique opportunities for students, teachers, and administrators to learn how to communicate and to engage in alternative ways with social conflict and social hierarchy. Understanding the key challenges and principles of Circle processes could better equip them to implement restorative and dialogue pedagogies amongst themselves. With this understanding, they can then collectively analyze how their choices might facilitate greater and more authentic inclusion.

DISCUSSION QUESTIONS

1. In responding to "who's in and who's out" of restorative practices, what characteristics define the *in* group and the *out* group? Include

behavioral characteristics. Describe how these behavioral characteristics have been taught or learned. And what kind of unlearning is necessary to offer restorative and equitable spaces, so that marginalized voices are consistently *in*?
2. When conducting research with communities of color or with Indigenous Peoples, how can we frame questions and methodologies in ways that control for essentializing identities and reduce further marginalization and stigmatization?
3. How and in what areas does your school seem to be using, promoting, or supporting restorative principles and practices?
4. Which youth would most benefit from opportunities to practice constructive conflict dialogue? What opportunities are available to critically reflect on social issues from the news, literature, or lesson material? What is the role of the engaged/disengaged youth in these types of conflictual discussions?

ACTIVITIES

1. *Facilitate Circles of identity or affinity.* Honor youths' multiple and intersecting identities and honor the various experiences connected to their identities. Reflection questions could include: "To me, oppression looks like . . . ," and "I honor my identity by . . . and I honor your identity by . . ."
2. *Facilitate empowerment within Circles.* Encourage young people of color to recognize their power to facilitate change. Complete sentence starters like this one: "I use my power for constructive change by . . ."
3. *Conduct research with communities of color or Indigenous Peoples on restorative justice practices through collaborative methods.* Design an action research project in collaboration with youth of color where they choose the questions and design and conduct the project. Engage in weekly research debrief sessions with these youth in Circle processes. Reflect on how this shared leadership into research with communities of color or Indigenous Peoples contributes to inclusion, engagement, and equitable research methods.

RESOURCES

Evans, Katherine, and Dorothy Vaandering, *The Little Book of Restorative Justice in Education: Fostering Responsibility, Healing, and Hope in Schools.* New York: Skyhorse, 2016.

Freire, Paulo. *Pedagogy of the Oppressed*, trans. Myra B. Ramos. New York: Continuum (1970), 2007.

Parker, Christina. *Peacebuilding, Citizenship, and Identity: Empowering Conflict and Dialogue in Multicultural Classrooms.* Rotterdam, the Netherlands: Sense, 2016.

NOTES

1. Christina Parker, *Peacebuilding, Citizenship, and Identity: Empowering Conflict and Dialogue in Multicultural Classrooms* (Rotterdam, the Netherlands: Sense, 2016).
2. Brent Davis, Dennis Sumara, and Rebecca Luce-Kapler, *Engaging Minds: Cultures of Education and Practices of Teaching* (New York: Routledge, 2015).
3. Simone Ispa-Landa, "Racial and Gender Inequality and School Discipline: Toward a More Comprehensive View of School Policy," *Social Currents* 4, no. 6 (2017): 511–17.
4. Kimberlé W. Crenshaw with Priscilla Ocen and Jyoti Nanda, *Black Girls Matter: Pushed Out, Overpoliced, and Underprotected* (New York: Columbia University, Center for Intersectionality and Social Policy Studies, 2015).
5. Paulo Freire, *Pedagogy of the Oppressed*, trans. Myra B. Ramos (New York: Continuum, [1970] 2007).
6. Heather Knight, "Articulating Injustice: An Exploration of Young People's Experiences of Participation in a Conflict Transformation Programme That Utilises the Arts as a Form of Dialogue," *Compare: A Journal of Comparative and International Education* 44, no. 1 (2014): 77–96.
7. Gayatri C. Spivak, "Can the Subaltern Speak?" in *Can the Subaltern Speak? Reflections on the History of an Idea*, ed. Rosalind Morris (New York: Columbia University Press, 2010), 21–78.
8. Judith Torney-Purta, Rainer Lehmann, Hans Oswald, and Wolfram Schulz, *Citizenship and Education in Twenty-Eight Countries: Civic Knowledge and Engagement at Age Fourteen* (Amsterdam: IEA Secretariat, 2001).
9. Kathy Bickmore and Christina Parker, "Constructive Conflict Talk in Classrooms: Divergent Approaches to Addressing Divergent Perspectives," *Theory and Research in Social Education* 42, no. 3 (2014): 291–335.
10. Jeannie Oakes, *Keeping Track* (New Haven: Yale University Press, 2005).
11. US Department of Education, *Guiding Principles: A Resource Guide for Improving School Climate and Discipline* (Washington, D.C.: US Department of Education, 2014).
12. Yolanda Anyon, Anne Gregory, Susan Stone, Jordan Farrar, Jeffrey M. Jenson, Jeanette McQueen, Barbara Downing, Eldridge Greer, and John Simmons, "Restorative Interventions and School Discipline Sanctions in a Large Urban School District," *American Educational Research Journal* 53, no. 6 (2016): 1663–97.
13. See Stephen Jull, "Youth Violence, Schools and the Management Question: A Discussion of Zero Tolerance and Equity in Public Schooling," *Canadian Journal of Educational Administration and Policy* 17 (2000), www.umanitoba.ca/plublications/cjeap.2000; and Russell J. Skiba, Robert S. Michael, Abra Carroll Nardo, and Reece L. Peterson, "The Color of Discipline: Sources of Racial and

Gender Disproportionality in School Punishment," *The Urban Review* 34, no. 4 (December 2002).
14. Christina Parker and Kathy Bickmore, "Peacemaking Circles in Diverse Classrooms: Professional Learning and Implementation," paper presented at the Canadian Society for Studies in Education (CSSE) Conference, Canadian Association of Curriculum Studies (CACS) SIG, Toronto, Ontario (2017).
15. See Parker, *Peacebuilding.*
16. Christina Parker and Kathy Bickmore, "Conflict Management and Dialogue with Diverse Students: Novice Teachers' Approaches and Concerns," *Journal of Teaching and Learning* 8, no. 2 (2012): 47–64.
17. Hilary Lustick, "'Restorative Justice' or Restoring Order? Restorative School Discipline Practices in Urban Public Schools," *Urban Education* (November 14, 2017), https://doi.org/10.1177/0042085917741725.
18. Katherine Evans and Dorothy Vaandering, *The Little Book of Restorative Justice in Education: Fostering Responsibility, Healing, and Hope in Schools* (New York: Skyhorse, 2016).
19. Russell and Diane Crocker, "The Institutionalisation of Restorative Justice in Schools: A Critical Sensemaking Account," *Restorative Justice* 4, no. 2 (2016): 195–213.
20. See Parker, *Peacebuilding.*
21. Michalinos Zembylas and Pavlos Michaelides, "The Sound of Silence in Pedagogy," *Educational Theory* 54, no. 2 (2004): 193–210.
22. Lisa D. Delpit, "The Silenced Dialogue: Power and Pedagogy in Educating Other People's Children," *Harvard Educational Review* 58, no. 3 (1988): 280–98.
23. Zvi Bekerman and Michalinos Zembylas, "The Emotional Complexities of Teaching Conflictual Historical Narratives: The Case of Integrated Palestinian-Jewish Schools in Israel," *Teachers College Record* 113, no. 5 (2011): 1004–30.
24. Katherine Schultz, "After the Blackbird Whistles: Listening to Silence in Classrooms," *Teachers College Record* 112, no. 11 (2010): 2833–49.
25. Stanton Wortham, "Listening for Identity Beyond the Speech Event," *Teachers College Record* 112, no. 11 (2010): 2850–73.
26. John W. White, "Resistance to Classroom Participation: Minority Students, Academic Discourse, Cultural Conflicts, and Issues of Representation in Whole Class Discussions," *Journal of Language, Identity and Education* 10, no. 4 (2011): 250–65.
27. Audre Lorde, "The Master's Tools Will Never Dismantle the Master's House," in *Feminist Postcolonial Theory: A Reader*, ed. Reina Lewis and Sara Mills (New York: Routledge, 2003), 25–28.
28. Kevin G. Welner and Prudence L. Carter, "Achievement Gaps Arise from Opportunity Gaps," chap. 1 in *Closing the Opportunity Gap: What America Must Do to Give Every Child an Even Chance*, ed. Prudence L. Carter and Kevin G. Welner (New York: Oxford University Press, 2013), 1–10.

Chapter 4

Burn the Bridge

Erica Littlewolf, Michelle Armster, and Christianne Paras, with Lorraine Stutzman Amstutz

A bridge has often been used as a metaphor to talk about how restorative justice (RJ) is a link from Aboriginal and Indigenous communities around the world who have lived out what restorative justice means. Yet it is false to claim that restorative justice in its current iteration is honoring the traditions of Indigenous people. We are not living out the values from those original traditions, and restorative justice does not truly honor the roots of Aboriginal/Indigenous in its current colonial form. Instead, restorative justice is rooted in a Western, white supremacist, cisgender, male-dominated system.

While a bridge has frequently been used as a metaphor to describe restorative justice, the bridge-metaphor framework has often been understood as the only way to reach a destination of healing and justice and to journey toward reconciled communities. This chapter reveals that a broader landscape exists—and has always existed—for the three individuals who were interviewed for this chapter. They discuss how their communities use their own wisdom to determine the meaning of healing and justice.

Where Are We in Our Work and What Are the Challenges?

Erica Littlewolf: I am a Northern Cheyenne woman and am biracial. I grew up on the Northern Cheyenne reservation in Montana. I have now lived off the reservation longer than I have lived on, mostly in urban areas with small Native American populations.

I am not sure when I "formally" began restorative justice work. I believe I was born into it as a way of life. I currently work on Indigenous justice issues within a Christian organization. The majority of my work has focused on the Doctrine of Discovery (DOD). I work toward educating mostly non-Indigenous Christian people on the Doctrine of Discovery. My work involves explaining the Christian roots of the DOD and how they were used to justify the extermination and enslavement of Indigenous Peoples globally. For example, using scripture, the concept of *Terra nullius*, and referring to Indigenous Peoples as non-humans, the doctrine set the tone for US policy regarding Native Americans, which included taking land and killing Indigenous Peoples.

It is challenging to educate Christian people who are restorative-justice oriented about how their religion and current way of life exist at Indigenous Peoples' expense. Indeed, lack of individual ownership in systemic problems continues. I often hear people say, "I cannot be held accountable for what my ancestors did." Yet they continue to farm and live in excess, while Indigenous Peoples live disconnected from their homelands and in poverty. I do not blatantly frame my work as "restorative justice," but it involves individual, familial, community, ancestral, and systemic restorative justice that will take generations. I find it is challenging to get dominant society to do work when they may not be able to see results in their lifetime. Dominant society tends to want immediate satisfaction.

I find it is challenging to get dominant society to do work when they may not be able to see results in their lifetime.

It is also challenging when non-Indigenous people recognize the harms of the DOD, take responsibility for the harm, but then immediately want to jump to reparations. The harm gets framed as the taking of land and the reparation immediately revolves around returning land. Some Indigenous communities are having this conversation, but not widely. I see the assertion of returning land both as a way in which non-Indigenous people can feel better about themselves and as a means of dominating the process. They are naming what needs to be done, instead of waiting for Indigenous people to name what is needed by them and their communities.

Another unanticipated challenge is with educated, anti-oppression individuals working in Indigenous communities. Such individuals tend to come to Indigenous communities with an idea of how things need to be done in order to implement a restorative justice process with an anti-oppression lens. They do fabulous listening processes, but they often question the results they gain from these processes. Because many Indigenous communities are at various levels of colonization and recovering from its effects, they are all different and have different needs. Often communities want things implemented in "colonial" ways. This colonial way is often the desired approach, because they know this is a step in the healing process; in contrast, implementing programs that are completely "decolonized" would cause more harm to the community than healing. Each Indigenous community is different. Doing what a community desires may seem "oppressive," but a community knows what is best for it in regards to healing and restorative justice, and outsiders do well to recognize and abide by the community's wishes. The important thing to remember is that Indigenous communities are complex, and it is best to develop a tone of "learner" and "co-journeyer" rather than expert.

Michelle Armster: First, I am a woman of African descent born in the United States. Also I am a womanist and a follower of Jesus. All of these identities are important in order to be transparent about what shapes my restorative justice lens.

I started in this work in 1985 and was drawn to it through my profession as an insurance claims examiner. At that time, insurance claims and suits were being referred to mediation for resolution. Because I was a representative of an insurance company, the success of responding to conflict with mediation caught my attention. As a result, I decided to pursue education and training in the field. It was through not "restorative justice" but "mediation" that I also facilitated divorce cases, domestic violence cases, victim-offender cases, community disputes, and justice of the peace disputes. Later, when I was introduced to the concept of restorative justice, I became aware that there was a territorial distinction between restorative justice and conflict transformation. The difference seemed to be in the articulation of the concepts, philosophies, or understandings.

As a practitioner of color, I noticed that if the person who did harm was White, then that person was going to have an opportunity to engage in a dialogue. If the person who harmed was a Person of Color, I hardly ever saw the same opportunity provided.

However, I saw no difference in the practices. In both fields, the disparity in who were afforded the opportunity to engage with restorative justice or conflict transformation troubled me. When I was assigned more serious cases, I began to notice connections with police and courts that were problematic. As a practitioner of color, I noticed that if the person who did harm was White, then that person was going to have an opportunity to engage in a dialogue. If the person who harmed was a Person of Color, I hardly ever saw the same opportunity provided.

As a womanist restorative justice practitioner, I am guided by three principles:

- Seek wholeness for all: women, men, children, and the community.
- Spirituality and ethics are essential in order to dismantle the oppressions of race, gender, class, and sexuality.

- The people have the power and wisdom to determine their needs and what is good for them.

At their core, the principles of restorative justice are wonderfully aspirational and have the potential to be powerful, humanizing, and transformative. However, some of the ways that restorative justice is being practiced is disturbing. Unless the field acknowledges its complicity in perpetuating racist and sexist systems, it will never be a "safe" place for people and practitioners of color. Furthermore, unless the field speaks up and begins to address the historical, systemic, and continued harms from the extermination of Indigenous people and the enslavement of Africans, people and practitioners of color can never feel fully part of restorative justice. Lastly, as long as Whites continue to articulate, dictate, and appropriate restorative justice and restorative practices, the field will continue to be racist and sexist and not live up to its ideals.

Christianne Paras: I am an Ilokano and Kapampangan woman from the Philippines, its colonized name. A significant part of my journey and identity is also as an immigrant-settler and Person of Color living and working on the traditional, ancestral, and unceded territories of Kwantlen, Musqueam, Tsleil-Waututh, Squamish, and Kwikwetlem, where I currently reside. *Agyamanak unay and maraming salamat.* I am deeply grateful for the land in which I live, work, and play.

The first time I sat in Circle among restorative justice practitioners to talk about "race," I spoke to the experience of being labeled as the "face of diversity." First, I shared about how much time and effort I have given to deepening my understanding of restorative justice philosophy and practice over the years, and the gratitude I felt for being part of the movement—part of this community that held values such as compassion, inclusivity, and respect. Then, I spoke to the impact of being called and treated as the "face of diversity"—an example of "tokenism"—which minimized the time and commitment I had given to restorative justice. I spoke about how this tokenism corroded my sense of belonging in the restorative justice community. The White restorative justice practitioners viewed referring to me in those terms as an acknowledgment, a compliment, an endearment. For me, it was a reminder that, as a Person of Color in a predominantly White field, I was alone and marginalized.

The first time I sat in Circle among restorative justice practitioners to talk about "race," I spoke to the experience of being labeled as the "face of diversity."

Additionally, the recognition the White RJ practitioners bestowed upon me as a person symbolizing diversity was not really about me but about them personally and about the organization for having a Person of Color working

The White restorative justice practitioners viewed referring to me in those terms as an acknowledgment, a compliment, an endearment. For me, it was a reminder that, as a Person of Color in a predominantly White field, I was alone and marginalized.

alongside them. It was a self-congratulatory statement about meeting some perceived requirement for being diverse and inclusive. After the Circle, a colleague approached me and said that I seem to have many "triggers around race that I needed to work on" and shared how they wished I had spoken up sooner so that they could have "exercised more awareness around my sensitivities." This pivotal moment made clear the lack of cultural humility and safety in the practice for authentic, transformative conversations around race. The moment began my journey into exploring the landscape of restorative justice through colored lenses. I began to critically examine how values such as community, inclusion, and diversity were being interpreted in the practice of restorative justice in Canada. How was restorative practice plagued with "colorblindness"? How were White practitioners not really seeing the different experiences of marginalized groups, particularly communities of color, who frequently and continuously encounter various forms of exclusion and oppression?

While we need to have more conversations around restorative justice to respond to social justice issues, my journey as an immigrant, woman of color engaged in this work has raised for me more questions than answers. For example:

- What are the experiences of People of Color who work in restorative justice, and what challenges have come up for us in doing the work?
- How does the restorative justice community respond to the needs of People of Color in addressing experiences of exclusion and prejudice?
- How does the impact of colonization, power, and privilege manifest in the field of restorative justice?
- How does restorative justice perpetuate oppressive processes?
- How do we go about making restorative practice a truly diverse and vibrant field that upholds the values of inclusivity and equality?

If we do not recognize and understand the impact of colonization and systemic oppression as well as the issues of power and privilege, restorative justice will have neither the capacity nor the capability to address the racist, sexist, and classist injustices at the core of our oppressive social institutions.

What Is Justice?

An area of concern around restorative justice is how we define "justice." Presently, definitions revolve around crime, conflict, and harm, yet these definitions fail to reflect the systemic issues that are often factors to crime and conflict. The harms that restorative justice processes address are focused on the chargeable criminal act and are considered resolved when addressed, which is often limited to the victim-offender binary. Dialogue is typically around the impact of the actions of the "offender"/person who commits harm on the "victim"/person who was harmed, situating the participants' identities around the criminal event or conflict. Factors such as systemic issues and power relations as well as the impact on one's sense of identity—whether it be race, gender, age, or class beyond the victim-offender binary—are often left unacknowledged and unaddressed.

For example, racially charged offenses—harms that should be identified as "hate crimes"—are limited or reduced to the chargeable criminal offense. This chargeable offense becomes the overriding focus, which means the "hate crime" context goes unrecognized and therefore is overlooked in the restorative justice response. For example, a group of White youth may be charged with repeatedly vandalizing the home of a student of color, but the discussion focuses on the vandalism, not on the racial terrorizing that was the motivation and impact of the harm. When this limited response happens, the lived experiences of disenfranchised and marginalized groups, particularly communities of color, are erased, made invisible, and ignored. The individualistic approach to responding to harms lacks the understanding of justice that includes the broader, dynamic contexts in which we live and that continually evolve. The individualistic approach functions instead within a stagnant, singular reality, serving to perpetuate that reality by allowing it to go unnamed and unaddressed.

When this limited response happens, the lived experiences of disenfranchised and marginalized groups, particularly communities of color, are erased, made invisible, and ignored.

Current definitions of restorative justice, limited as they are to individual actions, exclude a response to the larger social [in]justice contexts, yet this narrow framing centers "whiteness." That is, the social system built on white supremacy remains the central power precisely by remaining unnamed, unrecognized, and invisible, at least to Whites. Excluding social justice from the restorative justice process, then, centers the criminal "justice" that benefits Whites: whiteness, white power, and white privilege and the structural and systemic hierarchy that these create. Ruth Morris, Euro-Canadian, a leading advocate for prison abolition and transformative justice, stated, "Restorative justice is not enough if it doesn't address fundamentally the issues of racist and classist"—and we would add patriarchal—"injustice which lies at the root of every one of our systems."[1]

Assumptions/Questions

Restorative justice practices tend to operate on assumptions formed through a White, colonized, Western modality that is experienced as normative. These assumptions often silence, erase, and harm both those of us who are practitioners of color and the People of Color who participate in restorative processes. Here are a few of these assumptions:

- *Everyone is equal*: This assumption is problematic because it fails to recognize identity, intersectionality, and the different lived experiences of disenfranchised, marginalized groups. Instead, as Ragnhild Utheim, White cultural anthropologist and professor of Liberal Studies, states, "The notion of a colorblind collective identity . . . is used to denote common experiences, understandings, and sense of belonging that members of society purportedly share but . . . fails to account for race-based inequalities and institutionalized injustice."[2] This assumption makes power and privilege in the intersections of race, gender, and class invisible. Embedded in the colorblind collective identity is the implication that everyone has the same needs and that those needs can be met in the same ways—without understanding and recognizing the disparities in equity and in having voice and choice in social institutions and processes. This leads to a false sense of equality in restorative processes: participants of color are not truly seen nor are their experiences acknowledged.
- *This is a safe space*: This assumes that restorative justice can create spaces "devoid of power," as if we could ignore the operation of social constructs among us, such as race, gender, and class, or ignore the impact of power and privilege on the feeling and experience of safety.[3] The operation of whiteness, race, and gender can create potentially marginalizing power dynamics—both among participants and between participants and facilitators. Ignoring or being "blind" to the various aspects and intersections of identity can silence and further marginalize participants of color. Kimberly J. Cook, White professor of sociology and criminology, states that by not acknowledging these social dynamics and not attending to unequal power in processes, restorative justice potentially "sets up a smokescreen" that reconstructs privileges around identity such as race, gender, age, and class.[4] For participants to truly feel a sense of safety, restorative

processes must acknowledge social and power dynamics, have open and honest conversations about what is present in the space, and inquire how—for the facilitator or as a group—these dynamics can be minimized.

- *Circle symbolizes community*: This assumes a singular, collective understanding of "community" and the values associated with it, disregarding how communities of color define and experience community. This assumption also disregards the tension that exists between the hegemonic mainstream narrative and counter-hegemonic cultural narratives.[5] The notion of a colorblind collective narrative suggests a common experience of community and a specific understanding of belonging and connection in that community. Linwood H. Cousins, an African American author and professor of anthropology, states that embedded in the mainstream collective narrative of belonging is the "silencing, exclusion, and subjugation" of the realities of marginalized and disenfranchised groups.[6] By uncritically adopting and endorsing a singular, Western definition of community, restorative justice risks perpetuating the erasure and structural oppression of People of Color.
- *Facilitators are impartial/neutral/detached*: This assumption proposes that every practitioner is able to facilitate any process, independent of their racial or cultural background, and without attachment to a particular worldview or social/political stance. For restorative justice practitioners to critically assess and remove any form of oppressive practice within their work, however, they must be able to examine how all aspects of their identity and experiences have shaped them as justice practitioners and the values and worldviews that guide their practice. The idea that facilitators must remain impartial/neutral/detached in their role contradicts the practice of self-reflection, which is an important aspect of facilitation. Susan Kamuti-Gaitho, RJ scholar of color in Canada, states, "If practitioners fail to do this, they may be unaware of their own and their client's identity and how this can impact interactions, inadvertently causing them to minimize and ignore issues of race, gender, class, ability, and sexual orientation; fail to share power with clients; and link individual issues to structural inequalities."[7] By recognizing their own lived experiences and worldview, facilitators are better equipped to identify and reflect on assumptions and biases that affect their interactions. They can be more curious about and understanding toward participants who have different lived experiences and perspectives. They can also develop a capacity to respond to the social power dynamics that can manifest in the restorative process.

Case Study

A community restorative justice organization, P&P Consulting, was invited to come to an urban, predominantly African American school to lead a one-day workshop on restorative justice approaches and violence prevention with a group of students and teachers. The well-intentioned P&P Consulting sent an all-White facilitator team to the school. Within the first hour of the session, the students and teachers began asking questions: Who were the facilitators? What were they doing in the school? Who were they to talk about violence prevention in a setting where they would have had no lived experience? Why did they think it was okay for them to offer solutions to the violence happening in their school? The students and teachers were understandably upset and felt they were being disciplined and judged through this process. Not surprisingly, the White facilitators were asked to leave.

These assumptions and this case study raise questions that practitioners would be wise to ask, leading to critical inquiry and a critical analysis of the process. (Practitioner: a person actively engaged in an art, discipline, or profession.)

- How are the issues of race, class, and gender recognized (or not) within restorative justice?
- What additional resources do we need before engaging in dialogue around issues of race, class, and gender?
- Who is the community? What do we need to consider when we ask that question?
- What practices within restorative justice perpetuate colonization and oppression?
- How do we talk about good intentions and unintended consequences?
- How do power and privilege impact our processes?
- If we come from outside the community, how do our own assumptions and perceived roles contribute to further harm?
- How would you engage an inquiry process around issues of bias, power, and privilege?

The process starts with identifying the problem, issue, or concern and then asking:

- What are the impacts to you, to community?
- What would you want to see different?
- What is your personal and institutional power?
- Where are your points of access?
- What systemic things need to change?

- What are we willing to do individually?
- What should we be willing to do as a community?

Conclusion

As women of color in and around the restorative justice field, we know that our perspective challenges some, is dismissed by some, and is welcomed by others who deeply resonate with the struggle at the bridge. Our expectation is that the restorative justice field will admit the inadequacies and limitations of how it is currently defined and practiced, and will embrace the broadening and deepening that our worldviews provide. We also expect that the philosophy will begin to more fully align the restorative work with authentic and diverse cultural perspectives of justice.

We need to burn the bridge in order to see, honor, and recognize the rootedness of the land that the bridge is built on.

Perhaps we won't need to rebuild the bridge. We may need to enter the stream and plant a tree on the other side.

And this is just the beginning.

A Vision for Justice by Michelle Armster

Long, long time ago
Or was it last year
Or was it yesterday

A seed was planted
A seed

A seed was planted
A justice tree seed

But

How will it grow
This justice tree

When the ground is poisoned
With lies and broken treaties

How will it grow
When water spills the blood of African and Indigenous blood

How will it grow
When the stories of settlers is the sun that scorches the earth,
burns our backs and drinks our tears

And
We

Know

That Our stories are not the same
And we know
That justice is a verb

And WE know

That it is all about the babies
Taking care of the babies
The babies until the 7th generations
The babies we must love
In ourselves
In our homes
In our communities
In the streets

Bearing witness
Creating Brave spaces
Learning from the past to see the future

Sankofa

Telling our stories

And
Then
Maybe then

This moment becomes a movement

We would also like to thank Lorraine Stutzman Amstutz for her willingness and commitment to facilitate our dialogue and serve as a scribe. It is difficult to find a White ally, and she continues to prove herself as such. Her questions, insights, and challenges helped us to more clearly articulate our thoughts and philosophy.

DISCUSSION QUESTIONS

1. What are the experiences of People of Color who work in restorative justice, and what challenges have come up for us in doing the work?
2. How does the restorative community respond to the needs of People of Color in addressing experiences of exclusion and prejudice?
3. How does the impact of colonization, power, and privilege manifest in the field of restorative justice?
4. How does restorative justice perpetuate oppressive processes?
5. How do we go about making restorative practice a truly diverse and vibrant field that upholds the values of inclusivity and equality?
6. How are the issues of race, class, and gender recognized (or not) within restorative justice?
7. What additional resources do we need before engaging in dialogue around issues of race, class, and gender?
8. Who is the community? What do we need to consider when we ask that question?
9. What practices within restorative justice perpetuate colonization and oppression?
10. How do we talk about good intentions and unintended consequences?
11. How do power and privilege impact our processes?
12. If we come from outside the community, how do our own assumptions and perceived roles contribute to further harm?

ACTIVITIES

Design an inquiry process around issues of bias, power, and privilege. For example, such a process might start with identifying the problem, issue, or concern and then posing questions such as the following:

1. What are the impacts to you, to your community?
2. What would you want to see different?
3. What is your personal and institutional power?
4. What leverage for change do you have but may not yet be using?
5. Where are your points of access?
6. What systemic things need to change?
7. What are we willing to do individually?
8. What should we be willing to do as a community?

RESOURCES

D of D Menno. "Doctrine of Discovery in the Name of Christ." Filmed June 2015 at various locations. Video. https://dofdmenno.org/movie/.

Jenkins, Morris. "How Do Culture, Class and Gender Affect the Practice of Restorative Justice?" In *Critical Issues in Restorative Justice,* edited by Howard Zehr and Barb Toews, 315–40. New York: Criminal Justice Press, 2004.

Johnson, Allan G. *Privilege, Power and Difference.* New York: McGraw-Hill Education, 2018.

McCaslin, Wanda D. *Justice as Healing: Indigenous Ways.* St, Paul, MN: Living Justice Press, 2005.

Mirchandani, Kiran, and Wendy Chan. "From Race and Crime to Racialization and Criminalization." In *Crimes of Color: Racialization and the Criminal Justice System in Canada,* ed. Wendy Chan and Kiran Mirchandani, 9–22. Peterborough, ON: Broadview Press, 2001.

Newcomb, Steven T. *Pagans in the Promised Land: Decoding the Doctrine of Christian Discovery.* Golden, CO: Fulcrum Publishing, 2008.

Phillips, Layli. *The Womanist Reader.* New York: Routledge, 2006.

Saskatoon Community Mediation Services and the Mennonite Central Committee Ministry. *Restorative Justice: Four Community Models* (a presentation paper). Saskatoon, Saskatchewan: MCC Canada Victim Offender Ministries, 1995.

Utheim, Ragnhild. "Restorative Justice, Reintegration, and Race: Reclaiming Collective Identity in the Postracial Era." *Anthropology and Education Quarterly* 45, no. 4 (2014): 355–72. Retrieved from http://onlinelibrary.wiley.com.libproxy.uregina.ca:2048/doi/10.1111/aeq.12075/.

NOTES

1. Ruth Morris, "Transformative Justice Tackles Structural Inequality," in *Restorative Justice: Four Community Models* by the Saskatoon Community Mediation Services and he Mennonite Central Committee Ministry, a presentation paper (Saskatoon, Saskatchewan: MCC Canada Victim Offender Ministries, 1995).
2. See Ragnhild Utheim, "Restorative Justice, Reintegration, and Race: Reclaiming Collective Identity in the Postracial Era," *Anthropology and Education Quarterly* 45, no. 4 (2014): 355–72, DOI: 10.1111/aeq.12075.
3. See Oko O. Elechi, "Repairing Harm and Transforming African-American Communities Through Restorative Justice," *Community Safety Journal* 4, no. 2 (2005): 29–36.
4. See Kimberly J. Cook, "Doing Difference and Accountability in Restorative Justice Conferences," *Theoretical Criminology* 10, no. 1 (2006): 107–24.
5. See Utheim, "Restorative Justice, Reintegration, and Race."
6. Linwood H. Cousins, "It Ain't as Simple as It Seems: Risky Youths, Morality, and Service Markets in Schools," in *Childhood, Youth, and Social Work in Transformation: Implications for Policy and Practice,* ed. Lynn M. Nybell, Jeffrey J. Shook, and

Janet L. Finn (New York: Columbia University Press, 2009), 92–112, http://www.jstor.org/stable/10.7312/nybe14140.

7. Susan Kamuti-Gaitho, “Diversity in Restorative Justice: A Research Practicum Report” (master’s thesis, University of Regina, 2017), https://ourspace.uregina.ca/handle/10294/7809.

PART II

Negotiating RJ/RP as Professionals of Color

In part 2, the authors reflect on how mostly White or White-led workplace environments impact their work as restorative professionals. People of Color regularly face these challenges, no matter what our work or profession. The academy, for example, is notorious for its blatant and subtle ways of marginalizing students and scholars of color. We face a chronic battle, no matter how "woke" we would like to think our field or profession might have become. As part of a mainstream white supremacist society, the restorative justice movement is no different. To be different, the intention to incorporate racial justice, social justice, and decolonizing justice into the restorative work must be set. So far, as the authors explain, this incorporation has not happened. Being woke about racial and social justice and decolonization requires a long process of waking, just as the process of waking to ways of responding to harms other than punishment has taken intention, time, and effort—and still we are working on it.

Chapter 5

Calling Out Whiteness

Sheryl Wilson

Surviving in White Systems

I had just received a request to speak at an event to discuss restorative justice. While I'm happy to receive the invitation, it will be nearly impossible for me to be there. When the person who extended the invitation asked me to consider someone else of color who can present in my absence, I grew silent. I couldn't come up with the name of a single person living in my area who worked in the field.

In the early 2000s, when I began my career as a restorative justice practitioner in Minnesota, I rarely came across other practitioners of color. While I felt the support of many of my White restorative justice counterparts and mentors, I found it difficult over the years to digest that, even though more practitioners of color were being added to our numbers regularly, we still have been isolated, working in predominantly White systems. This discussion is not new in many all-White/White-dominated fields where People of Color (POC) carve out a living daily. Practitioners of color who are involved in restorative justice work have had opportunities to share and compare our stories, and we have realized that many of our restorative justice experiences are similar.

As a practitioner, I experience isolation on two levels. First, I feel it because I work in an emerging profession that makes my role hard to distinguish by others. The type of work I do can be very nuanced and some may wonder whether it is needed. Second, as a Person of Color, I am often the only one like me who does this work. When I work with White practitioners, it disturbs me that we are often serving diverse communities and yet we don't accurately resemble them.

We are in very odd times in the US. On the one hand, POC are often being penalized for everyday activities that we do but that Whites perceive as a threat. On the other hand, Whites who witness other Whites doing the same

Our everyday reality is hyper-racialized: Whites get to dictate what POC can't do, though we are doing exactly the same things they do.

activities give each other a pass. For example, driving while Black has been something that African Americans routinely face. Many POC have found themselves having to engage with law enforcement—sometimes with deadly effect—to justify why they are doing these everyday activities: shopping, getting coffee, taking an elevator to one's own apartment, and, most recently, being a college student asleep in a dorm-study area. Our everyday reality is hyper-racialized: Whites get to dictate what POC can't do, though we are doing exactly the same things they do.

In my role as a practitioner of restorative justice, I do not believe I face the threat of being persecuted by law enforcement or being marginalized by the powers that be for "facilitating while Black." However, I and others are fully aware that, as People of Color, we are not the field's "normal" face.

Recognizing All-White Spaces Dismantles Them

Over the years, I have become more emboldened to "call out" whiteness and white privilege in many settings, most especially in the spaces where I am working as a practitioner of restorative justice. By saying that I call out whiteness, I mean that I inform those who are in power or leadership that, as a Person of Color, I recognize that the creation of predominantly white work settings is a form of white supremacy, and I ask them to recognize it as well.

Recognizing all-White environments is critical to dismantling systems where whiteness prevails. It is necessary to define whiteness in order to discuss it. People of Color in the US often swap stories of how they have been in all-White spaces, because it happens for us in so many contexts. In his article "The White Space," African American sociology professor Elijah Anderson describes the estrangement Blacks experience when they enter white spaces:

> For black people, in particular, white spaces vary in kind, but their most visible and distinctive feature is their overwhelming presence and their absence of black people. When the anonymous black person enters the white space, others there immediately try to make sense of him or her—to figure out "who that is," or gain a sense of the nature of the person's business and whether they need to be concerned. In the absence of routine social contact between blacks and whites, stereotypes can rule perceptions, creating a situation that estranges blacks.[1]

We still live in a very segregated, polarized society. Whites can still create white flight by moving away when POC begin to populate predominantly white neighborhoods. Or, Whites can choose to exist in whiteness by opting out of diverse spaces. Unfortunately, whiteness remains in force—invisible to Whites, visible to us. In "Hypervisible, Invisible," Dr. Ciera Graham, a sociologist and a Black woman, writes:

> Although science today denies race any standing as objective truth, and the US census faces taxonomic meltdown, many Americans cling to race as the unschooled cling to superstition. So long as racial discrimination remains a fact of life and statistics can be arranged to support racial difference, the American belief in races will endure. But confronted with the actual existing American population—its distribution of wealth, power, and beauty—the notion of American whiteness will continue to evolve as it has since the creation of the American Republic.[2]

Being the Only Person of Color in a White Space

Many POC first experience estrangement in White-dominant schools, from preschool to graduate school. For young people, being the only Person of Color in a classroom is a very familiar context. We are keenly aware that we are "seen." We know what this feels like, and we know that we cannot "blend in" with the other students who look different from us but who look like one another. How does one advocate for others or for oneself in these circumstances?

When we make a mistake, other people see color and not us as individuals. We are mindful that any mistake of ours makes it that much harder for the Person of Color who comes after us.

Being an African American woman, I feel the pressure of always being seen, and because of that, I often find it difficult to recover from mistakes I make. People of Color have often expressed that we are never doing anything just for ourselves; we carry a whole race of people with us. So, when we make a mistake, other people see color and not us as individuals. We are mindful that any mistake of ours makes it that much harder for the Person of Color who comes after us. Dr. Graham explains how always being seen affects the dynamics between races and gender:

> Like many women of color, I feel this strange and pervasive sense of both *hypervisibility* and *invisibility*. Race is omnipresent and operating in a system that continues to uphold racist and gendered

> institutionalized practices and has severe consequences for Black women who are trying to be both seen and valued in predominantly white spaces.
>
> You find that your Blackness is always on display, while also feeling constantly ignored and alienated by the whiteness surrounding you. It is the hypervisibility that propels white people to involve law enforcement when they perceive Black people to be "criminal," "suspicious," or as not belonging in particular spaces. It is the hypervisibility that forces women of color to change their tone, be less direct in communication or use inflection when they speak in order to not be perceived as "angry," "hostile," or even worse "sassy."[3]

Some of the most difficult conversations I have had about race have been with well-intentioned White people, especially when it comes to helping them to understand what it is like to be a Person of Color in all-White spaces. Ironically, the worst offenders I have encountered are my colleagues, practitioners of restorative justice. The reason I say well-intentioned is because this particular group of people tend to be convinced that their "understanding" of the experiences of POC is entirely accurate. They possess a confidence as to how POC should be treated, such that there is no room to teach them anything new. They consider themselves "woke." The *Urban Dictionary* describes "woke" as "a reference to how people should be aware in current affairs." It elaborates further: "Getting woke is like being in the Matrix and taking the red pill. You get a sudden understanding of what's really going on and find out you were wrong about much of what you understood to be truth."[4] Being "woke" entails recognizing how asleep you have been and how not being woke distorted your thinking and sense of reality. Many well-intentioned, progressive Whites assume they can become woke while still taking the blue pill—whiteness.

What is so disheartening is that I am often torn when I interact with these un-woke individuals: the potential exists for them to do better, but their privilege and arrogance prevent them from hearing voices different from their own. This misguided mental state is why "calling out" whiteness is necessary, because I have to be unapologetic in my delivery for them to hear me.

"Calling out" whiteness is necessary, because I have to be unapologetic in my delivery for them to hear me.

Often, I've had the same well-intentioned Whites provide justifications for racism other than what lies in the spheres of their privilege. I call this "whitesplaining." White fragility prevents Whites from owning their whiteness and the privilege that goes with it. Dr. Robin DiAngelo, a White diversity trainer and author, describes how whiteness enables Whites to avoid confronting their racial privilege and how such fragility creates challenges for POC:

> Whites invoke the power to choose when, how, and how much to address or challenge racism. Thus, pointing out white advantage will often trigger patterns of confusion, defensiveness and righteous indignation. . . . [These responses] enable defenders to protect their moral character against what they perceive as accusation and attack while deflecting any recognition of culpability or need of accountability. Focusing on restoring their moral standing through these tactics, whites are able to avoid the question of white privilege.[5]

Wanted: Accomplices Against Whiteness

Whiteness is greedy. When POC try to claim their hard-won spaces, whiteness retaliates out of insecurity. In other words, whiteness has to hold all the power. Whiteness is different from having white skin, but people with white skin have been experientially conditioned since birth to take on the mindset and behavior patterns of white supremacy—the arrogance, the greediness, the privilege, the presumed superiority, and the entitlement and stolen power to own, control, dominate, exclude, and harm others. This mindset is whiteness, and it is what needs to be called out.

For Whites who wish to join the struggle against whiteness, Dr. Jalane Schmidt, professor of color in Religious Studies, advocates that they learn how to notice their whiteness, name its patterns, and then act in opposite ways. Schmidt discusses how Whites can become *accomplices* instead of *allies* to POC. White accomplices follow the leadership of POC; the accomplice role is not about holding the power, taking control, or calling the shots. During a talk at Bethel College in North Newton, Kansas, Schmidt, both an activist and scholar of African religions and decolonization, called on the Whites in the audience to recognize the difference between being an ally and being an accomplice and to become the latter. In her article, "Bethel Speaker Says Movement for Justice Needs 'Accomplices, Not Allies,'" Melanie Zuercher, White, journalist, reports on Dr. Schmidt's campus talk:

Whites can become accomplices *instead of* allies *to POC. White accomplices follow the leadership of POC . . .*

> Being an ally, you can "pat yourself on the back" for being supportive while not actually doing a lot, she says. But an accomplice is "a co-conspirator, someone with skin in the game, willing to take a risk."

Being an accomplice also implies you are taking your orders from someone else, which is imperative, Schmidt says.

"White people, you are joining in a struggle that people of color have been carrying on for centuries," she says. "You have to give up the need to be in control" and take cues and directions from People of Color.

"Resist white supremacy. Inconvenience yourself. Stop being polite. Get comfortable with making racists uncomfortable.. . .

"Do what you can to throw a monkey wrench in this thing called white supremacy. White supremacy only functions with collusion. It doesn't take that many people to stop cooperating or colluding for it to fall."[6]

Schmidt's research on White accomplices identifies Whites who have expressed this passion for justice and died for POC causes. For example, Viola Gregg Liuzzo, a White civil rights activist and mother of five, traveled to Alabama in March 1965 to help the Southern Christian Leadership Conference—led by Rev. Dr. Martin Luther King Jr.—with its efforts to register African American voters in Selma. Not long after her arrival, Liuzzo was murdered by members of the Ku Klux Klan while driving a Black man, Leroy Moton, from Montgomery to Selma. Moton survived the attack by feigning to be dead. Liuzzo was the only known White woman killed during the Civil Rights Movement.[7]

White accomplices are more than advocates for their counterparts of color. They serve in a dual capacity: for POC, they serve as trusted foot soldiers; and for their White peers, they serve as a voice of reason that can influence them to think differently.

Restoratively Changing an All-White Space

Challenging whiteness does not happen by negotiating space for a few People of Color to coexist with Whites; rather, change requires dismantling the systems that produce all-White environments. The existence of all-White restorative spaces is difficult to justify in view of restorative justice principles, especially those that embrace inclusivity.

Early in my restorative justice career, I developed many of my practice's

Challenging whiteness does not happen by negotiating space for a few People of Color to coexist with Whites; rather, change requires dismantling the systems that produce all-White environments.

foundational parts from working with White leaders in restorative justice. I now desire to see other practitioners of color increase our numbers and become leaders in the field. Just like any other area of my life as a Person of Color, in the restorative justice field I want to see other people who look like me doing the work and sharing similar career trajectories.

What would it look like to restoratively change an all-White space?

The process has definite steps:

- It first requires naming the situation—that a space is all-White or White controlled and dominated. When White restorative justice practitioners own their privilege and whiteness, both personally and in the worlds they create and perpetuate, reform begins.
- Next comes recognizing that an all-White environment perpetrates harm to POC and naming specifically how this harm is done.
- Transforming all-White spaces also requires education: anti-racism training/anti-oppression training and implicit bias training are imperative. Whites' edification in racial dynamics and institutional harm provides a foundation for systemic change.
- Educating on inclusivity and learning how to recognize blind spots become critical for developing an authentically diverse space. Such spaces have the capacity to stay alive to the issues that white supremacist institutions kick up and to keep calling them out.
- Transforming an all-White space requires the assembly and participation of a diverse group of people, so that POC take an active role in deciding how their needs and interests are properly addressed. This transformation and participation require that practitioners and educators of restorative justice commit to being transparent.
- Transforming an all-White space requires a commitment to using restorative practices in order to build community and handle future conflict or discord.
- Partnering with accomplices calls Whites to step into their responsibilities for changing all-White spaces. They must learn how to carry their own weight in this change and not put it all on their colleagues of color. The collaboration builds buy-in from Whites and gives them an experiential education in how they can be accomplices with People of Color.

Repairing Harm as a Social Movement

Philosophically, we need to include the language of anti-racism and anti-oppression in restorative justice principles. Much of its language alludes to this but falls short of truly communicating a clear connection to diversity, anti-racism, and the call to dismantle white supremacy—the source of the catastrophic harms committed prior to and since the founding of the US.

Restorative justice seeks to repair the harms created by crime or wrongdoing. Sharon Kniss, White, education and training director at Bethel College in Kansas, writes, "Restorative justice is a framework of principles and values which focus on addressing the needs of those impacted by harm through relational processes of accountability and repair. Restorative Justice values and principles are applicable in response to harm as well as in its prevention and cessation through relational community building and problem-solving."[8]

Although my orientation to restorative justice is strongly connected to it in practice, over time I have realized that I also relate to restorative justice as a social movement. I have seen restorative justice evolve toward becoming more inclusive. I have also seen how the intersectionalities of race, colonization, sex, gender, and wealth operate within restorative justice.

I have seen restorative justice evolve toward becoming more inclusive. I have also seen how the intersectionalities of race, colonization, sex, gender, and wealth operate within restorative justice.

It is my sincerest hope that, as a body of RJ practitioners, we will adopt language within the principles of restorative justice that embrace anti-racism and anti-oppression. For example, in *The Little Book of Restorative Justice*, Howard Zehr, a White leader in restorative justice since the 1970s, lists these principles in this way:

1. Focus on the harms and consequent deeds of the victims, as well as the communities and the offenders.
2. Address the obligations that result from those harms (the obligations of the offenders, as well as the communities' and society's).
3. Use inclusive, collaborative processes.
4. Involve those with a legitimate stake in the situation, including victims, offenders, community members, and society.
5. Seek to put right the wrongs.[9]

These principles open a framework for expanding the harms we address restoratively from those in school or those defined by the criminal legal system to the racial harms that lie at the foundation of US society and keep white supremacy going. Both the call to repair harms and the principle of inclusivity steer the movement in this direction. Unfortunately, while restorative justice principles are aspirational and allude to inclusivity, they don't actually detail how to achieve this.

Despite my tremendous respect for Zehr, who I think is one of the most woke White people I know, the origin of restorative justice's definition is through a Eurocentric lens. For restorative justice as a practice and as a social movement to continue to evolve, the lens that we use to define it must become intersectional. The term "intersectionality" was coined in 1989 by civil rights activist and legal scholar Kimberlé Crenshaw in a paper she wrote for the *University of Chicago Legal Forum*. Intersectionality is defined as "the complex, cumulative way in which the effects of multiple forms of discrimination (such as racism, sexism, and classism) combine, overlap, or intersect especially in the experiences of marginalized individuals or groups."[10]

What Does an Inclusive Restorative Process Look Like?

When engaging in restorative practices of any kind, RJ practitioners of color should experience a process that embraces us at a project's very inception: this awareness of who is at the table from the start is what inclusivity looks like. To envision such a fully inclusive restorative environment, we might imagine a peacemaking Circle's equity and draw guidance from that.

When engaging in restorative practices of any kind, RJ practitioners of color should experience a process that embraces us at a project's very inception: this awareness of who is at the table from the start is what inclusivity looks like.

For example, the Circle provides a balance of power for all participants. This balance means that White restorative justice practitioners do not dominate or set the tone for the direction of a particular group. Restorative justice practitioners of color can all probably share stories of being a "diversity choice" for a project, class, training, or event. Often, being a diversity choice means that the Person of Color is chosen after all the White members have begun their process and have figured out a role for a Person of Color, so that they fulfill a grant or state requirement or can claim diversity for the process. By contrast, in a fully inclusive project, restorative justice practitioners of color participate on the same terms and basis as White participants.

In Circle process, participants reserve the right to pass. Even if a person passes, he or she has an opportunity to hear others in the Circle. Outside of Circle process, though, people "pass" by opting out of the situation entirely. This passing can be done either mentally or physically. Unlike Circle process, when people opt out of diverse restorative processes, they do not get the benefit of hearing others in the group. Whiteness leads a group to routinely opt out. They self-isolate.

In Circle process, all participants are valued and respected theoretically. When White participants dominate projects, though, they automatically elevate their knowledge, experiences, visions, interests, and needs above those of participants of color. In a fully inclusive process, all people are valued and respected equally. They embrace a shared governance of the process and this allows each participant's creativity, knowledge, gifts, and experiences to come to bear on whatever is before the group.

What can potentially happen when a restorative environment is fully inclusive?

- Programs, projects, or initiatives experience the collective buy-in of many groups.
- Collaboration, though challenging on a personal level, yields stronger, richer, and more effective outcomes.
- Outcomes last longer, because more people and groups are vested in making them work and respond when problems arise.
- Problem-solving draws on a wider pool of knowledge, experience, creativity, and networks.

Looking Ahead: Authentic Diversity Overcomes Whiteness

What is the future of whiteness? In the world, POC are a vast majority, much larger in number than Whites. Over the next thirty years, experts predict that "White" will be another minority in the United States. In a review of the book *Diversity Explosion,* Christopher Caldwell writes:

> The Brookings Institution demographer William Frey would seem a good candidate to lead readers to a clear, propaganda-free understanding of what diversity is. The title of his new study on ethnicity and population change is *Diversity Explosion*. While he never defines the word explicitly, he means the decline—in both population and vitality—of America's European-descended population, and its replacement by more recently arrived population groups from everywhere in the non-European world. Frey sometimes describes this change as "the browning of America." More than half (53%) of the country's 3,100 counties had declining white populations by the first decade of the century. In the current decade the white population has begun to decline in the nation as a whole. . . . Three years from now most Americans under 18 will be "minorities" of one kind or another.[11]

As I write this chapter, my television is set on MSNBC, which is reporting on the 2018 mid-term election results. I have heard a few victory speeches. However, in several concession speeches, all of the would-be politicians stated that now is the time for both sides to come together and work as one. It is important that Whites develop a similar dream for diversity as POC.

To get there, though, Whites must become as skilled as POC are at recognizing whiteness, naming it, and throwing their weight—institutional, political, economic, social, and personal—at calling out whiteness, so that together we can dismantle it and benefit from each other's energies, gifts, and experiences. The world of the future, fully diverse, simply has no place for whiteness as we understand and experience it today.

DISCUSSION QUESTIONS

1. Whether you are a Person of Color or White, when and how have you called out whiteness? What was that experience like for you? Did you get support from either POC or Whites? Did change happen? Were you retaliated against for doing so?
2. How do you feel about the changing US demographics? What impact do you see this color shift having on society—politically, economically, socially, and educationally? As a result, how might the lives of your children and grandchildren be different from yours? How can we respond to fear-based whitelash against this trend?
3. What makes a good White accomplice to POC? For POC, what do you want and need from Whites in this capacity and what don't you want or need? For Whites, which White patterns do you need to notice and change in order to develop your skills and awareness as an accomplice to POC? How is that different from being an ally? Can you think of examples of both from your experience?
4. Share some instances of "whitesplaining." What do Whites often try to whitesplain away? What is the effect of whitesplaining on POC? What is the benefit of calling it out?

ACTIVITIES

1. Describe an all-White space that most everyone in the group has experienced. Drawing from the steps for transforming such a space, what might these steps look like in this situation? Brainstorm the possibilities. Brainstorm how to respond to resistance to changing power and privilege. Brainstorm how to respond to retaliation.
2. As a group, consider how whiteness has shaped restorative justice as we know it today. How has whiteness seeped into the restorative justice mindset, orientation, and practice? Consider how increasing the voice, power, and leadership of POC in the movement can and will change restorative justice. What might RJ's future look like?
3. As a group, explore the difference between authentic diversity and tokenizing diversity. What does authentic diversity require that

tokenizing diversity does not? What benefits does the first have that the second does not? What would the impact of one versus the other have on the practice of restorative justice and the integrity of the movement?

RESOURCES

Anderson, Elijah. "'The White Space,'" *American Sociological Association* 1, no. 1 (2014): 13. https://doi.org/10.1177/2332649214561306.

Graham, Ciera. "Hypervisible, Invisible: How to Navigate White Workplaces as a Black Woman." *Career Contessa*, August 29, 2018. https://www.careercontessa.com/advice/black-woman-white-workplace/.

Painter, Nell Irvin. "The History of White People." *The History of White People*, W.W. Norton & Company, 2010, xii.

NOTES

1. Elijah Anderson, "'The White Space,'" *American Sociological Association* 1, no. 1 (2014): 13, https://doi.org/10.1177/2332649214561306.
2. Ciera Graham, "Hypervisible, Invisible: How to Navigate White Workplaces as a Black Woman," *Career Contessa*, August 29, 2018, https://www.careercontessa.com/advice/black-woman-white-workplace/.
3. Ibid.
4. "Woke," *Urban Dictionary*, 2018, https://www.urbandictionary.com/define.php?term=Woke.
5. Robin DiAngelo, "White Fragility," *The International Journal of Critical Pedagogy* 3, no. 3 (2011): 64, https://libjournal.uncg.edu/ijcp/article/viewFile/249/116.
6. Melanie Zuercher, "Bethel Speaker Says Movement for Justice Needs 'Accomplices, Not Allies,'" *The Mennonite*, April 17, 2018, https://themennonite.org/daily-news/bethel-speaker-says-movement-justice-needs-accomplices-not-allies/.
7. Biography.com editors, "Viola Gregg Liuzzo," *Biography*, 2014, updated 2016, accessed November 7, 2018, https://www.biography.com/people/viola-gregg-liuzzo-370152.
8. Sharon Kniss, "Restorative Justice | KIPCOR," *KIPCOR*, 2018, http://kipcor.org/training-education/restorative-justice/.
9. Howard Zehr, *The Little Book of Restorative Justice* (Intercourse, PA: Good Books, 2002).
10. Kimberlé Crenshaw, "Demarginalizing the Intersection of Race and Sex: A Black Feminist Critique of Antidiscrimination Doctrine, Feminist Theory, and Antiracist Politics," *University of Chicago Legal Forum*, vol. 1989, article 8 (1989) HeinOnline — U. Chi. Legal F. 168 1989.
11. Christopher Caldwell, "The Browning of America: A Review of *Diversity Explosion: How New Racial Demographics Are Remaking America*, by William H. Frey, "*Claremont Review of Books* XV, no 1 (Winter 2014/15), https://www.claremont.org/crb/article/the-browning-of-america/.

Chapter 6

Using Restorative Practices to Climb the Leadership Mountain

Gaye Lang

Black Educators: The Historical Context of Racial Bias

For Black educators, achieving leadership success within the K–12 environment is fraught with racial bias, condescension, and other obstacles that prove difficult to navigate, much less overcome. Historically, White educators considered Black educators to be inferior—a belief that goes back to the turn of the twentieth century when historically Black colleges (HBC) were producing a cadre of Black teachers. This belief became more overt during the nascent days of the public school desegregation initiatives of the late 1950s and throughout the 1960s. Examinations of the public school integration scheme, such as busing, frequently overlook the lack of racial diversity among the teaching staff. Black children placed in classrooms devoid of Black teachers experienced and continue to experience unfamiliar, hostile environments. To remedy the racial disparities in teaching staff at the White schools where Black students were being bused, school districts developed initiatives to hire Black teachers. The thinking was that hiring Black educators would validate public school integration and stave off other court- or federal-ordered integration reforms. Tragically, White parents or educators did not welcome the integration of both students and teachers in White-dominated, public school districts.

The teaching profession confers authority onto its practitioners. Consequently, Black teachers in these newly integrated schools held positions of authority over White students. Of course, Black teacher authority proved a real concern for White parents. As Wendy Parker, White, civil rights scholar, writes in her article "Desegregating Teachers": "Specifically, white parents often doubted the competency of minority teachers and generally resisted giving a minority teacher power over a white student."[1] Many Black teachers and principals who met the professional standards and possessed the appropriate classroom experience were not afforded opportunities to enter the career development paths that would culminate in a principal-ship at newly integrated White schools. Parker continues: "School districts also shared these concerns, contending that minority teachers were incompetent to teach white students, and minority teachers were better teachers for minority students."[2] Unfortunately, this left qualified Black teachers and principals in a dilemma: they could remain at integrated White schools and be subjected to unrealistic professional objectives and ridicule; or they could return to predominantly Black schools where some opportunities were available and supportive professional development pathways were in place. In many cases, though, returning to a Black school was disastrous. The "Separate but Equal" doctrine led to inferior conditions of the buildings, substandard teaching materials, diminishing resources, and overcrowding. As a result, the neighborhood schools to which Black educators often returned ultimately closed. Many conscientious, young Black educators lost their jobs, and finding another job was a challenge. Parker explains: "Teachers and principals working in the closed [Black] schools could not compete against those at the formerly white schools on the standard set by the school board and were not retained."[3]

How have racial bias and stereotypical assumptions negatively affected Black teachers and principals?

Given this historical context, this chapter examines the barriers and challenges that confront Black teachers, principals, and leaders in the K–12 environment. It highlights how restorative practices could be employed at critical junctures in the educator's professional development. It demonstrates the effective implementations of restorative Circles to deter implicit (vs. explicit) racism in K–12 school systems. And it explores critical questions: How have racial bias and stereotypical assumptions negatively affected Black teachers and principals? Additionally, what positive coping strategies can lead to an upward career path and professional success far beyond the primary and secondary educational environment?

Negotiating the Racial Speed Bumps for Black Educators in K–12

The road to success for Black educators is pockmarked with racially tinged Black and White speed bumps. Black educators are not appreciated for the many years of training, which frequently include advanced degrees, that they bring to the classroom. These professionals are not valued for the years they have spent raising the academic standards at schools that have required improvement. Black educators—and sadly, Black women in particular—are not prized for their problem-solving skills in environments with a dearth of resources nor are they appreciated for their high emotional quotients, which enable them to establish relationships with some of the more challenging students. These assets buttress the intellectual bona fides of seasoned Black education practitioners.

Black educators are not appreciated for the many years of training, which frequently include advanced degrees, that they bring to the classroom.

However, some White school administrators frequently diminish these qualities or consider them irrelevant for the K–12 leadership office. The negative feelings of White teachers with regard to well-qualified Black professionals is intensified by Whites' contempt for a perceived arrogance that they impute to Black professionals. They are simply unwilling to openly welcome Black educators onto their team. When they do, Whites relegate Black educators to limited teaching and leadership roles. Within the various academic departments in K–12, for example, White educators incorrectly assume that Black teacher skills and abilities are best suited for slow learners. Additionally, White educators place very few Black students in the gifted and talented programs, so the White leadership does not see the need to "allow" Black teachers the opportunities to teach the gifted classes. This fallacious assumption has been the norm historically, and the pattern continues.

Black women who are teachers face many challenges at the beginning of their career, as I did. During the early days, no novice teacher could possibly map out the precise path her career development would take. She could not imagine the personal affronts and constant disregard for her diligent training and hard work, nor could she foresee the pinnacle of a potentially long career. What follows is my story.

As one female Black teacher, I faced many uncertainties after completing my bachelor's degree in elementary education. In the early 1970s, I obtained my first teaching assignment at an inner-city Los Angeles school. At this time, the community was dealing with the devastation of urban unrest—where homes and businesses once stood had become scorched earth. My first assignment placed me as an acolyte in a school that was the focal point of the neighborhood, situated as it was on a main boulevard. Most students walked to the school. In this particular neighborhood, the middle and elementary schools were next to each other. Frequently, I would see older siblings accompanying their younger brothers or sisters to school. The teaching staff and leadership were predominately Black educators. Unlike the prevailing White stereotypes, the school was replete with respect and professional admiration—a very collegial setting.

However, initiatives to desegregate the teaching staff at Los Angeles County's predominately White schools gave me, as a new teacher with just two years of experience, the opportunity to transfer to an affluent school and receive a pay increase. The transition to a suburban school outside the razed urban center of Los Angeles made an impression on me. The school had a robust gifted and talented pull-out program. This suburban school's student population was 70 percent White, 25 percent Asian, and 5 percent Black. The teaching staff was 95 percent White and 5 percent Black. The K–5 magnet school had one Black teacher per grade level. The Black students who attended were either part of the district magnet program or residents of the surrounding affluent community. And while Black teachers did not share lunch breaks or conference periods with each other, we would gather in the parking lot after work to talk before going home.

Racial Vetting and Responding with a Parent-Teacher Circle

As a new transfer educator, I was accustomed to being observed by the school's administrative staff. Yet, a peculiar incident occurred during the first six weeks of the fall term at my new school. That incident involved a Japanese parent of one of the students in my math class. Each day during class, this parent would come to the door, stand, and peer in. After a week of her observing from the hallway, I invited her in. She refused the invitation to enter. Later that week, she asked for a parent-teacher conference. During the conference, this parent, to ascertain my qualifications to instruct gifted math students, asked me numerous questions: Where did you attend college? In what field was your degree? And, how long have you been teaching? My answer was simple. I had placed on prominent display the undergraduate and graduate degrees I had earned and the content certifications I possessed. Would this parent have put these questions to a White male teacher? When the Japanese parent returned, I once again invited her into the classroom. This time she accepted the invitation, entered the room, took a seat, and quietly observed that day's instruction.

Would this parent have put these questions to a White male teacher?

The rubric outlined for the gifted and talented class emphasized problem-solving, which fostered higher-level thinking. My class gave students opportunities for innovative expression as they approached rigorous, challenging lessons. The parent wanted reassurance that her child was receiving quality instruction. Unfortunately, the Japanese parent's bigotry had stunted her worldview. She did not believe a Black teacher could deliver the rigorous instruction that superior academic achievement required and that would support real-world learning. The parent erroneously perceived my loud voice as frightening the students; this, in fact, had prompted her visits.

Throughout this episode, I did not deviate from the prescribed mode of instruction. In addition to teaching the textbook lesson on banking and bookkeeping, I required the fourth- and fifth-grade students in the gifted and talented program to maintain passbook savings and checking accounts as well as a weekly budget. For six weeks, the students received a different sum of script to budget and from which they could purchase various items. Through these experiences, they learned the basic arithmetic operations: addition, subtraction, multiplication, and division. They also learned to use decimals and fractions. The culminating activity was a field trip to a local bank that allowed my class to speak with the tellers. Persistent, deliberate, creative, and focused actions transformed a racially negative situation. The Japanese parent's negativity was challenging, but with patience and an awareness of the racial dynamics, I overcame it. The educational experience so impressed the parent that she made effusive positive comments about my teaching to the principal and other parents. Notwithstanding, the White male principal reminded me on a weekly basis to be respectful and not to upset the parent.

Research shows the pattern of negative racial stereotypes against Black professionals persists across social groups.

While this anecdote features a Japanese parent, I do not intend to single out this group as harboring poor impressions of Black teachers' qualifications and competency. Research shows the pattern of negative racial stereotypes against Black professionals persists across social groups. In "Through Our Eyes: Perspectives and Reflections from Black Teachers," researchers Ashley Griffin, African American, psychologist, researcher, and educator, and Hilary Tackie, researcher, write:

> [Black educators] reported being pigeonholed by peers, parents, and administrators into specific roles based on these strengths, thereby limiting and diminishing their capabilities. Without the acknowledgment of (or the chance to build) the pedagogical and subject matter expertise essential to their profession, they felt they lacked opportunities for advancement and were undervalued and unappreciated.[4]

Undaunted, I, as the beginning teacher, remained steadfast and continued to excel at my vocation in an effort to retain my job. While some may have succumbed to the frequent negative feedback, I was able to steel my resolve and persevere—failure was not an option. As a footnote, I later discovered that this parent and others engaged in a similar vetting process of other Black faculty members. All of this occurred with the approval of the White male principal.

Today, this vetting of faculty of color can be addressed in a more respectful and productive way. For instance, the principal can offer a restorative conference between a parent and a teacher. A restorative conference allows a parent and a teacher to express their concerns respectfully. The conference process works as follows:

- It starts with preparing all parties. The principal or a designee serves as the facilitator and invites a parent to meet with a teacher in a parent-teacher conference Circle.
- The principal then explains to the parent the purpose of the meeting, emphasizing that this meeting will give the parent an opportunity to meet with the teacher, to voice any concerns, and to share information about the parent's child with the teacher.
- Additionally, the facilitator explains the guidelines or ground rules of the conference Circle. Customarily, Circle guidelines include respect the talking piece; speak from the heart; listen from the heart; agree that what happens in the Circle stays in the Circle; trust you will know what to say; and say just enough. Everyone's voice is valued and will be heard.
- During this preparatory time, the facilitator also describes the use of a talking piece and its purpose.
- Finally, the facilitator develops several prompting questions for Circle rounds. These questions are designed to allow the parent and teacher to share information. Similarly, the facilitator invites the teacher to the conference and reviews the same process and guidelines, suggesting that this Circle would be a good time for the teacher to share her experience and background with the parent, if she chooses to do so.

When the Circle or conference convenes, the teacher and the parent discuss ways to improve their relationship and then write them down. Their insights can now be developed collaboratively into a plan that can be monitored or adjusted by the principal, teacher, and parent. Plans usually include a timeline, the length of which varies and depends upon the issues being discussed. The timeline is an effective tool to monitor progress and to make adjustments as necessary. The goal is to establish a respectful relationship between the parent and teacher. In *Circle Forward,* Carolyn Boyes-Watson and Kay Pranis, White women committed to RJ for decades, discuss the importance of parent-teacher conference Circles. It is "to empower parents to sit in the conference process as an equal; to more fully access the wisdom of the parents about the student; and to strengthen the relationship between the family and the school."[5] When people get to know and trust one another, their relationship improves. The restorative process provides a safe place to talk and build respectful relationships.

Responding to Racial and Gender Biases with Peacemaking Circles

Climbing the leadership ladder—scaling the academic mountain to the top leadership positions in education—is no easy task; yet trying to climb it as a Black woman adds difficulties that those of the dominant culture do not appreciate. We hear a great deal about the glass ceiling and the inability of Black women executives to break through it. As of 2018, only one Black female holds the position of chief state school officer in the United States. This obstacle—indeed, ceiling—that blocks the upward trajectory of Black women's careers is not due to a lack of requisite qualifications, far from it. As a group, Black women possess many advanced and professional degrees and certifications. Moreover, their experiences surpass those of many White educators: Black female educators have had the lifelong challenge to negotiate not one but multiple worlds—Black, White, and diverse communities of color—and to deal with racism daily. Whites never have these experiences and so are not challenged to develop appropriate relational skills from them. However, despite their high levels of training and experience, academic and real world, Black female professional educators are still rarely offered the chief educator job in a state or school district.

Moreover, their experiences surpass those of many White educators: Black female educators have had the lifelong challenge to negotiate not one but multiple worlds—Black, White, and diverse communities of color—and to deal with racism daily. Whites never have these experiences and so are not challenged to develop appropriate relational skills from them.

Those few who do make it to this coveted position or its equivalent find that they are frequently confronted with vicious stereotypes, especially when they demonstrate strength and decisiveness: Black women are accused of being overly aggressive, which is a double-edged razor. On the one hand, a key factor hampering the upward mobility of Black women in education is that they are often assigned to schools with significant disciplinary and academic problems. This assignment, of course, would require strength and decisiveness—the two qualities that in another context are deemed too aggressive. On the other hand, while others would consider such challenging assignments a career-ending move, Black women take on these challenges, identify strategies for success, and generally exceed the expectations of their superiors and subordinates.

To continue with my own story, during the next decade of my teaching career, I began to consider educational leadership positions. My first experience at applying for an assistant principal position in a middle school was met with several disappointing interviews. However, a Black male assistant superintendent in the central office noticed me (which is racially telling, is it not?). He asked if I would apply again for an assistant principal position in one of the middle schools on Fort Bend's east side (Texas). This time, I was given an opportunity to be an assistant principal at a very large middle school in the suburbs on the east side of the district. The population was 75 percent Black, 15 percent Latino, 10 percent "other." During my tenure at this school, the district made administrative changes at the central office, so the Black male, who was once my advocate, moved to another district. A White female replaced him as the new area superintendent. After five years, though, this woman harbored resentment because she was not given the principal-ship at the modern new middle school. Ultimately, a Black man who was neither a disciplinarian nor an instructional leader was hired for that position.

In my new role as assistant principal, I received very little mentoring from the principal. I performed many key administrative and supervisory functions that were normally responsibilities of the principal. On my own initiative, I was able to maintain school discipline, parent-teacher relationships, and academic success. During my second year, the principal resigned to take a job outside the district, at which time the area superintendent offered me the position of interim principal.

At the annual back-to-school staff meeting, the area superintendent addressed the faculty and staff. Following the meeting, I, as the new interim principal, was inundated with expressions of horror and frustration by the school staff at the condescending tone of the area superintendent's address. In a telephone conversation, I attempted to relay these concerns to the superintendent. Rather than attempting to understand the staff's dismay, she responded in anger and demeaned the competency of the educators. She formed this conclusion without observing any of the teachers. Needless to say, all parties were upset, and the matter remained unresolved.

My experiences in the field of education reflect a pattern that research about racial and gender biases confirm.

After three months in the role as interim principal, I applied for the principal position. Unfortunately, the area superintendent chose not to grant me an interview but hired a Black man for the position instead. I finished out the school year and then resigned to pursue my doctorate degree—a fact I relayed to the area superintendent. My experiences in the field of education reflect a pattern that research about racial and gender biases confirm. Tia Kathleen Gueye, African American, scholar of Black educational leadership, writes:

"Stereotypes, prejudice, and discrimination all contribute to the perpetuation of negative views of potential Black leaders. Stereotypes contribute to racist biases in overt or subtle ways."[6] In the larger picture, this educational hiring process was a missed opportunity not only for building trust but also for establishing a respectful working relationship.

How could positive outcomes be achieved, especially when relationships have broken down because of racial biases? I come back to peacemaking Circles, which Westerners have appropriated from various Indigenous practices of dialogue, healing, and community. Circles have a humanizing effect. Sharing stories of what happened and exploring together how to fix or repair relations is the Circle's goal. It typically involves three or more people sitting in a circle without tables and using a talking piece. The peacemaking Circle process provides an opportunity for everyone to tell his or her story to get a full picture of what happened. In cases of conflicts or harms, the Circle should address three questions:

1. What was/is the harm?
2. What led to the harm?
3. How can the harm be repaired?

The Circle keeper holds the Circle space through the following stages:

1. *Voluntary participation.* No one is forced or coerced into participating; all parties must agree to be present and want to participate.
2. *Preparation.* The keeper arranges a private pre-conference with each party to get an understanding of the issues or harm, to explore any potential problems or needs, and to ensure that the participants understand the process and know what to expect.
3. *Gathering.* The Circle convenes, which means all participants come together in the peacemaking Circle. They share their stories, express their feelings, and find solutions.
4. *Follow-up.* The keeper checks in with the participants to assess progress and to see if another Circle is needed to adjust the agreement as conditions change.

Of the several Circle keeper's roles, one is to support the Circle participants in achieving consensus. In this role, Circle keepers have a dual responsibility: they function both as participants and as keepers of the integrity of the process. Peacemaking Circles can be employed as often as necessary and for a variety of situations.

When I was going through these experiences of racial and gender bias that affected my career, I did not know about restorative practices or the Circle process. In hindsight, I wish I had. Perhaps some of the frustrating and painful experiences I had as a Black female educator could have opened spaces for repairing relationships and dispelling racist biases.

How Circles Can Address Racial Biases among Colleagues: Another Case

With my doctorate degree in hand, I landed a principal's position in Houston. I then became a project manager for developing the first virtual school, which was another first: a public school district designed, developed, and built this virtual school. I was now a part of the superintendent's cabinet. Although these positions were upwardly mobile, I still faced doubts from others about my credentials: Did I know enough about the use of technology in the classroom, or did I have the expertise to manage a project to build a virtual school? The doubters this time were three Whites: two women and one man. None of these cabinet members believed I was a good fit for the superintendent's team, which had otherwise been formed before I was hired. These doubters consistently questioned my ability to develop the virtual school that the superintendent wanted. Needless to say, as I have demonstrated in the past, despite others' challenges and doubts, I succeeded—creating the nation's first virtual school to be developed in a public school district. Not only did I surpass the district superintendent's expectations, I also noted my former detractors' amazement at my achievement. Plus, I won an award for instructional materials developed by a public school.

I succeeded—creating the nation's first virtual school to be developed in a public school district.

The roadblocks and doubts I faced came as no surprise to me. Again, failure was not an option. In their article, "Racial Microaggression Experiences and Coping Strategies of Black Women in Corporate Leadership," Aisha Holder, Margo Jackson, and Joseph Ponterotto describe the climate of racial and gender bias that Black women face on the job: "Black women also experience the perception of being intellectually inferior, which can undermine their credibility. African Americans report having to constantly prove their ability and observe the surprise of managers and colleagues who may have had initial assumptions about their competence."[7] In order for Black women to succeed, we must surpass all of the competition—a racial-gender reality that, no matter how immoral, has been engrained in us early in our professional lives.

A peacemaking Circle would have been appropriate in this circumstance as well. The reparative process starts with naming the harm: my colleagues' continual questioning of me about my experience and intelligence as a leader. Next, the Circle could have addressed what led to the harm—namely, the race- and gender-based programming that affects us all, and that, I believe, led the superintendent and other members of the cabinet to doubt my credibility, competence, and abilities. I did not receive the support to do this groundbreaking work that I should have received as a professional and that would have been accorded my White male colleagues. Finally, the Circle could have explored how to repair the harm. For this reparative work, an experienced Circle keeper trained in diversity and anti-racism would have been a must. Over time and with regularity, the Circle process could well have established a better working relationship among the three individuals as well as among all members of the cabinet.

Over time and with regularity, the Circle process could well have established a better working relationship among the three individuals as well as among all members of the cabinet.

Using Circles to Repair Harm within the Restorative Justice Community

With perseverance, I became a senior executive in government. This position required that I oversee educators' professional development—a role that has enabled me to mentor future educational leaders. Implementing restorative practices throughout the state of Texas has been an opportunity to improve student-teacher relationships, particularly in an effort to reduce school suspensions of minority youth. The implementation has taken several years, but the time and effort have shown its worth. The restorative movement is proving a success in the state and has garnered the support of business, government, educators, and parents. The entire process has been a rewarding experience for me as a seasoned professional educator.

Success has not come without a price, though. I have encountered many obstacles that have required tremendous energy to overcome while shepherding in the statewide adoption of restorative practices. To start, the implementation required six months of research, training, and evaluation of the effectiveness and benefits of the restorative process. During this time, I was introduced to some of the restorative movement's leading practitioners. As a result of my advocacy, the state moved forward with the adoption of restorative practices, which included a two-phase rollout for educators—an overview and implementation models.

New ideas and new methods frequently encounter resistance, and restorative practices are no different. Ironically, the most combative interchanges came from within the restorative community. I witnessed frequent negative behaviors among restorative practitioners. Disagreements arose about what occurred during a training session. Some leaders exhibited domineering behaviors to control the interactions among trainers/practitioners. Some demanded loyalty and respect but did not demonstrate these traits with others. The well-being of individual team members was not considered or respected. To put it bluntly, some leaders in the restorative community behaved in non-restorative ways. Furthermore, People of Color in the restorative movement frequently observed white privilege at the root of these behaviors.

However, to be fair as the person in charge of the rollout, I also was not without blame. With this self-realization, I corrected my behavior and became more restorative with the other practitioners. Finding myself in the middle of a situation, I tried to reason it out—to think self-reflectively, which is part of the restorative approach. Why were these restorative trainers/practitioners, including myself, not behaving more restoratively? I came up with a list of possibilities.

- All of the trainers and practitioners were new to the process.
- The trainers had not become a community and did not know how to respect and value one another.
- No one had enough experience to lead the process or to model restorative leadership.
- The trainers/practitioners were embarrassed to bring in outside help from an experienced practitioner, assuming they should know everything from one or two trainings.

So how can we apply the restorative process to restorative practitioners? Are the practitioners exempted from being restorative with one another? Providing opportunities and avenues to deliberately and intentionally repair the harm among the practitioners is more than necessary—*it is vital to the restorative process.* Ideally, the peacemaking Circle's capacity to repair harm and establish respectful relationships is the goal. If restorative practice is truly what we believe, then participating in several peacemaking Circles to repair the harm should not pose a problem. Indigenous Peoples have used this process over millennia, but the Western world has managed to take the process in a different direction, co-opting and institutionalizing it, managing it within the dominant racial frame of white supremacy. What can be done? STOP, LISTEN, and LEARN from those who came before and those who live the process today as a way of life.

> *How can we apply the restorative process to restorative practitioners?*

Using Restorative Processes to Transform Workplaces

Black women in leadership roles are marginalized. We are subject to harsh judgment, stereotypes, and differential standards for achieving goals. In short, we are being judged by at least two double standards (race and sex) in our abilities to lead, plan, and make decisions. Today's Black executives often feel burdened with expectations of perfection and a need to be overqualified for the job. To engender a safe space to voice concerns and promote fair treatment, workplaces implementing restorative practices must mandate training in these practices for new hires. If senior management values a salubrious work environment and believes in clear, honest, and respectful relationships, then implementing restorative practices among colleagues is a step in the right direction of climbing this mountain. Robert W. Livingston, African American professor at Harvard's Kennedy School of Government, and Ashleigh S. Rosette, African American professor of management at Duke University, conducted a study of minority leaders. One message that emerged is "that minority leaders face unique challenges because they are not seen as 'prototypical' leaders. That is, when someone thinks 'leader,' they typically don't think 'woman' or 'black'; therefore, minorities don't always enjoy the same level of perceived legitimacy as white males when they occupy these positions."[8]

In the workplace, restorative justice and restorative practices are important processes. They are foundational in promoting a safe culture and environment. In these spaces, employees can become great leaders who garner the respect and appreciation they deserve. Why? The focus of RJ is on establishing personal relationships, including repairing relationships through community building and peacemaking Circles. It also opens spaces for pushing dialogue to deeper levels, which requires challenging the racial and gender status quo. A restorative workplace is filled with opportunities to bridge the empathy gap between supervisors and staff. Dr. James Comer, African American, founder of the Comer School Development Program at Yale University, and one of the world's leading child psychiatrists, is widely quoted as saying, "No significant learning will take place without a significant relationship." Restorative practices are built on accepting differences, understanding that relationships are complex, trusting others, and agreeing on shared values. We learn from each other by sharing our stories. A restorative approach brings fairness and transparency, which is a real benefit in the workplace. Indeed, Ryan Fehr, professor of management, and Michele J. Gelfand, professor of cultural psychology, write, "Restorative justice ideally facilitates outcomes such as relationship repair, closure, and fairness."[9]

In closing, our workplaces can commit to dismantling glass ceilings and roadblocks and becoming environments where Black women are empowered, respected, and given opportunities to excel without limitations. Restorative practices and Circles can help us transform our workplaces into true game changers—both for Black female professionals and for the effectiveness of what we aim to achieve together.

DISCUSSION QUESTIONS

1. When have you felt you were not being respected?
2. When has someone told you he or she respected you but the person's actions showed the opposite?
3. When has someone told you that you were being disrespectful?

ACTIVITIES

Scenario 1: An African American woman who works in a predominantly White work environment is confronted by a White woman who has nothing to do with the training that the African American woman is conducting. However, the White woman works in the location where the training is being held. Conflict arises, because during each of the last three trainings, the White woman has found a reason to send the African American woman an email requesting that furniture be moved or the door be closed during training, even though she knew the air conditioning was not functioning properly, or questioning whether selling books that are a part of the training was legal. The African American woman asked the White woman why she was emailing her and asking these questions. The White woman's response was that she was documenting. The African American woman explained to the White woman that no rule, guideline, or policy had been violated. Discuss how restorative practices could be used to resolve this situation. What would you do?

Scenario 2: An African American man in a leadership role is questioned repeatedly by White men who are his subordinates, which undermines his plans and authority. This causes the higher-ups to think that he is incapable of handling the position. How could this scenario be resolved in a fair and restorative manner?

Scenario 3: While leading a restorative training, an African American woman is bantered and questioned by a White woman and a White man to the extent that the training was nearly derailed. The trainer kept her composure and finished the training with respect. What suggestions would you give this trainer? How should this behavior be addressed?

RESOURCES

Gueye, Tia Kathleen. "Race in the Appointment and Daily Leadership of African American Independent School Heads." Dissertation proposal, Fordham University, New York, 2015, 27. https://www.nais.org/Articles/Documents/Race%20in%20the%20Appointment%20and%20Daily%20Leadership%20of%20African%20American%20Independent%20School%20Heads.pdf.

Livingston, Robert W., and Ashleigh Shelby Rosette. "Failure Is Not an Option for Black Women: Effects of Organizational Performance on Leaders with Single versus Dual-Subordinate Identities." *Journal of Experimental Social Psychology* 48 (April 26, 2012): 1162–67. http://gap.hks.harvard.edu/failure-not-option-black-women-effects-organizational-performance-leaders-single-versus-dual.

Livingston, Robert W., Ashleigh Shelby Rosette, and Ella F. Washington. "Do Black Women Have More or Less Freedom as Leaders? Understanding the Roles of Race and Gender." *Kellogg Insight*, February 2, 2012. https://insight.kellogg.northwestern.edu/article/do_black_women_have_more_or_less_freedom_as_leaders. Accessed 2 September 2018.

NOTES

1. Wendy Parker, "Desegregating Teachers," *Washington University Law Review*, 86, no. 1 (2008): 13.
2. Ibid., 14.
3. Ibid., 15–16.
4. Ashley Griffin and Hilary Tackie, "Through Our Eyes: Perspectives and Reflections from Black Teachers," *The Education Trust* (November 2016): 1.
5. Carolyn Boyes-Watson and Kay Pranis, *Circle Forward: Building a Restorative School Community* (St. Paul, MN: Living Justice Press, 2015), 222.
6. Tia Kathleen Gueye, "Race in the Appointment and Daily Leadership of African American Independent School Heads" (Dissertation proposal, Fordham University, New York, 2015), 27.
7. Aisha M. B. Holder, Margo A. Jackson, and Joseph G. Ponterotto, "Racial Microaggression Experiences and Coping Strategies of Black Women in Corporate Leadership," *Qualitative Psychology* 2, no. 2 (2015): 165.
8. Robert W. Livingston and Ashleigh Shelby Rosette, "Failure Is Not an Option for Black Women: Effects of Organizational Performance on Leaders with Single versus Dual-Subordinate Identities," *Journal of Experimental Social Psychology* 48, no. 5 (April 2012): 1162–67. See also: Based on the research of Robert W. Livingston, Ashleigh Shelby Rosette, and Ella F. Washington, "Do Black Women Have More or Less Freedom as Leaders? Understanding the Roles of Race and Gender," *Kellogg Insight*, February 2. 2012, accessed September 2, 2018, https://insight.kellogg.northwestern.edu/article/do_black_women_have_more_or_less_freedom_as_leaders.
9. Ryan Fehr and Michele J. Gelfand, "The Forgiving Organization: A Multilevel Model of Forgiveness at Work," *Academy of Management Review*, 2012, https://journals.aom.org/doi/10.5465/amr.2010.0497.

Chapter 7

Women Colorizing Restorative Justice in White-Led Institutions

Rochelle Arms Almengor

I started my work in restorative justice over twenty years ago as a young Latina, when the words "restorative justice" were strange to the ear and its definition unwelcomed in the socially conservative state I lived in. Since then, I have seen our movement grow by leaps and bounds. Restorative justice now regularly appears in mainstream media as a viable response to crime and wrongdoing, and—even in rural areas—schools normalize its use. Yet, despite this progress, critical aspects of it remain fixed to our societal status quo. For example, the dearth of organizational leadership by women of color remains an issue even within the restorative justice revolution and demands that we pay special attention to the reasons and solutions surrounding it.

Background

My first real entry into restorative justice (RJ) was through a small nonprofit organization started by a fiercely dedicated woman who became my first professional mentor and remains a dear friend and cheerleader. With the help of volunteers, we designed and carried out restorative justice seminars for men and women who had committed homicide throughout our state. I learned early on about the colorization of RJ work, seeing that most of our core volunteers were White, including our well-loved founder and director.

When I moved to a major metropolis to advance my conflict resolution career after graduate school, I found similar demographics among volunteers and organizational leaders, even though the city's general population was much more diverse than where I had worked before. I managed a criminal court program where a majority of staff and volunteers were White-identifying, including the senior administrators in the organization. Interaction with other social service agencies in the city reflected a similar pattern, wherein the majority of staff, especially managers and directors, were not People of Color, even though most of their clients were. In 2013, my colleague and I started the first restorative justice professionals' network in our diverse city, reaching out to existing RJ leaders and practitioners. Again, most of the inaugural and subsequent members were White, even though most of the people we served were from underprivileged communities of color.

I am an immigrant biracial woman, and my experience with race in the US is largely a story of code-switching to "whiteness." Code switching refers to altering one's way of sounding or acting in order to gain legitimacy within the dominant group. While I do not experience the levels of discrimination that African American women face daily in the US, I understand what it means to be "the other" with respect to my skin color and culture in White-dominated spaces. Living with racial and gender consciousness has brought to light how regularly and starkly "the other" is missing from positions of influence and leadership in a field that aims for equity and justice.

Living with racial and gender consciousness has brought to light how regularly and starkly "the other" is missing from positions of influence and leadership in a field that aims for equity and justice.

The race and opportunity paradoxes I experience as a restorative justice practitioner are corroborated in recent research. Although little formal research focuses on how restorative justice practitioners of color encounter their work in White-led spaces, philanthropic agencies have become more interested in studying the equity gap in the nonprofit sector, where restorative justice initiatives are largely based.

Women of color are subject to double intersectionality, which counts against them through the prism of gender *and* race. Women compose about 75 percent of the nonprofit sector, yet only 45 percent of us make it to top positions in our organizations, despite our strong will and plenty of experience to get there.[1] Additionally, even though nearly half of nonprofit workers are People of Color, studies show that we occupy less than 20 percent of executive director posts in nonprofit organizations.[2] Research also indicates that People of Color working in the nonprofit sector have comparable amounts of training and education and are more interested in executive positions in our organizations than White-identifying nonprofit workers. Lack of preparation and lack of ambition are *not* the barriers to our advancement; the barriers lie within our inherited systems of inequality.[3]

Because many female RJ practitioners work in schools, where restorative programs are growing in acceptance and funding, a look at research on educators of color also frames the disparity and thus the hardships female practitioners of color encounter in the school system. A 2016 article in *The At-*

lantic noted that "in 2012–13, nearly 22 percent of Black public-school teachers moved schools or left their profession altogether, compared to 15 percent of White and non-Hispanic teachers."[4] Though 16 percent of the US population is Black and the majority of students in urban public schools are students of color, only 7 percent of teachers are Black.[5]

The US Department of Education's 2012 Schools and Staffing Survey showed that teachers of color often feel "pigeonholed" into working with Black students, both because White colleagues expect it more of them and because they feel personal responsibility to *do* more for Black students. Due in part to their capacity (or the perception of their capacity) to connect better with Black students, Black teachers are often relegated to disciplinary roles.[6]

The disproportionate number of White teachers to students of color in US schools is an increasing concern for education researchers, policy makers, and communities of color. Though half of US students in public schools are children of color, 80 percent of teachers are White. Schools remain functionally segregated despite *Brown v. Board of Education*, meaning that Black and Brown students do not see themselves reflected in the adults who aim to prepare them for future success. Studies also tell us that White educators hold lower expectations of Black boys and girls than they do of other students, creating a powerful and implicit self-fulfilling prophecy.[7] Black girls in schools, in particular, struggle with the negative stereotypes assigned to them by virtue of race and gender, resulting in harsher and disproportionate punishments from teachers.[8]

Though half of US students in public schools are children of color, 80 percent of teachers are White.

Like Black girls in schools, female Black educators also encounter negative pushback when they choose to speak out among their White peers. Women of color who advocate and express dissatisfaction or frustration are likely to be stigmatized by their White peers as "rocking the boat." This negative pushback results in Black women, as well as other women of color, sometimes remaining silent or "ignoring" the discrimination they personally experience or witness.

Case Studies: Female Restorative Justice Coordinators of Color in Schools

For women of color who work in the school system, these findings are not news. They resonated with me during the year I worked as a restorative justice coordinator in a highly policed urban high school, dominated by White teachers and deans. Like many coordinators, I experienced a sense of isolation as one person working to counter the punitive paradigms that normalized shaming of troubled young people, rather than supporting them. Schools are

Schools are microcosms of the greater society; they concentrate the strengths and ills of their members' communities. This social concentration means that racism, violence, and other challenges to mental and emotional well-being are felt more intensely within the pressure cooker of a school environment, where almost everything occurs in plain view.

microcosms of the greater society; they concentrate the strengths and ills of their members' communities. This social concentration means that racism, violence, and other challenges to mental and emotional well-being are felt more intensely within the pressure cooker of a school environment, where almost everything occurs in plain view. Schools are therefore fertile breeding ground for negative feedback, but by the same token, positive change can quickly amplify when school leaders make a concerted effort in that direction. Because of their intricate and tangible networks, schools are ideal communities for experimenting with new approaches—like restorative practices.

To support such positive efforts, my colleague Arthur Romano and I have tracked the learnings of Black female restorative justice coordinators (RJCs) who seek to address embedded racism, colorism, sexism, adultism, and punitive zero tolerance approaches to discipline in urban high schools. Operating under a mandate to carry out their work with a racial justice lens, these women have tried to support changes in school climate that take into account the needs of Black and Brown students, the ones disproportionately affected by disciplinary methods and all the "isms" mentioned above. I share a few iconic vignettes from conversations with two RJCs. In particular, I try to illustrate the challenges they faced and the lessons they learned about how to navigate these challenges, both in their home organizations and in the schools where they work. To protect participants' confidentiality, I changed or omitted identifying details. It also bears noting that the barriers highlighted here do not fall strictly along color lines. All educators and organizational leaders can individually choose to propagate either oppression or liberation in their work, even as the larger structures in which we operate make real distinctions among socioeconomic, gender, and color divides.

Case 1: Getting It When Others Don't

In line with research about female teachers of color, RJCs who participated in our study expressed a need to be present to and with students of color in ways that their White colleagues and administrators could not or would not be. RJCs of color "got" the pain of students of color. They intuitively understood that "acting out" very often meant "hurting out," and they were able to support these young people when their expressions of pain went unnoticed, or—worse—when students were ostracized for ineffectually channeling their pain through anger or violence.

One coordinator I interviewed in 2016, whom I will call Carol, told about the experience of a Black girl in her school who became the target of racist name-calling. As a Black woman herself, Carol could deeply understand the young woman's pain and this allowed her to support the student in ways that her White counterpart could not. As she put it:

> She's a young Black girl who just had her magic attacked. . . . She's crying because she has to navigate the system that [teases you] about being Black, right? About being dark-skinned, right? Not only in this place [school], but you live in a society that doesn't support it either. So, when you go to Google and you type in "beautiful woman," 99 percent of the women that'd pop up are White. She's not being validated anywhere else. And I'm very much in my blackness. I walk around with shirts that say, "Black girl is like God." So . . . I can talk to her about why the teasing is taking place. Right? I can talk to her about white supremacy and how it's indoctrinated within us, and talk to her about the issues of colorism. And [one of my White male colleagues] is very well equipped to have those conversations. But he can't talk to her as a Black girl, as a Black woman, to validate that. He hasn't been—I *can*. You know, *we* [the girl and I] can have that conversation.

Carol understood that she was in a unique and indispensable position to be able to connect with young women of color around racialized images of beauty, and yet, like many People of Color in White-led spaces, she found herself needing to skillfully educate White colleagues about the oppressive systems they unknowingly propagate for the people they work with. Her White male colleague had intended to meet with the young woman to explain to her that they were going to "sit down and talk about why we're teasing each other and that it's not good to tease anyone." Carol insisted that he hear her perspective:

> No, it's deeper than that. The conversation has to be deeper, because this isn't just about teasing people for the fun of it. There's a reason why, and that needs to be made known [to the students] because we don't take it for granted that they're too young [to understand]. . . .

> They're going to continue to repeat it, right, so we have to have the conversation as to why. . . . This is bigger than [teasing and bullying]. This can't be a conversation on the surface.

Though she received a formal restorative justice training, the lived experiences of racism and sexism cannot be fully taught or conveyed. Carol's experiences as a Black woman are what made her intervention with this particular student so vital.

Another RJC, whom I will call Jasmine, found herself having to bridge the experiences of students when White colleagues were unable to understand them. She shared the example of a young woman in her school who was in a conflict with another student over the use of racial slurs. As she recounts:

> The reason why the biracial young lady was referred to me . . . by the principal [was] because he thought she was too sensitive or hypersensitive. Her teacher actually came to see me. . . . He feels that she kinda just needs to thicken her skin, 'cause this is the world and it is what it is. Now, the people who thought she was hypersensitive were two White males. . . . She's a very lovely, smart, good kid. But they felt that she's just too sensitive when it comes to everything. So [what bothers her is] not just matters of race, it's sexism, so like "slut shaming," like all the -isms . . . offend her. Um, I'll be honest with you. I was a little sad in talking to her the first time, 'cause I was like, "Oh, you know, the world doesn't get better." But I wanted to validate her feeling—of feeling uncomfortable.

Though other adults in the school minimized this young woman's experience by calling her "too sensitive," Jasmine had experienced her own history with minimization that allowed her to fully understand the disappointment awaiting her student and to empathize with her in ways her White male colleagues could not.

Case 2: Going Against the Grain

Attempts to advocate for a different way of seeing or knowing put women practitioners of color in vulnerable positions. Jasmine goes on to share that racially derogatory terms are so normalized in her school that teachers simply brush them off or even use the terms themselves. Not being a teacher, she questioned when it would ever be appropriate to say to an adult in the school, "Don't say that." As a racialized person herself, Jasmine wondered if she would come up against White men who would deem her response to racial slurs as just another woman of color being "too sensitive"; such a response would send a clear signal about the parameters of "acceptable complaints" within her institutional setting.

Jasmine experienced the challenge of cultural translation and advocacy not only within her predominantly White school setting, but also within her home organization, where she worked under a White female supervisor. Though Jasmine was in the school daily, her supervisor rarely visited. When she did, however, she sometimes reprimanded Jasmine for not doing more to advance the ostensible goals of the restorative justice program. Jasmine often felt undermined during official meetings. She sensed that her supervisor prioritized the needs of the other adults in the school, even though, from Jasmine's perspective, the teachers regularly underestimated their students. Jasmine regularly felt caught between desiring to advocate for the young people she worked with and fulfilling the bureaucratic deliverables that her boss required of her. She also felt that her efforts to build trust and community in the school went unrecognized in the face of her supervisor's expectations. She felt intimidated to speak up in formal meetings and was generally told to leave the "important" conversations for her supervisor to lead. Given that Jasmine had built her own relationships with school administrators and felt she knew them better than her supervisor did, being relegated to structured silence in formal conversations felt demeaning. Yet challenging her supervisor's diagnoses of the school's needs meant risking her job and paycheck.

She felt intimidated to speak up in formal meetings and was generally told to leave the "important" conversations for her supervisor to lead.

Struggling against White educators' counterproductive ways of relating to youth of color in the school was one of the major challenges of the RJCs. Carol put it this way:

> Early on, I got a glimpse that a lot of things that were happening at school were not because of the kids. . . . I felt like a lot of that stuff that was happening could have been because of poor class structure, the way teachers responded to them. . . . Most of the teachers don't look like the students. . . . You will walk through the hallways and you will hear some of the ways that teachers—key teachers—the admin, would speak to kids, you know, in a way that they probably didn't find problematic . . . but, you know, when you talk to [students] in a condescending way, in a way that doesn't leave them in a place to walk away with their dignity, that is not restorative. And when it's done by key players . . . in an institution and the school, who claim that they believe in and support restorative justice, it does more harm than good because now it's like . . . a wolf in sheep's clothes.

Jasmine recalled a time when a White male teacher, who had been sitting in the same room as one of her Circle processes, interrupted the Circle to offer his own assessment of the problem. This man's behavior reinforced to Jasmine—and to others in the Circle—not only how little importance he placed on both the space she was trying to hold and on the Circle's participants, but also how little regard he gave her person and leadership. The teacher evidently considered himself entitled to interrupt her process and to "educate" young people by delivering his perspective on a problem.

Case 3: Being Overlooked for Training and Leadership Positions

While RJCs in schools and other settings have by now garnered a great deal of experience, they are still overlooked for training contracts. Many organizations hire outside trainers based on their reputation, even if these trainers have limited experience in urban or other unique settings. Rather than cultivating training skills for experienced mid-level RJCs of color, most of them women, organizations opt first for "recognized" names in the field. Seeing the potential of restorative justice coordinators of color to take leadership positions means also prioritizing their growth as thought leaders and educators for future generations of practitioners. Just as young people need to have adults in their lives who look and sound like them to validate their importance, female restorative justice practitioners of color need to have more models of women of color in positions of influence within their field.

Case 4: Strategies to Negotiate Subjugated Positions

Women of color in predominantly White-led institutions have to negotiate their own legitimacy in addition to the legitimacy of the people whose struggles are dear to them. June Jordan, speaking of Black English's power, said it was "a system constructed by people constantly needing to insist that [they] exist."[9] Not having ready access to expressions of power, female RJCs of color go about this insistence in different ways. Some, like Jasmine, are strategic about when to speak their own opinions and working "behind the scenes" to effect change, rather than always going through official channels. Whether deliberately or not, RJCs find ally-ships with White colleagues who understand

---

. . . meaningful cultural change requires a strong foundation of dialogue and education around racial justice, white supremacy, and the legacies of trauma in underserved communities of color.

---

their own privilege and are actively working to dismantle it. Female RJCs of color working on the front lines also recognize that change is a long-term process. Though not all of them have the luxury of time on their side due to limits in funding or contracts, they agree that meaningful cultural change requires a strong foundation of dialogue and education around racial justice, white supremacy, and the legacies of trauma in underserved communities of color.

All the female RJCs of color we spoke with recognize that being a sole voice in promoting restorative approaches to wrongdoing is a losing proposition. Their interest in collaborating and sharing the successes of their efforts with like-minded members of the school community helped them in building their legitimacy and also in multiplying their impact. Unlike the concerns of Jasmine's supervisor, whose focus was on the reputation of her parent agency, Jasmine's concerns were intricately tied to the students and community that she saw herself supporting. This attitude of collaboration and "sharing the wealth" was common to all RJCs, a testament to their integrated understanding of restorative justice philosophy. Though it would stand to reason that practitioners who remain true to the principles of the philosophy would be rewarded by their organizations, it seems the aims of nonprofits and the aims of female RJCs of color have not necessarily complemented each other.

As research indicates, women of color are not disadvantaged in our workplaces because they lack training, experience, or ambition. Rather, they are disadvantaged because they work within biased systems that overlook them as executive directors, trainers, or thought leaders. These systems also miss recognizing many of the skills that are essential to supporting youth of color in schools that women of color possess. Given the lack of women of color in top positions, people in systems must make conscious and intentional efforts to ensure paths for their advancement. Programs like "Cultivate" in Chicago that provide mentorship and support for women of color in community justice work are important models to replicate.

With the steady growth of restorative justice and the widespread recognition of its potential to address key issues of racial justice, such as the school-to-prison pipeline, facilitating women leaders of color in bringing their valuable skills and knowledge to the table is critical if the field is to achieve its aims.

DISCUSSION QUESTIONS

1. Questions for White leaders in institutions:
   a. Does racial and gender equity matter in restorative justice work? Why?
   b. Are women of color differently situated or affected by your organizational and leadership structure?

c. What barriers does your institutional makeup or culture pose to the advancement of women of color in this work? Explain.
d. How can you support female practitioners of color in achieving leadership milestones within your institution? What needs to change in order to make this happen?
e. Given your position of power, what concrete steps can you take to help ensure that women of color are supported in holding leadership positions?

2. Questions for female RJ practitioners of color:
   a. What are your goals in this work? Where would you like to be, and what change would you like to effect?
   b. What barriers do you experience to achieving these goals—to being seen and heard?
   c. Who are your allies, and what resources can you access (alone or with help) in overcoming these barriers?

ACTIVITIES (FOR INSTITUTIONS)

1. Create mentorship and peer-support programs for emerging Black RJ practitioners and would-be organizational leaders of color.
2. Implement race-conscious organizational practices—workshops, conversations, guest speakers, etc.—to uncover implicit biases that form barriers for women of color to lead and have legitimacy at high levels of influence.
3. Work with funders and organizational leaders at all levels to incentivize equitable hiring and promotion practices and to change the narrative of what a "qualified" leader looks and sounds like.

RESOURCES

Readings

The Annie E. Casey Foundation. "Race Equity and Inclusion Action Guide: Embracing Equity: 7 Steps to Advance and Embed Race Equity and Inclusion within Your Organization." http://www.aecf.org/resources/race-equity-and-inclusion-action-guide/.

Jones, Nikki. *Between Good and Ghetto: African American Girls and Inner-City Violence.* New Brunswick, NJ: Rutgers University Press, 2009.

Thomas-Breitfeld, Sean, and Frances Kunreuther. "Race to Lead: Confronting the Nonprofit Racial Leadership Gap." The Building Movement Project. www.buildingmovement.org; www.racetolead.org.

Websites

"Cultivate: Women of Color Leadership." https://crossroadsfund.org/cultivate. Cultivate offers a model of a mentorship and training program aimed at women of color working within justice fields.

"Equity Resources for Philanthropy." https://putnam-consulting.com/philanthropy-411-blog/equity-resources-for-foundations/. This site offers an extensive list of toolkits, action guides, and other resources for philanthropic institutions seeking to increase equity (applicable beyond philanthropy).

"Race Matters Institute." http://viablefuturescenter.org/racemattersinstitute/. This site offers resources to help organizations provide equitable resources.

The Truthtelling Project. http://www.thetruthtellingproject.org/. This project implements and sustains grassroots, community-centered truth-telling processes to amplify voices about structural violence.

NOTES

1. Rachel Renock, "Sexism and Nonprofits, Dismissing a Sector Run by Women," *Medium,* July 19, 2017, https://medium.com/the-nonprofit-revolution/sexism-nonprofits-dismissing-a-sector-run-by-women-dc7d71790307.
2. Sean Thomas-Breitfeld and Frances Kunreuther, "Race to Lead: Confronting the Nonprofit Leadership Gap," an initiative of the Building Movement Project, accessed July 1, 2018, http://www.buildingmovement.org/pdf/RacetoLead_NonprofitRacialLeadershipGap.pdf.
4. Emily DeRuy, "The Burden of Being a Black Teacher," *The Atlantic*, November 7, 2016, https://www.theatlantic.com/education/archive/2016/11/the-challenge-of-teaching-while-black/506672/.
5. Ibid.
6. Ashley Griffin and Hillary Tackie, "Through Our Eyes: Perspectives and Reflections from Black Teachers," a publication of the Education Trust, 2016, https://edtrust.org/wp-content/uploads/2014/09/ThroughOurEyes.pdf.
7. Jill Rosen, "Race Biases Teachers' Expectations for Students," Johns Hopkins University, March 30, 2016, http://releases.jhu.edu/2016/03/30/race-biases-teachers-expectations-for-students/.
8. Tanzina Vega, "Schools' Discipline for Girls Differs by Race and Hue," *The New York Times*, December 10, 2014, https://www.nytimes.com/2014/12/11/us/school-discipline-to-girls-differs-between-and-within-races.html.
9. Patricia Hill Collins, *Black Feminist Thought: Knowledge, Consciousness, and the Politics of Empowerment,* Routledge Classics Series, vol. 138 (New York: Routledge, 2008), 261.

Chapter 8

Co-opting Restorative Justice in Higher Education

Desirée Anderson

Introduction

For colleges and universities, colorizing the restorative justice movement means being critical of how white supremacy has affected the implementation of restorative practices in higher educational institutions. White supremacy is a part of every interaction we have, and it influences the ways in which we participate (and show up) in all spheres of life. The experiences of practitioners of color within institutionalized spaces speak to the ways in which we are further marginalized when we engage in restorative practices with White practitioners. When White practitioners fail to critically examine their identities as they relate to power and privilege, the voices and experiences of People of Color get silenced, if not erased. Additionally, when we expect restorative justice to solve problems that institutions neglect, the work gets watered down without institutional prioritization, and restorative justice's transformative potential gets lost in the process. Decolonizing the use of restorative justice within institutions is the only way to address systemic harm and oppression and to dismantle the ways in which these structures influence interpersonal harm and conflict.

Recent events have seen a discernible rise in the use of restorative justice, mostly as a response to harm on college and university campuses. For example, in 2011, Justine Darling, restorative justice coordinator, found that an estimated 2 percent of public institutions of higher education use some form of restorative justice or restorative practices. This number did not include private institutions, and presumably many more institutions have since begun to incorporate restorative justice and practices into their policies and procedures.[1] Restorative justice's introduction comes on the heels of what some scholars argue is an overly legalistic response to harm on campuses across the United States.[2] Restorative justice as a paradigm is framed as a tool to repair harm and rebuild community.[3] Practitioners place special emphasis on community. Restorative justice's theory thrives on the foundational belief that people want to make amends for wrongdoing for two reasons: to return to the community,[4] and to return a community to its relational balance.

Tom Sebok and Andrea Goldblum, facilitators in the restorative justice program at the University of Colorado at Boulder, argue that higher educational institutions possess resources to implement restorative justice:

> [They are] well-defined communities, which work to promote an ethos of care and integration and have ready opportunities for collaboration; diverse populations, which deserve the flexibility of a restorative justice approach to offenses; support systems normally available, such as counseling services, health centers; alcohol, drug, or anger management programs; and numerous other services, student judicial and residence-life missions and processes for which restorative justice is a complement.[5]

However, introducing restorative justice to these institutions, while fundamentally ideal for a "community," is problematized even by the way it is introduced. Restorative justice is often described as an *alternative* approach, when in reality it is a way of being and a way that communities once operated. Viewing restorative justice as an "alternative" makes it easy to co-opt its processes and, in essence, water them down. The result is that RJ's foundations are more readily lost. They become embedded in a structure that arguably is designed to work within the confines of an individualized justice system—not within the reality of community or collectivism. Mara Schiff, professor of criminology and criminal justice, posits the ultimate restorative justice question:

Viewing restorative justice as an "alternative" makes it easy to co-opt its processes and, in essence, water them down.

> Is it possible for restorative justice to survive and transform such systems to produce socially just results, or is restorative justice more likely to get compromised and co-opted by the overwhelmingly dominant cultural ethos (and corresponding power structures) of the organizations it seeks to transform? Ultimately, is restorative justice strong enough to co-opt the co-opters?[6]

Institutions of higher education operate within a hierarchical structure. The literature shows this structure is founded in white supremacy—indeed, race and racism are embedded in the very fabric of institutional policies and practices.[7] Institutions of higher education are not designed to benefit all of society but rather a select few or elite. As such, the goal of welcoming with open arms a more representative student body on college and university campuses has not been met. It is unclear if the presence of historically underrepresented students has increased harmony or exacerbated White-based, racial tensions on campuses across the country.[8] As more "minority" groups have entered the traditional White domain of higher education, a "quiet shift" has begun, one by which whiteness has shifted from the narrative of dominance and superiority to one that centralizes whiteness as normal.[9] As institutions and individuals treat whiteness as normal, they actually work to further the superiority of whiteness, whether intentionally or not. This whiteness-as-normal view most poignantly manifests in the denial of racism and bias. Nolan León Cabrera, professor of the study of higher education, focusing on racial dynamics, expands the presence of white supremacy to include other manifestations of whiteness:

As institutions and individuals treat whiteness as normal, they actually work to further the superiority of whiteness, whether intentionally or not.

> An institutional stance on racism that is reactive instead of proactive, the exclusion of diversity in the mission statement, concentration of institutional power in white (often male) administrators, minimal representation of faculty of color, and a reliance upon "traditional pedagogies" that disregard teaching across racial difference.[10]

As institutions have searched for ways to mitigate racial tensions of the campus climate and culture, they have done so mostly as a response to demands, public criticism, and the potential loss of funding avenues, rather than through developing ways to educate the campus community about racism's prevalence. Glyn Hughes, professor of sociology and racial justice, explains that "institutions with professed 'commitments to diversity' have felt a new sort of pressure to have well-organized mechanisms in place for responding to incidents [that pose a risk] . . . to a school's branded image."[11] The introduction of restorative justice is, in many ways, an attempt to reduce the critique of racism and to minimize the reliance on traditional pedagogies. However, when this process is used to "fix" the problems that institutions of higher education neglect, restorative justice is more likely to be co-opted and dangerously misused.

Historically, institutions of higher education have attempted to create "race-neutral" laws and policies that unintentionally—or perhaps intentionally—disproportionately impact students coming from marginalized communities. This impact is evident in what Daniel G. Solorzano, professor of education and Chicano/a Studies, and his colleagues discuss in relation to *Grutter v. Bolligner*—a 2003 Supreme Court case that upheld an affirmative action admissions policy but stated that race would become an irrelevant factor in twenty-five years. Solorzano and his colleagues assert: "Clearly, one of the major outcomes of the Supreme Court's opinion in *Grutter* was to forewarn higher educational institutions that race should become an irrelevant measure of the educational achievement or academic potential for students of color."[12] Colorblindness and race neutrality allow for the ideology of meritocracy and equal opportunity to permeate institutions of higher education without critically analyzing how history shapes cultural understanding and capacity to navigate these institutions.

White Supremacy as Policy and Practice

US higher educational institutions, as a whole, are a microcosm of the United States. As a result of a seemingly colorblind and race-neutral policy, Shaun R. Harper and Lori D. Patton, both scholars in racial equity, write in *Responding to the Realities of Race on Campus*, "it is entirely possible for students to graduate from college without critically reflecting on their racist views, or having engaged in meaningful conversations about race."[13] Whiteness is operationalized as the default in terms of representation in curriculum, pedagogy, and physical bodies. While most institutions have incorporated course requirements to encourage students to engage in diversity, developed cultural centers, and added key positions on campuses to address inclusion efforts, much of these efforts are still operating from a reactionary lens. Little is being done to address white supremacy's prevalence, how it manifests on campuses, and how it structures interactions between people. Institutions have not always been intentional about the types of interactions individuals are having on their campuses, particularly in creating opportunities for facilitated dialogues around issues of racism, classism, and other forms of oppression.

The introduction of restorative justice and its practices are no different. Restorative justice has been described in an "unequivocally positive—even idealized—light; as an exclusively benign and unquestionably progressive mechanism for facilitating inclusivity, reparation, resolution and, ultimately,

This description of restorative justice fails to consider the typical liberal, individualistic paradigm, which is hierarchal and emphasizes consequences that form the structure of higher education.

healing and satisfactory closure."[14] This description of restorative justice fails to consider the typical liberal, individualistic paradigm, which is hierarchal and emphasizes consequences that form the structure of higher education. Institutions of higher education have mostly implemented restorative justice as a tool to address disciplinary issues. These issues range from alcohol violations and bias incidents to, in a very few cases, sexual misconduct.

While, as David Karp and Susanne Conrad of Skidmore College observe, the "restorative justice approach promotes inclusion over social distancing, emphasizing instead those sanctioning strategies that rebuild conventional social ties to the college community," much of the work in higher education has failed to consider what community means: Who is included in that community?[15] Because the restorative work focuses mainly on disciplinary issues, little to nothing has been done on what it takes to build community. This community-building work must involve having honest and difficult dialogues about issues of oppression that impact individuals within the walls of the campus "community." Dorothy Vaandering, professor of restorative justice in education, explains, for example, "Some early proponents of restorative justice warned that restorative justice initiatives risked being co-opted by institutional hierarchies if they focused only on conflict management procedures after individual incidents, and ignored the necessity of transforming governing structures and relationships."[16]

Vaandering suggests that restorative justice requires a community perspective; it requires no hierarchies to dictate what is acceptable—and what is not—in terms of forgiveness and accountability. By focusing only on conflict management, institutions of higher education fail to build community; they fail to develop a structure necessary to adequately implement restorative justice and restorative processes based on relationships. In the latter regard, restorative justice differs from traditional retributive justice. In other words, restorative justice sees offenses as damage to relationships and seeks to repair those relationships. Nevertheless, what do we do when there are no relationships to build on? What happens when there is no community established to which one might return?

By focusing only on conflict management, institutions of higher education fail to build community.

Institutions of higher education are, by definition, "communities"; however, many sub-communities play a more active role in people's lives than the institution itself. Belonging to clubs and organizations, athletic teams, individual schools, etc., all offer subsets of community on college and university campuses. Similarly, self-identifying with historically marginalized groups creates an out-group experience, and that may limit what it means to be a member of the larger campus community or even some of the many sub-communities.

Chris Cunneen and Barry Goldson, professors of social science and criminology, argue that structural divisions around race, class, gender, etc., may inadvertently exclude individuals from restorative practices, "because they are without a community or without the right community."[17] Without the right community or affinal group, instances of injustice can be viewed as business-as-usual; the injustices can be seen as too small, irrelevant, or not big enough to warrant change. Without the right community or affinal group, racism looks natural and ordinary. The focus falls on the extreme and shocking forms of injustice that are often individualized. But, as Richard Delgado and Jean Stefancic, leaders in critical race theory, write, this does "little about the business-as-usual forms of racism that people of color confront every day and that account for much misery, alienation, and despair."[18]

Viewing acts of racism as only the individualized acts of extremism increases the prevalence of white supremacy, as it allows those who hold power and privilege to define what is racist and what is important to address. Shaun Harper explains this racial dynamic: "The minimization of racism frame compels Whites to view discrimination through the narrow lens of overt, outrageously racist acts. Anything that falls short is often misperceived as minoritized persons being 'hypersensitive' or unfairly playing the 'race card.'"[19] Institutions must do the work of building a cultural competency and dismantling white supremacy to ensure that everyone has the "right" community or affinity group. Implementing restorative justice is vital to developing community.

How we implement restorative justice is, of course, crucial to its success. Restorative justice is not meant to be only a reactionary tool. Lewis Schlosser, professor of psychiatry, and William Sedlacek, professor of counseling, explain that administrators often work in a reactive mode rather than in a proactive manner. Solutions of the former are designed to provide a quick resolution, one that places "emphasis . . . more on 'putting out the fire' than working toward preventing future 'fires.'"[20] Restorative justice, as a relationship-building process, slowly changes the campus ethos. On one hand, it ideally puts out fires, while on the other hand, it proactively prevents future fires. Restorative justice is both reactive and proactive and, as discussed below, should be implemented as such.

Restorative justice, as a relationship-building process, slowly changes the campus ethos. On one hand, it ideally puts out fires, while on the other hand, it proactively prevents future fires.

For instance, Gillean McCluskey, professor of restorative practices in Edinburgh, and her colleagues describe three specific ways to implement restorative justice in school environments.[21] Among these three approaches, the most effective method they identify is "ethos building," i.e., a whole-school approach. The ethos-building approach encompasses both a proactive approach (using preventative and educational tools) and a reactive approach (an operational response to wrongdoing). As for the reactive approach on its own, the authors explain that such interactions of restorative justice are limited to those responsible for student behavior, like disciplinary officers, and are used only in response to events and issues, not with any proactive measures. In the third approach they describe, restorative justice is used only for serious incidents that could result in immediate school expulsion or would result in criminal charges. This approach did see positive gains for the individuals involved but had no impact on the overall school climate.

In order to implement the ethos-building approach, an institution has to be committed to a cultural shift—one that requires achieving buy-in from a variety of campus partners and other community stakeholders. It also means creating some structural and systemic changes to policies and practices. Additionally, this approach requires having conversations with those committed to improving the campus climate and reducing racism and other forms oppression on the campus. What this commitment means boils down to answering: What exactly is justice, and how do we understand it? The whole-school approach requires sufficient time and resources devoted to improving the overall campus climate. Institutions addressing isolated incidents cannot expect restorative justice to fix school climate, since they are a manifestation of campus culture. Gerardo R. López, professor of education and critical race theory, explains further the difference between explicit and structural incidences:

Institutions addressing isolated incidents cannot expect restorative justice to fix school climate, since they are a manifestation of campus culture.

> This focus on explicit acts has ignored the subtle, hidden, and often insidious forms of racism that operate at a deeper, more systemic level. When racism becomes "invisible," individuals begin to think that it is merely a thing of the past and/or only connected to the specific act.[22]

Individuals who commit harmful acts against those in their community must believe that such behavior is acceptable—moreover, that those in their community would not find their behavior and actions indefensible or disrespectful. Treating these harmful acts as isolated incidents only furthers the disconnect that students experience when they try to engage around incidents of campus-related harm.

The use of a whole-school approach to restorative justice aligns with the steps outlined by Sylvia Hurtado, professor of education, and her colleagues.[23]

They assert that in order to improve the campus climate, the following things should occur simultaneously:

1. Campus administrators should reflect on their institution's history of inclusion.
2. They should take intentional steps to actively recruit and retain People of Color on the campus.
3. They should make serious efforts to attend to the perceptions and attitudes between and among groups.
4. They should improve the inter- and intra-group relations among groups in college.[24]

This whole-school approach would ask that campus partners institute proactive restorative practices, such as community Circles and other forms of social engagement that emphasize relationship building. This focus on relationship is similar to the dynamic-diversity approach. According to Liliana Garces, professor of law and educational policy, and Uma Jayakumar, professor of racial justice in higher education, this approach fosters the "interactions among students within a particular context and under appropriate environmental conditions needed to realize the educational benefits of diversity."[25] In essence, Shametrice Davis, professor of education, and Jessica Harris, professor of critical race theory in education, observe, "Conversations on racism should not be just that, but rather purposeful dialogues that are cross-racial, sustained, and deconstruct the normality of whiteness."[26] Intentional cross-racial and cross-cultural conversations in the many spaces that students, faculty, and staff cross paths on the campus (e.g., classrooms, the residence halls, orientation, student organizations) should be normalized. These conversations should not only center the voice of the marginalized in an effort to deconstruct the normalcy of whiteness, but also challenge all parties to re-evaluate what they hold to be true and either change those held beliefs or further fortify them.

Failing to engage the campus in the work of dismantling white supremacy—such as engaging in intergroup dialogue and making building community across subgroups a priority—relegates restorative justice to another ineffective tool because it was not implemented properly. Nevertheless, restorative justice's transformative nature makes it more than an ideal candidate for adoption in higher education. Nancy Geist Giacomini, private educator and mediator, and Jennifer Meyer Schrage, conflict management specialist, assert, "The diversity of our students and the issues they face demand creative and educational solutions in addition to the conscientious application of procedural safeguards traditionally provided by campus disciplinary processes."[27]

It will take some time over the course of several semesters to build to these types of dialogues, but offering spaces to engage in these dialogues can build stronger and more connected communities. Here are some sample questions, adapted from Occidental College, to ask students and others in this process:

1. How has your high school or pre-college experience differed from your college experience in terms of diversity, equity, and inclusion?
2. Based purely on how you look or present yourself, or on how someone else you know looks or presents themselves, what is an incorrect assumption someone has made or could make? How do these assumptions make you feel? What is an attribute or trait you would like people to recognize in you?
3. The country has been engaging in discussion this year around ________, ________, and ________; how have these topics impacted your home community?
4. At the time of ________ within the US, many people thought it was a good thing. Today, most people think it is unimaginable that ________ occurred, but it is important to recognize that ________ still exists in various forms in the US and around the world. What current commonly held belief or practice do you think will seem unimaginable fifty to one hundred years from now? What social injustice are we, as a society, currently overlooking or condoning?
5. What is your understanding of power, privilege, and oppression? Where have you heard or learned about these terms and their meanings in your life? How do you understand these terms as both academic concepts and lived experiences?
6. How can you use your time at ________ to connect with others different from yourself and contribute to an inclusive community?

Responses to Harm

Steps to build community and relationships within and between groups will need to be a principal element of the restorative paradigm. According to Vaandering, all four corners of a school must be included in this work:

> In theory, facilitating circle conferences to address specific incidents of harm involving a few people should become the tip of the triangle, with the need for such post-incident repair reduced by foundational building work where the whole school population is enfolded in building and maintaining and repairing relationships in all aspects of the educational experience.[28]

If restorative justice and restorative practices are to be advantageous for everyone and not just for those who are able to benefit from the normalcy of whiteness, then restorative justice facilitators must do the work of decolonizing their ideas about justice and who is deserving of that justice.

The whole-school approach is most beneficial, but for this process to be truly effective, facilitators—even at the basic level of restorative practices—must challenge their held beliefs about justice and social groups. If restorative justice and restorative practices are to be advantageous for everyone and not just for those who are able to benefit from the normalcy of whiteness, then restorative justice facilitators must do the work of decolonizing their ideas about justice and who is deserving of that justice.

Restorative justice and traditional justice are most often described as polarized rather than as compatible. While Gregory Paul and Ian Borton, both professors of communication, assert that "at their core . . . an offense is a violation that produces a need for condemnation, reparation, and accountability . . . and it is possible for people to pursue both 'retributive' and 'restorative' aims within RJ practices," the two forms of justice respond to harms differently. Traditional justice seeks to hold those who have done harm accountable through punishment, while restorative justice seeks to hold them accountable through their desire to return to, and be welcomed by, their community.[29]

According to a study conducted by Huang, Braithwaite, Tsutomi, Hosoi, and Braithwaite—professors of sociology, justice, and international relations in Australia and Japan—those who seek punishment as a form of accountability hold more traditional and socially conservative attitudes, while those who can access higher levels of social capital adopt a restorative justice orientation.[30] The authors found that the preference for more punitive measures was "fueled by fear of crime, fear of the poor, and belief that traditional values are decaying."[31] Conversely, the preference for restorative justice reflected a valuation of victim voice and amends. This binary result is not surprising when we consider the notion of social capital, defined as "the connections among individuals within networks and across networks."[32] The authors further distinguish two forms of social capital: "bonding social capital" refers to associations within groups where trust is thick and cohesion is high, while "bridging social capital" refers to between-group associations where trust is thin, values and norms are heterogeneous, but social exclusion is low.

The process (of facilitating restorative processes) requires that we negotiate justice among all the participants. The facilitators "can exert a particularly strong influence on this negotiation and enactment simply by virtue of their position."[33] We may reasonably believe that those who make the choice to become restorative justice facilitators hold particular beliefs and values about justice and may have high social capital. However, we may also reasonably assume that individual facilitators hold unconscious biases that may limit their ability to see harmed parties or offenders as deserving of restorative processes. The facilitators' social identities may allow for strong-bonding but low-bridging social capital, and this incongruence may influence facilitators' capacities to offer or adequately provide restorative practices as a response to incidents of harm.

Facilitators of restorative justice must do the work of developing their multicultural competence. Raechele Pope, professor of educational leadership and policy, and her colleagues define multicultural competence as the "awareness, knowledge, and skills that are needed to work effectively across cultural groups and to work with complex diversity issues."[34] Restorative processes are intended to correct the perceived shortcomings of the judicial process.[35] However, traditional judicial systems or a campus's cultural environment may co-opt the restorative process and lend opportunity for forgiveness to some populations more than for others. The result? An unfair or biased process may develop that favors students who mirror the dominant culture. By contrast, facilitators who are committed to rethinking and unlearning their conscious and unconscious beliefs have the potential to undo systems of injustice and inequity.

The tenor of not just the facilitators' but also the community's social capital also affects opportunities for forgiveness. In addition to biased, disproportionate access to restorative practices, it is all too easy to operate with binaries. The language of "victim" and "offender" or "harmed party" and "responsible party" limit the way facilitators and institutions both perceive and address harm. Often those who have either caused or suffered harm have likely been harmed or caused it themselves, but binary terminology gets in the way of recognizing this. The more that restorative practitioners explore harms' complexities, the more restorative processes on college and university campuses can address not just the incident of harm but also the harm's root causes. Facilitators begin to dig deeper into the "what happened" question. When higher educational institutions use restorative justice and restorative practices, their desire to resolve conflict quickly may result in processes that do not dig deep enough. In trying to address a harm, institutions may fail to invest in understanding "The Why." Without a whole-school approach, restorative justice's transformative benefits will be lost, either swept up into the hierarchal structure of higher education or used only for a select few, mostly those who are already beneficiaries of current justice systems. The goal of restorative justice is to bring harmed parties

In trying to address a harm, institutions may fail to invest in understanding "The Why."

and responsible parties (those who have done the harm) together. However, a substantial amount of pre-conference, pre-Circle work is required for both sides; otherwise the process may do more to harm the situation rather than resolve it. In the process of unlearning, advocates of restorative justice and restorative practices must engage in dismantling notions of who is deserving of justice. This self-change begins with believing in the power of stories. The stories we need to hear are not only the stories of individuals but also the stories of peoples. To engage this unlearning process, I suggest reading two books by Waziyatawin, Wahpetunwan Dakȟóta: *What Does Justice Look Like? The Struggle for Liberation in Dakota Homeland* and *For Indigenous Eyes Only: A Decolonization Handbook.*

The stories we need to hear are not only the stories of individuals but also the stories of peoples.

Those wishing to advocate for restorative justice and restorative practices in higher education should ask themselves and these institutions the following questions:

1. What are your (vs. institutional) goals and intended purpose in using this model?
2. What resources (time, staff, and money) is your institution willing to offer for its implementation?
3. Is your institution committed to instituting the community-building and relationship-forming aspects of restorative practices? If not, then perhaps this practice should not be implemented at your institution.

Decolonizing restorative justice in higher education means moving beyond person-to-person harms. All four corners of a campus must be committed to digging down to and pulling up the roots of harm. Institutions of higher education must be willing to name white supremacy, name racism and oppression, and name the ways they and their institutions have been complicit in upholding these models. Institutions have to be about building relationships and dismantling white supremacy. Traditional notions of justice must be challenged through sustained dialogues and intentional cross-cultural communication—initiatives that are fully within the power of higher educational institutions to make happen.

DISCUSSION QUESTIONS

1. What steps has your institution taken, intentional or not, to preserve whiteness as normalcy, and what specific measures can be taken to uproot those practices, procedures, and policies?

2. How do we reimagine the college campus and the communities within? What can community look like if we invested time and money in building and expanding relationships? What would that investment look like in ten years?
3. How do we get colleges and universities to go beyond what critical race theory calls "interest convergence"? How do we get institutions to care about diversity, inclusion, and community because that is essential to our well-being and not because it supports the bottom line?

ACTIVITIES

1. For practitioners who are training other facilitators, consider having them unpack their identities in relation to their work as facilitators. This identity activity can be done in a variety of ways; one of those may be to use the activities found at this link with the perspectives of current RJ facilitators in mind: https://intraweb.stockton.edu/eyos/affirmative_action/content/docs/Interactive%20Diversity%20Booklet%2010-14-2011%20Rev%203_1_16.pdf.
2. As many people are aware, bias runs deep in our everyday lives. Engage facilitators and the campus community in discussion with our own biases through the use of the implicit bias test available through Harvard University: https://implicit.harvard.edu/implicit/.
3. Facilitate Circle lunches with people in positions of authority to walk through the discussion questions. Allow them to practice the community-building Circles that a whole-school approach desires for the larger campus community. Ideally, the activity will give them insight into the power of Circles.

RESOURCES

Blackwell, Angela Glover, Stewart Kwoh, and Manuel Pastor. *Uncommon Common Ground: Race and America's Future.* Revised and updated edited. New York: W. W. Norton, 2010.

Skidmore Project. Those interested in restorative justice in higher education may want to look at the Skidmore Project as a starting point to connect with other campuses with restorative justice programs: https://www.skidmore.edu/campusrj/index.php

Winn, Maisha T., and H. Richard Milner IV. *Justice on Both Sides: Transforming Education Through Restorative Justice (Race and Education).* Boston: Harvard Education Press, 2018.

NOTES

1. Justine Darling, "Restorative Justice in Higher Education: A Compilation of Formats and Best Practices" (manual) (San Diego: University of San Diego, 2011).
2. Michael Dannells, *From Discipline to Development: Rethinking Student Conduct in Higher Education, J-B ASHE Higher Education Report Series (AEHE)*, (Book 70) (Hoboken, NJ: Jossey-Bass, 1996).
3. Gillean McCluskey, Gwynedd Lloyd, J. Stead, J. Kane, S. Riddell, and Elisabet Weedon, "'I Was Dead Restorative Today': From Restorative Justice to Restorative Approaches in School," *Cambridge Journal of Education* 38, no. 2 (2008): 199–216.
4. John Braithwaite, "Restorative Justice: Assessing Optimistic and Pessimistic Accounts," *Crime and Justice*, vol. 25 (1999): 1–127.
5. Tom Sebok and Andrea Goldblum, "Establishing a Campus Restorative Justice Program," *Journal of the California Caucus of College and University Ombuds* 2, no. 1 (1999): 15.
6. Mara Schiff, "Institutionalizing Restorative Justice: Paradoxes of Power, Restoration, and Rights," *Reconstructing Restorative Justice Philosophy* (Furnham, UK: Ashgate Publishing, 2013), 163.
7. Edward Taylor, "Critical Race Theory and Interest Convergence in the Desegregation of Higher Education," in *Race Is . . . Race Isn't: Critical Race Theory and Qualitative Studies in Education*, ed. Laurence Parker, Donna Deyhle, and Sofia Villenas (Boulder, CO: Westview Press, 1999): 181–204.
8. US Department of Justice, Community Relations Service (CRS), *Responding to Hate Crimes and Bias-Motivated Incidents on College/University Campuses*, 2003, https://www.justice.gov/archive/crs/pubs/university92003.htm.
9. Michael Omi and Howard Winant, *Racial Formation in the United States* (New York: Routledge, 1st ed., 1986, 3rd ed., 2015).
10. Nolan León Cabrera, "Exposing Whiteness in Higher Education: White Male College Students Minimizing Racism, Claiming Victimization, and Recreating White Supremacy," in *Race, Ethnicity and Education* 17, no. 1 (2014): 32.
11. Glyn Hughes, "Racial Justice, Hegemony, and Bias Incidents in US Higher Education," *Multicultural Perspectives* 15, no. 3 (2013): 127.
12. Daniel G. Sólorzano, Octavio Villalpando, and Leticia Oseguera, "Educational Inequities and Latina/O Undergraduate Students in the United States: A Critical Race Analysis of Their Educational Progress," *Journal of Hispanic Higher Education* 4, no. 3 (2005): 273.
13. Shaun R. Harper and Lori D. Patton, eds., *Responding to the Realities of Race on Campus, New Directions for Student Service* series, no. 120 (Hoboken, NJ: Jossey-Bass, 2007), 2.
14. Chris Cunneen and Barry Goldson, "Restorative Justice? A Critical Analysis," in *Youth, Crime and Justice,* 2nd ed., ed. Barry Goldson and John Muncie (London: Sage Publications, 2015), 139.
15. David Karp and Susanne Conrad, "Restorative Justice and College Student Misconduct," *Public Organization Review* 5, no. 4 (2005): 318.
16. Dorothy Vaandering, "Relational Restorative Justice Pedagogy in Educator Professional Development," *Curriculum Inquiry* 44, no. 4 (2014): 514.

17. Cunneen and Goldson, "Restorative Justice?" 147.
18. Richard Delgado and Jean Stefancic, eds., *Critical Race Theory: The Cutting Edge* (Philadelphia, PA: Temple University Press, 2000), xvi.
19. Shaun R. Harper, "Race without Racism: How Higher Education Researchers Minimize Racist Institutional Norms," *The Review of Higher Education* 36, no. 1 (2012): 9–29.
20. Lewis Z. Schlosser and William E. Sedlacek, "Hate on Campus: A Model for Evaluating, Understanding, and Handling Critical Incidents," *About Campus* 6, no. 1 (2001): 25.
21. McCluskey et al., "'I Was Dead Restorative Today.'"
22. Gerardo R. López, "The (Racially Neutral) Politics of Education: A Critical Race Theory Perspective," *Educational Administration Quarterly* 39, no. 1 (2003): 70.
23. Sylvia Hurtado, Jeffrey Milem, Alma Clayton-Pedersen, and Walter Allen, *Enacting Diverse Learning Environments: Improving the Climate for Racial/Ethnic Diversity in Higher Education, ASHE-ERIC Higher Education Report* 26, no. 8 (Hoboken, NJ: Jossey-Bass, 1999).
24. Ibid.
25. Liliana M. Garces and Uma M. Jayakumar, "Dynamic Diversity: Toward a Contextual Understanding of Critical Mass," *Educational Researcher* 43, no. 3 (2014): 116.
26. Shametrice Davis and Jessica C. Harris, "But We Didn't Mean It Like That: A Critical Race Analysis of Campus Responses to Racial Incidents," *Journal of Critical Scholarship on Higher Education and Student Affairs* 2, no. 1, article 6 (2016): 75, http://ecommons.luc.edu/jcshesa/vol2/iss1/6.
27. Nancy Geist Giacomini and Jennifer Meyer Schrage, "Building Community in the Current Campus Climate," in *Reframing Campus Conflict: Student Conduct Practice Through a Social Justice Lens,* ed. Nancy Geist Giacomini and Jennifer Meyer Schrage (Sterling, VA: Stylus Publishing, 2009): 7.
28. Vaandering, "Relational Restorative Justice Pedagogy," 512–13.
29. Gregory D. Paul and Ian M. Borton, "Toward a Communication Perspective of Restorative Justice: Implications for Research, Facilitation, and Assessment," *Negotiation and Conflict Management Research* 10, no. 3 (2017): 203.
30. Hsiao-fen Huang, Valerie Braithwaite, Hiroshi Tsutomi, Yoko Hosoi, and John Braithwaite, "Social Capital, Rehabilitation, Tradition: Support for Restorative Justice in Japan and Australia," *Asian Journal of Criminology* 7, no. 4 (2012): 295–308.
31. Ibid., 305.
32. Ibid., 296.
33. Gregory D. Paul and Julia A. Dunlop, "The Other Voice in the Room: Restorative Justice Facilitators' Constructions of Justice," *Conflict Resolution Quarterly* 31, no. 3 (2014): 258.
34. Raechele L. Pope, Amy L. Reynolds, and John A. Mueller, *Multicultural Competence in Student Affairs* (Hoboken, NJ: Jossey-Bass, 2004), xiv.
35. Cunneen and Goldson, "Restorative Justice?"

Chapter 9

"What Do You Want, Reparations?" Racial Microaggressions and Restorative Justice

Anita Wadhwa

A few years ago, I worked with two other educators, one White and one Black, to craft what I believed was a highly successful restorative justice program. The impact of the program was measured not by increases in participants' GPA or attendance—two indicators often valued by foundations and some researchers who don't question the paradigm they work in—but by the social bonds created among youth, the conflicts averted, and the high-level conversations and vulnerability displayed in peace Circles.

So it was a surprise to me when, by the end of the program's third year, our united front on restorative justice disintegrated. Nothing prepared the three of us for the breakdown in communication, save for our own training in RJ and my hope that we would, as adults who expected the same of our youth, be able to model restorative communication with each other when conflicts arose. It seems our racial identities—Black, White, and South Asian, as well as those of our predominately Latinx students—created conflicts over what we saw as restorative justice's purpose in schools. A year of conflicting cross-purposes left me depleted, angry, and hurt, and later I found work at a new school where its leadership supported restorative practices.

This chapter addresses the racial microaggressions that I, and other colleagues of color, have experienced working in the restorative justice field. Ultimately, I write with the hope that my experience will shed light on how we can maintain multiracial coalitions that do not feed into systemic oppression. This systemic oppression is what I feel we must work so hard to resist, as well as expose, and doing so entails questioning the direction of restorative justice's implementation—in schools and in general.

The School

The high school in Houston where I worked years ago is unique in that it is small—fewer than 200 students—with a student body drawn from all over the district. These youth sought the school's smaller classes and alternative forms of teaching, which distinguished it from the larger high schools in the district. Many youth in this school had long histories of feeling dispossessed within the school system—they had been suspended or expelled or had dropped out. Some were young parents; others had anxiety issues; and others attended simply to try to graduate more quickly through the school's credit advancement opportunities. Latinx youth comprised the majority of the school's student population, and they came from low socioeconomic backgrounds.

I brought a youth apprenticeship model to the school five years ago. My principal at the time hired me because she wanted to institute restorative practices. My doctoral work for the prior five years had centered on restorative justice programs developed at two urban Boston high schools. The two high schools' programs had one overwhelming feature in common: they used a social justice agenda to promote restorative justice. Circles were not simply constructive spaces where interpersonal conflicts were resolved; rather, they were spaces to teach youth about the school-to-prison pipeline and institutional practices that create oppressive conditions in their communities.

This restorative/social justice approach had very clear political intentions, and it inspired youth to address problems, embrace new people, and become agents of change. These programs embodied Brazilian educator Paulo Freire's concept of *conscientização*—critical consciousness—to mold students who are informed and inspired to act. My goal was to import the best features of these programs to Houston, my hometown where I planned to return after graduate school.

I began my first year at the school in Houston as an in-school suspension (ISS) teacher, and but after discussion, the principal agreed to recast my position as that of restorative justice coordinator (RJC). When I introduced restorative justice to the staff during year 1 of our implementation, I did so explicitly with a focus on healing Circles as a way to break the school-to-prison pipeline and build relationships.

Hiding the Ball

My work is built on the foundations of social and racial justice, and I believe restorative justice's philosophy can end systemic oppression. However, at my school, I never made this intention explicit for two reasons. First, I knew from growing up in Houston and from experience that starting off with those

By depoliticizing RJ at my campus, I hid the ball to make the concept more palatable, . . .

concepts (social and racial justice) would alienate many people, particularly in Houston. "Critical pedagogy" and "white privilege" are not terms thrown around as easily in Houston as they were in Boston. Second, I felt the urgency to complement in- and out-of-school suspensions with an alternative that seemed so commonsense—Circles. I had seen youth sent to ISS for a variety of small infractions, such as not having materials, being tardy, or not shaving one's facial hair.

I now look back on the decision to defang restorative justice with some discomfort. When the US Supreme Court heard a case on using race as a factor to desegregate schools, it decided that zip code could be used as proxies for race in order to integrate students. A perplexed Justice David Souter stated that such a policy forced school systems to "hide the ball" and to "seek racial diversity without relying on race."[1]

By depoliticizing RJ at my campus, I hid the ball to make the concept more palatable, employing critical race theorist Derrick Bell's notion of *interest convergence*.[2] My thinking was that teachers weren't going to change their attitudes on addressing perceived misbehavior simply because they were genuinely interested in questioning their own privilege. However, I knew they *would* get on board with a revolutionary alternative if it served their own interest of having improved order in the school.

Youth Apprenticeship Model

That first year, I introduced a restorative justice leadership course and trained young people in Circles. They learned about restorative justice and then co-facilitated healing Circles with me when conflicts were referred to the RJC. The course was housed inside the classroom of a White coworker, Ms. Rose.[3] She was often in the room handling her own classroom matters, and occasionally she would join the students and me in Circle or in discussions. She quickly took to the practice and began brainstorming with me about how we could expand the work.

Another colleague, Ms. Pickard, who wanted to teach leadership, also approached us. She was training to be a counselor and found that Circles complemented her beliefs in youth empowerment. I connected both women to different people in the field. For example, a colleague and friend requested that I conduct a restorative justice training out of state, but when I could not make it, Ms. Pickard and Ms. Rose went in my place.

Institutionalizing the Philosophy

The second year of our program, the surveys we conducted with students who participated in Circles revealed high levels of satisfaction, and the trained youth leaders traveled all over, including Harvard, to teach others about Circles. The third year of our program, we decided to work with the assistant principal, Mr. Lewis, to make sure restorative justice was considered for every disciplinary referral he received. We split the duties of restorative justice coordination. I was the primary RJ coordinator, allotted with five out of eight class periods to plan and run Circles, while Ms. Rose and Ms. Pickard were provided with one and two periods, respectively, to do RJ. The rest of the time, they taught their core content classes, Social Studies and English. In this way, an RJ coordinator would be available every class period during the day.

Restorative justice had a much stronger presence on campus that year. Ms. Pickard and I taught leadership to students who facilitated Circles for community building, academic content, support, healing, truancy, reentry, and accountability. Ms. Rose was responsible for tracking the data on our disciplinary referrals and Circle surveys. We three met weekly at first to share lessons and plan for how to mobilize more teachers to buy in and participate in the program. Over time, Ms. Rose faded away from the program. She did not reach out or show up to my class during her RJ time to consult about which students she could be meeting with. She seemed to be avoiding me, and mid-year, when I asked if she would organize some community Circles, she said she was not available.

White Privilege

Over the years, Ms. Rose, Ms. Pickard, and I had become friends, planning curriculum during the summer, sharing meals and laughter, and generally enjoying one another's company the way colleagues who bond over a common mission do. So I approached Ms. Rose hoping we could air out why she seemed so distant. When I did, she said she was not ready to talk about it. She admitted she was very angry and had been avoiding me. I pressed on. She began explaining:

"I don't agree with what we are teaching our kids."

I asked for examples. She thought we were teaching kids to blame their circumstances on White people. She said a student told her, "I can't relate to you because you're White."

"What does that have to do with the program?" I asked.

"He was one of the students in our program. I feel like, as a White person, I've been left out of a lot of things. Maybe you don't do it on purpose, but that's how I feel."

After that, much of what she said was a blur. I felt blindsided and could only register individual comments. Why couldn't she have come to me to talk about this before getting, in her words, "pissed" at me to the point of avoiding me?

"I know white privilege is real, but I've been through things too." *I know white privilege is real, but . . .* I had heard the phrase so many times that I started to zone out after hearing the "but." Ms. Pickard tried to mediate a conversation with all three of us about a week later. She asked if we felt we could repair the relationship. I told Ms. Rose, "I just feel used—like you learned about RJ from me, I gave you opportunities to do it when I couldn't, you got paid to do it, and you use it on your résumé. Now it's like you don't even believe it."

"I *do* believe in it, just not your version of it," she said. "And I don't use it on my résumé."

"It doesn't matter." I pushed on, "You have that bank of experience to draw on in your interviews to be an administrator."

She was quiet for a second and shrugged, almost in disinterest, before she said, "What do you want, reparations?"

Reparations

I remained silent. Ms. Pickard flinched a bit. If Ms. Rose thought I wanted reparations, the framing that she invoked was this: she was the descendant of White slave owners who had capitalized on my labor, body, blood, and tears. She was mocking the term and somehow reinforcing the notion that she had appropriated something from me—also mocking the idea that I somehow "owned" restorative justice. Did she think I was this egotistical?

In "The Case for Reparations" in *The Atlantic*, Ta-Nehisi Coates wrote,

> The popular mocking of reparations as a harebrained scheme authored by wild-eyed lefties and intellectually unserious black nationalists is fear masquerading as laughter. Black nationalists have always perceived something unmentionable about America that integrationists dare not acknowledge—that white supremacy is not merely the work of hotheaded demagogues, or a matter of false consciousness, but a force so fundamental to America that it is difficult to imagine the country without it.[4]

Coates rightfully notes that the mockery of the term and concept of reparations is, indeed, "fear masquerading as laughter."

Fear. Somewhere along the way, I felt Ms. Rose thought I was teaching students to ostracize themselves from White folks, to reject them entirely, to blame them for all of their problems. Ms. Rose's White lens placed her in an

She was the subtle white supremacist—not the card-carrying KKK kind—but the liberal who believed in RJ, but just didn't want to talk about race.

uncomfortable position. Maybe this unfolding is not what happened. I won't ever know, because the conversation got shut down.

"What do you mean *reparations?*" I retorted. Ms. Pickard exchanged glances with me, but she was doing her best to mediate. We kept talking and she didn't answer. Two minutes later I said, "Reparations is such a loaded term. *Why would you say that?*"

No answer.

To me, Ms. Rose suddenly became the opposition to what I was trying to accomplish in the program. She was the subtle white supremacist—not the card-carrying KKK kind—but the liberal who believed in RJ, but just didn't want to talk about race. Coates was right: "that white supremacy is not merely the work of hotheaded demagogues, or a matter of false consciousness, but a force so fundamental to America that it is difficult to imagine the country without it."

Ms. Rose said, "You are so rigid in your definition of restorative justice. I don't think the goal is to end oppression. That is just one of the goals."

"Isn't that a conversation we should have had months ago?" I blurted out.

A shrug.

Later, upon processing the conversation, I realized what I should have said when Ms. Rose said, "What do you want, reparations?"

I should have said, "Yes."

RJ Establishment Politics

Reparation is a loaded term in the United States, but it is also used, with a lower-case "r" in the field of restorative justice, in a practical way. It means to repair, to fix, to heal—and, indeed, to restore. I saw Ms. Rose's comment as part of a pattern of racial microaggressions I had experienced while doing restorative justice work. During one restorative justice conference, participants were asked to discuss a moment where they first became cognizant of race and racism. Three out of twenty were persons of color. The exercise generated some conflict as one of us three said bringing up such memories made her physically uncomfortable, and she felt unsafe. We circled up to address our concerns. When I received the talking piece, I stared at the floor as I spoke. I really didn't feel safe either. The crowd was mostly academics, and who was I—even with a doctorate from Harvard—but a lowly practitioner in a high school?

So I looked down in Circle and talked about racial bullying, which I had experienced on a daily basis the year that I was in sixth grade. "But it's not my fault!" blurted out a White woman. I had to hold down the space once again, and she called up the same oppression I had felt as a child being silenced. "I have the piece," I boomed. She interrupted again. "I HAVE THE PIECE," I repeated. I felt foolish, belittled. Like the muted brown child I once was. And instead of being silent, I had to get loud. Alienate White folks. Be that loud Brown woman.

The Bind

How do I call out racism, tell these stories, without distancing myself or being distanced from others in the very community I seek to learn from and with? It is easy to lose alliances and close doors by talking about race. Many White scholars who are deemed experts receive praise for their courage when they talk about race. In some ways, they should. The fact is that by having white privilege—a concept so many people reject—they have the responsibility to speak on it. But they also get to be the gatekeepers. When I went on a restorative justice Facebook group to ask folks whether the goal of restorative justice was to end oppression, I was trying to generate dialogue. Someone asked how I described oppression. I wrote, "Behaviors, practices, laws, beliefs, systems that privilege some groups and demean and subjugate others physically, mentally, materially, or otherwise."

An older White male wrote, "We look for common ground. A key word is 'respect.'" I didn't understand his response. Since I was asking my community of practitioners—member to member, not as an outsider new to the philosophy—I felt excluded by his use of the word "we." "Who's we?" I asked. "You are right to call me out," he responded, "but many people would endorse what I wrote." I didn't care what "many people" would endorse; I wanted to know if anyone at all agreed with me, since it seemed "my version" of restorative justice strayed from Ms. Rose's version.

Someone else wrote, "I would think no longer working with people because they don't see oppression as the end goal would be a not very Restorative Action. Oppression much like privilege is a topic scary to many and very misunderstood even by some RJ folks."

Who comprises the "many"? Oppression, much like privilege, is *not* a scary topic to my friends, White and of color. So, I ask, who makes up the RJ community, and am I truly a part of it? My own student Chris Mendez, who has facilitated dozens of Circles and discussed "white privilege" with his grandmother way before he heard it as a young adult, feels the urgency around having such a conversation. In Circle, he once noted, "We have the privilege to help those with privilege."

They zoom in on building healthy communities and reducing punitive disciplinary measures but steer clear of focusing on the history of racial exclusion in our country.

President Obama made racial disproportionality in school discipline a priority issue and ordered the Department of Justice to investigate and mandate school districts to lessen the amount of unnecessary suspensions.[5] Still, people taking on this charge sometimes do not use the moniker "restorative justice"; they opt for the more palatable "restorative discipline"—"RD." They zoom in on building healthy communities and reducing punitive disciplinary measures but steer clear of focusing on the history of racial exclusion in our country.

Multiple experts and practitioners have told me that they are uncomfortable with the term restorative "justice"—preferring the term "restorative discipline" instead. Yet this phrase puzzled some visitors from the restorative city of Wuanajato in New Zealand and prompted my mother-in-law to ask, "Is that like restorative spanking?"

Ms. Pickard and I purposely chose and welcome the term "justice." We believe restorative justice is a philosophy that can create space for us to dismantle systems of inequality, and this is how we practice restorative justice with our youth. To me, you cannot have restorative practices without referencing justice—you cannot refer to ethnic disproportionality without addressing how to dismantle inequality. Implementing Circles might reduce your in-school suspension rates, but, as youth practitioner Travis Medley once told me, "Restorative justice is not just about reducing suspensions."

Showing People Grace

A huge part of me flinches at the idea of even discussing this real-life experience. I sat on this draft for a year before finally deciding to put it out into the world. My thought was this: if Ms. Rose felt comfortable saying words to me that seemed inherently harmful, hierarchical, and racist, then I should feel comfortable putting those words back out into the real world to see if others could prevent this from happening again. But in addition to keeping people accountable, I also want to show grace. My relationship with Ms. Rose is far from repaired, and all I can do is learn from the experience and write about it to heal myself in some shape or form. My greater wish would be to have an empathy-rooted conversation with any of my former colleagues about the discomfort they feel when reflecting on their whiteness, but alas the relationships were not built enough for us to go that deep. But also, I have to show grace.

I was on a panel at the New Schools Venture Fund's 2017 Summit,[6] which the former Secretary of Education under President Obama, John King, moderated. During the summit, he said something obvious and wise. Just as we have to provide unconditional support to our youth, we have to not give up on adults. I write this chapter not simply to itemize microaggressions in the work on restorative justice—or at least not only to do that. The challenge I face is showing people grace, a phrase we constantly use at my current work environment, YES Prep Northbrook High School.

As far as RJ coordinators go, I'm probably one of the angriest RJ coordinators you will meet, and that is okay. My words and actions are not always restorative. As I grapple with trying to emulate peaceful mentors, such as Stephen Jackson in Chicago or Howard Zehr himself, who has posted ten beautiful ways to be restorative,[7] I am reminded of a phrase that Dr. Morris Jenkins said when he was a professor of criminal justice and social work at the University of Toledo. "Race is here. Racism is here. We have to deal with both, not only on the outside, but within our own movement as a people who are progressive."[8]

I'm probably one of the angriest RJ coordinators you will meet, and that is okay.

I cannot converse only with others who agree with me. And I have to contend with myself and my own need for self-care. Why do I react so often from a place of anger or self-righteousness? How can I not dismiss or give up on practitioners who are going to stay in the classroom for years and who are going to fiercely disagree with the notion that institutional racism even exists? Audre Lorde eloquently states this tension of being drained:

> Black and Third World people are expected to educate white people as to our humanity. Women are expected to educate men. Lesbians and gay men are expected to educate the heterosexual world. The oppressors maintain their position and evade their responsibility for their own actions. There is a constant drain of energy which might be better used in redefining ourselves and devising realistic scenarios for altering the present and constructing the future.[9]

The answer for me—and the answer for Ms. Pickard—was to unite forces and find a way to unapologetically promote our vision of restorative justice. From our experience, we knew instinctively it would appeal to people because we had had so many guests from the community wowed by what they saw in Circles. They always returned to us and said, "How can I do this in my school?" So we started our own business, hiring youth who had been apprenticed in the program. They co-facilitate sessions so that the people who attend our trainings can learn from the constituents and change agents—our young people.

Restoring Myself

Ultimately, I am grateful for the race-based conflicts that arose in our restorative justice program, however painful. Through this disintegration, something new has been created. Because of my skin color, my Indian heritage, or my sex, I have experienced the stories that emboldened me to embrace my stance on social justice, rather than stray or shy away from it. At age eleven, I cried daily under a tree when faced with microaggressions in my middle school in Toledo. Now at age forty, I celebrate these stories, because they planted my desire for a more just world. Those experiences are "the why" I teach in a high school: restorative justice has empowered me, restored myself, and nurtured my capacity to continue to appreciate the power of youth. My hope is that through being vocally committed to social justice, while at the same time showing grace to others, I can grow restorative practices in a manner that is genuine and fosters sustained multiracial coalitions. My other hope is that practitioners can live with discomfort in our discourses and still create bonds strong enough to sustain us when the need for reparations arises.

Ultimately, I am grateful for the race-based conflicts that arose in our restorative justice program, however painful. Through this disintegration, something new has been created.

DISCUSSION QUESTIONS

1. Can you foster relationships in multiracial coalitions? Explain. Do they allow for spaces to broach the topic of race and implicit and explicit biases?
2. Can you proactively create spaces in multiracial coalitions that are readily available when difficult conversations around race and other identity markers are necessary? How so?
3. How do you balance speaking up against injustice with not giving up on practitioners who (unwitting or not) engage in microaggressions?

ACTIVITIES

1. Whenever microaggressions do occur, reach out to other practitioners. Share experiences, feel heard, heal, and think through ways to respond to other practitioners when racial issues arise.
2. Journal about microaggressions as they arise and use these journal entries as case studies in professional development sessions on restorative justice to elicit conversation.
3. Collaborate with other practitioners of color and White allies to write about issues that impact our work, and publish articles in multiple arenas—academic and nonacademic—to further the field's understanding of our lived experiences.

RESOURCES

Readings

Holtham, Jeannette. *Taking Restorative Justice to Schools: A Doorway to Discipline.* Allen, TX: Del Hayes Press, 2009.

Vaandering, Dorothy. "A Faithful Compass: Rethinking the Term 'Restorative Justice' to Find Clarity." *Contemporary Justice Review* 14, no. 3 (2011): 307–28. DOI:10.1080/10282580.2011.589668.

Wadhwa, Anita. *Restorative Justice in Urban Schools: Disrupting the School-to-Prison Pipeline.* London: Routledge, an Imprint of the Taylor & Francis Group, 2017.

Websites

https://implicit.harvard.edu/implicit/takeatest.html
http://irjrd.org/
http://restorativeempower.wixsite.com/arey
www.restorativejustice.org
http://restorativejusticeontherise.org

NOTES

1. Joel Roberts, "High Court Considers Racial Diversity," *CBS News*, December 4, 2006, https://www.cbsnews.com/news/high-court-considers-racial-diversity/. The cases are *Parents Involved in Community Schools v. Seattle School District No. 1, 05-908*, and *Meredith v. Jefferson County Board of Education, 05-915*.
2. Derrick A. Bell, "Brown v. Board of Education and the Interest-Convergence Dilemma," *Harvard Law Review* 93, no. 3 (1980): 518, DOI:10.2307/1340546.
3. Names are pseudonyms.
4. Ta-Nehisi Coates, "The Case for Reparations," *The Atlantic*, June 2014, accessed April 28, 2018, https://www.theatlantic.com/magazine/archive/2014/06/the-case-for-reparations/361631/.

5. "ACLU Hails Obama Administration's Supportive School Discipline Initiative," *American Civil Liberties Union*, accessed April 28, 2018, https://www.aclu.org/news/aclu-hails-obama-administrations-supportive-school-discipline-initiative.
6. https://www.newschools.org/.
7. "10 Ways to Live Restoratively," *Zehr Institute for Restorative Justice* (blog), Harrisonburg, VA: Eastern Mennonite University, November 27, 2009, accessed April 28, 2018, https://emu.edu/now/restorative-justice/2009/11/27/10-ways-to-live-restoratively/.
8. Morris Jenkins, "Next Ooze," April 6, 2012, accessed April 28, 2018, https://nextooze.com/dr-morris-jenkins-on-restorative-justice-and-the-african-american-community/.
9. Audre Lorde, "Age, Race, Class and Sex: Women Redefining Difference," in *Sister Outsider: Essays and Speeches* (Freedom, CA: Crossing Press, 1984), 114.

PART III

POC Experiences of RJ/RP and Circle Work

What makes People of Color different from Whites in what we bring to the restorative work? Experience, community, and knowing structural oppression. No White person can fully know what it is like to be a Person of Color or an Indigenous person in a society steeped in white settler supremacy over centuries. No White settler experiences the multigenerational impact of catastrophic violence against us as peoples, violence that can erupt at any moment as we go about our daily lives. When relationships matter, as they do in restorative work, the solidarity of community born of lifelong experiences of racial and social harm makes mutual empathy around race a base-level bond. So, it is not a surprise that the restorative practitioners of color in this section bring a depth of experience with race in the restorative work that is distinct and instructive. Experience matters. Whites in the restorative justice movement have yet to value how our experiences as People of Color and Indigenous Peoples equip us to engage the restorative work in ways that White experiences do not. We feel what is at stake in our bones and not only for our own communities and peoples. We carry critical messages for the restorative justice movement and its transformative role in our societies, yet when we raise our voices, we are too often met with marginalizing, patronizing, and tokenizing responses. These *CRJ* authors will have none of this.

Chapter 10

Passing the Cup of Vulnerability: Offering Vulnerability as a Challenge to White Fragility through the Elements of Circle

Gilbert Salazar

As a restorative justice coach and strategist on the "RJ in Schools" team at the California Conference for Equality and Justice, an applied theater artist, and a playwright, I find my worlds are often integrated, particularly in the intimate, vulnerable, and playful space of restorative justice training. These training spaces are where I've been activated to put the best of myself into action, while inviting challenges for participants to share in story and give witness to each other. At times, this process—combined with restorative justice topics—sparks either discomfort or activation from participants, including what is now referred to as white fragility.

As a way to understand the experience of white fragility in these spaces, I have collected stories I have witnessed and stories that I asked for from female-identifying colleagues. These stories helped me create a short play about women of color sharing their experience with white fragility. The following excerpts from the play *Sippin'* unmask two central questions: How can Circle, with the elements of container[1] (as I explain on pp. 183–84) and witnessing shift the rupturing paradigms of whiteness that white fragility exposes? How can vulnerability and storytelling call forth accountability when whiteness is named and called in during training spaces, especially when feelings described as "discomfort" or "being unsafe" occur?

SCENE 1

Lights fade in on stage with four women of color seated at a table with separate sets of very fancy and dainty tea sets of which they are sipping from small delicate teacups. The women are wearing hoop earrings, bright clothes with cultural patterns and fabrics. Their hair is up in buns or in a natural state. They sit with legs open, some reclining. All very confident.

WOMAN 1
It tastes salty.

WOMAN 2
I'm not surprised.

WOMAN 3
Mine doesn't taste that way.

WOMAN 4
For real?

WOMAN 3
Yeah, it tastes bitter!

WOMAN 2
Mine is sour, but I'ma sip it anyways. Tu sabes.

WOMAN 3
The other day I was at work and we had done this activity. I was facilitating the training. It went fine, everyone participated, and then the next day when I went back to this school to facilitate the next part, this chick interrupts me and she stops and says to everybody, "Let's be sure to make sure that we make this a space for everyone, because although we were laughing and having a good time yesterday in the activity, I heard some people laughing at me, and I went home and I cried because I felt so unsafe in the space, so let's please remember, to be kind to each other." And everybody sat there, confused. Nobody said a damn thing. From the look on people's faces, it looked like they were wondering, what the hell is she talking about?

WOMAN 4
And what did you say?

WOMAN 3
I said, "Let's remember that what is safe for some, might not be safe for others."

WOMAN 2
What did you wanna say?

WOMAN 3
Nobody was laughing at you!

WOMEN laugh. WOMAN 3 takes a sip from her cup.

WOMAN 3
I mean, if in the game that I was facilitating, I heard people laughing at other people or going against building relationship, I would've called it out. But I swear I didn't hear any of that. I heard people having a good time and I heard what sounded like people joking with each other because they knew each other. I didn't hear anything that to me sounded like what she described. (Pause) I mean, I could have missed it, yes —

WOMAN 1
The problem was not your facilitation or maintenance of that space. The problem was—it wasn't all about her.

WOMEN make an affirming sound to agree to that statement and all collectively and at the same time reach for their cups to sip, then put cups down at the same time.

White fragility is a state in which even a minimum amount of racial stress becomes intolerable for Whites, triggering a range of defensive moves. These defensive moves are invoked to ease or detract from experiencing further racial stress. They can include the following patterns: outward display of emotions, such as anger, fear, guilt, and defensive behaviors, such as argumentation, silence, and leaving the stress-inducing situation.[2] On occasion, I have observed how whiteness has interrupted, impeded, or shifted the openness of storytelling, dialogue, or conversation during the work that my colleagues and I do.

A relationship-based paradigm centers the work we do with restorative justice in schools. Intentional relationship-building through dialogue and Circle practice facilitate how we meet and balance needs, both of individuals and of a community. Our work trains school staff in practices that identify these

---

I have observed how whiteness has interrupted, impeded, or shifted the openness of storytelling, dialogue, or conversation during the work that my colleagues and I do.

---

needs and show how to take tangible actions to meet them. Within a justice lens, our work models how to identify, expose, and dismantle biases and exclusionary practices that target youth of color and other marginalized youth. We recognize that, in public schools, these exclusionary practices and biases create the all-too-familiar school-to-prison pipeline. We know that restorative justice as a paradigm has Indigenous origins, so we do our best to honor and respect Indigenous frameworks, such as Ubuntu, "I am because you are" or "My humanity is tied to your humanity."

When I facilitate training spaces, my personal framework is that identities and stories are our greatest resources for teaching and learning. Identities shape our experiences, and the stories that rise from them give us narratives for understanding our relationships, both within ourselves and with others. My own life experiences, emerging from my own identities, have created the narratives that shape my expectations about safety, relationships, and communication. These narratives also shape how I engage with others, and they shape what conflict looks like for me and how I respond or engage when conflict arises.

When I facilitate training spaces, my personal framework is that identities and stories are our greatest resources for teaching and learning.

These narratives, which I believe to be true for me, become the paradigms or archetypes through which I center myself, and they move with me as I move through the world. When a narrative or schema comes into question, such as when its validity is challenged, conflict occurs: I experience a rupture in my understanding of this paradigm. As I've witnessed paradigm shifts in my own life and from others, something has to break, something has to unravel, for transformative motivations and actions to be released. A paradigm shift, then, is where we sit in the unlearning of paradigms—especially those paradigms that are damaging and harmful. This intersection between rupture and unlearning is where teaching adults about restorative practices and restorative justice can be both a painful and a rewarding process.

WOMAN 1
Alright—so since we're talking about work. Our office had this week-long training on trauma. Well, it was supposed to be a week, but it ended early. The facilitators showed us these images of trauma and then asked questions connecting the images to communities of color—who they themselves were not. They kept pushing us to talk about our own damn traumas!

WOMAN 2
Oh no.

WOMAN 1
Of course, nobody wanted to say anything to them, because . . . one called our intern—"articulate."

WOMAN 3
Ha!

WOMAN 2 shakes her head to the side.

WOMAN 1
One of them asked us to call her by the Spanish pronunciation of her name. She wasn't Latina!

WOMAN 2
Ay, no me diga!

WOMAN 1
Then the other one asked us to share out our personal traumas on a personal trauma mother fuckin' timeline without—hearing anything from them first!

WOMEN laugh.

WOMAN 1
And on the fourth day when we called her out on her shit and told her, "You're not getting what you're doing—you're creating trauma for us," do you know what she did?

WOMAN 3
What?

WOMAN 1
She stopped the conversation—

WOMEN 2, 3, and 4 quickly reach for their cups to sip as they utter sounds or shake their heads.

WOMAN 1
—she said, "This work is important to me because of my grandkids. I do this for their safety," and then she takes out a picture of her goddam grandkids and passed it around the damn circle.

WOMAN 2
So?

WOMAN 1
They were Black!

WOMEN 2, 3, AND 4
Oh!

WOMEN 2, 3, and 4 beat on the tabletop and move in their seats.

WOMEN 1
Then some Black folks get up to leave, right? And she stops them and says, "I want you to listen to me" and starts crying about how she's worried about her grandkids.

WOMAN 1 reaches for her tea pot, all other women reach for theirs and pour more tea into their cups. After they pour, they take long sips and make slurping noises as they drink.

When I draw on the roots of restorative justice to examine this White female trainer's response and how the entire office experienced it, I observe that:

Needs: Her unmet needs in that moment were understanding, clarity, wanting to be heard, and wanting to be seen.

Harms: She felt those needs were not being met, and she felt personally attacked, so she offered a personal story and shared an identity of hers. Unfortunately, this crucial moment was the only time she did so during the training.

Accountability/Obligations: She held herself accountable only to herself in her work. Starting earlier in the week when a White ally and colleague asked us if she could speak to the trainer about the harm she was doing, she responded out of threat and stuck to her identity as a facilitator of trauma work within her concept of justice. Her response to the unraveling was to move into a place of vulnerability, offering her home life and her identity as a grandmother to honor herself. In doing so, she negated our unmet needs of being heard, listened to, treated fairly, and being visible—of having our harms addressed. Fueling these unmet needs that became more harm for us, she offered up one of the worst possible trespasses for folks of color in a container of space: she placed her own White, perceived connection to identity and oppression at the center of the activation. By referencing her grandchildren, she blocked our needs. She effectively denied and neglected these needs, while offering no accountability for her previous actions that had created a container of harm for us.

We were further harmed by being forced into a container of listening, in the practice of Circle, as she passed the picture of her grandchildren around the Circle. When she positioned her vulnerability over the vulnerability of those who had expressed the impact of her actions, she expected us to be held accountable to her. Instead of the restorative practice of listening or asking open-ended questions, i.e., "restorative questions," she used her grandchildren's identity and her relationship with them to justify her work—as if this reverse restorative practice would negate the impact she had initially created. She avoided taking accountability for her actions. Her obligation was to protect herself and leave town, while the rest of us were left to create a container of resiliency and preservation and to do that work for ourselves.

To examine further how white fragility showed up in the space she created for us, I'll break down how it functioned. This trainer invoked the Privileged Identity Exploration (PIE) model. The PIE model traces how "social justice issues" or "difficult dialogues" often activate privileged folks.[3] Its eight behaviors offer a conceptual framework that White folks can assume when they experience cognitive dissonance, which is often brought on by a new awareness about self and other(s).[4] The PIE model also identifies six assumptions that can help White people explore their privileged identities.[5]

The PIE model is useful for analyzing White women's tears when women of color bring up race in a discussion.[6] The PIE model is a tool not only to help educators anticipate defensive behaviors but also to prevent conversations from being derailed. By identifying these behaviors, educators can then strategize how to prevent conversations from being hijacked.[7] With the PIE framework in mind, the behaviors I observed from the trainer include:

> *Rationalization:* An individual presents an alternative reason that does not require him or her to explore the roots of an injustice in more depth.[8] The trainer/facilitator chose to focus on her grandchildren as the reasons for her actions as a facilitator and not to explore what we were bringing to her as our harm and the impact of her actions.
>
> *False Envy:* False envy is a common defense tool. It positions the person with white privilege not only as someone who understands difference across race but also as someone who transcends it, because she has positive relationships with POC.[9] When this trainer revealed that she was a grandmother of Black grandchildren, she attempted to insert herself into the narrative that mostly POC and White allies were telling her about understanding harms and oppressions towards POC.
>
> *Benevolence:* This behavior displays an overall sensitive attitude based on a charitable act. However, as the PIE model explains, it serves as "a defense tool that shifts the conversation to make the person with privilege and her good intentions the central focus of the discussion, further privileging her identity."[10]

"Safety" proved a key word that the trainer used to defend her rationalization of why she does this work: she did it for her grandchildren's safety. She positioned her commitment to them and her relationship with them as the central focus of the conversation. Her rationalization cemented her stance in our physical circle as the most important thing. Because her grandchildren were Black, she attempted to convey the message: "I know what I'm talking about, and you need to listen."[11]

The trainer further framed the narrative of White-woman helplessness within the narrative of White-woman goodness—making her someone deserving of and entitled to sympathy. In "When White Women Cry," Mamta Motwani Accapadi, university administrator of student affairs, deconstructs these White-serving narratives: "This powerlessness informs the nature of White womenhood."[12] "Our societal norms inform us that crying indicates helplessness, which triggers automatic sympathy for the White woman."[13]

Here, I want to lean into the curiosity of crying: it may be a sign not of helplessness but of paradigm rupture. Mario Martinez described Thomas Kuhn's analysis of the stages of paradigm shifts in scientific beliefs. These stages are threefold: disdain, then denial, followed by acceptance.[14] In my experiences with adults in learning spaces, I have witnessed that, when a new learning awareness occurs, it often challenges maintained belief systems, triggering the stages of denial, rupture, and acceptance. If I think of denial as a behavior of "new awareness," crying could be a response that a White person—or in these stories, White women—hold on to once their framework is challenged. In other words, when their white-privilege framework is challenged, their responses reveal that these trainers have not done the hard work of really examining themselves. In both scenarios, these White women were educators, both in communities of color, and both in the job and position of holding or creating spaces or "containers" of learning. Yet, when they were called in to such a container of learning to examine their own actions and impacts, their responses indicated a paradigm shift underway, leading to a response of vulnerability through crying.

When White women weaponize their tears in these spaces, they impact participants, particularly participants of color, in at least four dangerous ways:

1. Halting of space and halting of dialogue
2. Unilaterally forcing all participants to stay and listen—or conveying the feeling that we should do so
3. Neither seeking nor waiting to receive choice or consent before releasing their vulnerability on us
4. Halting and forcing of witness: those witnessing in this forced container have the perception that they need to (or are expected to) respond to comfort the White women

In these incidents, the White women neither showed nor expressed accountability for their behaviors and their impact. This can make POC want to sip on White tears.

How do we uphold accountability without comforting? Is there something more we need to understand about whiteness when it shows up this way in our training and restorative spaces?[15] White fragility is not weakness. On the contrary, it is a performance of invulnerability. As I understand it, as performance, white fragility attempts to use a mask of vulnerability. Sherry K. Watt, professor of higher education and student affairs, explores this defensive response in "Difficult Dialogues, Privilege and Social Justice: "White people actively perform fragility and continue to perform it in a way that consolidates white narcissism and white arrogance—signs of power and privilege, not weakness."[16] "These performances are defenses on display to protect the ego when one has a provoking experience; especially when an experience puts one's concept of the self into question."[17] Fragility is not a reaction or response to feeling unsafe, but a feeling of discomfort when privilege, power, and status are called into question and critiqued. This performance of invulnerability under a mask of vulnerability attempts to create aims to save face; to retain the schema of accepted power; and to prove oneself emotionally impenetrable by others' narratives.

When the mask is noticed and called into question or observation, a stage of rupture ensues, which is extremely uncomfortable and painful. When something is uncomfortable, many of us are inclined to retreat and back away. Or we react through defensive behaviors that create in us movement, which gives us the ability to back away. However, moving toward rather than away from discomfort can create greater change. This paradigm rupture or shift is needed for the justice work to seed, as well as for authentic relationship-building to root.

Yet carefully preserved and maintained narratives of dominance and power—maintained by gloved hands, primed into delicate, flowering, clinging vines, and woven into garden tresses—can make it hard to see native plants and trees being choked. Discomfort and change are hard, and few people want to remove what may look like delicate flowers. "White fragility is a stance that enables one to ignore those aspects of existence that are inconvenient, disadvantageous, or uncomfortable for us.... As fragile, we cannot be affected by what might unsettle us. Like invulnerability, white fragility is about closure to a certain understanding of our relations with others as well as closure to

---

Fragility is not a reaction or response to feeling unsafe, but a feeling of discomfort when privilege, power, and status are called into question and critiqued.

---

certain features of ourselves."[18] Whereas vulnerability can mean openness and willingness to listen or be heard, invulnerability can mean closure to growth.[19]

I tell adults in training that extracting the root of restorative justice, accountability, or obligation is restorative practice's most dirty work during dialogue and sharing. At the heart of it—and what adults, regardless of race, often have trouble understanding—is that holding a mirror to ourselves is a great tool for working through a troubling conversation with a young person or colleague. Bringing your own self and your own story is a tool to challenge invulnerability. So at the heart center of restorative practices—at the core of its impact and effectiveness—is vulnerability and the responsibility we have to be vulnerable.

At the heart of it—and what adults, regardless of race, often have trouble understanding—is that holding a mirror to ourselves is a great tool for working through a troubling conversation with a young person or colleague.

By contrast, the dominant narrative across patriarchy, sexism, white supremacy, heteronormativity, and other narratives of power internalize vulnerability as a deficit, as weakness. This dominant narrative is not the restorative paradigm or mindset of vulnerability. Instead, the restorative paradigm views vulnerability as a strength, as an asset, and as a necessity. For many colleagues, when we see a person cry in Circle, we don't run to a Kleenex box and place it in the person's lap; instead, we sit and witness that person in their moment of vulnerability in what they are allowing us to see. For many of us, it is a moment of strength, not to be wiped away, but one in which my role is to witness you. In this moment of your healing and experience, my role is to give witness.

Conditions are ripe for giving witness, I have found, when I have been either prepared or prepared to be unprepared, when I am completely open, when I am most vulnerable, even when I have been least ready with little sleep, little information of who was expected, or no idea how many would show up, when I am anticipating a fight and my adrenaline has surged, or when I am afraid of what heavy emotions might come up in a question. Being in the moment is when a community-building Circle provides the greatest gifts for its participants. I have witnessed this action whether the participants were young students, campus aides from the community unsure of why they were in this space, teacher leaders just beginning their careers, or veterans—seasoned administrators and survivors of school systems and school districts. Willing or hesitant, they all recognized Circle as a space to be vulnerable. In all of these Circles, I recognize a presence and energies of something greater than any of us. I also recognize a container that had been created to offer an opportunity for witnessing.

I use the term "container" as a carry-over from having worked in ritual spaces of theater, classrooms, workshops, and on the floor of Cabin 5.[20] In all of these spaces, the container is the same: a physical space where participants build from each other and become accountable to each other's growth and experience. To create a container, a facilitator is responsible for initiating the building of this space and setting expectations in ways that participants, including the facilitator, will be accountable to the shared space. The facilitator leads the group in creating norms or agreements for what the space will look like and how it could feel. The participants decide what language, what gestures, and what tone support the work to be done as well as what the space's physicality should be. When the facilitator intentionally pauses to share and reflect on the objective or meaning for the gathering—either as it is happening or afterward—the container comes into being as another body. Participants listen and hold the container to listen to each other. Like a deep conscious breath, the container actually grows and expands as a collective. When this deep listening and receiving happens, some call it magic, some call it spirit, while others may call it something else. On a "basic" level, I call it witnessing.

To be ready to model witnessing, the Circle keeper needs to meet conditions within. In my own experience, I bring myself completely, fully, at my best in that moment in what I can offer in listening and receiving. I need to be available as a witness and willing to disturb my own sense of self.[21] I also need to be willing to be exposed and have something at stake.[22] In other words, I must be ready and willing to be accountable to people with whom I am in space at this moment. In Circle, the container is a space for witnessing, for risk-taking. Circle can hold the possibility for needs to be addressed and, if possible, met, and it can generate a desire to listen to the other. Other necessary elements in the container are permission and consent. No one should be forced to witness other people in ways that go against the work or that harm the individual, the group, or the container. The container is a separate but connected entity—a liminal space where folks should consent to enter willingly.

Other necessary elements in the container are permission and consent. No one should be forced to witness other people in ways that go against the work or that harm the individual, the group, or the container.

When these conditions are structured or are the result of what is—or seems like—chaos, I can attest that what can erupt within the container are stories. Storytelling is the thread that ties witnessing to the container. Stories emerge with intentional listening and create the roles of storyteller and listener or receiver. Relationships are built on listening and stories. How we begin to become accountable comes from sharing our stories, as stories play a central role in learning about each other. Because restorative practices can create containers for both witnessing and stories, folks can be invited into the practice of vulnerability. These are the "conditions necessary for transformation" that Barbara Applebaum, professor of cultural foundations of education, writes of.[23] We can seed accountability amongst White folks by challenging discomfort into witnessing—both of self and of the other.

Taking ownership for how a choice has harmed someone is a difficult truth to accept. It requires some action for amends. In the attempt to make amends and to make things right, one has to remove ego's several masks and invulnerability to sip on one's own accountability. Harmful choices and behaviors can have or leave a bitter taste.

One of the most amazing experiences I've had of late was as a student in a plant medicine class called Hood Herbalism. In one of our first classes, we learned about teas and the healing properties of herbs, flowers, and roots. Burdock has one of the deepest root growths, growing several feet into the earth. It is rich in many minerals and can be taken for a variety of ailments. When its root is made into a tea, it clears out toxins from the blood, but it has a very bitter flavor. Bitter is not a preferred flavor. Chemically and culturally, we are programmed to want to drink what is sweet. But in order to practice accountability, much like burdock root, we must dig in, uncover, chop up, steep, and finally sip the bitter flavor. For white accountability to exist, White folks have to sip their own tears.

We can seed accountability amongst White folks by challenging discomfort into witnessing—both of self and of the other.

In the winter of early 2017, Murphy Robinson, a White woman, spent six weeks with the Water Protectors at the Očhéthi Šakówiŋ Oyáte camp, near the Standing Rock reservation, to support the Indigenous defense of the Missouri River from the Dakota Access Pipeline, the #NODAPL resistance. Of the sixteen people she camped with, over half were Indigenous. Of her Očhéthi Šakówiŋ experience, she writes, "Nearly daily, I would receive feedback about my unconscious acts of racism: using a phrase with derogatory roots, displaying impatience that betrayed my sense of entitlement to any space I was in, making a joke about Spirit Animals that made light of the sacred traditions of Lakȟóta culture."[24] Indigenous people expected that they would give this feedback to the non-Indigenous allies who joined them.

In the following quote, Robinson describes the decolonization framework that White allies were given:

> One of the most impactful concepts taught in the orientation was this: When an Indigenous person corrects you, the proper response is gratitude. Rather than being offended or defensive, recognize that it is a

huge gift and act of trust for someone to take the time to tell you how to do something properly in our culture. When you react with resistance and protest, you dishonor and reject that gift. Just say thank you and change your behavior, that is all that is required.[25]

I believe that restorative justice, through restorative practices, can offer whiteness an opportunity to taste itself, an opportunity to taste accountability. Murphy Robinson witnessed this impact on white fragility through five experiences, which the Indigenous Water Protectors intentionally created:

1. Bring people together over a common cause greater than themselves
2. Create a community where White people are in the minority
3. Create a standard of People of Color being in leadership
4. Give everyone a basic orientation to how privilege works and why we are trying to dismantle it
5. Create a norm of prayer, ceremony, offerings, and gratitude[26]

When I design a new agenda for a group of adults, especially if I sense they may show resistance, I craft the agenda with the image of weaving a container so tight that it can hold water. Then, when someone goes to find a hole (defensiveness, avoidance, etc.), the container is so tightly woven that no hole exists. Thus, the truth of relationships is the container's woven material. Tending relationships is a cause greater than individual selves, and relationships know no resistance, not at least to their authentic truth. Relationships are a necessity for all of us. A cranky person who has remained at a school site only to make it to retirement, having felt burnt out long ago, might just say, "I don't need to be in a relationship with anyone!" My response—one I hope I never have to use—is, "Tell me a story about your relationship with yourself, or a pet, or a favorite plant or location on this earth." The desire, the effort, and the necessity of being in mutually positive relationships are such expansive experiences; they are connected to Robinson's experience of dismantling her white fragility mentioned above.

In many of the schools our team serves, White adults are in the minority, both in the student body and among faculty. At many sites, administrators of color are also in the majority; White administrators have the experience of being a minority. Our RJ in Schools team comprises mostly men and women

Tending relationships is a cause greater than individual selves, and relationships know no resistance, not at least to their authentic truth. Relationships are a necessity for all of us.

of color. We weave in the second and third experiences that dismantle white fragility.

The fourth experience—and perhaps the most challenging one—that Robinson describes is discussing privilege. But the fifth experience is where restorative practices give the greatest offering within a container for witnessing: vulnerability through questions to elicit story. Circle and restorative dialogue offer a "secular" experience of ceremony, in which soul and spirit are centralized. The word "container" comes from the Greek, *temenos*, meaning a sacred space and time specially prepared and set apart in order to reconnect with ancient energies.[27] I don't often name or label Circle as ritual with folks, especially not at the beginning of this work. But once having experienced Circle, most groups share an unspoken understanding that our Circle experience felt sacred, in community, and one of "bringing us back to ourselves."

Heart work
courage
allowing
submitting
risk
exposure
allowing others to see you
allowing you to be exposed, in honest form,
in authentic self,
sitting in story

I am often surprised to hear White participants in Circle with mostly colleagues of color say, "I don't have culture." But then there is a story of picking blueberries with a grandmother outside the house to make pancakes, and I think, "That doesn't sound that different from picking figs or pomegranates with my grandmother." As a Chicano, male-identified, cisgender person, I sometimes forget amongst my witnessing of oppression—my active work in recognizing moments of when to be an ally and when not to be—that systems of racism also impact White people, though not to the same degree as non-White folks. But in that moment when Whites say "I don't have culture" and then give a story about being with an elder or with nature, I see racism's impact on them.

Skillful questions spur us to share our stories. Practitioners of RJ know very well the power of a question perhaps not to disrupt but certainly to disturb and how a question creates an opportunity to give story. To speak without statement or to speak forcibly of feeling or to be challenged to create a defense is the opposite of what a solid question can do. Questions can contain the permission for a person to crack a seed and tell a story. It's in the sweetness of telling others who we are that I've seen folks expose themselves. They show up with who they are (the self-image), what they come with (the baggage), and where they come from (the journey). It isn't just the darker stories that we sip from but also the sweet stories that reveal lessons and meanings.

The practice of a question within Circle invites adults who are professionals—overworked, overstimulated, overexposed to stress, all of which shuts down the channels of vulnerability—to open themselves. Restorative practices create opportunities for loosening, sharing, or increasing the desire and motivation to want to share just by listening to someone else. Stories are inherent in us, but often adults—in particular, adults who work hard to maintain invulnerability and to maintain dominant narratives of identities—can forget their stories. So we attempt to bring them back to those stories, to bring them back to themselves. We invite them to remember, we activate them from within, and then we challenge them to speak.

I was once at a high school facilitating a "Games and Activities for Circle Preparedness" training with a small group of mostly male and mostly White staff. In this training, which lasted about two hours, I was facilitating games for teachers to learn and process so that they could facilitate them in their classes with youth. After each game, I would ask process questions to help the group reflect on their experience—I would do this protocol in any Circle training. But I was experiencing constant struggles in bringing the group back. Even through the elements of play and curiosity, I had to use strategies and techniques I use with youth for group management. Because of constant side conversations and laughter, they conveyed that they were not taking this training seriously, and I observed some teachers, the few women in the space, being silenced. All of this was activating for me, and as I attempted to check my own activations and self, the behavior seemed to heighten. All this was also contrasting with my need to be taken seriously and for the work to be taken seriously. Something had to be done to regulate them and myself.

So, I went to my golden question, I stopped and asked:

> "When you were younger, was there an adult that you felt you were in a positive relationship with? What did that person look like? What did that person sound like? Bring that person into the room with you right now. Some of us may not have had such a person when we were younger. That's alright, take a breath for you right now . . . and make one up. What would you have liked that person to look like or to sound like, so that you felt you would be in a positive relationship? Bring this person, real or imaginary, into this space. Think about what they did with you or what they said to you that made you feel as if you

A practice like Circle with its listening allows us to drink from a cup that we may have forgotten and then to sit in or own our vulnerability as we pass the cup, so that others may know who we are.

were in a positive relationship with them. In a moment, I'm going to ask what value or what quality they offered you or gave you."

The room shifted. The people whom they were remembering, whether on this earth or not, were being brought into the room. The energy from this question and the calling in of these loved ones are always powerful, but I had never had a room of mostly White men when I used this exercise. To my surprise, many of these men were in a quiet place. I could see tears and a softening of energy, an unmasking happening. I brought us back, and they shared those qualities and gifts. Then I continued on with the training of playing games, as all of us were now ready and focused. We had been brought together by a created understanding of an emotional center point, one that connected us back to our own narratives and gave us the opportunity to name something of value from that person or story.

I had a similar experience to this Circle exercise during the plant medicine class. On the same night that I tasted burdock tea, I also tasted lemon balm tea. Before taking the class, I had wanted to know which tea my abuela, my grandmother, had given me as a child for stomach pain. As one cup was being passed around a Circle for me to taste, I sipped it and immediately, my eyes opened, and I felt an awakening, a re-knowing. I saw leaves being dropped by my small hands into boiling water. I heard the sizzle of those leaves. I heard the sound of my tiny hands after someone had loosened the metal lid, pressing my palms down to unscrew the lid of the large jar that once held mayonnaise and now had the lemon balm leaves. I was trying to open the jar to pull them out. Instantly, I heard the plant say, "You know me, here I am." With one sip, I re-entered an old relationship with lemon balm tea.

The container of a Circle or of a restorative conversation is one where participants can sip on their own stories and pass cups among others to sip as well. The lemon balm brought me back into relationship and to the responsibility to use it. A practice like Circle with its listening allows us to drink from a cup that we may have forgotten and then to sit in or own our vulnerability as we pass the cup, so that others may know who we are.

DISCUSSION QUESTIONS

1. Have I checked in with the colleagues with whom I'm training about their activations and how I can support them?
2. What are examples in my life where a paradigm of mine was ruptured?
3. What are my own stories that connect me to a deeper sense of self and community?

ACTIVITIES

1. Imagine when you were younger, think about an adult you felt in a positive relationship with. Explain or describe what value or quality that person offered you.
2. Describe a favorite game or place you went for play when you were younger. Share why the game or place was a favorite.
3. When you are at your most stressed, imagine what your younger self would say to you. Explain why this activity is important or valuable.

RESOURCES

Accapadi, Mamta Motwani. "When White Women Cry: How White Women's Tears Oppress Women of Color." *The College Student Affairs Journal* 26, no. 2 (Spring 2007): 209.

DiAngelo, Robin. *White Fragility: Why It's So Hard for White People to Talk About Racism.* Boston: Beacon Press, 2018.

Robinson, Murphy. "Moving Beyond White Fragility: Lessons from Standing Rock." *Communities, Class, Race, and Privilege Magazine*, no. 178 (Spring 2018).

NOTES

1. On the notion of Circle as a container, see Kay Pranis, *The Little Book of Circle Processes: A New/Old Approach to Peacemaking* (Intercourse, PA: Good Books, 2005), 9.
2. Robin DiAngelo, "White Fragility," *International Journal of Critical Pedagogy* 3, no. 3 (2011): 54. See also Robin DiAngelo, *White Fragility: Why It's So Hard for White People to Talk about Racism* (Boston: Beacon Press, 2018).
3. "A difficult dialogue is a verbal or written exchange of ideas or opinions between citizens within a community that centers on an awakening of potentially conflicting views or beliefs or values about social justice issues (such as racism, sexism, ableism, heterosexism/homophobia)." From Sherry K. Watt, "Difficult Dialogues, Privilege and Social Justice: Uses of the Privileged Identity Exploration (PIE) Model in Student Affairs Practice," *The College Student Affairs Journal* 26, no. 2 (Spring 2007): 116.

4. Ibid., 118.
5. Ibid., 119. Here are the six assumptions about PIE: (1) The exploration of privileged identity is an ongoing socialization process. (2) There is no ultimate level of consciousness that can be reached regarding one's privileged identity. (3) Engaging in difficult dialogue is a necessary part of unlearning social oppression (i.e., racism, sexism/heterosexism/homophobia, and ableism). (4) Defense modes are normal human reactions to the uncertainty that one feels when exploring their privileged identities in more depth. (5) Defense modes are expressed in identifiable behaviors. (6) Expressions of defense modes may vary by situation.
6. See also Mamta Motwani Accapadi, "When White Women Cry: How White Women's Tears Oppress Women of Color," *The College Student Affairs Journal* 26, no. 2 (Spring 2007): 209.
7. Watt, "Difficult Dialogues," 118.
8. Ibid., 120.
9. Accapadi, "When White Women Cry," 212.
10. Ibid., 213.
11. Watt, "Difficult Dialogues," 120–22. Other behaviors in the PIE model are denial, deflection, intellectualization, and minimization.
12. Accapadi, "When White Women Cry," 209.
13. Ibid., 209.
14. Mario Martinez, "The Mind and Body Code: How the Mind Wounds and Heals the Body," *Sounds True* (compact disc), May 2009, session 1.
15. In numerous incidents, I've witnessed whiteness to be more damaging and more discrete with female-identified colleagues. As a male-identified individual, when co-piloting a training space with a female-identified colleague, I've wanted to intervene but have been confused about what my role should be in the intervention. Intervening without my co-pilot's consent just doubles up the hegemonic system of patriarchy against my colleague, who is experiencing white supremacy in this moment. What I've learned is to ask my co-pilot beforehand during our prep work: What are your activations? What behaviors or attitudes might activate you in this training? What support do you need from me? Or to offer her, "Let me know by throwing me a sign or a look to know if you need me to step in." In the first incident described by Woman 3, my colleague, Jenny, handled it and didn't want anyone to step in. It took this incident for me to discover that I needed to ask her what support she wanted in the future.
16. Barbara Applebaum, "Comforting Discomfort as Complicity: White Fragility and the Pursuit of Invulnerability," *Hypatia* 32, no. 4 (Fall 2017): 868.
17. Watt, "Difficult Dialogues," 118.
18. Applebaum, "Comforting Discomfort as Complicity," 871.
19. Ibid., 870.
20. Cabin 5: I was a camp counselor while serving with the National Civilian Community Corps at a YMCA camp, having never been to camp. I found myself sitting on the floor late one night at camp soothing young boys afraid of the Lizard man. They were told he would watch for them if they left the cabin—a tactic that

harmed young boys who had experienced whatever trauma in their communities in North Charleston. What soothed us and created culture was that each night, we would share stories about our day and how we showed the values of camp to each other and to ourselves. These were my first Circles.

21. Julie Salverson, "Witnessing Subjects," in *A Boal Companion*, ed. Jan Cohen-Cruz and Mady Schutzman (New York: Routledge, 2006), 150.
22. Ibid., 146.
23. Applebaum, "Comforting Discomfort as Complicity," 863.
24. Murphy Robinson, "Moving Beyond White Fragility: Lessons from Standing Rock," *Communities, Class, Race, and Privilege Magazine*, no. 178 (Spring 2018).
25. Ibid.
26. Ibid.
27. Julie Salverson, "Performing Emergency," *Theatre Topics* 6, no. 2 (September 1996): 185.

Chapter 11

In My Rightful Place

Shameeka Mattis

When I reflect on restorative practices, I am transported to a serene place. In this place, I feel the strength and wisdom of my people and our ancestors, before we were stripped from or robbed of our lands as Africans and Indigenous Peoples. Because colonization and racism were imposed on us, we were then made to hate ourselves and destroy each other. I feel our fortitude and resilience in this present moment, generations later with a lifetime ahead of us.

The Safety of POC Circles for POC

For a decade, I have been blessed to serve as a restorative Circle facilitator within mostly Black and Latinx communities—much of what I will center on in this chapter. As a Black queer woman in restorative work, I am humbled and filled with gratitude. Even when in Circles with White people, I am still drawn to communities of color, because I am reminded that we have always had the tools to manage conflict effectively, including systemic oppression. Though race is a social—albeit tyrannical—construct that must be undone through the practice of restorative justice, White people as participants, not necessarily as facilitators, can learn to honor People of Color and humble themselves by accounting for and committing less harm.

In any case, to assist in, and bear witness to, naming and then the releasing pain, shame, and rage is an honor. Yet this assistance is also no small feat, as it requires me to be accountable—despite living in a country that is rarely accountable to me as a Black woman—before I can even think to utter that word to someone else. Being entrusted with convening my community in order for us to delve into trauma without certainty of the outcome requires self-care. I take care of myself, so that I can be a steward for others. Writing this chapter is another way to show up, because this work we do together should not be kept secret. It is also a way to say "thank you" to the sisters and brothers who let me bear witness to their reconciliatory processes.

One of the many reasons I am grateful to participate in restorative practices is because it's actually a privilege and not in some unearned way. I am fortunate to commune with People of Color on paths to healing and reconciliation, and these paths bring me closer to my own healing. With this privilege comes the responsibility of walking the talk, which is also requisite for my self-care. My identity as a Black queer woman (who doesn't always present as cis) does not exempt me from the restorative practices work. The work actually implores me to embrace my identity fully, as someone who lives on society's margins and therefore has to work through daily anguish to be present and whole. Similarly, my Blackness does not automatically qualify me for the role of facilitator, nor have the Circles I've been in made me an expert.

My Blackness does not automatically qualify me for the role of facilitator, nor have the Circles I've been in made me an expert.

Don't get me wrong: in Circles of color, I think that POCs as restorative justice practitioners are more effective than White people in the same role. For example, POC feel inherent safety and mutuality within Circles, which is due to POC's shared experiences with various forms of oppression.

Our spirituality as POC is also interconnected and is not voyeuristic or exploitative. White allies can be reliable, but this requires lots more unpacking over a period of time, and POC often have to second-guess what's operating in the room, especially if there's a hard moment concerning White allies. The truth and connection afforded me as a woman of color still does not grant me automatic access to my people in this way. As a facilitator, I still need permission from those directly impacted and from those who have the most to lose if I mess up. Humility is required for service in the restorative practice, and we must live this understanding in all areas to guide others through. Otherwise, we are merely spectators or frauds, and the power of true transformation will be lost on us. We can also cause great harm when we do not acknowledge how delicate relationships become when restorative justice or practices makes us vulnerable.

Facilitators as Servants to the People

As facilitators, we must first understand and trust restorative justice processes before we can ask others to go through it. This rootedness in the practice ensures that we contribute to a safe space. I am less likely to be opportunistic and abusive of my power if I, too, am steeped in restorative practices in my daily life, which includes my daily work life, accounting for my actions, and making amends. In safe communal spaces, we should ask ourselves the following:

- What am I doing to combat oppression in ways that also nurture my spirit and affirm my power?

- Who am I accountable to and why? How do I show up to them?
- Where do I feel powerless? How does that powerlessness impact my community?
- Where do I have to make amends?
- Where is whiteness overpowering my existence or co-opting my cultural experience?

After all, I'm a servant to, not a master of, my people and this ancestral process. That has to be felt from start to finish. I yield to the power of my people in the process. First and foremost, the process is theirs, because the experience is theirs. The process is mine as well only if I have some skin in the game. A critical incident or series of hurtful events, like the robberies and assaults I have helped to address, is what typically brings folks into the restorative practice. Restorative practices have also been used to reset or reconnect the community barometer by making space for intentions as a collective—embracing someone, sharing stories, and honoring the past.

Challenges: Control Issues and the Court System

Because I have worked through a court-based initiative with People of Color in cases of physical violence, I have had to live my life in restorative practice. This life-work should not lend itself to self-congratulation, nor did I go around fishing for credit or pats on the back. No, the stakes in restorative practice are too high to engage in self-adulation; instead, I had to find a way to level the playing field for all participants, so they were heard and seen by each other, including the court system we were all struggling through. I wasn't always conscious of this deeper purpose around restorative practice, though. Thankfully, I had the benefit of working within community for longer periods of time, which meant I have been shown my missteps. As I relinquished my control issues and returned to my purpose, I remembered my role as a servant to my people.

Giving up control has not meant being passive or too accommodating. For example, I did not insult anyone's intelligence by downplaying my skill as a facilitator. And, because of the court-based circumstances, I didn't act as if I weren't responsible to the court to at least report that a restorative practice had occurred and produced resolutions. I did not lie about my power in that

No, the stakes in restorative practice are too high to engage in self-adulation; instead, I had to find a way to level the playing field for all participants, so they were heard and seen by each other, including the court system we were all struggling through.

arrangement or about my role as gatekeeper. I maintained confidentiality, so the courts weren't privy to Circle questions and actual processes. As a balancer and servant, I shared power by asking people who were preparing for Circles what they needed, how they wanted to be protected in the space, what they hoped to gain, who they wanted to accompany them, and anything they were willing to leave behind. I also shared with them every step that the Circle process would entail, so that they could interrogate it and me and know in advance what to expect. This practice not only created buy-in but also most certainly supported their agency. It also created a way to opt out, for those who desired. Conversely, in too many restorative practice spaces, POC have been told how to exist. I am, as a conscious choice, not for replicating that abuse.

From Hierarchical Thinking to Creating Space within Diverse Communities of Color

Though it seems obvious, it is important to note that communities of color are not monolithic. As non-White peoples, we are certainly marginalized with respect to white supremacy, albeit systemically and universally to the point that it can feel counterproductive to differentiate our experiences. We instead focus on uniting, so that we can end this vicious caste system racially, socially, economically, and politically. However, as a woman of color, I, too—so that I do not discount anyone—have had to learn to acknowledge, understand, and appreciate the myriad of POC cultures and systemic barriers. Not to discount others means that I am always learning. I am also mindful not to engage in "oppression Olympics" with other POC—the urge to position my Black American or Caribbean story over that of my Native or Filipino sisters and brothers. I am able to manage this one-up oppression, while still recognizing and calling out anti-Black and other anti-POC sentiments and practices in communities of color.

Though it seems obvious, it is important to note that communities of color are not monolithic.

Internalized oppression is one of the master's—i.e. White—tools, and I'm conscious of how it can pit us against each other. Internalized inferiority via white supremacy asserts that I am of lesser value than White people in all cases. If I believe this power hijack, then I am compelled to also believe that I must be better than someone else, and if I'm not supposed to be superior to Whites, then it must be other POC, right? This logic or framework is also where I check the model minority who believes they are exceptional to their race or ethnic group. This exceptionalism, which is a White American attribute, could not be further from the truth. But so much conflict within communities of color is bred and fueled by this very toxin. It posits that some of us "make it" because we are the exception to the rule and therefore leave the rest of our brother and sisters of color behind.

Hence, being accountable as a woman of color means that I have to know we are not the same and yet also know that there is no hierarchy among us. Audre Lorde said it best, "Difference must be . . . seen as a fund of necessary polarities between which our creativity can spark like a dialectic."[1] Lorde's quote helps me in restorative practices to feel true power—power with instead of power over—and to regard stakeholders in the process as equal, capable beings. Furthermore, it means that I will not view myself or the communities of color I serve as inherently marginal, despite how we are treated and labeled systemically.

Similar to the monolithic fallacy, succumbing to this myth of inherent marginalization already taints the process and offers my people a disservice that can be detrimental. However, being critical in this way also means I get to make space for everyone's uniqueness and beauty in the room. It keeps my language open and inviting, even when presenting guidelines and parameters about the direction of a speaking rotation and the use of talking sticks. Mostly it keeps me quiet. With my quietness, I listen with clarity to the perspectives of everyone around me and, like everyone else, I get taught something special and necessary to move us forward and in connection with one another.

Being Restorative Comes with Listening

This discussion on quietness brings me to the next point, which is an overt mainstay in restorative practices, but an underrated and underutilized one in mainstream society (especially when dealing with Whites in POC spaces or POC in White spaces): listening. Whether I am involved in Circle preparation sessions or an actual Circle, I genuinely listen to everyone. I have to listen for what is spoken and what is not, paying attention to someone's use of verbal and body language, and minding my own. To bear witness is oftentimes to shut our mouths and open our ears and hearts.

To bear witness is oftentimes to shut our mouths and open our ears and hearts.

This intentional listening is especially critical among communities of color. White society has historically disregarded and silenced us, and it does a great harm to our communities in times of crisis and pain to mute one another because we have internalized our silence. This learned silence should not be viewed as a lack of basic empathy toward each other but as lacking either the capacity or a willingness to make space for them. Intentional listening ensures that we have not heard it all before, nor will we. We should not begin to think that we can articulate someone's story or understand it better than they do. Our voices carry generational legacies as well as historical traumas and triumphs—because we literally contemplate life and death in our words. Who are we to shut down the voices of others?

As a facilitator, I've rarely been alarmed by anything I've experienced in restorative justice spaces. However, if I am operating from my ego or the socialized constraint of time, I might try and hasten someone to their point, or give them a wary eye if they muse about their homicidal thoughts as a response to being hurt or witnessing their loved ones being harmed. When not truly listening, I might insert my own agenda for the group and/or use my time with the talking stick to analyze someone else's thoughts that were spoken, instead of speaking from my own perspective. Mediation and some group therapy use this model, and it should not be confused with Circle facilitation. When failing to listen, I could also become repetitive and annoying, or worse, shun someone for their opinion, making it clear to the community that I'm not focused, responsible, or invested. In other words, when I display an unwillingness to listen, to make a space, the Circle becomes less restorative.

Listening to Silence

Many people in the Circles I've participated in have hit impasses temporarily because, even on a good day, reaching consensus is hard work. Our socialization in dealing with this impasse could lead me to become chatty and close my ears or only listen to others so that I can form my next point or rebuttal. Yet insight is not usually in what we are about to say, but instead in what we genuinely hear and how it transforms us from within. As facilitators in restorative practice, we must model that which does not exist in popular culture: being silent, paying attention to the people communicating, and being open to what is being said. We must speak only what is true for us, and we reflect back what we heard only when we have the stick and when necessary for the purposes of moving forward.

There is also purposefulness in listening to the silence. Eckhart Tolle, spiritual teacher and author, states, "Whenever there is some silence around you—listen to it. That means just notice it. Pay attention to it. Listening to silence awakens the dimension of stillness within yourself . . . see that in the moment of noticing the silence around you, you are not thinking. You are aware, but not thinking."[2] When I just listen to my people and speak when I'm supposed to—i.e., when I have the stick (even though I've often passed up the oppor-

---

As facilitators in restorative practice, we must model that which does not exist in popular culture: being silent, paying attention to the people communicating, and being open to what is being said.

---

tunity to speak when it's my turn or just held the stick for a few moments to allow for silence)—and follow the very structure of the questions I've asked others to prioritize, people have expressed that they felt respected, equitably heard, and honored in the Circle's space. And imagine this scenario: no one got hurt, and the primary issues at hand were resolved! By modeling this listening, people have access to one another in meaningful and necessary ways.

Holding Each Other in Values

Another facet of Circles is how we enter the room. Opening the space thoughtfully is key. At the start of all Circles, I offer a brief guided meditation, asking people to silently remember their true power. This Circle space is preceded by an equitable seating request that everyone expects and follows, so that the illusion of opposing sides is diminished. Then I give thanks to our ancestors for their presence and the gift of restorative practices across cultures, followed by specifically honoring everyone in the room and naming the reason we need them in Circle. After hearing the reasons we agreed to come together, i.e., the conflict, I list specific oppressive structures (e.g., law enforcement, colorism, patriarchy) relative to that incident and how those structures might operate in the room to lead us to fail and return to our powerless spaces. In addition to the preparation that has occurred days to weeks in advance to get to this moment, I now restate my value of investment and belief in them and in the Circle. Circle participants usually appear encouraged by the fact that I will push us to hold each other in love and constancy until the end of our time together. We stay connected to the values that we are worth the struggle to restore ourselves and that we can become stronger than oppression.

I always remind folks that POC used to engage in restorative processes, much like the ones used in restorative practices, as effective rituals before colonial obstructionists riddled us with genocide. These tools for healing and transformation are still within us. Opening in this manner and then circulating the talking stick enables us to open up our minds to setting agreements for a safe conversation. Personally, I encourage everyone to remember their power, because it activates people to be connected and intentional, which has the dual effect of curbing self-conscious fear or diminishment.

Using the Restorative Ways to Hold Each Other Up

It is crucial for me to set the stage in this ritualistic, restorative way, because along this journey, I've paid attention to and quieted the noise in my head—the self-doubt that tells me I'm not good or competent enough, that I'm not seasoned in the work to navigate it responsibly, that I will fail, or that I will let my people down. This self-doubting is the noise that sexism, homophobia, classism, and most certainly racism have planted in my consciousness—not to mention the other battles with oppression I've had to fight as a woman of color. When I sit with White people in restorative justice spaces, I'm aware of the ways in which I sometimes feel displayed or perceived as a minstrel show. Or that I'm being tested through Whites' microaggressions, because they don't believe I'm skilled. Instead of letting this internalized inferiority dominate me, I take slow, deep breaths and name what's showing up for me internally. This meditation-like exercise affirms the people who are around me, including myself. Managing myself in this actualizing way helps me to see fully in the space and to be (in the) present. It also emboldens me when it's my time to speak to confront oppression outright, without fear, no matter the community that I'm sitting with at the time.

I am empowered by our use of these tools that are rightfully ours. They assist each of us in managing the problems that oppression gave us.

Whether through relatable stories, brief definitions, or breaking down the conflict by pointing to one facet of it that's operating in the room, I go there. All the while, I self-check, making sure never to shame anyone or to speak to their experience as if it's my own. And I'm held to the same standard where my people can call me out or ask me to make it plain. If one falters, the lot of us picks the other up. I am empowered by our use of these tools that are rightfully ours. They assist each of us in managing the problems that oppression gave us.

Recovering What Is Ours

We should remember that conflict is natural—a part of living, and from our human design, we carry it with us in myriad ways: by just walking in the room with others or by simply looking at ourselves in the mirror. Hell, just by thinking, we are in conflict. Thus, we should neither fear it nor shirk our ability to manage it. Yes, the lift is harder. Structures like racism have distorted everything, and we have to deal with micro- and macro-aggressions constantly. And we deal with racial aggression before we even get to the more basic issues that all people deal with in their lifetime. But combatting oppression remains possible and only through a process of reconciliation.

This understanding about conflict is why restorative practices cannot be a behavior modification tool. The restorative work cannot masquerade as zero tolerance in schools or victim exploitation in the courts. It can't be used to make People of Color "act right" or white—walking around deeply repressed but on the surface playing politically correct and passing, until our privilege gets challenged and we flip. People of Color have historically known the ways in which to resolve this racist conundrum, and perhaps that is why white systems fear, stifle, or kill us. If we were all at peace, then there would be no need for hierarchy.

These same communities of color can heal systemic trauma and oppression that communities of color have endured. I am living proof of this healing from within community and self, and, so too, are many others. So is bell hooks, when she states, "There should be books that do nothing but accentuate the positive, sharing theories and strategies of decolonization that enable self-love."[3] Restorative process simply asks if we will account for what we did and commit to something higher, such as making amends with ourselves and with our people. It reminds us that we are love and loved. It is innately harmonious. And so, beloved POC, I'm committed to returning to our roots with you to recover what is ours.

DISCUSSION QUESTIONS

1. What am I doing to combat oppression in ways that also nurture my spirit and affirm my power?
2. Who am I accountable to and why? How do I show up to them?
3. Where do I feel powerless? How does that powerlessness impact my community? Where do I have to make amends?
4. Where is whiteness overpowering my existence or co-opting my cultural experience?

RESOURCES

hooks, bell. *Salvation: Black People and Love.* New York: HarperCollins, 2001.
Lorde, Audre. *Sister Outsider.* New York: Ten Speed Press, 1984.
Ruiz, Don Miguel. *The Four Agreements: A Practical Guide to Personal Freedom.* San Rafael: Amber-Allen, 1997.
Senghor, Shaka. *Writing My Wrongs: Life, Death, and Redemption in an American Prison.* New York: Drop a Gem, 2013.
Tolle, Eckhart. *Stillness Speaks.* Novato and Vancouver: New World Library and Namaste Publishing, 2003.

NOTES

1. Audre Lorde, *Sister Outsider* (New York: Ten Speed Press, 1984), 111.
2. Eckhart Tolle, *Stillness Speaks* (Novato and Vancouver: New World Library and Namaste Publishing, 2003), 4.
3. bell hooks, *Salvation: Black People and Love* (New York: HarperCollins, 2001), 92.

Chapter 12

The Cipher, Circle, and Restorative Practices with Black and Brown Boys

Abdul-Malik Muhammad

We struggle to turn the tide in the school-to-prison pipeline and mass incarceration. In our struggle, we ask, "How must we organize our classrooms and organizations to connect, to value authentic voice, and to use our authority for the optimal development of the personalities of Black and Brown males?" Of course, restorative practices and justice play a significant role in this struggle. However, as a movement, we have often failed to explore how notions of culture, manhood, hope, and bias affect our restorative work with our boys. This essay explores how our use of authority impacts our Black and Latinx boys, and how both Affective Language and the Cipher, an Indigenous Circle process, are transformative, restorative tools for empowering and liberating youth of color.

Authority and Our Boys of Color

The question of authority's use is central in our collective analysis and self-reflection. Particularly, how are we serving this young population to build social capital on the one hand and to respond effectively to wrongdoing on the other? Through our restorative practices work with Black and Brown boys in public, charter, and alternative schools, we have found that practitioners can transform, internally, our use of authority—in schools, law enforcement, service agencies, families, and the community—to make the most fundamental and radical shift that saves their lives. Too many of our Black and Latino boys indicate that they often do not feel connected to, valued, or uplifted by public institutions, including schools. They find support and relationships among their peers, outside of the influence of adults who wield authority and bias toward them. For many

Too many of our Black and Latino boys indicate that they often do not feel connected to, valued, or uplifted by public institutions, including schools.

Black boys, the cycle of punishment–disconnectedness–negative behavior replicates itself throughout their school/life tenure.

In the simplest terms, we can understand authority as being the intersection of both control and support. By control, we are referring to setting limits, establishing expectations, providing structure, holding folks accountable, and providing norms and standards. Control's continuum, represented on the Social Discipline Window (SDW) in Figure 1,[1] is the vertical axis on the left, and it ranges from low control to high control. By support, we refer to being nurturing, compassionate, empathetic, and loving. The support continuum is the horizontal axis at the SDW's bottom, and it also ranges from low support to high support. The quadrants thus created reflect the intersections between the degrees of control and support in how we use authority.

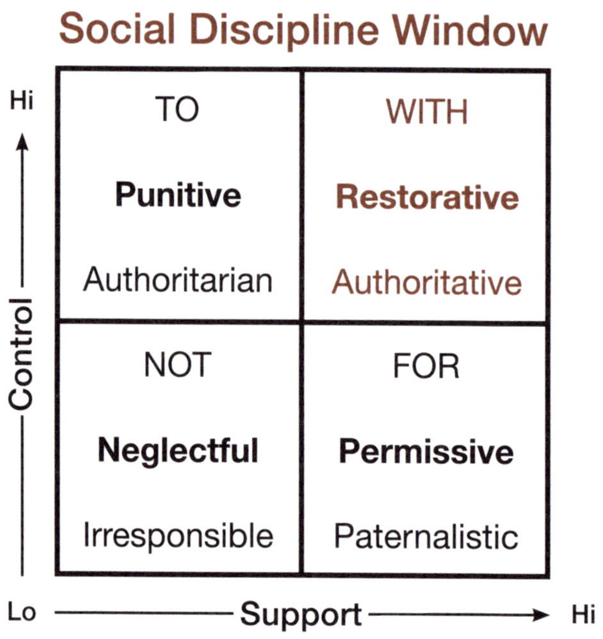

The SDW's framework provides a powerful insight concerning the synergistic effects of race, class, and gender for our boys of color.

The NOT Box: Passive Violence. For instance, in our trainings with adults, I have never had a participant admit that they primarily operate in the NOT box. The twin pressures of shame and self-preservation keep some participants from admitting it. However, in visiting schools and organizations and in talking to many Black and Latinx boys themselves, we see—and they describe—some environments that certainly fall within the NOT quadrant. For our boys of color (and other students), the adults are the ones whom they describe as not caring about them at all. Not surprisingly, they see these adults who operate in the FOR and WITH box as caring; they can even see the TO folks' behavior as manifesting care and concern. However, for those in the NOT box, the depersonalization and non-engagement that the adults project communicates a clear negative message for these boys. In fact, for an adult to hold a place of authority and influence in the lives of our most marginalized and at-risk youth and yet to not "see" them or to ignore their behavior and need for connection and support might just be the worst form of passive violence against them. I believe that this violence is rooted in a belief that these boys are not worthy of our attention and best efforts. It sends a message to the boys that this part of the battlefield—serving these youth—is where adults *have* to be, not where they *want* to be. "Having to be" means adults give only minimal effort—just enough to remain employed.

The TO Box: Authoritarian Control through Punishment. Many adults internalize, and then operate from, the dominant societal mindset that our Black and Latinx boys need to be controlled. This need-to-control approach replicates the discredited plantation and inhuman prison strategies that induce and activate trauma while producing hypermasculinity, disengagement, or passivity.

Whereas the NOT box ignores the value and needs of our boys of color, the adults in the TO and FOR boxes have biases that cloud their perspective when they interact with youth of color. The TO box in particular operates from the dominant societal mindset that needs to control others who are disempowered. Supposedly, the others' very nature requires a heavy hand—a dominant authoritarian figure whose primary role is to ensure obedience. The paradigm, however, is crafted and communicated under the guise of more structure and order. For instance, in his book *Crazy Like a Fox*, which includes some thoughtful insights from a strong practitioner, Dr. Ben Chavis also embodies this TO mentality when he states that "when you look at the areas in which minorities succeed—sports, military, and church—you realize what they have in common . . . they are all highly structured and have serious consequences for stepping out of line."[2]

This authoritarian approach has three fundamental and significant errors. First, it replicates (and justifies) centuries-old oppressive and violent tactics used on Black and Latino males. Plantations used and prisons continue to use the strategy of control and domination in the absence of support.

Intimidation, threats, punishments, and hierarchies characterize these interactions. We know them well as America's societal tools to manage People of Color historically and now. Even more heartbreaking is that our boys replicate this TO approach toward their peers and others.

Second, the TO approach, not surprisingly, induces and activates trauma. It invokes the survival mechanism that produces hypermasculinity (fight), disengagement (flight), or passivity (freeze) as methods of coping. In any case, inducing the survival mechanism virtually stops our boys of color from learning.

Third, disproportional discipline finds its genesis in the TO quadrant. Teachers and administrators believe that they must control our boys of color. As a result, disproportionate punishing, suspending, and expelling them seem natural and inevitable outcomes—and also seem self-fulfilling, naturally.

The FOR Box: Not Holding Youth to Standards. More subtle but equally damaging to our youth of color is when adults offer only support and yet refuse to establish restorative norms and accountability. Adults' support-only mode is born of an assumed-deficiency mindset—the FOR quadrant. Adults' lack of faith in youth of color, combined with a heavy dose of savior syndrome, produces a set of negative mental habits FOR our boys and young men. "I won't set high standards, or any standards at all, because they are incapable of meeting them. I won't push them and apply pressure because the answers lie in me (to do it for them) and not in them. They are deserving only of my praise and rewards, not challenge and correction." Given that over 90 percent of America's teachers are White and mostly women, one wonders what role White guilt plays when they operate from the FOR box toward our boys of color.

Dependency, of coure, is the most expected outcome from the NOT, TO, and FOR boxes. When our boys are not required to carry their own weight regarding their education or family and societal responsibilities, then literally and figuratively their naturally strong shoulders atrophy. If they wait it out, our youth grow accustomed to teachers giving them answers to the hardest challenges. And an uncomfortable truth is that parents and community members could be enablers as well. For instance, our youth become comfortable with community workers giving them a pass on arriving late to programs. They come to expect that their parents will accept (and even provide) their excuses for why they behaved in a negative way. Mwalimu Bomani Baruti is correct about this point:

> By running interference for our sons when the tasks are hard and challenging and within their capacity, we are weakening them for their life's responsibilities, therefore, making them 1) unprepared, 2) dependent and soft, and 3) ripe for the whim of anyone who will feed them.[3]

Dependency encourages youth to develop a manipulative mindset. If we treat our boys of color as highly breakable glass, as though they should be fused over, then they expect us to do things FOR them. Manipulation, cajoling, and/or coercing them into behaving (or at least liking us) sends a message to our youth that these methods are acceptable to use with authority and to manage behavior.

What happens when they direct this quid-pro-quo attitude toward a young woman? What happens when they attempt to cajole her by doing something FOR her (providing a gift or compliment) and she doesn't respond as intended?

Last, the FOR quadrant cripples motivation and the internal drive that boys of color need to struggle through challenges. It weakens their spiritual and emotional fighting capacity and their sense of authentic achievement. To tell our Black and Latinx boys that they can become anything they want is cute encouragement—if we don't have them carry the weight of anything. Without the internal humility to accept both help and responsibility, they will rise no further than our lowest expectations. In *The Fire Next Time*, James Baldwin eloquently explains this limiting mindset for men of color:

To tell our Black and Latinx boys that they can become anything they want is cute encouragement—if we don't have them carry the weight of anything.

> The limits of your ambition were, thus, expected to be set forever. You were born into a society which spelled out in brutal clarity, and in as many ways as possible, that you were a worthless human being. You were not expected to aspire to excellence; you were expected to make peace with mediocrity.[4]

The Restorative Response: From a Relationship's Inside

For our boys of color and all youth, restorative practices provide the opportunity to create school and community environments that do not respond to wrongdoing from the SDW's NOT, TO, and FOR boxes. In the restorative model, the infraction/harm is identified, but much more attention is given to who was harmed/affected and in what ways. Addressing and undoing harm is an inclusive perspective, often looking at and beyond the person harmed to others who have been affected as well. Likewise, we explore and attempt to understand a person's needs that a harm has created. For instance, someone who has been assaulted may have a real need to feel safe and to receive monetary support for the resulting medical bills, while the one who did the assault may have a real recipocal need to apologize, express remorse, or be removed from others for a time period. Lastly, the restorative model places great emphasis on restorative actions, both by those who have caused harm as well as by a community: What must be done to repair and restore relationships, balance, and peace? These "consequences" should be directly linked to addressing the personal and community needs created by a harm.

In the absence of a relationship, we are, at best, guessing as to what will have a meaningful impact on youth to transform their behavior. What happens when our suspensions don't work on Anthony because we just rewarded him with a three-day vacation from school, a place where he would rather not be anyway? What happens when a reward of cute, little fuzzy pencils don't induce Jamal to return a failed test signed by a parent or other caretaker? How are we going to handle Javier when he could care less about not being allowed to go on the upcoming field trip to the library?

In the absence of a relationship, we are, at best, guessing as to what will have a meaningful impact on youth to transform their behavior.

It is through a relationship's inside with these young people that we can accomplish at least two things. First, we can begin to understand what their leverage points are. That is, what has meaning to them. More importantly (and less manipulatively perhaps), they establish emotional belonging and deeper connections. Belonging and connecting make them police their own actions, which would otherwise threaten to disappoint, to harm, or to cause them to lose a relationship much more significant to them. Ultimately, if we really want our consequences to have effect or meaning beyond simple punishment, then we must connect school-age youth with our school community through respectful, youth-adult interactions.

Wielding Affective Language

Dr. Christina Watlington, a trauma and anxiety expert, teaches that, in the absence of a strong emotional vocabulary, we all rely on our behavioral vocabulary—girls and boys, adults too.[5] In other words, when we lack the language skills to express affect, emotion, and feelings, we instead communicate what is going on within through our behavioral vocabulary. If a student doesn't feel safe or skilled enough to raise their hand to express the frustration and/or confusion within, as Watlington points out, then they will show how they are feeling through nonverbal behavior, from a dazed look of mental detachment to an aggressive backlash against the teacher or other students. If a behavioral specialist doesn't "have the words" to express their burnout and/or their feeling of being overwhelmed, then their behavioral vocabulary might kick in: avoiding work or disrespecting their colleagues. When we understand that this absence of a strong emotional vocabulary is a universal phenomenon affecting us all, we are more able to have patience and to recognize our youths' humanity as they struggle.

Now, what happens when a student doesn't just struggle to verbally express emotion but, even more, finds it socially unacceptable and, in some cases, dangerous to do so? What happens when the pressure to deny all but a few emotions is intimately wrapped up in the core of one's self-identity? What happens when anger, pride, and happiness are the extent of a young person's emotional continuum, and only these emotions become the filter through which they manifest shame, humiliation, sadness, and fear? Such is the case with many males in general, but specifically with our boys (and men) of color, who, in the Western psyche, represent the quintessential male "other." This culture of masculinity and hypermasculinity prevents them/us from expressing what George M. Taylor, an author and counselor in the Bay area who conducts men's groups, refers to as "our inner lives and truths."[6] Tupac, legendary hip-hop and rap artist, in the powerful song "Gotta Keep Ya Head Up," said it so eloquently: "Dying inside, but outside you're looking fearless."

I refer to "wielding affective language" as the ability to express the full range of emotions verbally. Our boys of color need nurturing to further develop this ability, particularly when they are sad, frustrated, overjoyed, ashamed, and fascinated. Just like the development and understanding of any language, the language of emotion is taught, encouraged, and refined by adults who care about the youth they serve. We teach affective language through both modeling and explicit instruction. Our Black and Brown boys need this modeling and instruction so desperately.

I refer to "wielding affective language" as the ability to express the full range of emotions verbally. Our boys of color need nurturing to further develop this ability, particularly when they are sad, frustrated, overjoyed, ashamed, and fascinated.

The Cipher

According to Carolyn Boyes-Watson, director of the Center for Restorative Justice at Suffolk University, the Circle is powerful because it doesn't include the traditional symbols of power and significance. Circles offer no table to hide behind, no podium for power, no back of the room, no symbols of hierarchy. This transparency is precisely what speaks most to youth who, by definition and custom, are without power or position, and therefore voiceless.[7]

In our experience, many practitioners have too often engaged in cultural imperialism; that is, they believe and act as if they are "bringing the Circle" to a poor, marginalized community. On an authentic, restorative level, we should invite the community to sit in our Circle, but more importantly, we should explore ways to join theirs. This restorative value means that we have to understand them, and they us. However, we can find a dynamic **WITH** practice within the culture of our young men of color. When we genuinely begin to understand them, we discover that, within the culture of many urban (or urban-oriented) Black and Latino boys, an Indigenous Circle process already exists. We could be so lucky to be invited into this Circle. It is called the Cipher.

Imagine a spontaneous circle formed by seven middle school boys of color immediately after school in the courtyard. Their bodies are huddled tight, and there is an intensity in the boys' energy. Voices grow louder and other students begin flocking toward the group. As the closest adult, you intervene and elbow your way into the center, since your voice and shouts don't seem to have any effect. Bodies are swaying closer to the epicenter and some hands are in the air. The "ooh," "damn," and "whaat" coming from the crowd tell you that an afterschool fight is happening. You know these kids. You didn't hear about anyone having "beef" with anyone today that would lead to this. When you finally reach the center, you bump into Ali, a physically underdeveloped, rambuntious sixth grader, as he shouts something to the inner circle. Now at the center of the circle, you look around to see who Ali is fighting, but you see only him and everyone else looking back at you with angry eyes.

Unbeknownest to you, you just interrupted one of the strongest lyricists in the school—he was just twenty-four seconds into his freestyle flow. When you scan the inner circle, two other boys have their hands to their mouths delivering the bass and rhythm beats for Ali, while another one had his phone out live streaming the whole process. Beyond the inner circle are twenty more fully engaged youth, the same students who fall asleep during your math class and never have questions when you bring in a guest speaker. There was no fighting, no crisis, just connection. You just broke up a Cipher.

The Cipher is a uniquely pan-Indigenous phenomenon that urban youth adapted to the modern context as a dynamic way to express themselves. Its modern manifestation serves as an outlet for various expressions of hip-hop culture, including mc'ing (rap lyrical expression), beat boxing, and b-boying (dancing). Additionally, several conscious groups, like the Five Percenter Na-

Beyond the inner circle are twenty more fully engaged youth, the same students who fall asleep during your math class and never have questions when you bring in a guest speaker. There was no fighting, no crisis, just connection. You just broke up a Cipher.

tion of Gods and Earths, used the Cipher to "Build" (share knowledge and co-create culture) with each other. The Cipher is a site for sharing, for free and authentic expression, for connection, and for "battle." It is a street-based cyclical exchange of energy. It is a *sacred* space that one does not enter into lightly, and it has its own set of norms and structure, including the following:

- Only one person has the floor at a time.
- One must be invited/embraced by the collective.
- Everyone contributes, no matter how small.
- Challenging another is acceptable.
- Contributions determine length.
- Participation is authentic and freestyle.
- Everyone flows with the rhythm of the collective.
- We celebrate each other.

The Cipher's most sacrosanct norm is *authentic* expression. One must come only from the "top of the dome" or "from your heart," or your contribution will be questioned and collectively and publicly critiqued. This shaming can be reintegrative, as those who violates this cardinal rule might remain within the Cipher and be given another chance to share their authentic voice/contribution.

Authenticity and sincere voices rarely conform to traditional schools' acceptable and stale methods of expression and decibal levels.

Authenticity and sincere voices rarely conform to traditional schools' acceptable and stale methods of expression and decibal levels. Therefore, Ciphers almost always find home within the uninhibited and open spaces of youths' free time, i.e., street corners, parks, afterschool settings, etc. Additionally, Ciphers create and build energy from energy. This wielding of affect language is certainly problematic in a society that has outlawed and criminalized, within the context of school, our boys' of color energy. The Cipher's unpredictability and dynamicism are two creative traits that traditional and oppressive environments, such as schools, cannot and will not tolerate with Black and Latinx boys.

The connection made through the Circle's use goes deep into the historical memory of boys of color. For example, we leaned into the Circle to sustain life and humanity even in our darkest hours of enslavement. Marimba Ani, anthropologist African Studies scholar, writes in *Let the Circle Be Unbroken*:

> We gathered and enjoyed the warmth of our commonness, of our togetherness. We would form a circle, each touching those next to us so as to physically express our spiritual closeness. We "testified," speaking

on the day's or week's experiences. We shared the pain of those experiences and received from the group affirmations of our existence as suffering beings. As we "lay down our burdens," we became lighter. As we testified and listened to others testify, we began to understand ourselves as communal beings, no longer the "individual" that the slave system tried to make us. . . . Through our participation in these rituals, we became one. We became, again, a community. Each of us gained the strength necessary to deal with our incarceration. Sometimes we prepared for rebellion.[8]

Further evidence of this circular collectivity lies in the Adinkra symbols of the Akan, the Indigenous African Peoples' philosophical references. The Adinkrahene, which is a set of concentric circles, is the oldest and chief of these ancient symbols. The Akan believe this to be the origin of all other symbols and to represent leadership, greatness, and charisma. When we tap into a Circle's power, we validate and empower a natural method of interaction for our boys (and girls and ourselves).

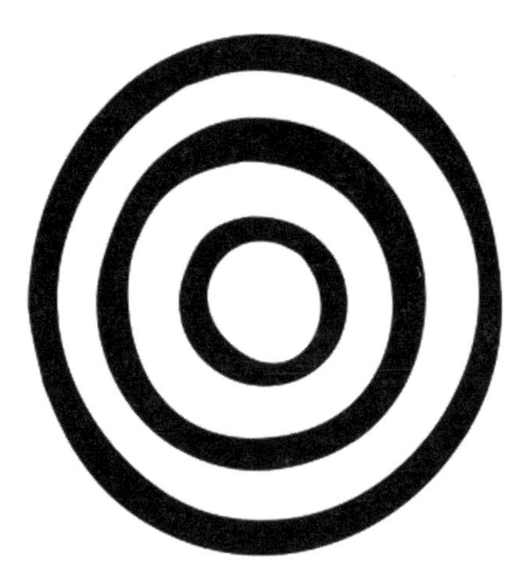

Adinkrahene is "Chief of the adinkra symbols." It is a symbol of greatness, charisma, and leadership. This symbol is said to have played an inspiring role in the designing of other symbols. It signifies the importance of playing a leadership role.[9]

Baba Kwame Agyei Akoto, an amazing elder and profound voice in the African Centered School movement, is one of the founders of NationHouse and Watoto Shule in Washington, D.C. He argues that Circles are the preferred and most culturally sound methodology of instruction between the *mwalimu* (teacher) and *mwanafunzi* (student). In his seminal work, *Nationbuilding*, he

Circles are the preferred and most culturally sound methodology of instruction between the mwalimu (teacher) and mwanafunzi (student).

explains that the teacher-student connection should be "interactive, meaning that there is a vibrant exchange of information, mutual learning and inspiration" and that "this interactive and reciprocal act of communication . . . is exemplified by the communal circle in traditional Afrikan societies."[10] According to Baba Agyei, the Circle's force releases to its participants several relationship-building features. For example:

- It facilitates the spiritual communion in traditional spiritual systems.
- It includes the family elder or griot and represents the intergenerational flow of history and culture.
- It is explicitly collective and communal and can best facilitate the kind of dynamic and reciprocal discourse that is essential to the development of the truly liberated Afrikan personality.
- It is particularly well suited to facilitating the active participation of all its members, and it allows the *mwalimu* (teacher) to easily adjust from an egalitarian posture to that of mediator, facilitator, lecturer, adversary, and various degrees in between.
- It is fluid enough to allow opportunities for *mwanafunzi* (student, learner) initiative and creativity.
- It can further the development of cooperative skills and a sense of reciprocity and mutual accountability.
- It can also facilitate the development of leadership and constituent skills.

For our boys of color, the use of the Circle goes beyond the simple, procedural implementation of a restorative program. It also has the power to tap into both their Indigenous and culturally normative mode of exchange as well as to indigenize modern expression through the Cipher.

A Challenge to Restorative Practitioners

We owe a great debt and appreciation to our colleagues within the restorative practices movement for championing and broadening the use of these powerful practices, including affective statements and Circles, with schools and beyond. As we imagine this work's next evolution, we argue that the evolution must consciously and explicitly address the challenges facing our Black

Teaching restorative skills to our participants without having them challenge their own biases does not go far enough. In other words, sharpening our restorative practices' tools of equity and liberation is the challenge, rather than simply dulling the negative effects of oppression.

and Latinx males, perhaps the most marginalized amongst us. This restorative practitioners' work will require us to overtly confront issues of power disparities, oppression, racism, sexism, white privilege, male privilege, and sexual-orientation privilege. Teaching restorative skills to our participants without having them challenge their own biases does not go far enough. In other words, sharpening our restorative practices' tools of equity and liberation is the challenge, rather than simply dulling the negative effects of oppression.

To truly move beyond anti-racist and anti-oppression platitudes, our work must include deeper explorations of how what we do impacts—and is enlivened by—our Black and Brown boys' culture and lives.

DISCUSSION QUESTIONS

1. Think about how our boys of color interact inside a positive relationship they have with an adult. What are the relationship's characteristics?
2. How can we display care, concern, and love in our connections with Black boys?
3. Other than Circles, what are other Indigenous sites of connection and restoration often overlooked by practitioners of restorative practices and justice?

ACTIVITIES

1. Teach the Social Discipline Window to your colleagues and explore the explicit impact of the NOT, TO, and FOR boxes on our boys of color.
2. Model and teach affective language (statements and questions) to build the emotional vocabulary of boys of color.
3. Integrate both the norms listed above and the structure of the Cipher into your restorative work with boys of color (and others too). Notice the energy and dynamic, authentic expression at work.

RESOURCES

Readings

Akoto, Kwame Agyei. *Nationbuilding: Theory and Practice in Afrikan Centered Education.* Washington, D.C.: Talkingstick Publishing, 1992.

Block, Peter. *Community: The Structure of Belonging.* San Francisco: Berrett-Koehler Publishers, 2008.

Boyes-Watson, Carolyn. *Peacemaking Circles and Urban Youth: Bringing Justice Home.* St. Paul: Living Justice Press, 2008.

Rios, Victor. *Punished: Policing the Lives of Black and Latino Boys.* New York: New York University Press, 2011.

Online

Akoben LLC. www.akobenllc.org.

Coalition of Schools Educating Boys of Color (COSEBOC). www.coseboc.org.

Watlington, Christina. https://drwatlington.com/about/ as well as https://drwatlington.com/blog/ and https://drwatlington.com/.

NOTES

1. Bob Costello, Joshua Wachtel, and Ted Wachtel, *The Restorative Practices Handbook for Teachers, Disciplinarians, and Administrators* (Bethlehem, PA: International Institute for Restorative Practices, 2009, 2013), 50.
2. Ben Chavis and Carey Blakely, *Crazy Like a Fox: One Principal's Triumph in the Inner City* (New York: New American Library, 2009), 55.
3. Mwalimu Bomani Baruti, *Asafo: A Warrior's Guide to Manhood* (Atlanta: Akoben House, 2004), 124.
4. James Baldwin, *The Fire Next Time* (New York: Dial Press, 1963), 7.
5. Based on conversations between the author and Dr. Christina Watlington. For more information about Dr. Watlington's work, see https://drwatlington.com/.
6. George Taylor, *Talking with Our Brothers* (Fairfax, CA: Men's Community Publishing Project, 1995).
7. Paraphrased from Carolyn Boyes-Watson, *Peacemaking Circles and Urban Youth* (St. Paul, MN: Living Justice Press, 2008), 92.
8. Marimba Ani, *Let the Circle Be Unbroken: The Implications of African Spirituality in the Diaspora* (New York: Nkonimfo Publications, 1980), 24–25.
9. Adinkrahene image by Vinay, "Download Free Famous Ghanaian Adinkra Symbols (Brushes and Shapes)," https://vincenttechblog.com/adinkra-symbols-brushes-shapes-download/. Caption from "Adinkra Symbols and Meanings," https://www.somervillenjk12.org/cms/lib5/NJ01001815/Centricity/Domain/89/Adinkra%20Symbols%20and%20%20Meanings.pdf.
10. K. Agyei Akoto, *Nationbuilding: Theory and Practice in Afrikan Centered Education* (Washington, D.C.: Pan Afrikan World Institute, 1992), 105.

Chapter 13

Colorizing Justice Practice: Afro-Caribbean Experience of Restorative Justice in Three World Areas

Leon Dundas

Colorizing cannot merely be changing the color of who is holding the whip but rather a revaluing of the experience of People of Color at all levels of decision making.

My aim is to explore potential themes for research, reflection, and action. My modus is narrative and descriptive, rather than research-based. This chapter shares stories and reflects on them: many come from direct involvement but also from recollections of experiences shared by service users, trainees, other trainers, program managers, policy makers, and practitioners. Due to the difficulty of accessing documents that are not in the public domain, as well as the desire to respect confidentiality and "protect the guilty," some material cannot be referenced or cited in the traditional manner. I will, however, always provide enough detail to produce the "knowing nod" from those who have worked or are working through similar issues.

This chapter considers experiences over more than twenty-five years of work in restorative justice in Jamaica, the US, and the UK around three key themes:

1. Are the systems for policy-making, funding, and practitioner accreditation, etc., fundamentally *restorative enough* to have a transformative impact on the nature of contact between dominant and nondominant groups?

2. Does the prevalent RJ focus on actual cases of harmful behavior actually contribute to repairing and/or reducing fundamental harm? Or does it deflect attention from the real systemic disadvantage—the disadvantages built into systems—of which harmful behavior is only a symptom?[1]
3. What alternative strategies and non-traditional approaches to the status quo have proven effective for People of Color who lead in developing RJ work?

Before exploring these themes in depth, however, a working definition of "colorizing RJ" emerged for me through the course of writing this chapter: an epithet for shared-power, dialogue-based approaches that invite excluded or marginalized individuals and/or groups into the center of decision making.[2] I shall use the terms restorative justice (RJ), restorative approaches (RA), and restorative practices (RP) interchangeably, but I prefer RJ. The preferred term reflects a focus on the restorative philosophy that is common to all three and to the myriad of slightly differentiated processes, such as Circles, panels, and conferences.

A Bit of Scene-Setting

I am Afro-Caribbean and, to put it crassly with tongue in cheek, "the right kind of Black"—the kind of Black as represented by Barack Obama and Meghan Markle: mixed race, light skinned, university educated, heterosexual, and protestant Christian with a very liberal outlook.[3] I grew up in Guyana, leaving at age eighteen to study in Trinidad and Tobago and later in Jamaica. Afterward, I spent eighteen years working in Jamaica's criminal justice system, volunteering in two key conflict resolution organizations and serving as a pastor. In 2003, I was offered the Hubert H. Humphrey Fellowship and spent a year based at the University of Minnesota. In order to build my understanding of restorative practices, I traveled across the US and farther afield. In particular, I wanted to explore RJ models that have the potential to shift the balance of decision-making from the national level back to local communities. In 2005, I moved to the United Kingdom and, though I returned to Jamaica to continue RJ work at different points in the early years, I have spent the past thirteen years developing restorative justice mainly in prisons and in local community settings.

I took my first steps into the restorative justice world in Jamaica in the early 1990s. The Jamaica Bar Association (JBA) and the Jamaican government were developing positive alternatives—"jungle justice" being a less-than-positive one—to reduce delays in getting cases through court and to address chronically high levels of crime and violence.[4] I was involved with setting up the Dis-

Over time, the alternative dispute resolution/mediation model began to morph from a more typical "Getting to yes" focus into a wider transformative, conflict resolution approach and then into formal restorative justice.

pute Resolution Foundation (DRF) in 1994. Over time, the alternative dispute resolution/mediation model began to morph from a more typical "Getting to yes" focus into a wider transformative, conflict resolution approach and then into formal restorative justice.[5] At the same time, my work was developing through the Peace and Love in Schools (PALS) program, which, in collaboration with the Ministry of Education and with youth, teachers, and parents, sought to bring about peaceable schools and communities.

My earliest consciousness of color and race relates to the ethnic divides and parallel issues of political tensions in Guyana, Trinidad, and Tobago. Always present—or at times hidden in the background—were the historical experiences of People of Color, either as slaves or indentured laborers in North America, the Caribbean, and Europe, not to mention political oppression in Africa and the capitalist/communist Cold War tensions. The resulting "war," to use the words of Bob Marley, was (and still is) as much international as it is national and local. This war manifests through poverty and other structures of inequality and exclusion, as well as through crime and violence.

At the core of all my work has been an ever-increasing commitment to a pluralistic and non-discriminatory way of working and relating. At the level of casework, this commitment means that RJ prioritizes the needs of those harmed, while simultaneously humanizing those who have done harm. For RJ specifically, this simultaneity has demanded challenging the narrative about the causes of harm and its subsequent disorder, while valuing as well as questioning the narratives around both the individuals involved in doing the harm and the communities that hosted them. In the words of Mallana, a female Afghan asylum seeker whom we trained recently, the most important word in the RJ definition is "hope"—a comment made even more poignant by the fact that the word "hope" was not actually in the definitions examined!

RJPoids vs. RJPoints

Central to the analysis I offer here is a two-tiered classification of persons working in RJ: RJPoids and RJPoints.[6] No slur is intended when the terms are used.

I will use the term "RJPoid" to describe a group that directs RJ and has set its course: researchers, consultants, policy makers, managers, grant writers, and trainers who are typically members of dominant social groups. They are either racially or by association lighter-skinned than those being harmed or causing the harm.[7] Because of their professional networks, RJPoids are more likely to hold decision-making, influencing, and (when funding is provided) paid roles in the RJ world. On the whole, RJPoids would have escaped—at least the most vicious but not necessarily the most insidious—aspects of ethnic penalty.

The term "RJPoint" refers to the group that RJ is for: those harmed, those who have done harm, and the community members and practitioners whose lives are most directly impacted by both particular instances of harm and/or by broader issues of inequity. Their communities retain a memory and models of justice and peacemaking that the prevailing criminal justice system, in some areas, is seeking to bring back. RJPoints usually claim only expenses and work on a voluntary basis. Effectively and happily, they subsidize RJ work at the grassroots level.

In Jamaica, RJPoids have tended to be public service professionals, lawyers, and academics who share concerns about the quality of justice and high levels of crime and violence. Their role as RJPoids is performed in addition to their regular jobs. A small group of paid staff provide organizational/administrative support. Many of the RJPoints delivering the frontline, traditional victim-offender-type mediation work are from a similar professional background as their RJPoid colleagues. But they are in their own league when it comes to hybrid RJ work such as peace dances, peace walks, and drama. Peace dances and walks are highly visible movements, able to impact relatively large groups of people. They provide lightning rods for volatile situations, while also allowing for critical information-gathering and influencing public awareness. Notably, RJPoints who "speak the same language" as those on both sides of harm and their community members are inevitably less visible and receive less plaudits and pay for their work.

RJPoids are at their best on the national stage, accessing various networks for funding and training as well as using local media to help frame dialogue around harm and injustice. Comparatively, RJPoints lead the community-based peace centers, which are satellites of national organizations, and they also lead on casework.

RJPoints who "speak the same language" as those on both sides of harm and their community members are inevitably less visible and receive less plaudits and pay for their work.

An example of this situation can be seen in Leicester, England, where Restorative Justice Initiative Midlands (RJIM) provided from their own pool of volunteers perhaps 80 percent of the facilitators in the Victim First Project launched in 2015. Except for the initial RJ training course and a train-the-trainers course, the training and development of new volunteers, as well as the awareness-building around RJ, continue to be led by the RJIM team of Black, Asian, and White volunteers. Many of its former volunteers have moved on to paid practitioner roles outside Leicester. While the Victim First Project imports its RJ practice managers, it continues to use RJIM volunteers as co-facilitators. In this scenario, as with PALS and the DRF in Jamaica, traditional victim-offender work witnesses a crossover between RJPoids and RJPoints. I'll discuss this dynamic more fully later.

In my experience of the US context, the RJ world appeared to be shared between dedicated RJ community organizations (e.g., Minnesota Restorative Justice Campaign and the Minnesota Restorative Services Coalition, Roca in Boston,[8] and Operation Ceasefire in Chicago) and public sector teams in prisons or probation services. As an outsider, I did not detect a significant class divide between RJPoids and RJPoints. Yes, except for enclaves in Minnesota and Chicago, the RJPoids were predominantly White, but the players I encountered often seemed to share the quintessential hippie or Rastafarian passion (whether Black, White, or mixed race) for social justice and change.

Expertise from People of Color has always been available, locally and internationally.

Reflecting on the ethnic profile of the US trainers who visited Jamaica to deliver RJ training or to give program advice, I remember them as "White people," except for two Black experts I was able to recommend from my US network. RJPoids from Canada Quaker Service and England's International Institute for Restorative Practices and Thames Valley Police also mirror this profile. As inevitable as the White presence may have been in the early stages of development, this colorizing RJ project calls us to reflect on a mindset that has created more travel miles, hotel bills, and fee payments than may have been necessary.

Expertise from People of Color has always been available, locally and internationally. For example, Jamaica's ninth International Restorative Justice Conference signaled a mindset shift. Craig Pinkney, an RJPoid Person of Color, also a British criminologist and urban youth specialist who serves as the lead for the European Union Gangs Project, held a position at the head table.

Standards, Accreditation, and Ownership: Resourcing or Blocking Colorizing?

For RJPoids and others, accreditation is important. It marks "professional competence" and ostensibly assures service users and funders. It also provides a mainstream structure of accountability at both individual and organizational levels. In England, full practitioner accreditation through the Restorative Justice Council costs 300 pounds (386 USD), requires thirty hours of online casework documentation, and involves further conversations with an assessor. (An RJ Quality Mark is also available for organizations intending to give confidence during tender processes.)

The requirements of up-front payment and a high level of literacy around filling out forms create barriers for those seeking accreditation, especially among People of Color. It is therefore simpler to complete a training course, move into a program, and then remain there without taking on the extra work of writing up case studies in order to achieve national accreditation.

As a person with some international RJ experience and significant experience with form-filling, I was simply told that my application did not meet the national standards. It took a threat of a racial complaint before I was taken seriously. In a telephone discussion, a new assessor agreed that I met the standards. In the end, I was not awarded accreditation due to, among other reasons, the RJ process being *too focused on the needs of the prison setting.* During the time of this application process, my RJ work in the UK—and therefore the cases that I submitted as evidence—were prison related.

In the US, I had no awareness of state or national RJ gatekeeping systems, certainly not of the type I experienced in the UK. In Jamaica, the accreditation process has developed very gradually and with very minimal requirements. A person simply needs to have done directly supervised casework and to have been recommended by more experienced trainers. Programs actively support their volunteers in getting up to the mark, with virtually no outright refusals as far as I am aware. Organizations, either government or community-based, charge for a range of educational, social, and criminal justice projects and use these funds to cover the costs of their volunteers' accreditation. Trainings include meals at no charge to participants, and organizations often provide stipends to cover participants' travel expenses.

In the UK, I fear that the accreditation process is leading to a centralization and rigidity that runs counter to the very essence of the restorative philosophy. The institutional setup prioritizes the needs and reputations of service providers, funders, and policy makers above the need to nourish RJ's ancient soul. For example, RJ practitioners need room for creative choice in how to serve people and communities and to attend to the more qualitative norms of reconciliation, forgiveness, truth-telling, respect, and justice. Fortunately, many RJ providers do not require national accreditation as a precondition for employment.

I find myself faced with the questions: Is the drive to accredit practitioners, which involves marking and branding them, driven by the need for consistent, evidence-based, professional standards, or is it driven by the strategy of the modern political economy that transfers resources from south to north by branding and monetizing products? Pushing the issue further, is our work, our labor, being treated as a commodity? These points of tension—as well as contention—call us, as People of Color, to consider what might lie beneath our frequent lack of interest in accreditation. Is it coming from a commitment to acting authentically? Is it laziness or tiredness, or is it coming from some other place?

How then do we colorize accreditation without "ghettoizing"—the fear of lowering RJ's "professional standards"? For starters, we can expand RJ's understanding and knowledge base—as *Colorizing Restorative Justice* is doing—pushing it to encompass knowledge and experiences that a White-only/dominant view lacks. Caribbean, African, and other Indigenous-based practices of Ubuntu, Sawubona, and community justice, which I explore later in this discussion, are a few of the better-known examples. People of Color, as storytellers, are capable of embracing a fluidity in language, underpinned by an alternative vision and understanding of justice. This fluidity may not be readily available to those who have not lived simultaneously in parallel worlds and the tensions that go with this.[9]

Hence, when it comes to frontline interventions, which of the following RJ models in table 1 is truly a separate brand worth differentiating? If we differentiate them, what is the value in doing so? Is it to understand a process and the sorts of needs or situations it meets, or is it to push a brand of process as the one and only?

Table 1: RJ Models and Processes

Restorative Justice	Relational Justice	Restorative Practice	Restorative Decision-Making
Conferences	Circles	Community Panels	Peace Walks/ Marches/Vigils
Truth and Reconciliation Commissions	Youth Justice Panels	Circles of Accountability	Appreciative Dialogue
Victim-Offender Mediation	Victim-Offender Restorative Processes	Victim-Offender Mediated Dialogue	Nonviolent Communication
Restorative Approaches	Resettlement Circles	Family Circles	Peace Dances
Restorative Drumming	Peace-Building	Peacemaking Circles	Stand Up RJ
Facilitated Dialogues	Transformative Justice	Transformative Mediation	Restorative Dispute Resolution

In my experience, none of the models in table 1 are exclusive; therefore, we must take a less formal approach that recognizes quality without compromising flexibility or grassroots initiative. Richness flows from flexibility, which allows for natural impulses. Consider, for example, the flexibility and hence richness in African and Caribbean music vs. music with a history of written scores; traditional/natural medicine vs. the patented pharmaceutical products of modern medicine; or cooking by feel vs. cooking by recipe. *Colorizing Restorative Justice* would do well not to demand or even expect clear ownership or credit for any given RJ model but rather to encourage and facilitate the fudging and mixing needed to fit the peculiarities of each local situation. In other words, we must resist the temptation to speak as if formal institutions have the last word on RJ.[10]

We must resist the temptation to speak as if formal institutions have the last word on RJ.

Another key strategy in this struggle has been to focus on the RJPoints' grassroots work without entirely ceding policy control or visibility to RJPoids. RJIM, for example, remains engaged with police, prisons, universities, the media, as well as with political leaders as key parts of its work, while also doing RJ Awareness Circles, leafleting, training, and assisting larger providers with casework. Fortunately, on the ground, a growing number of people recognize that the services of small, local providers, like RJIM and satellite peace or peace and justice centers (in Jamaica)—largely done on a voluntary basis—are critical to establishing the trust needed for people on either side of harm to access and benefit from RJ at the deepest possible levels.

Dr. Denis Tanfa, Cameroon-born founder and director of RJIM, cites research indicating that RJ service users trust volunteer facilitators more than they do professionals, such as housing, police, and probation officers. With the latter, issues of bias, conflicts of interest, and concerns about disclosure inevitably arise. In my own casework in the UK, I have often received comments around trust: "I could tell from your accent that we could trust you." University lecturers talk about the impact of RJIM presentations on students, who want to feel the energy from "real people doing RJ."

Colorizing as Staying Flexible in Process and Model

In Jamaica, unlike in the US and UK, the RJ provider organizations I encounter (e.g., DRF, PALS, Peace Management Initiative [PMI]) do not specialize in traditional RJ. They incorporate RJ as part of a suite of interventions, ranging from traditional arbitration and mediation to hybrid interventions, like peace dances. Their collective philosophies reveal a pragmatism, patience, and breadth of knowledge and praxis in the way that Black- and minority-led groups work, assuming that the leadership at the center of power supports or at least does not block them.

As a result, in Jamaica, policy most often follows practice. International funders and supporters, often with public sector coordination, tend to show a commitment to valuing local leadership, and they judge accountability largely in terms of project deliverables. Assessing the actual impact of RJ itself is limited and often left to the media's coverage of success stories. For example, the media reported zero murders in the Grants Pen area of Kingston in 2006, after reporting up to fifty murders in the previous year.[11] Notably, though, the number of cases they covered came from the practitioners who were trained and certified; they were not counting the actual number of cases that moved through the process.

While in the US, I was impressed by the role of grant-funded (philanthropic or state), community-based projects, such as Operation Ceasefire (in Chicago) and the Frog Town–Summit Circle Program in Minnesota, as well as a number of Anishinaabe Circles. Victim-led community lobbies in Minnesota set the agenda, which led to establishing an Apology Letter Bank at Minnesota's Department of Corrections.

It feels different in England. National standards and policy, underpinned by high-profile research, seem to be the key drivers of RJ's development. The not-so-subtle message is that the power/plaudits and pennies lie with research, training, and management—the RJPoids. By contrast, local volunteers—those directly vested in community-level peace and justice—facilitate the community-based casework. In the youth justice system and probation services, RJ functions as an add-on, rather than as the core way that programs work. Plus, race is far from being recognized as worth equal attention as other strands of diversity, such as gender.[12] Unsurprisingly, the "professionals"—perhaps a fudge word for "paid staff" that undervalues the highly skilled and motivated volunteer cadre—drive into a given community to do casework. Many of the case managers I know live forty-five to sixty minutes (thirty miles) away from where those dealing with harm live.

Situations that involve significant dislocation and risk may require an alternative approach to facilitate engagement in RJ. While not meeting the "fully restorative" criteria set out by Paul McCold and Ted Wachtel of the International Institute of Restorative Practices (IIRP), both White Americans,[13] affinity spaces allow participants who have a shared history (gender, race, experience, or circumstance) to engage in a depth of truth-telling. Indeed, perhaps this affinity approach cannot be replicated if the group were mixed with those who lack these experiences. I witnessed this depth of truth-telling—a deeply humanizing experience—during a number of Circles: for example, during the prisoner Circles I observed in a Minnesota prison; during others

The affinity of experience ensures that everyone understands what is at stake and will treat the relationship with understanding, care, respect, and trust. These safe, trust-building spaces (caucuses) often produce significant breakthroughs in transformative mediation work.

I facilitated as chaplain in a UK prison that involved Afro-Caribbean and a mix of Afro-Caribbean and Irish persons; and when I co-facilitated Circles of women-only survivors of arson attacks near Mountain View in Jamaica. What is "confessed" remains confidential, unless the party speaking wants it otherwise. The affinity of experience ensures that everyone understands what is at stake and will treat the relationship with understanding, care, respect, and trust. These safe, trust-building spaces (caucuses) often produce significant breakthroughs in transformative mediation work.

Political RJ: Colorizing as a Tool for Challenging and Changing the Structural Relationships between Dominant and Nondominant Communities

The policy, program work, and training around restorative justice/practices/approaches necessarily focus on how to hold Circles, conferences, panels, and other restorative processes effectively. Yet a more fundamental role for RJ is to challenge the dominant narrative that harms and conflict are predominantly a consequence of personal choice. People of Color recognize them as expressions of structural tensions between social classes or of the disproportional power dynamics between dominant and nondominant communities. RJ offers transformative opportunities for building alliances between people and communities who may otherwise be blissfully unaware of how the other really feels or thinks.

Restorative practices—and indeed the wider criminal justice system—in first-world societies assume a basic level of normality, safe functioning, and trust in formal institutions, such as the police and courts. However, this simply does not exist for many communities and groups: it is not the lived experience of many individuals. For many People of Color, our experience of the average police officer (or any other person in authority, for that matter) may be as an agent of oppression or dominance, rather than as a resource or peacemaker. Jamaican reggae musician Peter Tosh included a song on his 1977 hit album *Equal Rights* that sums up the problem powerfully: "I don't want no peace; I need equal rights and justice!"

This potent messy space is where many RJ practitioners work, whether they are engaged in local, national, or international processes. The clear moral line between those harmed and those who have caused harm gets fudged. RJ's spiritual core calls for a demonstrated commitment to taking seriously the experience of all participants, and this core commitment produces a humanizing if not equalizing impact. Real shifts in power and legitimacy happen when people understand the story and context of the other. The agenda for action may well change if, as I have seen, the underlying issue turns out to be the actions of another person or group—those in positions of power, authority, or dominance.

I have long been struck by the similarities between my RJ experiences in Jamaica and the experiences with introducing RJ in post-Apartheid South Africa, given what my Mennonite and Quaker colleagues who were actively involved in RJ trainings there described. In Jamaica, grassroots community members, who often included gang members, shared a common space with police officers, prison staff, businesspeople, and other professionals, and this experience challenged the latter's assumptions and social narratives of the proverbial "other half." Transforming the socio-political space had to precede RJ as we have come to know it—namely, the crime-event-focused RJ. Addressing safety issues and the mistrust of formal society meant that, instead of using the typical event-focused approach, RJ Circles were used as a medium for "public consultations" and action. For example, Peace Day (celebrated in Jamaica on the first Tuesday of March each year), Peace Walks, encouraging peace graffiti through competitions, balloon releases for abused children and young people (hosted by a victim support unit), street dances involving communities previously at war, and joint training events became critical avenues through which the different sides of a conflict were brought together.

These approaches reflect an awareness of the ubiquity of the experience of marginalization (often framed as victimhood and crime) and the further awareness that attending to the structural elements generating these experiences must be a priority. Think of the participants in RJ trainings in South Africa who had to eat meals in separate rooms for the first few days until bridges of trust began to emerge. Consider also a teenager, who was sitting

Consider also a teenager, who was sitting beside a man in a training sponsored by the Jamaica Chamber of Commerce, expressing shock when he realized that this father and singer was also a cop. Listen to the gasp of a well-heeled Jamaican woman at lunch in a major hotel when she was told that (alleged) gunmen were also in the group, wearing well-pressed shirts and trousers.

beside a man in a training sponsored by the Jamaica Chamber of Commerce, expressing shock when he realized that this father and singer was also a cop. Listen to the gasp of a well-heeled Jamaican woman at lunch in a major hotel when she was told that (alleged) gunmen were also in the group, wearing well-pressed shirts and trousers.

What Do We Aim Not to Restore?

Changing the status quo for individuals is where restoration starts. Those who have done harm, intentionally or not, must be challenged about narratives that may have justified, in their minds, a particular harm, crime, or misdemeanor. The restorative process reinforces civic responsibility. For example, in Hennepin County, Minnesota, I observed restorative conferences taking as much time to explore how the person who had done harm should restore the damage caused in community spaces as they did to map out how to incentivize a person back into education and work.[14]

Very often, what existed previously was unequal, unjust, or just plain wrong. To say that we need to "put right" these harms cannot be about restoration or reconciliation. RJ's idealism lies in building respect between persons and groups and reseeding ancient values, such as tolerance and patience. While researching Indigenous RJ principles, I came across a video documentary about the Accompong Maroon Community. The community was discussing theft as going against the principle of shared community ownership of resources, rather than as violating modern society's concept of private ownership. Indeed, a hungry person who steals to eat is not in the same moral situation as someone who steals to increase his or her wealth. Taking one breadfruit to cook is fine, but picking ten to sell is not, because the latter increases the potential for greater harm.

Very often, what existed previously was unequal, unjust, or just plain wrong. To say that we need to "put right" these harms cannot be about restoration or reconciliation.

Consider the following efforts to engage in "putting right." Which effort moves toward reinforcing a status quo, and which toward changing it? A White school principal attending an RJ conference in the US offers his contact information to another White person who is incarcerated. The principal has possibly shared the color of his power and privilege by offering the person access to support after his release. Consider that the White principal's offer may not be available to others, especially those of color who, like the White man being offered support, are incarcerated.

In another case, an African American man serving a life sentence offers to receive school reports and to help review the academic work of a White child whose parents he killed. Arguably, he could be helping to turn around the life chances of that child, while also discovering a level of personal legitimacy that he previously may not have experienced.

Music and arts are other ways of promoting consciousness change. LA Lewis, Jamaican, a DJ and singer, wrote a song on conflict resolution that a new RJ program incorporated into its marketing. Its decision to incorporate Lewis's song conferred some legitimacy on both the program and the singer, and it expanded the community's awareness of RJ. Also, when an RJ-activist group put human rights and conflict resolution information in cartoon format and distributed it free of charge, the police made the contents part of one of its promotion. This mutual awareness of people on both sides of power shifted the power dynamics between the police patrols and the poor communities on their beats.

Another example of using restorative practices to promote a shift in consciousness is the restorative justice work in schools. PALS Jamaica, a collaborative initiative between the private sector and the Ministry of Education, focuses on transforming the environmental aspects of crime and conflict. Without losing sight of the need for incident-focused interventions between students in conflict, PALS has shifted the focus to preventative work—to creating peaceable spaces.

A similar environmental or public health approach has emerged in the work of the Violence Prevention Alliance (VPA), launched in 2004. More than a decade into their journey, the VPA now uses hospital-based monitoring to identify hot spots and proactively facilitate coordinated multiagency responses. The Dispute Resolution Foundation's Youth program operates in the VPA vein, using "Restorative Justice Awareness" for desistence training with at-risk young people (those excluded from school) to help them stay on a steady, productive path with their lives.

In the UK, schools often use dialogue or Circles as an integral part of check-in or community building, but many seem not to have the resources to develop a full restorative approach to bullying scenarios or to train and support peer facilitators. Their use of restorative processes seems more like a complaint-driven, adult-led environment, rather than a peer-facilitated, adult-supported space for children and other youth to learn critical life skills. When problems become more acute, the default is still to use state-funded or credentialed actors—a default that remains problematic.

Sometimes opportunities arise to use RJ to challenge and transform structural relationships. In recent memory, for example, British citizens have had many such opportunities. I think of the Grenfell Tower Fire (2017), the Tottenham Riots (2011), the Brixton Riots (2011), and Stephen Lawrence's murder (1993). Yet at such times, judicial or quasi-judicial interventions dominate the official response. Professional and political actors in the officious, institutional

Taking Colorizing Restorative Justice *seriously brings considerable risks. An almost unquestioning loyalty to the rules of the dominant institutional setup, in terms of both RJ codes of practice and legislation, is an unspoken element of accreditation and funding processes.*

space draw their power from "the center" and statute, rather than from grassroots experience. As a consequence, momentum for deep change is difficult to initiate and maintain, and opportunities for changing consciousness are missed.

One wonders about the extent to which the creation of feature-length films, such as *Stephen: The Murder That Changed a Nation* that BBC aired in April 2018, helps to build momentum for consciousness change. Stephen, a Black teenager, was murdered by White men at a bus stop in London on April 22, 1993. His murder and the "institutionally racist" response by the police and courts are considered a watershed moment in race relations in the UK. Twenty-five years after his murder, Prime Minister Theresa May announced that April 22 would henceforth be observed as Stephen Lawrence Day.

Other shorter snapshots have contributed to reframing the collective narrative around crime and the criminal justice response, depicting pathways for how the status quo has changed and can continue to do so. *The Long Night's Journey into Day,*[15] *The Imam and the Pastor* (about interfaith conflict resolution work in northern Nigeria), the Anne Frank Trust UK Prisons Project, and the Kwanza celebration are culture-changing projects that have humanized both those who have harmed others and those who have functioned as oppressors.[16] They have also provided spaces for people to go deeper into the historical contexts surrounding crime and violence.

Ethical Considerations

Taking *Colorizing Restorative Justice* seriously brings considerable risks. An almost unquestioning loyalty to the rules of the dominant institutional setup, in terms of both RJ codes of practice and legislation, is an unspoken element of accreditation and funding processes. As we go down the colorizing road, I anticipate times when it will get messy, and decisions to support colorizing RJ will raise conflicts and tensions around fundamental RJ values. Several examples come to mind:

1. When we work to de-escalate the threat of gang violence in prisons or communities, personal credibility is key. Key players must

have no doubt that information will be held in strict confidence. Confidentiality raises issues of trust, and trust can be undermined if RJ practitioners are perceived as having easy and friendly relationships with authorities that the community does not trust. It may not (in the words of a gentleman in Chicago's Ceasefire Program) be possible both to maintain influence in disadvantaged communities and to be seen in conversation with "the authorities." We can derail our best efforts at trust-building if we do not pay attention to the people we are speaking to and to those who are observing us when we have conversations with institutional players. How much information does the formal security sector have a right to know? How does colorizing RJ negotiate such tensions between confidentiality and accountability?

2. A colleague who worked in the favelas in Brazil recounted how a member of his team complained that a teen with an assault rifle had interrupted a preparation Circle meeting. In my colleague's view, the teen, who was a stakeholder, was challenging his not being invited to the meeting. Was this a fair concern, even when carrying an illegal firearm? How does colorizing RJ negotiate the complexities of respect and participation?
3. Black prisoners who have successfully planned and delivered Black History Month lend their support to prisoners from minority White communities interested in having their own culture celebrated. Is this a powerful example of interracial collaboration for mutual transformation? What risk goes with disrupting the racial regime that prison complexes maintain?
4. Prisoners, after mediation and restorative justice training, form a Guiding Angels group to resolve conflict among other inmates and seize illegal items as part of their work. If the head of the prison or prisoner leadership do not give their blessing to this project, would the prisoners' actions still be empowering or would they actually be subversive?
5. Various groups fund and provide other resources to facilitate contact between former Irish Republican Army (IRA) members and those they harmed. However, as long as the wider public seems not yet ready to value this gesture as a good thing, are the groups causing conflict and tension? Should they make these overtures anyway?
6. Who gives an RJ practitioner the right, as one judge asked, to host an RJ conference to address the needs of parties in a sexual violence case when the case had not been brought to the attention of the police? Do RJ practitioners have the authority to convene a

restorative conference to address a case of homophobic behavior, when either the law or public opinion—or both—view gay people as valid targets for hate and exclusion? What does it take for RJ practitioners to do this? Courage? A commitment to social justice?

The Color of Money and Resources

In this short section, I wish to pay tribute to the work in Jamaica to explore ways to procure services, such as cleaning, food, and transport, for projects in non-traditional ways. Small, community-based businesses supply services that large companies would otherwise handle and possibly co-opt. This with-in community arrangement has many benefits. It allows funding to have a direct impact inside the community where events take place; it strengthens the level of community engagement and buy-in around problem-solving; and it builds community capacity at the grassroots level.

The Core of RJ: Spirituality

I find my work has increasingly focused on two core principles that have distilled from my training and casework:

- The first principle is to help participants "drop down from head to heart," using Indigenous or traditional rituals and spirituality to enhance awareness of our shared responsibility. By speaking truth from the heart, every participant contributes to their own process of *conscientization*. In 1968, Paulo Freire introduced and defined this term in *Pedagogy of the Oppressed* as developing a critical consciousness and acting from it to change reality. The intention is to facilitate a shift toward recognizing that each participant's (or social class's) narrative is important to hear and acknowledge in the consciousness-raising process. Storytelling, which is at the core of African and other Indigenous cultures, can rebalance attitudes and ground mutual trust in intuitive, spiritual, non-rational ways of expressing oneself.
- The second principle is to present RJ more as a values-based lifestyle and less as a model or specific approach facilitated by experts.

The first principle is to help participants "drop down from head to heart," . . .

For some People of Color, these two RJ principles may lead to acknowledging the importance of an explicitly religious or spiritual element of identity and using this identity as a bridge to restorative practices. For example, in Islam, the Qur'an teaches that human nature and society derive from God's nature, which is restorative in essence. "If any one does harm or wrongs his own soul but afterwards seeks Allah's forgiveness, he will find Allah Oft-forgiving, Most Merciful" (Surah An Nisa: 4:110). Also, "If you stretch your hand against me, to slay me, it is not for me to stretch my hand against thee: for I do fear Allah, God of the Universe" (Surah Al Maidah: 28). Sikhism speaks of forgiveness, love, equality, and eternal optimism. For example, the Punjabi term "chardi kala" expresses the aspiration to maintain a mental state of eternal optimism and joy.

Because values and moral considerations lie at the heart of many of life's most important decisions, I have found it very important to highlight restorative values as key—a priority that stands out in the following examples:

1. As a trade union leader, I once observed a decision to pursue another round of strikes "in an effort to force the employer to make payment before Christmas rather than at the end of January." This decision came after a successful strike action—with all the disruption that any strike inevitably creates—had already generated a much-improved offer. It took a real focus on restorative values to challenge and change the decision. Not only would the decision to continue the strike have risked causing additional harm and undermined goodwill, but also it would have laid bare a shallowness during a season when greater understanding and compassion are foremost in consciousness.
2. Employees and office holders (e.g., police officers, ministers of government, and ministers of religion) often are investigated and face disciplinary action in matters involving motives and cultural context, even when the facts give no grounds for disciplinary action. Allegations of corruption and whistleblowing come to mind as examples. I have been part of organizations that have supported staff who were open and honest about a breach of rules. But I have also seen organizations deprive themselves of the service and support of experienced staff, and this deprivation has contributed to an organization's dysfunction and mental health problems based on less-than-restorative values. Perhaps they prioritize upholding traditions and the status quo of powerful constituents, or they are unwilling to focus on the actual harm. Revisiting values could move an organization's dysfunctional behavior toward healthier relations and ways of working.

3. For those oriented to spiritual, religious, or cultural ways, singing, reading sacred texts, or introducing religious or cultural rituals and artifacts can have an impact. For example:
   a. I once co-facilitated an RJ conference with an Imam who led the welcoming ritual using Qur'anic verses and a prayer. He explained why the dialogue process would move from right to left around the room rather than from a conventional left to right direction that others might be accustomed to. While facilitating a preparation meeting with a family dealing with allegations of school bullying, I asked about the Arabic writing on a wall, and this genuine interest about things Arabic seemed to enhance the participants' willingness to engage with RJ.
   b. I recall the quieting effect when I invited two Sikh families in dispute over a parking matter to bring and share a verse that was important to them from the Guru Granth Sahib, the religious scripture of Sikhism. Inviting reflection on such stories as the woman caught committing adultery in John 8 in the Bible or the disagreement between two very different cultural groups in Acts 15 have had a similar positive effect in my work in church conflict situations.
   c. A community member accused of assault had been entirely unwilling to engage with RJ. However, he began to be more receptive once the facilitators accepted his invitation to "share a glass of good wine." Though the matter did not proceed beyond pre-conference preparation, the experience showed me that there is something to be said about valuing cultural norms and engaging with the common humanity of others. A similar situation is documented in the book *This Light That Pushes Me: Stories of African Peacebuilders*, edited by Laura Shipler Chico. An invitation to "eat food" at the home of a woman who had overheard plans for a gang reprisal led to a positive resolution.[17]

The RJ practitioner must always consider how power is being exercised and in whose interests. Justice is not, in fact, blind to the social context.

Other Hybrid RJ Applications

Having been on one side or the other of investigations, I cannot resist the opportunity to reframe the following investigations as Circles. Circles enable participants to transform a fraught encounter filled with many-sided stories into an opportunity to speak truth to power. Whatever the outcome, ultimately a Circle fails only if one's story is not spoken truthfully and with dignity. These are some of the key contributions that holding Circles in palliative care environments can offer.

As a hospice chaplain, I have hosted Circles with families doing funeral planning. In many cultures, funerals are not private spaces. As a pastor, the restorative instinct demands that, in leading funeral services, I consider the role of Circle keeper: accessing the healing power of the Circle; hearing the lament of harm experienced; holding the space for individual speakers; and filling in the grave by family and friends—a kind of "we will do it ourselves," rather than leave it to the professional grave diggers.

Whatever the outcome, ultimately a Circle fails only if one's story is not spoken truthfully and with dignity.

Consistent with my desire to avoid branding, I have not proposed a brand called bereavement Circles or some similar name. In these situations, the essence of my work has been to offer restorative principles and a talking piece into a natural—albeit emotionally challenging—conversation(al) space with families. The success of these interventions led to rolling out an RJ awareness training with spiritual and pastoral care staff, volunteers, and community clinicians. With any luck, an RJPoid will research the efficacy of RJ and Circles in de-escalating family conflicts and in supporting decision-making around key end-of-life matters. At some point, a narrative around standards for training, their use, and risk assessments will develop. Preferably, though, practitioners will share what they have learned about other end-of-life-related applications of RJ, such as grave talk, death cafes, good-death cafes, or pizza parties for family members planning their funerals around the dinner table, as my chaplaincy colleague from the University Hospital of Coventry and Warwick has done.

A well-developed instinct for restorative decision-making has meant, for me, challenging another racial, cultural, institutional norm: unfair prison practices. Prisons have allowed family Circles, family time, a meal, or an act of worship only for prisoners from the dominant community. As the injustice of these unfair practices has been named and exposed, prisons have had to rewrite the criteria to reflect the norms of minority groups as well.

Adhering to a restorative lifestyle demands that we use a talking piece and Circles in personal family life and parenting—another space where restorative values become visible. When it comes to teaching or presenting, can a lecturer not also be a Circle keeper? Communicating information means inviting youth to consider the need for personal transformation. To this end, we can use Circles to explore the ripple effects of a harm as well as to reflect on shared values and truths across the religious spectrum, which presentations by an African cosmologist, Imam, and Hindu priest can inspire. Notice again that RJ values for People of Color match dignity and respect. Hearing truth directly wherever possible takes priority over having it mediated through an expert, whether it be a lawyer, a lecturer, or a credentialed RJPoid.

Colorizing Games

Over many years, I have observed that those who are in dominant positions—whether individuals, groups, organizations, or systems—often do not find it easy to notice the value of prioritizing harm's repair, inclusion, and mutual interests over organizational rules and institutional structures.

Right-brain work can be critical in facilitating the shift in thinking. This right-brain awareness is why I often use movement, music, and games in my work as a trainer and facilitator. I have found these to be much more powerful than formal, technical skill-building and content-driven work (see activities section).

Some Positive Strategies Highlighted

Over the years, I have observed some of the strategies or accommodations that have allowed RJ provider organizations and programs to survive and grow.

1. Be fluid about process and flexible about language: these are important skills for this journey. The ability of People of Color to speak several "languages" is a unique gift that facilitates the emergence of a credible "we"—in the Ubuntu sense, not as the "royal we"! I believe a sense of "we" is central to peacemaking and healing.
2. Invest and be intentional about "identifying" and "projecting"—terms I use deliberately instead of the condescending term "developing"—RJPoids of Color. Opinion leaders of all stripes who co-opt messages—whether words or behavior, coded or otherwise—do so such that those on the other side of the table can recognize themselves in the process. Some reaching out or connection is made. Without this effort to find common ground, "white flight," heterosexual flight, youth flight, older person flight, or speakers of other languages flight could well occur.
3. Piggyback on wider community development, crime prevention, parenting education, and social support programs. This community outreach or collaboration is an effective way of multiplying limited resources, even though it risks diluting "YOUR OWN BRAND"!

4. Engage with people who have "coals in more than one fire" or "feet in more than one camp": consider it cross-fertilization or "networking," if necessary. A passionate generalist may have value far beyond that of a technically astute specialist. So, open the door for a lawyer, businessperson, minister of religion, medical professional, local politician, or senior from the public sector to explore their wider interests in social justice and community transformation. Call it role enrichment perhaps or symbiosis, but always keep space for an RJPoint at the table.
5. Indigenize messages and methods. I think of restorative drumming in Iraq or the community training in Jamaica called "Level de Vibes." Part of this indigenizing includes the skillful art that affirms informal community processes. When this impulse goes in the direction of restorative action, though, we may encounter "fowl coop" or "jungle justice"—the view that informers/snitches/grasses, i.e., people who take problem-solving outside their own community—should be "disciplined." This view rightly prioritizes community, but such disciplining must be open to incorporating more skillful and less punitive strategies for upholding community autonomy.

In Summary

Most Jamaicans would probably accept that inequity's structural problems persist and need addressing alongside RJ casework. Here, there is no easy "other person" to deflect attention from harm's core causes and conflict. In the US, communities of color seem to hold enough power, both economic and political, to drive change, even in the face of apathy or resistance from society's other sectors. The UK, however, seems to sustain much less consensus around the need for institutional change. Only when major events of injustice occur is there a spike in public consciousness about inequality. In all three areas, tribalism (expressed in partisan politics, anti-terrorism work, and anti-immigration sentiments) result in a kind of deprivation and injustice that cannot be readily separated from the first problem of historical injustices based on color.

Ultimately, I believe, a natural balance will emerge between individualism and collective responsibility (Ubuntu). The well-known maxim "It takes a village to raise a child" says it well. Those who share the power of vulnerability—slaves, immigrants, trafficked people, and victims of hate crimes, global trade deals, environmental crime, or corrupt banking practices, etc.—do not need to meet as individuals with those who harm them. Rather, they must work together to stop these harms and to repair them through transparent dialogue processes. Real RJ casework is the ground for all this. By analogy, "disease prevention" requires both great hospitals to deal with medical crises and good public health programs to make crises less likely and less intense.

DISCUSSION QUESTIONS

1. Consider the six cases presented under "Ethical Considerations" (pages 230–32): what questions do they raise?
2. In RJ practice, which efforts move toward reinforcing a status quo and which move toward changing it? How can we become more aware of the difference and point our practice in the latter direction? Consider the examples on pages 228–30.
3. Taking colorizing restorative justice seriously brings considerable risks. As we go down the colorizing road, it will get messy, and decisions to support colorizing RJ will raise conflicts and tensions around fundamental RJ values. Have you experienced this? What happened? How did you respond? What support or options did you have or would you recommend for others who are facing similar experiences?

ACTIVITIES

1. *"Guess the Rule" Game.* Resources needed: two to three lawn tennis or similar-sized soft balls. The purpose of the game is to explore the frustration people feel when they have not been consulted about the rules of the game or when the rules shift without their involvement. Advise participants that you will throw the ball to each of them in turn. Whether they catch it (or not) or throw it back to you or another person, you then randomly choose some to be "out" and say that's good. After a few instances, participants tend to begin guessing whether they caught the ball with the wrong hand or threw it back the wrong way or should throw it to another participant. Stand your ground—that is, remain silent about your rationale—and let the anxiety build as you continue to throw the ball around. Choose a moment to check if anyone thought they knew the rule. Comments such as "I am the trainer" or "Are you questioning my honesty and integrity?" help to get participants focused on the issue of fairness and exclusion. If some refuse to throw the ball in an attempt to stop the "injustice," introduce the second ball that you have kept out of sight in your pocket and continue to play as above. Debrief feelings and thoughts around democracy, rules in families, how leaders use power and their impact on others. Lead the discussion toward acknowledging how harmful it is to be excluded from having a say in the rules.

2. *Cross the Circle.* Ask participants to stand in a circle. Share that you will be making a number of statements that, if true for them and if they feel safe enough to do so, they should move to a different place in the circle. The participants are to be silent throughout the activity, with each person deciding how they wish to interpret the statement. The activity helps to explore the importance of creating choice and a sense of safety if people are to "speak truth from the heart" as well as to make visible the many shared experiences we have. Start with relatively benign statements like "I had breakfast today" or "I have a savings account." Build to more challenging ones, such as "I have a close friend who is gay or in prison." Later, explore admissions to statements like "I have used violence against another person in the last six months" or "I have done something in the past year that could have led to a criminal charge or disciplinary action." Be creative in your response to the local context of the group. I have often used the activity in conjunction with a discussion of the principle of *Sawubona*, a Zulu greeting meaning "I see you."
3. *Switching chairs.* I have used this technique both in training and in preparing for RJ meetings with those who have harmed others. Resources: one or more empty chairs. Ask participants to answer the relevant RJ questions while sitting in a different chair, as if they were the other party.

NOTES

1. My chapter has been edited to reflect US spelling and grammatical conventions.
2. Some might prefer terms such as Black, Asian, Minority Ethnic (BME or BAME) groups.
3. D. Shante, "I'm Exhausted from Trying to Be the 'Right' Kind of Black Girl at Work," *Huffpost Personal*, March 14, 2018, https://www.huffingtonpost.com/entry/codeswitching-while-black-at-work_us_5aa2b7dce4b07047bec60c5c.
4. There has always been a strong "jungle justice" alternative available to those who know where to look and who to ask!
5. Roger Fisher, William Ury, and Bruce Patton, *Getting to Yes: Negotiating Agreement without Giving In* (New York: Penguin, 1991).
6. Adapted from the classifications philanthropist, philanthropoid, philantropest, philanthropreneur, philanthropoint, which I first encountered at the University of Minnesota in 2004.
7. To use a concept from M. G. Smith, *Culture Race and Class in the Commonwealth Caribbean*, foreword by Rex Nettleford (Mona, Jamaica: Department of Extra Mural Studies, University of the West Indies, 1984).
8. I owe a tribute to the multicultural and child-focused work of Roca, Inc., in Chelsea, Massachusetts, which introduced me to the very impactful piece "A Prayer for the Children" by Ina Hughs.

9. For further reading on this subject, please explore the work of Professor Maduabuchi Dukor. See also Kathleen Daly and Julie Stubbs, "Feminist Engagement with Restorative Justice," *Theoretical Criminology* 10, no. 1 (2006): 9–28 (Sydney Law School Research Paper, No. 06/42), https://ssrn.com/abstract=699841.
10. See, for example, the video: Larisa Mann, "Decolonizing Copyright: Jamaican Street Dances," http://wilkins.law.harvard.edu/events/luncheons/2011-03-22_mann/2011-03-22_mann640.ogv, accessed February 2, 2018).
11. See Sherrian Gray, "Trends in Urban Crime and Violence in Kingston, Jamaica: A Case Study," in *Enhancing Urban Safety and Security: Global Report on Human Settlements 2007*, United Nations Human Settlements Programme (London: UN-Habitat and Earthscan, 2007), 307–8, https://unhabitat.org/wp-content/uploads/2008/07/GRHS.2007.CaseStudy.Crime_.Kingston.pdf.
12. Gus John, "Ethnic Penalty, Crime and Punishment," IARS International Institute, 2013, https://soundcloud.com/iars-1/theo-gavrieldies-achieving.
13. Paul McCold and Ted Wachtel, *In Pursuit of Paradigm: A Theory of Restorative Justice*, January 2003,https://www.researchgate.net/publication/237314664_In_Pursuit_of_Paradigm_A_Theory_of_Restorative_Justice, accessed June 23, 2018.
14. See "Diversion Programs: Offering Alternatives for Low-Level Misdemeanor Offenses," http://www.ci.minneapolis.mn.us/attorney/diversionprogram/index htm, accessed August 2017.
15. Frances Reid and Deborah Hoffman, *Long Night's Journey into Day* (Berkeley, CA: Iris Feminist Collective, 2000). This work is a documentary on the South African Truth and Reconciliation Commission.
16. In 1966, Dr. Maulana Karenga developed a celebration of African heritage to occur from December 26 to January 1. Initially, prisoners of African heritage and later from all racial groups sat in a circle in a facilitated conversation about the personal relevance of seven named Afro-centric values.
17. Laura Shipler Chico, *This Light That Pushes Me: Stories of African Peacebuilders* (Fitchburg, MA: Quaker Books, 2014).

PART IV

Restorative Lessons from within the Community

The power of restorative processes hinges on relationships, and relationships build community. Conversely, being in community, which restorative practices create spaces for, nurtures relationships and deepens them. As People of Color and Indigenous Peoples, we are community-minded, because our communities have been the means for our respective survivals since time immemorial and most certainly in the rough waters of white settler supremacy over the past five centuries. This acknowledgment of our survivability is not to say that our communities are free of dysfunction. Given the trauma we have had to endure over generations, PTSD patterns are ingrained and internalized. Dr. Joy DeGruy, Black, author and consultant on race, culture, and education, names these patterns in African American families and communities as the "post traumatic slave syndrome."[1] As the authors in part 4 discuss, communities are foundational to our identities, our healing, our safety, and our well-being. For a restorative philosophy and practice to work for us, we must operate from within and through our communities. Being restorative means being community-minded and community-committed. The trick is realizing that this calls us to think and act differently from Western ways. Consequently, we have some healing and relearning to do.

[1] See: Joy DeGruy, *Post Traumatic Slave Syndrome: America's Legacy of Enduring Injury and Healing* (Portland, OR: Joy DeGruy Publications, 2005).

Chapter 14

Restorative Justice through a Trauma-Informed, Racial-Equity Lens

Victor Jose Santana

Introduction

Since time immemorial, restorative justice has been a way of life for Indigenous Peoples globally. I am fortunate to have been introduced to the restorative justice practice of peacemaking Circles during a critical time in my life. I was transforming from a young person to an adult. I graduated from college with a communications degree and had been working for a couple of years in a graduate internship at the Publishing Services Bureau at the Massachusetts Institute of Technology (MIT). I worked on graphic design and every type of publishing imaginable. I enjoyed my time there, I learned so much, and I was being groomed for a position within the booming publishing field. However, my passion for grassroots community work was always at the forefront. In retrospect, recognizing that my passion differed from what I was being groomed for told me that what I truly sought was healing.

During my spare time (while not at work at MIT), I was a community organizer and activist. My passion around social justice concerned those issues important to many young people. A friend who had been a member of an organization (Roca) since she was thirteen invited me to a youth leadership conference the organization was holding. Roca, Inc., is a youth-serving, nonprofit organization based in Chelsea, Massachusetts. I soon learned that one of the youth leaders in the organization had died while playing with a gun among friends. The mood was very sad, yet the youth were transforming all this pain through their workshops, art, and performances. One workshop on LGBTQ awareness didn't have a facilitator because the facilitator had fallen ill, so my friend asked me if I would be willing to lead that session. Since I had already been leading workshops on gender identity and homophobia,

I said "yes" and had a dynamic workshop with fifteen young people. A few months later, I left my MIT position for a position as Roca's art programming coordinator. Every time I would hear about an injustice in my community, I would always try to take action. At the time, I thought this new opportunity would help the children in my community address injustice through artistic expression and education.

My parents' history and experiences, plus my own experiences as a Dominican, Black, Native, cisgender, gay man living in the United States of America, shaped the way I approached my work. These identities and experiences shape my understanding of race, restorative justice, and how they can be integrated to work toward healing. My convictions are that restorative justice peacemaking Circles can (1) raise trauma awareness and (2) promote healing among communities. In my own personal life, I have struggled to live and succeed in a world where I am often told or reminded that there is something wrong with who I am as a person. I have spent the last twenty-three years integrating my personal and professional work as an artist, leader, activist, mentor, trainer, and Circle keeper. In my pursuit of self-acceptance, leadership, and social justice, these roles have influenced my approach to restorative justice work.[1]

In my own personal life, I have struggled to live and succeed in a world where I am often told or reminded that there is something wrong with who I am as a person.

My father's political activism and his acceptance of a university scholarship from the Romanian (Communist) government in the late 1960s were the reasons for his exile from the Dominican Republic for more than ten years—and why I was born in Puerto Rico. When I was seven, my parents, sister, and I moved to Salem and then to Lynn, Massachusetts, where I grew up. Comparatively, both my parents grew up during a dictatorship and revolution in the Dominican Republic. Their experiences of political and social repression in the context of dictatorship, as well as exile, are part of my family history.

Through my Circle practice, I have become more aware of my own trauma and cognitive dissonance. Through this understanding, I began to use the wisdom and skills drawn from my life experiences to help young people and adults who have struggled with experiences similar to mine.[2]

Mark Wedge, elder/leader from the Carcross/Tagish First Nation; Judge Barry Stuart, Euro-Canadian, chief judge of the Yukon Territory, now retired; and Kay Pranis, White American, international restorative justice trainer, and author, are mentors who trained me in Circles. I was first introduced to restorative justice peacemaking Circles (Circles) while I was working at Roca. I attended a Circle training with forty people who represented community—young people, gang members, police officers, and clergy members;

representatives from juvenile corrections, social service agencies, and various community organizations; and community leaders. We spent four full days together learning about the Circle process. We had time and activities to help us get to know each other and reflect on ourselves. By the fourth day, compared to our initial day, we knew each other on very deep levels. We had learned about each other through the stories and activities we shared in the Circle process.[3]

"We are all related," stated Harold Gatensby, Dahka T'lingit, First Nations leader, at my first training at Roca. "If you can't seem to find a circle anywhere, just look into the pupil of another person's eye. The Earth is a circle and is made up of 80 to 90 percent water, and so are our bodies. People will always be 80 to 90 percent more alike than different."[4] The wisdom shared during that Circle process had a profound impact on the way I worked with people. It also helped me reflect on my identity and my own cognitive dissonance. During that time, I was not living my life in a way that reflected my values and who I wanted to be in the world.

Since then, I have come to understand that, in order to be effective in Circles and restorative justice work, I must engage in my own process of self-discovery. I have also come to understand that acknowledging restorative justice's Indigenous roots is critical to working with integrity. In addition to being transparent, an honest conversation about our commonalities and differences is critical to the peacemaking and the healing process, and one that I have learned to appreciate as restorative justice.

Stories of Building Trust and Resilience

Relationships are as important to the Circle process as water is important to life. I have devoted a lot of time in Circle to people getting to know each other before we dive into an issue and seek solutions. When you feel you know someone, conversations go to deeper levels, and leaving an uncomfortable dialogue is not an option until a consensus is attained. Trust in Circle is foundational; it is what can hold the hard conversations. When this norm is missing, it is difficult to gain consensus or an understanding of an issue. Common ground rules can be established through group agreements and additional icebreaker activities, which range from fun questions to something a little more personal. Sometimes things come up in the Circle process that we have no control over, no matter how much we have prepared.

Sometimes things come up in the Circle process that we have no control over, no matter how much we have prepared.

I have two stories that illustrate how sensitive and thoughtful we must be when we are asked to facilitate or keep a Circle.

In the early 2000s, the City of Chelsea and other communities in Massachusetts welcomed many Sudanese young men who were escaping from a civil war. Many of the young men were referred to Roca. They immediately engaged in the organization's educational and employment programming. Despite the "welcome" they had received, all the young men I worked with were experiencing discrimination. They told me of rocks being thrown at them while they were waiting for buses and people making fun of their dark skin. The executive director asked me to co-lead a few Circles in support of the twenty-four young men who were engaged in our programming.

I spent a few days with my colleague Raming preparing for the Circles. Raming and I worked closely with a young man named Samuel who spoke both Sudanese Arabic and English. He volunteered to serve as an interpreter for all the Circles and, as a result, his social and language skill set made him a leader. He invited most of the other young men to the Circle.

Although I prepared for the Circle, I didn't know enough about their experiences to avoid what would eventually disrupt our first Circle. During that Circle, we had a centerpiece and introduced the talking piece. We asked permission from those in Circle to burn sage and introduced the Circle process. We learned only one person had participated in a Circle before. We let the group know that we wanted to support them. Our first round responded to a check-in question, and you could already feel the tension in the room. Because we were pressed for time, we did not spend enough time building trust. One of the young men asked Samuel to ask me a question. What I heard Samuel ask was, "Are Circles a relief?" but what the young man actually asked was, "Are Circles a belief?" Once the group heard it was a belief, more than half the Circle got up and left very upset. I couldn't quite understand what had happened. What I later understood was that they had escaped religious persecution in Sudan. Religion was imposed on these young men, and the Circle felt like another forced ritualistic practice.

The other side to this story was that, for many of the young men, it was the first time they felt brave enough to say "no" to a practice they didn't understand. I found out later that they, being Indigenous, had a similar Circle process. Circles resembled some of their own rituals, which was another reason they felt so uncomfortable. It took days to repair relations and apologize for the miscommunication. Eventually, the entire group came back, and we mutually apologized for the misunderstanding. We all re-engaged in a second Circle and shared how we felt and what we had learned from the experience. *I personally learned how good intentions could have a negative impact or outcome.* Our ability to recover from the initial Circle experience created a greater bond that contributed to our resilience in a later Circle.

I personally learned how good intentions could have a negative impact or outcome. *Our ability to recover from the initial Circle experience created a greater bond that contributed to our resilience in a later Circle.*

As Circle keepers, we may be asked to facilitate Circles in different communities, and we have to carefully analyze how we are being utilized and for what purpose. A friend who is a community organizer from the Baltimore area invited me to lead a Circle bringing people together after the Freddie Gray case. Freddie Gray died a week after sustaining spinal injuries while being in police custody. The killing—some say murder—of Freddie Gray resonated nationally and internationally. I wanted to help. Yet I also understood that, if not planned well, this Circle could potentially be harmful.

I used the following tool (figure 1) to guide my decision-making process. The guide is a tool based on a framework and approach that I have used for years when I conduct Circles, community planning, community-focus groups, and/or speeches or presentations.

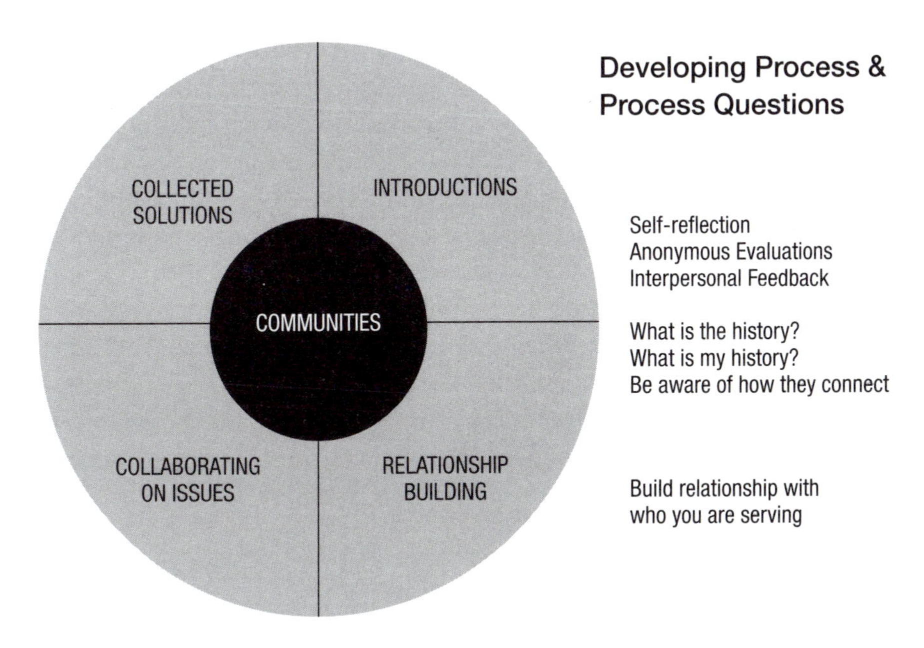

Figure 1. A Circle Process Approach to Community Engagement.

First Nations leaders Mark Wedge and Harold Gatensby in Yukon taught me about the Medicine Wheel (see figure 3). I apply the Medicine Wheel framework to many areas of my life. This particular Medicine Wheel is based on my approach to community work that involves focus groups, trainings, and preparing for a healing and/or talking Circle.

My approach is to always center the communities we are working with. The community's needs guide the decisions I make about any Circle I keep. Sometimes I know the community well and sometimes not. This community approach has always worked for me. So, when I used this tool to analyze whether I would go to Baltimore to help lead a Circle of support, I concluded that it was not a good idea. There would not be enough time to prepare and hold space in a good way. Moreover, my White male friend and co-facilitator had already encountered race-based resistance with some of the communities he was trying to support in Baltimore. I told my friend that we must be mindful of the racial dynamic and perception when a White person, who is not fully integrated or connected to a community, uses me, his friend of color, to lead a Circle process with people who are in the midst of so much pain: this dynamic could add more pain. My questions to him were: Who is already doing the work in that community, and how could he support them? Who has historically been doing the work there, and how can you become more of an ally?

My approach is to always center the communities we are working with. The community's needs guide the decisions I make about any Circle I keep. Sometimes I know the community well and sometimes not. This community approach has always worked for me.

Another example of the sensitivity and care needed in community and Circle work comes from when I worked at the Boston Public Health Commission (BPHC). I was tasked with developing and designing training for youth workers in the city of Boston. I was given a list of people to visit and talk with in order to organize focus groups centered around identifying themes for the curricula and ensuring that the curricula being developed for youth workers in Boston was relevant. I asked myself the following set of questions before I went to speak with the youth workers and their communities:

1. Who is my audience?
2. What are some existing networks? Informal or formal?
3. Who are the Elders, leaders in the community, community health workers (CHWs), curanderos (healers), and gatekeepers?
4. Can I—and is it appropriate for me to—help meet a need?
5. How is this training linked to their need?
6. What is the benefit? Who benefits?

7. Is this long term? Is this short term?
8. Am I that right person—even if it's a community I come from or work with?
9. Who is already connected?
10. How do I build trust?
11. Am I calling or emailing people back on time?
12. If my communication is inconsistent, whom am I calling back?
13. Whom am I not calling back?
14. Can I use this as an opportunity to balance how I distribute access and resources?
15. Am I being fair? Thoughtful? Considerate?
16. Am I being consistent?
17. Are there ongoing opportunities for engagement?
18. When am I going back? How am I giving back?
19. Is there a history of swooping in and out of this community? How do we not replicate this?

I used the Circle process tool to develop this training. In the *introductions* stage, I met with all of the leaders and elders, youth workers, young people, organizations, committees, and task forces identified for me. I then invited them to come together to introduce them to the project and myself. During the first round of meetings, I listened for stories that could help me identify themes. In addition, I asked about any upcoming events in the community that would be appropriate for me to attend. Another part of the introduction included being transparent about how this process would work and how the community would benefit—that the process would be appreciative of their time and feedback.

If you want to develop something that requires a community's input, then it is also important to have clear expectations about what is possible. For this project, I knew there would be a written document in the end. I also knew that the community had identified sharing or reciprocity as a need. Part of my expectation was that, once I developed the training, I would bring it back to the community for approval, which I did. I lived in Boston after I graduated high school. During this time, I was very involved in People of Color LGBTQ social justice work, which helped me establish strong networks of support with different community leaders and organizations. My history and reputation were a main contributor to establishing trust with the communities of Boston that work with young people.

As I attended events and continued to meet more people from the community, my Circle grew and so did the *trust-building*. I always make sure that, if I am invited to events, I am on time. Emailing and calling people back in a timely manner are also ways of building trust. When creating the curricula for the BPHC, I had to make hundreds of calls to community members. When I wasn't being consistent with the callbacks, I took a moment to reflect on whom I wasn't calling back and why that might be. Eventually, I was able to form fifteen focus groups. For example, one focus group was comprised only of young people who had worked with a youth worker before. That focus group talked about what they needed from youth workers and the training they would recommend.

Through the focus groups, I identified *issues and themes*. It was clear that youth workers already possessed many skills and more than sufficient knowledge, but they needed more support around trauma, resilience, restorative justice, and racial equity to unleash their talents. Applying this experience in a context outside of a talking Circle is an example of being "In Circle out of Circle." The Medicine Wheel process/framework allows us to think in equitable, trauma-informed approaches to developing and implementing Circles, trainings, presentations, and community organizing in communities of color.

This collective process of *seeking solutions* enhanced youth workers' capacities to serve young people whose lives have been impacted by violence and trauma. Through the extensive, two-year process of designing, facilitating, and evaluating four training institutes, we trained more than 5,000 youth workers in Boston who, in turn, served approximately 60,000 young people in the city. From this community-rooted process, the Boston Defending Childhood Initiative (BDCI, an Initiative of the Boston Public Health Commission) and the Boston Area Rape Crisis Center (BARCC) developed a training and facilitator's guide.

Circles and Tools for Racial Equity Circles

Restorative justice continues to gain popularity and momentum in the United States and beyond. As restorative justice becomes more mainstream, opportunities to co-opt and forget its origins grow. Academic institutions and local governments in particular tend to over-intellectualize or over-professionalize a field of work, respectively. Academia prioritizes a westernized point of view (at the expense of other worldviews) and money. Professionalizing a field via academia perpetuates inequities. For example, the work becomes about who the experts are, who has access, and who can pay for that knowledge. In contrast to this mainstreaming, restorative justice's practitioners earn their knowledge via hard work, experience, or as it is passed down through intergenerational relationships. When we recognize Indigenous Peoples for their resilience against harm, we are acknowledging that Indigenous Peoples historically have had knowledge about restorative justice that is valuable and contributes to the field. Noticing this contrast between frontline and professional restorative justice is a way to begin addressing inequities in the field.[5]

> *Addressing race and other inequities in a Circle format requires very thoughtful preparation. From my experience, I recognize that people are at different levels in their understanding of race, racism, gender, and identity.*

The notion that restorative justice is something new doesn't value its historical origins. For those of us who do racial equity work in Circle, we must start here. We must always respect and acknowledge restorative justice's Indigenous roots.

In the last few years, I have had many Circle requests to address race and/or racial tension in groups and organizations. Addressing race and other inequities in a Circle format requires very thoughtful preparation. From my experience, I recognize that people are at different levels in their understanding of race, racism, gender, and identity. There is a difference between preparing a restorative justice Circle in response to a racist incident versus people coming together to discuss and address issues of race and racism. The case studies I will share include both types of Circles.

Addressing Issues of White Supremacy in Youth-Serving Organizations

An organization I have worked with (which will remain nameless) is a national youth-serving organization. The organization has a dilemma that is very common in the nonprofit and private sectors: the staff does not reflect the population they serve. This dynamic leads to issues of guilt, accountability, trust, and perpetuating cycles of oppression.

This organization invited me to lead its staff in a Circle process focused on race and equity. They wanted to acknowledge the racist situations that young people and staff were experiencing at work and in life; identify tools they could apply; and spend some time on self-care and how this impacts them as youth workers. Approximately twenty-five youth workers attended—approximately ten People of Color and fifteen White people. All the youth workers who participated were in their mid to late twenties.

Whenever I speak about race, racism, and their impact, I approach the subject from a child-identity development lens. I provide the following tool to help youth workers reflect on their own identities (figure 2), which is critical in preparing to work with young People of Color.

As we reflect on the identities that we bring to Circles, it becomes clear that internal and external factors influence critical stages of identity development. We all bring our own identities and experiences to our work and to

Figure 2. Identity Maps: You and the Youth You Serve

other non-work activities. Our identities and experiences no doubt play a part in how we relate and then interact with each other and in our communities. Hence, being aware of identity is a key component to cultural competency and promoting equity.

This activity's goal is to understand what factors increase adolescent and youth worker awareness around identity development. When differences in race, gender, and class come up in this activity, the opportunity opens to reflect and have a conversation about what those differences and similarities mean. Even when we share an identity with someone, we can have unique experiences.

In this activity, I explain positive self-identity as an important part of healthy development. When applying some context, we think about the messages that young People of Color receive about their identity compared with your own and others. From this contextual contrast, we can start to see some similarities and some differences. I use the tool in figure 2 to help participants explore their own identities and those of the young people they work with. On the left side with "YOU" in the center, I ask participants to write, "What were important parts of your identity as a teenager? What are important parts of your identity now?" I then ask participants to reflect on the messages they receive and have received about their identities from media, family, their communities, their neighborhoods, and nation. Then I ask them to write down what the youth they work with have shared about these same questions (the right side with "YOUTH" in the center).

I have found this activity helpful when talking about race and identity issues between young people and the adults who serve them in Circle. This tool proved helpful for the predominately White staff of this organization. Their responses to the self-reflecting questions below revealed that almost all the participants affirmed the importance of understanding that we have experiential differences.

1. Why do I stay in this work?
2. What have I learned about race from my family? Culture? Community? Neighborhood? Nation?
3. What have I learned about gender identity from my family? Culture? Community? Neighborhood? Nation?
4. If I share the same identities as the youth I work with, how might that impact my response to trauma exposure at work?
5. If I don't share the same identities as the youth I work with, how might that impact my response to trauma exposure at work? How might the dynamics change?

Affirming our identities and reflecting on them are important components in addressing racial justice in Circle.

Seeking Solutions: Restorative Justice Policy and Legalization

Roxbury Tenants of Harvard Association (RTHA) is a nonprofit housing and human service organization founded by residents of the Boston neighborhood of Mission Hill in 1969. Jennifer Lewis, RTHA's community center program director, started applying restorative justice principles to the policies the center had developed. The organization needed disciplinary protocols and processes for when interpersonal violence, like bullying or humiliation, occurred among the young people who participated in their program. Jennifer, who was already familiar with restorative justice, attended the Trauma Awareness and Resilience Training Institute for Youth Workers, one that I lead with colleagues for the BPHC. The training institute is three days and includes a restorative justice module. The institute's participants sit in Circle, come up with group agreements, define the Circle's openings and closings, and use a talking piece when needed.

Jennifer made it clear that she wanted to use the Circle process as the institute used it. During one of our sessions, a point of tension arose when a participant called out one of the activities for being racially insensitive. Even though the facilitators apologized for what had happened, I felt that the tension in the room prevented us from moving forward with more learning. I asked the participants if it was okay to pause and process what had happened in our Circle and to use a talking piece. The group agreed, and we had a deep discussion about race that left people feeling united and empowered.

When things get hard, we suspend the agenda, revisit our agreements, and introduce the talking piece. What followed the pause was a challenging process, but the evaluations demonstrated people's gratitude for pausing and addressing a participant's concern about race. The participant was a respected youth worker, a community organizer, and one of the founders of the #BlackLivesMatter movement.

When confronting issues among young people at RTHA, Jennifer started out using restorative practices that involved disciplinary action. But she wanted to move from punishment to a trauma-informed accountability approach. Not so coincidentally, restorative justice is a trauma-informed approach that provides people an opportunity to repair harms done. Because restorative justice principles are sensitive to trauma, people are given choices and provided clear expectations. More important, the approach involves and maintains connection to community and resources. In accountability terms, restorative justice's approach is different from traditional punishment. Punishment triggers many people. Once a person shuts down and becomes resistant or apathetic, a power-over approach will not work: it will not create a space in which many people can see the larger implications of their actions or behaviors or can be open to self-change.

When things get hard, we suspend the agenda, revisit our agreements, and introduce the talking piece. What followed the pause was a challenging process, but the evaluations demonstrated people's gratitude for pausing and addressing a participant's concern about race.

Jennifer was able to make one small test of change by implementing a restorative justice policy: young people who had engaged in bullying and/or fighting would have an opportunity to repair the harm done, so they could then re-engage in programming and use the center's sports facilities. Not all cases ended up sitting in Circle. Circles were always an option, a free choice. Often, people come to consensus with their own solutions.

In Massachusetts, many people are concerned about S847 and H7923 Restorative Justice legislation. This legislation institutionalizes restorative justice within the juvenile justice systems. It is the policy of the Commonwealth of Massachusetts that principles of restorative justice are included as an option for criminal and juvenile justice practitioners and parties to address certain harms. Although the goal of this bill is for law enforcement officials to employ restorative justice wherever it is applicable, law enforcement receives no general or foundational training to support them in applying restorative justice practices.

The good news about this legislation is that both the state and law enforcement recognize that restorative justice and restorative practices can strengthen community, reduce recidivism, and lower the risk of more serious crimes.

An advisory committee is being put in place to track programs and to make legislative, policy, and regulatory recommendations to support the use of community-based restorative justice programs. The public's concern with the committee's makeup is that the original list of members did not include any restorative justice practitioners. Due to the great work of the Restorative Justice Coalition of Massachusetts (RJCM), of which I am a member, the committee will now include some restorative justice practitioners. If the RJCM had not been involved or hadn't forced the RJ community into this process, the people who are actually doing the work would have been left out. We must maintain not just the elements of restorative justice practices but also their spirit.

My hope is that this bill and others like it support Jennifer Lewis and others with some preventative restorative justice training and policy support.

Seeking Solutions: Spirit and a Culture of Care

When people come together in Circle, energy is awakened. This energy's potential can help connect us. In Circle, we can be vulnerable, and we learn from

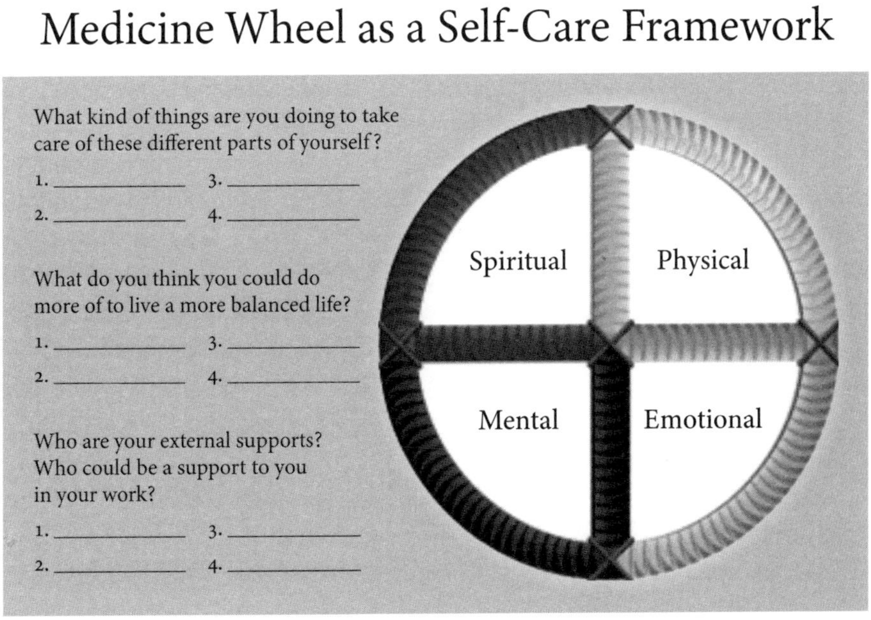

Medicine Wheel as a Self-Care Framework

What kind of things are you doing to take care of these different parts of yourself?

1. _____ 3. _____
2. _____ 4. _____

What do you think you could do more of to live a more balanced life?

1. _____ 3. _____
2. _____ 4. _____

Who are your external supports? Who could be a support to you in your work?

1. _____ 3. _____
2. _____ 4. _____

Spiritual
Physical
Mental
Emotional

Figure 3. Medicine Wheel as a Self-Care Framework

each other's stories and feelings about difficult things. When I am organizing a Circle process, I always think of the Medicine Wheel (figure 3).

In order to promote balance in the Circle processes I co-keep, I make sure that we are addressing our physical, emotional, mental, and spiritual selves. In our westernized thinking, we can forget to acknowledge Spirit—in and out of Circle. Some communities acknowledge Spirit by leaving an empty chair in the Circle. Some will acknowledge Spirit in an opening prayer, poem, song, or quote. Others will bring in sacred objects to be part of the centerpiece. I often acknowledge my ancestors and the people who made it possible for me to be here. When we acknowledge Spirit, we are respecting the energies that brought us together and the tone we are about to establish. Opening and closing a Circle in this way marks our time together in Circle as sacred.

As a Circle keeper, you have to tend to the Circle's energy. This means tending to your own energy from within before, during, and after a Circle process. Indeed, a practice of self-care is critical to sustaining your energy in this work and in the world in general. Our identities and how others perceive People of Color places us at intersections where we are on the receiving end of society's violence and oppression. For this reason, my self-care has grown into the most important part of my personal, restorative, and Circle practice. I approach my self-care with the Medicine Wheel framework. Within the context of the restorative and social justice work that I do, I look to my culture of care in two ways: understanding my triggers and understanding my limits. First, I seek to gain balance and to center myself the moment I encounter a trigger. Second, I do the daily things I can, so I am prepared for those unexpected triggers or life events. Yet regardless of how much I take care of myself, some topics still trigger me. Moreover, when I am not taking care of myself and stressed about things, the triggering impact becomes even more intense.

One of my mentors, Dr. Olivia Cheever, trained me in Leadership Embodiment techniques that are rooted in aikido, a nonviolent martial art. Through this training, I learned how to better understand my physical and emotional patterns while under stress and how to best transform that energy in the moment. No one can be centered 100 percent of the time. According to Cheever, if we were centered all the time, we would go insane. The trick is getting back to our center when our balance is thrown off. The main takeaway from learning this re-centering process is quite simple: it is always best to pause and

---

The main takeaway from learning this re-centering process is quite simple: it is always best to pause and breathe before we respond to any trigger. When we are off balance, we have an opportunity to learn something about ourselves.

---

breathe before we respond to any trigger. When we are off balance, we have an opportunity to learn something about ourselves. I meditate to center myself daily, and I also attend Leadership Embodiment trainings at least once a year. Even with this practice, I get thrown off balance often.

Another part of my self-care is my work with my godmother, Rosa Tupina Yaotonalchiuatli. Rosa is a licensed clinical social worker and heads the Native American Church (NAC), Kalpulli Teokalli Teoyolot (Church of the House of the Heart of God), of which I am a member. Rosa is also an internationally known herbalist and medicine woman. The NAC holds an annual Moon Dance ceremony in Austin, Texas, where 100 women come together to fast, traditional dance, drum, and sing. During this ceremony, supporters of the dancers are able to participate in workshops about traditional dances, herbal medicines, traditional music, and teachings given by Native elders from communities from all over the world. In addition to the workshops, the gathering gives us an opportunity to connect with people who are doing restorative justice work globally. The network that I have established through Rosa has also been critical to my growth and resilience. This work can be difficult, and having a strong network to lean on helps sustain me in the work.

The Circle offers many ways to model and promote a caring culture. You can use the tool in figure 3, and you can also make sure to take breaks as needed. For instance, ask Circle participants how they are feeling. Always have water and tissues on hand. And follow up with people if they need support or additional resources. Recently, Rosa and I have been working with a network of Zapotec women from Oaxaca, Mexico. We gather in Oaxaca a couple of times a year to exchange knowledge. They have taught us about how they treat trauma exposure with their traditional medicine and healing ceremonies. They have also helped us think about applying restorative justice principles to our self-care and healing. If we are the ones causing ourselves harm, how do we repair that? What is our obligation to ourselves when we are causing harm to ourselves, not to mention our obligation to others whom we could be impacting?

I have connected with Indigenous communities across the United Sates, the Dominican Republic, Puerto Rico, Mexico, and Chile. What I have learned through my relationships with these communities is that at the core of *their* restorative justice practice and philosophy are values such as honesty, integrity, being in community, having a relationship with all beings, generosity, and respect for Mother Earth. Additionally, these Indigenous communities think not only of their children's welfare or even that of their children's children but also of the welfare of seven generations to come. This cultural time frame is an essential part of the healing process. For justice to be, there must be healing. Those who live their Indigenous practices experience harsh punishment and discipline from the West, which isolates and disconnects them

Those who live their Indigenous practices experience harsh punishment and discipline from the West, which isolates and disconnects them from community. By contrast, healing happens in connection with others, not in isolation.

from community. By contrast, healing happens in connection with others, not in isolation.[6] People have different self-care recipes and therefore practice self-care in different ways. What is most important is to find what works best for you.

My hope is that, as the restorative justice field grows and the practice of Circles continues to expand, we maintain its integrity. My goal is that the Circle practice and its spirit are things that we do outside a circle of chairs. Circles are a way for us to get to know each other, build community, and model other relationship values we wish to see in the world. We have to be mindful of how we apply restorative justice and how we hold ourselves accountable to what it is—and what it is not. I conclude, however, that restorative justice existed well before we formally identified it, and it will continue long after us. In our practice of it, we must always be mindful. While its potential for good is limitless, if used inappropriately, its potential for harm is also limitless.

DISCUSSION QUESTIONS

1. When closing out a tense Circle in which there might not be consensus, I often pose the question: "For the children in your community, what do you hope for them?" Why would such a question be appropriate in closing out a tense Circle?
2. Since race and racism frames social interactions between communities of color and Whites, a significant question to consider personally as well as to ask in Circle is: "What did you learn about race from your family? Community? Culture? And how (or in what way) did you learn it?" This question's importance is based upon the fact that although race, much like gender, is socially constructed, it has real consequences.
3. Identity is a defining factor in a person's life. It not only guides how we perceive ourselves internally and in our relation to others, but it also defines how we will most likely experience life. How does your identity (i.e., race, ethnicity, culture) affect how you perceive and react to traumatic events?

ACTIVITY

Reflecting on Identity (Post-it Note Activity)

Goals:

1. To build relationship in the group
2. To build trust
3. To open up the conversation regarding identity: stereotypes; expectations we have of people based on our socialization; being vulnerable and authentic (depending upon group); the layers of ourselves and what we choose to share; what it's like to have layers of yourself that you know contradict expectations people have of you based on your identity

Instructions:

1. Give everyone three Post-it Notes.
2. Then give them the following instructions.
   - *Post-it Note 1*: Write down two to three things about you that someone knows (or thinks they know) by looking at you. Make sure at least one of these things is an aspect of your identity (example: I wear glasses, I'm short, I'm a woman; not I wear glasses, I have long hair, I'm short).
   - *Post-it Note 2*: Write down two to three things about you that someone would know about you from a brief conversation or that someone who is an acquaintance would know.
   - *Post-it Note 3*: Write down two to three things about you that only someone who knows you really well would know. Caveat: you won't have to share the exact thing that you wrote on your Post-it Note, but we will be sharing, so decide what you want to write and what you're willing to share or not.

GENERAL DEBRIEF QUESTIONS:

(Feel free to add questions specific to the composition and goals of the specific group.)

- What did this personal or self-inventory feel like?
- Was there a Post-it Note that was harder for you than others? Why?
- What is something on your third Post-it Note that may surprise people because it doesn't align with a stereotype about a part of your visible identity?
  - Have you ever been judged based on your appearance? What was that like? Can you think of a time when you judged someone based on their appearance? What was that experience like for you?

LEADERSHIP/MANAGEMENT QUESTIONS:

- Is there something on your third Post-it Note that would surprise people who work for you?
- What do you think the people whom you supervise/lead think about you based on your appearance? How might those expectations impact your relationship with them? What would it be like to allow people to experience something on your third Post-it Note? What gets in the way of being more vulnerable/authentic with the people you lead?

Note: Activity created by Rebecca Jackson, neuropsychological educator and co-author of *The Learning Habit.*

RESOURCES

"How Do We Fix the School-to-Prison Pipeline?" (podcast with transcript). http://www.abajournal.com/news/article/podcast_monthly_episode_53/ CIRCLES.

Lash, John. "Restorative Circles and the Heart of Justice." http://jjie.org/circles/92495/.

Pranis, Kay, Barry Stuart, and Mark Wedge. *Peacemaking Circles: From Conflict to Community.* St. Paul, MN: Living Justice Press, 2003.

NOTES

1. Victor Jose Santana, "Youth Leadership, Circles and Trauma Awareness," (master's thesis, Lesley University, January 11, 2012).
2. Ibid.
3. Ibid.
4. Harold Gatensby, personal communication, August 2000.
5. From Jean-Luc Pierite, board president, the North American Indian Center of Boston (NAICOB), personal communication, 2017.
6. See Richard Katz, *Boiling Energy: Community Healing Among the Kalahari Kung* (Boston, MA: Harvard University Press, 1982).

Chapter 15

Restorative Practices in Community

Belinda Dulin

What It Takes to Stop the School-to-Prison Pipeline

In 2009, the American Civil Liberties Union (ACLU) of Michigan produced a seventy-three-page report entitled *Reclaiming Michigan's Throwaway Kids: Students Trapped in the School-to-Prison Pipeline.*[1] This report, referred to as the *STPP* for *School-to-Prison Pipeline,* gave a compelling account of the disciplinary actions of Michigan's K–12 schools. The report's data suggested that students of color were subjected to disciplinary actions, such as out-of-school suspensions and expulsions, at a rate disproportionate to their Caucasian counterparts. In one local district, 18 percent of the secondary school population was African American, yet 58 percent of the students receiving disciplinary suspensions in one school year were African American. This report also pointed out that African American children were often disciplined at a higher frequency and for lower-level infractions—like talking back or being insubordinate—than Caucasian children. This phenomenon leads to school push-out, which often becomes the gateway to school dropout. The probability of their incarceration increases, thus the school-to-prison pipeline.

The *STPP* suggested several remedies to reverse this trend, one of which was restorative practices. The report identified a clear path of responsibility for practitioners to apply their knowledge and skills of non-punitive and collaborative problem-solving as a process for responding to conflict, thereby combatting the tendency to push children out of school. The restorative response to conflict is a fair process that embodies theories of communication, listening, de-escalation, and collaborative problem-solving. It empowers students and teaches them important life skills. Restorative practices appear to be a magical solution to an ongoing problem that greatly affects children, families, and communities. Practitioners can intentionally interrupt this push-out phenomenon and restore children's educational experience.

Key to Effective Restorative Practices

However, after almost ten years of watching programs start, stop, and get defunded, and after participating in never-ending policy discussions without any real outcomes of reducing suspensions, I have started to wonder what and who are missing from the programming discussion, design, and implementation of restorative practices. For example:

- Would the inclusion of People of Color change the dynamics and outcomes for children of color?
- Would educating parents and community members of color about restorative practices redefine a school's disciplinary standards and create a sense of advocacy among them?
- Would more restorative practitioners and process-supporters of color add value to school-based programs?
- Can existing practitioners of color expand our bandwidth to be more inclusive and to make this work more accessible for our most vulnerable stakeholders?
- Collectively, how do we contribute to this movement and reverse the school-to-prison pipeline trend for our youth?

This chapter will inspire readers and practitioners to critically expand their bandwidth and to include children, parents, and community members of color in dialogue, advocacy, program design, and training about the use of restorative practices for school discipline.

I have started to wonder what and who are missing from the programming discussion, design, and implementation of restorative practices.

On March 27, 2017, an online newspaper ran an article, "Low-Income, Black Students See More Suspensions in Ann Arbor Schools." The article describes a persistent disparity in one school district in how frequently low-income students, Black students, special education students, and male students in high school are suspended compared to the rest of the student population.[2] The suspension rates for these four groups were 56 percent (low income), 43.5 percent (Black), 29 percent (special education), and 71.2 percent (male) during the 2015–16 school year. These same four groups represented only 17 percent (low income), 16.4 percent (Black), 10 percent (special education), and 52.5 percent (male) of the high school population. The district's administration acknowledges its challenges in reversing these discipline outcomes. To its credit, the district is engaging several strategies to mitigate these disparities. It has, for example, implemented positive behavior strategies, restorative practices, and other incentive-based programs that address social-emotional learning. So far, administrators are not seeing the results they anticipated and that these strategies promised.

In many of our local schools, restorative practice programs appear to run on scarce budgets and with limited scope regarding the depth of restorative justice work. The Circle process includes a minimal number of questions—enough to lead children who caused harm to apologize for what they did and to make some reparation. The children who have been harmed are asked if they will accept the offered apology or other offers of reparation. The children sometimes sign an agreement that captures the outcome of their Circle and are then sent back to class. If the program is staffed, often it includes a school staff person who, after receiving a few days of training, is charged with bringing the children on both sides of harm into an office to quickly resolve a problem. These trained individuals often do not have deep knowledge or experience with restorative justice, are not the decision-makers on program development, and/or do not have the resources or power to determine when and how to best carry out a Circle.

So far, administrators are not seeing the results they anticipated and that these strategies promised.

Schools may contract with outside restorative practitioners to implement a school's restorative practice program, yet they are subject to the institution's rules and practices. On the ground, executing a successful restorative Circle is often tricky and challenging because of the rigidity of the school's rules and practices. As a consequence, practitioners are limited in exploring who has been impacted by the conflict. They are also limited by not having enough time to create an authentic Circle environment, even though this time element is essential for the Circle's effectiveness. Making time for a Circle honors the relational authenticity among its participants and acknowledges Indigenous Peoples from whom we adopted, as best we can, the Circle process.

Another consequence of these limits is that the practitioners are not able to engage other community members, including school staff, parents, and other stakeholders and partners. The absence of community members who have been affected compromises the quality of the Circle and the impact of this process. Moreover, a child who caused harm may not get the support needed to move forward or even to articulate the support necessary to do so. The child does not get the opportunity to see the full scope of their behavior.

Practitioners know that many youth and families need a support person to feel comfortable enough to be vulnerable, to have a sounding board to explore ideas for solutions, and, often, to follow through on the outcomes of the Circle. Instead, due to institutional constraints, practitioners are forced to abandon this valuable component of Circles. They are unable to make space for supportive community members to participate in the resolution of student conflict, thereby missing opportunities to build positive relationships between and among children, school staff, and other community members.

The following experience illustrates how powerful and essential it is to involve community members in the Circle process, if we are looking for real transformation:

> A few years ago, the opportunity arose for me to facilitate a restorative Circle involving two students who had had a fight during an after-school event early in the school year. The boys of color were about thirteen years old and had become bored at the event. They decided to go into a different part of the building and have a wrestling match that lasted a couple minutes. They were caught "fighting" and were suspended for the remainder of the school year—approximately five months. In addition to determining the educational requirements of getting schoolwork to the boys while they were at home, the school went further to question the boys' ability to return to school and re-engage the following school year. The boys' educational advocate sought to bring in restorative Circle services.
>
> Being very rooted in the Circle process and the components that make it effective, I insisted that the boys themselves, their parents, their teachers, other teachers who knew them, and a building administrator participate in the Circle. With the approval of the parents, other community members were also included. It was important for the boys and parents to see how many people cared about the boys and their educational experience. It was also important for the school staff to have responsibility in re-engaging these students in the school community. During the Circle, it became clear that the boys would need support in catching up academically and in getting over the stigma of the long-term suspension. The students also needed support in making good choices. The Circle ended with agreements that gave full support to the boys and their parents.

This Circle was effective and had a positive outcome, yet its very efficacy raises questions about restorative practices in schools. Academic and other articles related to restorative theory and praxis examine the impact of Circles for student conflicts on disciplinary suspensions throughout the United States.

Missing from these examinations of school-based and locally based restorative models and from their discussions of the Circle process is a key component: the community.

A number of them assert that very few schools have had similarly positive results in reducing suspension rates for children of color. A *Washington Post* article, "Implicit Racial Bias Causes Black Boys to Be Disciplined at School More Than Whites, Federal Report Finds," cites 2018 data from the US Government Accountability Office (GAO). The data demonstrates that Black male youth account for 15.5 percent of public school students, yet 39 percent of this group were suspended from school. Missing from these examinations of school-based and locally based restorative models and from their discussions of the Circle process is a key component: the community.[3]

Engaging Community Members of Color in Resolving Conflicts

Justice as Healing: Indigenous Ways, edited by Wanda D. McCaslin, Métis, is a compilation of writings on community peacemaking and restorative justice practices from the Native Law Centre at the University of Saskatchewan. The writings in this book have been a valuable resource for understanding the role and strength of community members in Circles. In chapter 4: "Respecting Community" and chapter 5: "Community Peacemaking," eight different articles underscore the importance of community members and the strengths that they offer Circles, particularly when these community members reflect those on both sides of harm ethnically and racially.[4] These chapters also offer examples of sentencing Circles, healing Circles, youth Circle programs, and other justice initiatives that include members of the local community. Moreover, these programs are flexible enough to engage community members in meaningful ways. Doing so further centers cultural norms, empowers community members to be responsible for their citizens, and teaches community members how to manage conflict.

Such regular engagement also helps practitioners avoid assimilating with the status quo and becoming institutional players.

By engaging community members, restorative justice practitioners can hold true to those restorative-work philosophies that include remaining connected with the community—not detaching from it—so that community members are informed and engaged with one another. Such regular engagement also helps practitioners avoid assimilating with the status quo and becoming institutional players. Practitioners can facilitate dialogue within the community on what justice can look like for its citizens, including children in their schools. Authentic Circles also foster healing as well as harmony for those who have done harm, been harmed, and been impacted by harm. Here is a story from my own experience as a restorative Circle keeper and practitioner:

Another opportunity arose for me to facilitate a restorative Circle involving two families, both residents of a public housing community. These neighbors had been having intense disagreements for at least six months. Both homes had large families and were single-parent homes with many stressors. The parents were doing the best they could with very limited resources and busy schedules, while trying to be compliant with the many housing regulations. Unfortunately, neither parent had big enough support systems to navigate the terrain of neighborhood conflict. After a number of police calls, fights between their children, and fights between themselves, these parents found themselves facing eviction. Their last resort was to work out their differences using a restorative Circle.

After meeting with each of them independently to hear their perspectives about the conflict, their lives as single parents, and their challenges as residents of a public housing community, I felt someone was missing—someone whose presence would give comfort, support, and wisdom to each of the parents; someone whose lived experiences would help point out commonalities and differences between the parents; someone whose availability could provide respite from the hustle and bustle of childrearing alone; and someone who would be trusted enough to provide a shoulder to lean on. This restorative approach incorporated the value of community. A grandparent of one of the residents agreed to participate and contributed many values to the process, including compassion, love, and a desire to support BOTH parents. The grandparent had to be part of the Circle.

The Circle went forward as scheduled and included the grandparent at the consent of both parents. The housing management was skeptical and struggled with institutional rules, noting that the grandparent was not a resident, not listed in the documents, and would not be allowed to live on the premises. As the facilitator, I moved forward anyway, and the outcomes of the Circle were amazing. The two residents shifted their energy away from being enemies to being good neighbors and role models for their children. The grandparent continues to be a resource for the parents, bringing compassion, love, and wisdom to them.

The grandparent in this case proved a valuable resource to the Circle participants and keeper. The grandparent added cultural depth to the conversation, had a calming voice, and, as an Elder, was able to both demonstrate respect for the residents and demand respect from them. The grandparent also supported the Circle process and the Circle keeper. This person's inclusion was essential to achieving a positive outcome.

Bringing Community Members of Color in on the Restorative Work

In addition to working in schools, restorative justice practitioners of color are responsible for engaging and preparing community members for restorative work. Practitioners of color must expand the bandwidth of this work by being more inclusive and making Circles more accessible to the most vulnerable stakeholders, including students of color.

I share the following reflections, based on my own experiences, to offer ways to accomplish this throughout communities of color.

- It is important to speak publicly about the cultural roots of restorative justice work. We know that it is rooted in Indigenous Peoples' lifeways and that its principles are based on relationships, responsibility, and respect within and for the community. Yet very often, mainstream restorative justice is commercialized, including marketing tactics and professional jargon. While these tactics are important for capturing the attention of institutions, community members need a person-to-person conversation to address questions, engage sensibilities, and connect with the work.
- It is important to engage parents and other stakeholders in discussions about justice. We know that traditional disciplinary methods often mirror those of the juvenile justice system. The three-strikes-and-suspend decisions, for example, clearly follow the juvenile justice model. How school rules are enforced follow this pattern as well: children are considered insubordinate when they are seen as breaking a school code or rule, whether they question school staff with confidence ("defiance") or wear a hoodie (in violation of a dress code). Parents and other youth stakeholders need a safe place to address the impact of these institutional approaches on youth behavior and to advocate for a different and just approach.
- It is important to help community members learn how to become accountable for our youth and to serve as mentors and surrogates when needed. Creating safe spaces through talking Circles can help community members address the need to heal.
- It is important to help community members understand the connection between systems, politics, and justice. Engaging political candidates in communities of color through community spaces like

---

It is important to remain proximate and to cultivate our own relationships within the community.

---

churches, schools, or community centers can help community members better understand the difference between system actors and system allies. Community members of color can advocate for redefining the standards of discipline within a school.

- It is important to remain proximate and to cultivate our own relationships within the community. Offers of trainings and orientations on restorative justice practices in informal and formal ways create new practitioners and advocates. This widens the circle of practitioners and process supporters of color, who add value to school-based programs.
- It is important to prepare community members to engage in a restorative Circle for conflict resolution that has been offered to children and youth.
- It is important to remain a resource for other practitioners and supporters of restorative practices and to share stories, challenges, and ideas with each other. This expands our toolbox of techniques, questions, and other resources, so that we continue to create safe spaces for our community members to heal and problem-solve.

Responsibility of Educational Leaders to Operate Inclusively

As in the case of the youth Circle, educators play a significant role in creating restorative spaces that include and empower both students and parents of color. These spaces need the practitioners' support.

- Educational leaders must be held accountable for restorative practice by educating themselves, their staff, parents, and community partners on the principles of this work. Also, on the principle that each stakeholder has a contribution that adds value, educational leaders must engage these stakeholders in the design, implementation, and evaluations of outcomes.
- Educational leaders need to create safe spaces to have honest and difficult conversations about race and equity in the community and in the educational experience. These conversations must include respect, patience, kindness, and openness to hear the lived experiences of People of Color. This space of safety can move us beyond awareness to acceptance of the impact of these lived experiences.
- Educators must value the relationships they have and need to have with each student and parent of color by making efforts to know the student and be inclusive. Greeting students by name, showing vulnerability, and engaging their voices for problem-solving helps.

Educational leaders need to create safe spaces to have honest and difficult conversations about race and equity in the community and in the educational experience.

- Educators must reframe the role of youth conflict as an opportunity for building critical thinking skills, developing empathy, learning decision-making processes, and cultivating relationships. Many of the offenses that lead to disciplinary suspension for children and other youth of color include behavior that is deemed inappropriate, insubordinate, or disruptive. The same behavior could be viewed and treated as a valuable opportunity for everyone involved and affected to make positive change.

By mindfully including communities of color, practitioners and educators can contribute to this restorative movement, address needs, and reverse the school-to-prison pipeline trend for students of color, creating stronger citizens, healthier families, and safer communities.

My Own Journey: Where Are the People of Color in the Restorative Work?

As a conflict resolution practitioner—specifically a mediator, facilitator, restorative justice practitioner, and a peacemaker—I assist community members in resolving their conflicts. I've co-created programs within institutions that provide an alternative path for dispute resolution. My journey began in 1995 as a graduate student at Wayne State University's Dispute Resolution Program. A few years later when the Columbine High School shooting occurred, I was an intern at a suburban community dispute resolution program. The program's leadership, like many other practitioners across the country, wanted to do something in their local community in response to the shooting. We began developing a peer mediation program and introducing the wonderful concepts and skills of conflict resolution to predominantly White, middle-class, suburban youth. This work was my first opportunity to process the experiences of the school and the community of color in the context of conflict resolution. It is also when I began questioning what restorative work could do for children of color, who were currently struggling with disciplinary systems and academic expectations.

Fast-forwarding a few years, I joined a suburban, community-based organization whose mission was to provide conflict resolution services that were affordable, constructive, and healing to local constituents. For fifteen years,

> *I am still questioning where the People of Color from the community are. . . . Why aren't they at the table contributing to the practical and aspirational conversations about restorative work for their children?*

I've witnessed the power of mediation and restorative practices in community, family, student, and organizational disputes. I've helped train hundreds of adults and youth to become mediators and restorative practice Circle keepers. In collaboration with many community leaders—judges, educators, faith leaders, and justice workers—I have created and implemented effective conflict resolution services for schools and court systems. But I am still questioning where the People of Color from the community are. Why aren't they in the room? Why aren't they getting trained? Why aren't they being asked about the needs of their community? Why aren't they at the schools? Why aren't they at the table contributing to the practical and aspirational conversations about restorative work for their children? Is their absence contributing to the challenges that restorative practitioners of color face in creating restorative models with fidelity?

As a practitioner of color, I realize I'm charting new waters locally to ensure that high-quality services are available for communities of color. I'm inviting them into these sacred spaces, believing that our collective wisdom will help dismantle the school-to-prison pipeline.

DISCUSSION QUESTIONS

1. Are you engaging the most vulnerable community representatives in your work—for example, seniors, youth, and those formally incarcerated?
2. Does your partnership network include local groups, spiritual leaders, block-club leaders, local business owners, and other community members?
3. Do you engage youth in discussions about their perceptions of school discipline and justice?

ACTIVITIES

1. Examine your network and determine who is missing from the justice discussions. Volunteer with local justice initiatives to see who shows up and who doesn't.

2. Engage with community members by attending events, providing educational forums, and inviting them to share their stories and insights.
3. Create a forum for discussing issues of justice by using films, books, presenters, etc., to stimulate thought and inspire change at a community level.

RESOURCES

Communities for Just Schools. http://www.ytfg.org/2015/07/communities-for-just-schools-fund/.

National Association of Community and Restorative Justice. https://www.nacrj.org.

School-Justice Partnership National Resource Centers. https://www.schooljusticepartnership.org/.

NOTES

1. Mark P. Fancher, *Reclaiming Michigan's Throwaway Kids: Students Trapped in the School-to-Prison Pipeline* (Detroit, MI: American Civil Liberties Union of Michigan, 2009), http://www.njjn.org/uploads/digital-library/resource_1287.pdf. See also "ACLU of Michigan Releases Report Identifying School-to-Prison Pipeline in State," https://www.aclumich.org/en/press-releases/aclu-michigan-releases-report-identifying-school-prison-pipeline-state.
2. Lauren Slagter, "Low Income, Black Students See More Suspensions in Ann Arbor Schools," *MLive.com*, March 27, 2017, updated May 16, 2018, https://www.mlive.com/expo/erry-2018/05/92b69e7aba9550/ann_arbor_schools_suspension_r.html.
3. Valerie Strauss, "Implicit Racial Bias Causes Black Boys to Be Disciplined at School More Than Whites, Federal Report Finds," *Washington Post*, April 5, 2018, https://www.washingtonpost.com/news/answer-sheet/wp/2018/04/05/implicit-racial-bias-causes-black-boys-to-be-disciplined-at-school-more-than-whites-federal-report-finds/?noredirect=on&utm_term=.78c7bf24f844.
4. Wanda D. McCaslin, ed., *Justice as Healing—Indigenous Ways: Writings on Community Peacemaking and Restorative Justice from the Native Law Centre* (St. Paul, MN: Living Justice Press, 2005), chap. 4: "Respecting Community" and chap. 5: "Community Peacemaking," 161–211.

Chapter 16

"There's No Place Like Home!" The Secret That Restored Me

Janice Jerome in collaboration with Jessica A. Hicks

As I think about colorizing restorative justice (RJ), I am reminded of the scene in the 1939 *The Wizard of Oz* film where Dorothy clicks her heels three times and repeats, "There's no place like home." This refrain is repeated throughout the movie. Dorothy is right: there really is no place like home.

For me, "Home" has never been a house or a specific residence. "Home" is where I am in a good space with others, sharing and practicing my values. Home is where I am allowed to thrive and be who I am—fully and completely. I have had many different homes, but one of them has been a secret for most of my life. Only recently did I reveal this secret, and it has transformed me.

As a channel of reflection, I will share my story of how I, an African American woman born in the early 1960s, carried the shame about my family's humble beginnings and transformed it into pride. My introduction and belief in restorative justice principles freed me from a life of hidden and suppressed emotions. As I open this door to my past and allow you in, it is not recognition or the badge of bravery I seek, but the healing that comes through the restorative justice process that I have totally committed to and proudly acknowledge as a way of life for me: RJ is my ministry. Jessica Hicks, a restorative practitioner with a master's in social work from Georgia State University, conducted this interview with edits.

Life in Pitsburgh

Pitsburgh is a neighborhood community in Atlanta, covering about 324 acres. It was founded in 1883 by working-class Blacks. By the 1940s and 1950s, Pitsburgh was still a working-class, racially diverse, non-incorporated community in Atlanta. In spite of its poverty level in the early Pitsburgh years, well-educated and progressive residents lived there. Before the 1930s, Pitsburgh housed Clark College, a well-known private, historically Black university, currently located in Atlanta.

By the 1960s, the City of Atlanta—like many places in the United States—was experiencing a mass exodus of White residents or white flight. During this mass movement, middle-class White folk moved from racially mixed urban cities to more racially homogeneous areas. During this same time, my parents (both in their early twenties) moved into Pitsburgh and were one of the Black families who were better off.

The 2000 Census listed Pitsburgh as having 3,286 residents. Pitsburgh is spelled with one "t" and was named after Pittsburgh, Pennsylvania, because the community looked like the steel mill communities there. Today, Pitsburgh is considered an at-risk neighborhood with signs of gentrification spreading rapidly. It is part of the NPU-V community—Neighborhood Planning Unit V of the twenty-five NPUs in Atlanta. NPUs are citizen advisory councils that make recommendations to the mayor and city council on zoning, land use, and other planning issues. With the help of many activist groups, concerned citizens, and organizations like the Annie E. Casey Foundation, Pitsburgh's NPU is developing plans for better parks and roads and for rezoning areas for the betterment of Pitsburgh.

Meet My Family

James, my father, and Louise, my mother, had known each other since the age of five, which is not an uncommon experience within communities of color and Indigenous communities. They grew up on the same street and attended the same school in Forest Park, Georgia. In 1956, my father purchased a $200 diamond gold band wedding ring and presented it to my mother while they were visiting my maternal aunt Grace, who lived in the Summerhill, Mechanicsville, area near the Pitsburgh community.

My father was a large-framed man. He easily weighed more than 250 pounds and stood around six feet five inches. My father served as a supply handler in the United States Army (Korean War era). He was stationed at Fort McClellan, Alabama, and received an honorable discharge in 1956. My father went on to complete his education at the Carver Trade School in Atlanta. It was there that he received his brick-mason skills, which became his life's profession as an entrepreneur until he retired.

In contrast, my mother was barely five feet tall and weighed around 120–140 pounds. My mother's identical twin sister, Aunt Betty, had nearly the same physical makeup as Mom. My mother studied nursing at Belmont Nursing School and retired after nearly thirty years as a nurses' assistant from Piedmont Hospital in Atlanta in the prestigious community of Buckhead.

On September 28, 1957, my parents were joined in holy matrimony in Clayton County, about fifteen miles south of Pitsburgh. Their first residence was a small one-bedroom apartment in Pitsburgh. After a couple of years renting, they bought a multi-family, ten-room, two-story house on Smith Street in the same neighborhood. As a Black family, we lived comfortably in Pitsburgh.

At that time, our family had five members—my dad, my mom, myself, my oldest sister Maya, and my younger sister Sue (I am using pseudonyms for their privacy). I remember living in Pitsburgh as a tiny child. I remember how much fun I had playing outside with my sister Maya. We would play games like hide-and-seek and dodgeball with our friends in front of the house as the smell of Mama's homemade banana pudding engulfed the community. My older sister and I attended Crogg Elementary School. Jessica, who interviewed me, said she overheard a resident of Pitsburgh say that Rev. Dr. King's daughter Yolanda once taught in Pitsburgh at Crogg Elementary School for several years. I was fortunate to have many other family members living in the Pitsburgh neighborhood, including my paternal great-aunt Maggie, uncles, and cousins along with Aunt Grace. Watching TV, following the news, or reading, I am often reminded of the stoops in Harlem where everyone had an integral part in shaping each other's identity. So, too, in Pitsburgh, I am who they were. I am a part of those integral pieces, and they have given me the relationships that have helped me in life's important moments.

I am often reminded of the stoops in Harlem where everyone had an integral part in shaping each other's identity.

The Violence Begins

My early growing years should have been a happy time, and I wanted them to be. The truth is, despite our seemingly tight-knit, familial community, my childhood was plagued with violence in the home. I always wondered how would it feel to hear my mother say "I love you" to my father or to see my father hold my mother in his arms and protect her. My parents showed love, kindness, and accountability to my siblings and me. However, my mother and father shattered my family unit through their tumultuous relationship, yelling at each other and calling each other names.

My mother always was a member in good standing in the faith community and believed in paying her tithes to the church. Every Sunday, she took us to Sunday school, wearing our best dress clothes. So, in our home in Pitsburgh, we did not hear a lot of cursing. My mom did not use profanity, and my father was the same. There was no substance abuse or smoking in our home. However, we were aware of thousands of fights—or at least that is what it felt like to me. I remember once they both participated in a brick-throwing fight, trying their best to hit and hurt each other. Threats with knives, brooms, and even guns were often part of their exchanges. It seems to me the issues that led to the violence were about my father's infidelity and my mother's refusal to go along with it. She demanded respect through violence. I wish they were both living now—I would have loved to share a conversation with them about "What is respect?"

These violent exchanges were a precursor of worse things to follow. I witnessed my mother putting a gun to her chest and my father looking at her, then turning and walking away. This was not the only episode I witnessed where my mom contemplated suicide or was in harm's way of a gun. When I was around five years old, I remember a very heated exchange of words between my mother and a tenant who was renting a room from my parents. My mother accused the tenant of having an affair with my father. The tenant pulled out a gun as I stood in front of my mother—the gun pointing at me. My mother slowly pulled me away, as we both left the scene and went inside the house.

To survive the things I witnessed, I found happiness in books. Reading was my escape. If I wasn't not reading a book, I would read labels on anything within reach, such as soap containers, cleaning solutions—whatever was handy. I became a counter: I would count squares, lines, dots—anything to preoccupy my mind.

Through all of this, rarely did my parents argue about finances or the children. The physical wounds they left on each other, though, could not compare with the emotional trauma their fighting caused me and possibly my oldest sister, Maya. After school every day, before I would enter my home, I would stop and stare at the door, wondering what was going to happen or what I would see once I walked in. During the most violent times in the home, I experienced unexplainable physical illnesses. For example, my nose would start bleeding as I stood there staring at the door—nosebleeds happened quite often. Or, on many occasions, Maya and my cousin Don (my aunt Betty's son) would be outside playing with me and the others kids on the block when suddenly they both would rush into the house for help, because they thought I was "sleeping in the street." Little did they know that I was having one of my many seizures, brought on by the things I witnessed at home. This home environment was the root, the cause, of my health condition and the catalyst of the deep shame I carried but kept buried deep within my soul. The pain was locked away, never to be acknowledged or shared—or so I thought.

This home environment was the root, the cause, of my health condition and the catalyst of the deep shame I carried but kept buried deep within my soul.

Moving to Atlanta

After living in our ten-room home in Pitsburgh for about a decade, in 1965 my parents decided to leave Pitsburgh and buy a home in the heart of Atlanta. As a veteran of the Armed Forces, my father had GI benefits that afforded him the opportunity to buy a home in East Atlanta. By the time we left Pitsburgh and moved to idyllic East Atlanta, I was almost six years old.

East Atlanta was a predominantly White, middle-class community. As time passed, the City of Atlanta grew larger, and by the 1970s, my former Pitsburgh home transformed from a stable, mixed-income community into a low-income community with high violence. Ashamed of my hometown's rapid decline and even more ashamed of my parents' tumultuous relationship, I began to hide behind the fear of being labeled as "the girl from Pitsburgh." For years, I could not admit that I, Janice Jerome, was a product of there. Pitsburgh was a place that I hid in the back of my mind, and I vowed never to return. Where I never felt safe, I felt ashamed. This shame weighed me down for decades. My thoughts of Pitsburgh became a place of hell in my mind and I did not want to go back.

Our new home in East Atlanta was on a dead-end street with about twenty single-family homes. Our house was yellow and white and sat on a hill with a garage, huge attic, two fireplaces, and a large backyard. This new home was in a beautiful, mixed-race neighborhood. It was in that home that three of my younger siblings—Ron, Rita, and Elliot—were born.

My family has more than 160 years (since 1858) of family history living in the metro Atlanta surrounding areas. Life in the 1960s and 70s in East Atlanta could be described as idyllic. Our new home in East Atlanta was less than five miles from Dr. Martin Luther King Jr.'s birth home and the church he pastored (Ebenezer Baptist Church). I grew up in a familiar city of nonviolence marches and watching People of Color work together in their neighborhoods. Atlanta was once called "The City Too Busy to Hate." The homes in the neighborhood slowly became full of Black families who celebrated life but also faced similar challenges of respect toward death that would visit a home. My mom often hosted neighborhood-watch meetings. The concerns were many, from paper being thrown on the end of the street to dogs running loose. The community members had relationships with each other and shared similar values about how to raise children. As kids, we would invent new games to play in the street. We enjoyed skating and played hopscotch, Punchinello, and dodgeball frequently.

Our families knew each other, and the adults knew the names of all the children in the twenty homes that decorated the neighborhood. There were no conversations about drugs in our community and no homeless people on our block; family disputes were worked out in the home in secrecy. Police

Police were absent, unless it was a very severe matter like death or accidental injuries, because families talked out problems in the neighborhood.

were absent, unless it was a very severe matter like death or accidental injuries, because families talked out problems in the neighborhood.

The violence between my parents did not end when we moved to East Atlanta, though. I lived through this family violence until I was eighteen years old and left home for college. East Atlanta was its own place, as Pitsburgh had been. However, East Atlanta was a community of which I was proud—a place where I felt like I belonged.

My parents never discussed the Pitsburgh community with me or my siblings. I joined my parents in this silence and never brought up Pitsburgh. Through my years in East Atlanta, no one even whispered the word "Pitsburgh" in our home; it brought me unbearable memories and shame. I attended Charles Hubert Elementary and Franklin D. Roosevelt High School in Atlanta. I never spoke of or allowed any of my school friends to know the big secret that I had spent my earliest years in the community of Pitsburgh. We were middle class and happy in East Atlanta. I wanted to forget that I was from Pitsburgh and its product. Instead, I projected myself as a proud product of East Atlanta.

Looking back, I have heard people in other communities in Atlanta refer to Pitsburgh as the "Pitts." I guess that is why the shame ran so deep inside me. Unwilling to unlock the baggage from the Pitts, I carried it around for years, only to pick it up for a new look at it years later.

Around the late 1970s, Pitsburgh was labeled an "at-risk" community. At that time, the City of Atlanta's mayor, Maynard Jackson, often spoke of how communities similar to Pitsburgh—Mechanicsville, Peoplestown, Summerhill, and public housing communities—needed financial and social support because of the high crime rate, the drugs flowing in, and the low economic status of the residents.

All Grown

By the time I left home for college around 1980, I felt grounded in family values, born of the love my mom showed us and the relaxed relationship my dad built with me and my siblings. While I attended undergraduate college in Alabama, Pitsburgh was a long-forgotten place in the back of my mind. As normal, I never mentioned the word Pitsburgh to my new college friends.

Around 1985, I married and moved from Alabama back to Atlanta, and my then-husband and I started our family and lived in the Greenbrier area of Atlanta. My husband joined the City of Atlanta Police force and moved his way up to detective. Still, after years of marriage and finally divorce, I kept my secret and never told him about my roots in Pitsburgh. In the mid-1990s, I married again and repeated the same process of not sharing with my second husband my beginnings in Pitsburgh.

As I continued to become a seasoned adult, a mother, a wife, and a professional in government, the hidden shame of my past continued. Around 1992, I applied for a job (and was hired) with the United States Department of Justice—a job for which I had to have a sensitive clearance from the Federal Bureau of Investigation (FBI). The clearance application asked many questions about home, work, and family. I was very anxious to make sure I included all information about my personal life, which included residences and work experience. However, I never whispered a word about Pitsburgh because, by now, it honestly had become a blank in my mind.

Meet My Aunts

I remember one day around 1999, I visited my paternal grandmother Ethel Willis, who lived in Forest Park, Georgia, a small suburb about fifteen miles from Atlanta. That day, Ethel, who lived to the age of 105, was sitting under her big tree in her front yard with her sister and my paternal great-aunt Maggie, who was also visiting her for the day. My aunt Maggie was having small talk with my then thirty-something self about how I was doing and how my parents were. On this day, my great-aunt Maggie outed me: "You know, you came out of Pitsburgh." I felt so ashamed and embarrassed, yet relieved that no one but Grandmother Ethel was around to hear this comment. Anytime I would see Aunt Maggie, who was proud of her community of Pitsburgh, I would be a little nervous that she might make the statement out loud and others would hear her.

Actually, Aunt Maggie moved into the neighborhood of Pitsburgh around the late 1940s or early 1950s when it was still middle class. She was instrumental in her church, and she seemed to be proud of her community, still holding that pride and fond memories of Pitsburgh, despite its downturn. My aunt Maggie died at the age of 97 in 2006, sitting on her front porch in the Pitsburgh community.

My aunt Grace (born in 1924) also lived around the Pitsburgh community (Summerhill and Mechanicville). I would visit her often as a teenager and as a married woman. Aunt Grace would babysit my oldest son, Michael, while I went to work. I really enjoyed being around Aunt Grace, because she never mentioned my immediate family's history in Pitsburgh, and I was so happy and relieved she did not. Aunt Grace and her husband, my uncle Lenard, purchased their first home in the Pitsburgh area around the early 1950s. Uncle Lenard died before Aunt Grace. She lived there until the mid to late 1990s, when she had to move in with her son and his family in California for health reasons.

Community Policing Utilizing Restorative Justice

As I continued to grow into a seasoned woman and have a family of my own, my parents continued to argue and fight and show hatred toward each other. When my siblings and I began to grow up and move out, my parents had more time to attack each other. I remember one of the most powerful moments in their conflict that involved the police, the community, and my parents. One day, I stopped by to visit my parents. They were the only ones in the house at the time. As I walked in the door, I observed my mother pulling her hair out at the roots and throwing it on the floor. She kept repeating over and over, "I am going to beat Carol's ass." Mom did not have a history of using curse words, so I was very surprised. I kept asking Mom, "Who is Carol?" She never answered. She had a strange look in her eyes, as if she was not able to comprehend my questions. My father was standing outside the house in the front yard during all this. I went out and asked my dad, "Who is Carol?" He never replied; he just held his head down. I later found out Carol was a woman who had moved into a neighbor's house several doors down from my family home in East Atlanta.

Mom was getting louder and louder, and I knew I needed help, so I called 911 for police and an ambulance. They both arrived and found Mom in the same state of being incoherent, belligerent. At one point, she picked up the "fireplace poke stick" and told the police she would "beat their ass." The police informed me that my mom would have to be removed from the house in a straitjacket and taken to Grady Memorial Hospital's mental patients floor. As I looked out the window, I could see a crowd of neighbors building up around my parents' house. There were at least five police cars and an ambulance in front of the house. All the people I saw outside the house looked like the neighbors who had been in the neighborhood as long as my parents had. My heart began to beat fast, because I did not want my mother to be brought out of the house in a straitjacket. I felt Mom deserved respect as my mom. I told the police I would get my mom to come out the house and ride to the hospital, and I pleaded to the officer, "Please do not take her out in a straitjacket."

As I stood next to my mom, another policeman, whom I did not know and who was African American, began to sing my mom's favorite church song, "I Will Trust in the Lord until I Die." The policeman did not know this was my mom's favorite song. As he continued to sing, my mom began to calm down. She became very relaxed as I walked with her hand in my hand out of the house toward the police car. The other policemen (about six other Black men) did not say a word. They just stood still in a respectful way toward the matter. The neighbors who had surrounded the house were standing in total quietness, as if something beautiful was happening instead of a bad situation. The majority of the neighbors knew my mom well and showed her total respect for what they were seeing. Tears began to roll down my cheeks, as I felt my mom was moving at the speed of trust. She trusted me to hold her hands, it appeared that she trusted the policeman who was singing, and she trusted the neighbors who created an atmosphere of humbleness. The policeman who was singing did not stop when Mom was placed in the police car. He continued to sing as we arrived at the hospital and even as she was placed on the elevator. As the nurses began to assist my mom and the situation, the policeman stopped singing. When he stopped, she appeared to immediately go back into a severe mental state. She was hospitalized for a while and placed on medication, and eventually she returned home in a good way.

In the African American community, singing songs during difficult times is, I believe, embedded in the descendants' memories, passed to us from the ancestors. Beating drums brings in music, song, and dance. I believe this rhythm is the heartbeat of Mother Earth. I believe African American communities prefer music, song, and dance in the opening and closing ceremonies of restorative Circles, rather than poems and quotes. The police and the community showed a level of values-driven respect, and because of their relationship with my mom, the community was able to provide her a safe space during a very difficult time. By treating her so respectfully, neither the police nor the community created another harm in her.

By treating her so respectfully, neither the police nor the community created another harm in her.

As I continued to grow and my own family grew, I never had a conversation with my three children or siblings, nieces, nephews, cousins, neighbors, spouse, or best friend about Pitsburgh. Again, the shame from the violence in my home and from being from Pitsburgh was deep inside of me. No one would ever know the heavy load I was carrying from my parents' violent and ugly relationship, which in my mind had become tied to my earliest memories of place. I had become numb to the violence and the shame I carried around it.

The Fork in the Road

Around 1998, I was visiting my parents' house. My father was in the basement and Mom was hitting him with objects (workmen tools). My father, who suffered from diabetes, neuropathy, and arthritis, was trying to sit in a chair. My mom was so angry at him (I never knew what started the argument) that I thought my father might be in danger. I contacted my siblings, and we decided together my father would stay at my house for the weekend until Mom could calm down. Well, the weekend turned into nine years that my father lived with me. During the time he lived in my house (1999–2008), I had already been introduced to restorative justice. I began to practice this way of life with my family, including with my father. When I was a child, my father never raised his voice at me, never hit me as a disciplinary measure, and never said any unkind words to me. Although my parents fought each other, they were gentle and caring with me and my siblings. However, they did not respect each other. As the years rolled by, my father became comfortable living with me. He began to work around my house: he built an extended front porch, and he planted a large vegetable garden in my backyard.

Often, we would sit on the porch until dark. I began to notice how peaceful he seemed to be, and he started sharing things about his life I never knew. He talked about the military; he talked about how his father was abusive to his mom; he talked about terrible and scary moments with White people, who threatened not to pay him for honest work he had done or to lock him up for things he was not guilty of. In many of those quiet moments, he would talk about my mom and he would cry, saying he was "stuck in the marriage." During this time, my father would cry hard and long. He cried so hard that his dinner would just roll down his mouth. Little did I realize that I was learning what a "safe space" looked like with my own family members. As Dad would talk, I listened with my heart. I did not interrupt him, and I did not comment on his sharing, his stories, and his experiences. This time with my father was one of the beginning moments when I started living my life with my family in a restorative manner. In contrast, I never had the opportunity to share this space with Mom. Her mental state declined too rapidly.

This time with my father was one of the beginning moments when I started living my life with my family in a restorative manner.

A Career as a Restorative Practitioner

During the early 1990s, I started my work in justice with the US Department of Justice, the Executive Office for Immigration Review, the Immigration Court in Miami, and then the Immigration Court in Atlanta. In the early 2000s, I started working with the Juvenile Court of Clayton County, Georgia. This was when I started my walk as a restorative practitioner. I was introduced to restorative justice by the Honorable Chief Judge Steven Teske (Clayton County Juvenile Court), along with John Manelos (former BP Oil executive), and Ansley Barton (former director of Kennesaw University Conflict Resolution Department).

Around 2004, Kay Pranis and Gwen Chandler Rhivers, now Gwen Jones, trained me in restorative justice. I managed juvenile court officers and was responsible for the mediation department. The mediation department used restorative justice processes to come to meaningful, accountable agreements with those who caused harm or had made some misstep. The vast majority of the juveniles referred to the court were African American youth. Most notably, many of their cases were minor offenses and charges, such as runaway, truancy, affray, disorderly conduct, and disrupting public school.

During this time, I acknowledged that my humble beginnings were in East Atlanta. As a manager and court officer, I often had to do prescreening and background history on youth and their families. I enjoyed building relationships with families and sharing small talk; however, at no time did I mention my humble beginnings in Pitsburgh. I have always boasted about being a Grady Baby—born in Atlanta's Grady Memorial Hospital. There was no way that I would mention Pitsburgh to anyone.

One of my proudest moments in working for the Juvenile Court was managing the Diversion Department. I was the lead designer of a restorative process called Project HIP (Handling It before Prison). Clayton County's Diversion Program had a large number of youth, especially African American youth, on probation and/or detained. This program diverted youth from going to court and allowed the youth an opportunity to have their cases dismissed without prejudice.

Project HIP operated in collaboration with the Clayton County Sheriff Department, the Georgia branch of the Innocence Project, and the Clayton County Public Schools system. The Innocence Project recipients were mostly exonerated Black men who went to prison for years for crimes they did not commit: new DNA testing later proved their innocence.

Project HIP also invited guest speakers, often African American young adults who had been sent to prison at an early age, such as thirteen or fourteen, and had done at least ten years before they were freed. Through dialogue and the use of a values-driven process, guests would tell their story to youth and their families. The stories of wrongdoing and harm always got the attention of the youth. Again, I was glad to be part of this creative diversion process, which utilized restorative principles for youth and their families. However, I still had no plan or intention to deal with any of the buried stuff that I kept so deep inside of me, covered with shame and embarrassment. The violence in my former home had me bound.

The Faith Community

As a restorative practitioner, I found myself providing training and consulting services in various areas of my life. One of the greatest personal moments for me happened around 2011, when I was working for a total of six months with fourteen leaders of two different church congregations. I called this six-month training Restorative Justice Conflict Management among Church Leaders. The Circle process training among the church leaders (ages thirty-four to seventy-five) culminated in a cap-and-gown graduation ceremony. Many of the families of the church leaders attended the restorative graduation. Some of the graduates had doctoral degrees, while others had not finished high school. However, restorative justice brought them together as equals in the graduation process.

Circling My Neighborhood

In 2012, I moved to Conley, Georgia, which is a suburb of Atlanta. Here again, I found myself bringing restorative justice to those in my new neighborhood, while ignoring the needs in my very own Pitsburgh neighborhood, less than fifteen miles away. The Conley neighborhood is not much different from Pitsburgh in terms of being an "at-risk" community, yet I chose to rent a place in this community. I started a neighborhood watch committee, utilizing restorative justice. I did preparation by getting police statistics on crime in the neighborhood and passing out flyers to all the homes in the neighborhood. I participated in purchasing hot dogs and treats to have a restorative meeting. During this restorative neighborhood meeting, I introduced neighbors to the talking piece, discussed our respective values and guidelines, and, most of all, had respectful conversations about our community problems. In the restorative community meetings, we posed such questions as:

- What do you like about your community?
- What do you dislike about your community?
- What are you willing to do to make Conley a better place to live?

When I reflect on these restorative neighborhood meetings, I did not have any guidance about how to provide restorative principles to an at-risk neighborhood that I was also living in. However, I trusted the process and invited the neighbors, police, sheriff department, and firefighters to the meetings. The restorative work in Conley paid off! After doing restorative Circles through community meetings, in a very short time, the neighborhood changed. A drug dealer was evicted from the community. We had no more burglaries reported to the police, and the landlords committed to screening potential residents more carefully. One landlord, who, with his family, owned at least forty of the fifty homes, placed burglar bars on the back of every home that his family owned. No car thefts were reported, and we had no gun shootings. Cars were not cruising with loud music, and youth stopped walking around late at night talking loudly. Neighbors began walking their dogs, waving, jogging, and sitting outside on their porches. Best of all, the entire police department and sheriff's department officially certified the neighborhood as a registered Neighborhood Watch Community. But what about Pitsburgh, my home, my beginning?

Pre-Trial Services and Theft Prevention Utilizing RJ

As I continued to help others—still ignoring my own deeply rooted issues about my beginnings—I decided to set up my legal structure as the Restorative Justice Institute of Atlanta, LLC (RJIA), which created a unique Theft Prevention and Impact Utilizing RJ diversion workshop for adults facing misdemeanor and felony charges. The majority of the clients on probation with the Atlanta Fulton County Pre-Trial Services are African American (the US Census estimates for 2017 that African Americans constitute only 45 percent of Fulton County's population). This new venture with the Atlanta Fulton County Pre-Trial Service started in 2014. Fulton County is Georgia's largest county, and its pre-trial service has a unique theft-diversion process. The one-hour class meets twice a month, with up to fifty participants per class. The classes introduce the participants to the restorative process and, from the reservoir of values, offer the experience of safe spaces in which to talk and have respectful dialogue. The RJ Theft Workshop contracts trained RJ theft instructors from RJIA, and RJIA has provided instruction to over 400 adults (per year) on probation for theft charges. An RJIA instructor opens and closes with a ceremony, explains the talking piece, and also discusses values before the workshop begins. By the workshop's end, the court clients draw on what they have learned about their values, and they are invited to voluntarily share in answering the five affective, restorative questions:

1. What happened that got you here today?
2. What were you thinking of at the time?
3. What have you thought about since?
4. Who has been impacted by what happened?
5. What do you think you need to do to make things right?

At the end of the workshops that I conducted, the time together always left me with a great feeling of having shared a beautiful space with those who have allegedly committed a wrongdoing.

Going Home by Way of Texas

In April 2016, I moved from Atlanta to Texas to accept a job as an assistant director at the University of Texas, the Steve Hicks School of Social Work, and the Institute for Restorative Justice and Restorative Dialogue (IRJRD). While working for IRJRD, I also continued with my private company RJIA to offer trainings and consulting.

While sitting at home in Austin in 2017, I received an email from an organization named Chris 180 (https://chris180.org), which pilots healing Circles in the communities of Pitsburgh, Mechanicsville, and Peoplestown. In the overall planning design of Atlanta, these neighborhoods fell within the NPU-V (Neighborhood Planning Unit V) area. I was asked to train community members in healing Circles, and I was excited to do any work in Atlanta, my hometown. At this point, my roots started to look different, yet I was realizing that Pitsburgh was the community I never claimed.

The Annie E. Casey Foundation provided the grant funds through Chris 180. The goal for this project was to ensure safer, resilient communities for NPU-V neighborhoods. The deliverables were trainings in trauma recovery, first responding, keeping and holding Circles, and establishing a referral network for those seeking support in their healing process.

The Healing Begins

I accepted the Chris 180 agreement to do the trainings for Pitsburgh, Mechanicsville, and Peoplestown. My first training for this organization began in August 2017 at the Dunbar Recreation Center in Atlanta, and the training was a truly transformative experience. I worked with participants from these three different communities—the very communities I am rooted in. Something spiritual—a healing journey—took hold of me when I returned to the Pitsburgh community and met the people.

The atmosphere of my humble beginnings emotionally moved me. As I began the training, memories of my mother and father arguing, fighting, and showing other violent behaviors flashed within me. As I started the talking piece around the Circle, I realized that the violence I had experienced was not from within me, nor was it about me. The violence belonged to my parents. I did not have to be ashamed as I listened to those in the healing Circle. Their spirit of love for Pitsburgh became contagious, and I wanted to shout, "Yes, I am a Pitsburgh girl." During this training, I willingly admitted—for the first time—that I was from Pitsburgh. And for the first time, too, I also felt so safe, included, and so much relief that I exclaimed to those in Circle: "WOW, why have I kept this secret for so long?"

In October 2017, I was asked to come back a second time by the same

Something spiritual—a healing journey—took hold of me when I returned to the Pitsburgh community and met the people.

organization. Little did I realize that the address given to me to conduct the training was a school that had been repurposed into lofts and had a community room for events. As I drove up to the school in Pitsburgh, I began to experience that déjà vu feeling. I realized that this training site was the first school I had ever attended. It was as if God said, "I have work for you to do—for others and for yourself." Suddenly, the memories started flowing. I began to feel something I have never felt before because shame had never permitted me to feel it: freedom from this secret that I held within me for years.

As I conducted the training, I could feel my heart opening, while simultaneously my own deep pain was being addressed—and it *felt* so good. I shared all that I could with the participants about my shame around my formative years in Pitsburgh and how that shame was transitioning to pride. Finally, I admitted to others and myself my connections to Pitsburgh—that it was my heritage. I became so proud. My shame dissipated in a great inner shift that moved me from embarrassment to pride, from exclusive to inclusive, from rejecting to embracing, and from dodging to shouting, "THIS is MY community!"

Given my experience, I now encourage all restorative justice practitioners to return home.

My life's values are deeply rooted in the belief that anything is possible. After fifty years, I felt a release as I announced to the participants that this place was my humble beginning and roots—my home. I was proud to say, "I am from here, and some of the Circle participants could be my blood relatives."

Given my experience, I now encourage all restorative justice practitioners to return home. Home may be a physical place of upbringing, it may be a current home, or that place in the heart and mind that feels like home—where we go back to and can meet our needs for self-care. It reminds me of the African symbol "Sankofa," which means to "return and get it."

For me, things came full circle when I returned to Pitsburgh to conduct a healing Circle, entirely unaware of the self-transformation that I would experience while there. This experience was truly a turning point in my life, unlocking my potential to do the restorative work fully and with authenticity. Looking back, I realize how my years of reflecting on RJ values and processing them prepared me to embrace Pitsburgh.

Dorothy repeats, "There's no place like home." Restorative training lifted me higher than I had ever been or could anticipate. The shame and fear I once felt and held deeply—I came to realize that I had created it and given it a place to live inside of me. This fear was not real, but shame made it emotionally and spiritually real for me. When "the right place," "the right time," and "the right reason" intersected, I was ready to release my shame and embrace Pitsburgh, and my home restores me. My growth in restorative justice made me realize I could be as proud of Pitsburgh as I was of East Atlanta, Clayton County, and

Conley, Georgia. I was able to address my shame through community—this was truly transformative justice.

As one of my mentors, Jamie Williams, shared with me, this work is about "moving at the speed of trust." There is no place like home—I truly trust the process at home!

DISCUSSION QUESTIONS

1. What childhood trauma did you experience, and how might that have influenced your work with restorative justice?
2. Who were your family members that surrounded you during your childhood?
3. To be Black and middle class in the 1960s was a great feat for many Black folk. How did you and your family experience and negotiate race and class?
4. Did you have a "Pitsburgh" that you carried shame around? If so, what contributed to your shame? How did that shame affect your life?
5. Has restorative justice helped you deal with the shame of being from your Pitsburgh?
6. How have your personal values and RJ values helped you to embrace your Pitsburgh?
7. What type of transformative experiences have you had from the intersection of working in RJ and being a Person of Color?
8. How has your work experience with RJ affected your life?

ACTIVITIES

1. Choose a discussion question and write about it, perhaps in a journaling style. This activity is for you to explore your memories, thoughts, and feelings about your original family experiences. How have these experiences played or continue to play a role in your development and work in restorative justice/practices?
2. Develop a support/dialogue group of People of Color in the restorative work. This activity can be two or three RJ/RP People of Color or ten or twenty. The discussion questions can provide starting questions for dialogue. Perhaps folks may like to share with each other what they have written in the first activity. Also, in the Resources section, Joy DeGruy has a study guide to go with her book *The Post Traumatic Slave Syndrome* (PTSS). On her website, she writes: "Post Traumatic Slave Syndrome: 'The Study Guide' is designed to help individuals, groups, and organizations better understand the functional and dysfunctional attitudes and behaviors transmitted to us through multiple

generations. The Guide encourages and broadens the discussion and implications about the specific issues that were raised in the PTSS book and provides the practical tools to help transform negative attitudes and behaviors into positive ones." See www.joydegruy.com/published-works/.

3. Meet your ancestors: Trace your family's ancestors. Many resources are now available to do this. I myself am a professional genealogist. I have come to the conclusion that researching the family history of People of Color carries a different acceptance than it does for White families. For example, I once researched a White family back to the Czar of Russia. In this research, one of the ancestors had been in prison. The White client immediately said, "This is not my family member." However, I have run into the same situation with Black families, and their responses are usually, "WOW, do you know what he or she did?"

Through various research approaches, place as many of your ancestors' names on a genealogical chart as possible. If any older family members are still living, have a restorative chat and build additional trust with them for more information about family values. I credit many of my values from the wisdom of my elders—my grandparents and great-aunts and uncles.

I believe identity is linked to feeling safe. I feel in the past many moral values were held very seriously by the ancestors of People of Color. The history of People of Color comes with a lot of poverty and lack of education, which meant that, as was commonly said, "all a man of color had was his words"—his values.

RESOURCES

DeGruy, Joy. *The Post Traumatic Slave Syndrome: America's Legacy of Enduring Injury and Healing.* Portland, OR, and Atlanta, GA: Joy Degruy Publications, 2005; revised edited edition, September 11, 2017. DeGruy shows powerfully how multi-generational trauma from slavery and racism affects family and intimate relationships today. This book also has a companion study guide that provides useful and practical tools to help the reader develop skills aimed at transforming negative attitudes and behaviors into positive ones.

DiAngelo, Robin. *White Fragility: Why It's So Hard for White People to Talk about Racism.* Boston, MA: Beacon Press, 2018.

Menakem, Resmaa. *My Grandmother's Hands: Racialized Trauma and the Pathway to Mending Our Hearts and Bodies.* Las Vegas, NV: Central Recovery Press, 2017.

Chapter 17

Creating Safety for Ourselves[1]

Johonna McCants-Turner

#SayHerName. #SayHisName. #SayTheirNames. The spirits of Black and Brown people killed by police officers bear witness to police as a common source of danger rather than a prevailing source of protection within many of our communities. In some situations, calling the police even when we need help can result in greater violence—for example, the police murder of a loved one experiencing a mental health crisis or the deportation of an undocumented immigrant family. And our #MeToo stories attest that we, too, experience sexual violence and other kinds of abuses. How can we secure our own safety given that White government institutions for "keeping the peace" have never functioned for our safety, freedom, and self-determination? This question is not new, and our communities have been innovating answers for centuries. As people committed to a healing justice that resists oppression in all its forms, we inherit this legacy. And as with those before us, it is crucial that we not only rethink our journeys toward justice, but also reimagine our strategies for safety.

This chapter tells how People of Color, particularly women of color and queer and trans People of Color, in this generation are creating safety without relying on a violent and oppressive criminal legal system. I first became aware of these efforts more than ten years ago as a young activist and artist involved in juvenile justice organizing and the prison abolition movement. Around that time, I began to think more about the domestic violence and sexual abuse I had witnessed and experienced within my own family. As I reflected on my own experiences, I came to realize that the threat of intervention by the police and social services systems kept me and others in my family from talking about what was happening and seeking assistance. After a next-door neighbor tried to rape me when I was in college, I called the police. But the officers who responded and the broader criminal-legal system did not help in meeting my needs or keeping my other neighbors safe. Rather, it was a friend, a mentor, and other people I knew who provided me with safe housing and physical and emotional support and who set me on the path toward healing. In contrast, I came to know policing as an occupying force that was especially brutal to members of my family and community.

Over the last two decades, a movement has emerged to offer us solutions—strategies that address the realities of violence *against* and *within* our communities and the need to transform them both simultaneously.[2] Collectively, this movement and its body of practice is called different things: transformative justice, community accountability, community interventions, community-based responses to violence, or simply community safety. Grassroots organizing for community safety, while distinct from restorative justice, reflects many perspectives that restorative justice practitioners of color share, particularly those grounded in social justice activism. This movement also offers analysis, vision, and strategies as well as language, lenses, and tools to expand the liberatory possibilities and potential of restorative justice.

I came to know policing as an occupying force that was especially brutal to members of my family and community.

I now teach courses on restorative justice—a master's degree and practitioner training program—at the Center for Justice and Peacebuilding (CJP), located at a small Christian university in Virginia's Shenandoah Valley. I also co-direct the Zehr Institute for Restorative Justice, which is located at CJP. I came to this work because of what the transformative justice movement taught me about addressing harm through processes that center healing, relationships, and accountability. A few years ago, some of my graduate students asked me to help them better understand how restorative justice could address systemic injustice and structural oppression. I responded by leading them in a small study of transformative justice the following semester.

This chapter is organized around the primary questions we studied together: What is the contemporary transformative justice and community accountability movement? Where did the movement come from? And what are transformative justice practices and processes?

For this piece, I begin with a look at the history of grassroots organizing for community safety. Next, I turn to definitions of transformative justice and community accountability, providing central principles, goals, and values. Thirdly, I provide examples of how various projects have taken shape and of specific steps activists have taken to respond to harm and cultivate safety. Finally, in the last section, I discuss differences and similarities between restorative and transformative justice, as well as how leaders in each sector can learn from one another.

Like my course, this chapter is primarily about learning from the individuals and groups who have put in the work of creating and experimenting with community-based responses to violence. The ideas and examples I provide in this chapter are not my own, but come directly from the resources and materials created by movement leaders. Mimi Kim, Nat Smith, Rachel Herzing, Shira Hassan, Cara Page, Dominique McKinney, Mariame Kaba, Nia Wilson, Isaac Ontiveros, Andrea Ritchie, RJ Maccani, Ejeris Dixon, Nathan Shara, and Mia Mingus: these are but a few of the people who have been critical resources of insight and wisdom for me. I consulted their articles, book chapters, videos, and websites in the process of developing this piece. The projects they birthed—such as the SpiritHouse's Harm Free Zone in Durham, NC, and the Young Women's Empowerment Project in Chicago (which continues as Street Youth Rise Up)—are living libraries. I participated in workshops, convenings, and other gatherings with these groups and others from 2007 to 2010, and also collaborated with some of them as I directed a small youth-led anti-violence organizing project in Washington, D.C., called the Visions to Peace Project. For this chapter, I interviewed two leaders with extensive experience in transformative justice whom I first met during that period. I also drew on previous interviews with two restorative justice practitioners whom I have known and worked with more recently. Finally, I intermingle stories of my own lived experience with this story of a movement for safety, accountability, and self-determination.

Building Holistic Anti-Violence Movements

What is the history of grassroots organizing for community safety?

Our communities have never been able to fully rely on government systems for safety. Historically, we were defined as threats, deemed unworthy of protection, or targeted for violence by the state.[3] The contemporary roots to create safety for ourselves can be found in this historical context. Black and Brown feminist movements have organized against sexual violence; LGBTQ groups have rallied resistance to police and transphobic violence; and immigrant women have created alternative interventions to domestic violence.[4] Ejeris Dixon, who has been organizing for community safety within Black queer communities, told me that this work not only has a long history in the efforts of groups like the Black Panthers but also within many of our families.

Our communities have never been able to fully rely on government systems for safety. Historically, we were defined as threats, deemed unworthy of protection, or targeted for violence by the state.

"I learned strategies from my mom talking about what used to happen in her own neighborhood growing up when it was segregated," she said. Educator, writer, and organizer Mariame Kaba sees the Underground Railroad as one of the earliest, boldest, and most extensive models of what it means to create safety through entirely community-based strategies.[5] Seen from this perspective, we can understand abolitionist Harriet Tubman's work as organizing communities to provide liberation from violence.

Black women have been at the helm of resisting multiple forms of violence. For example, Ida Bell Wells's anti-lynching campaigns in the late nineteenth and early twentieth centuries challenged acts of terrorism against Black people. Simultaneously, she chipped away at the cultural violence—the widespread myths about Black men as rapists—that Whites used to justify lynchings, which were also acts of state-sanctioned sexual violence.[6] Beginning in the 1940s, Rosa Parks built upon Wells's work in her advocacy for the Black women whom White men raped with impunity.[7] Parks and numerous associations of Black women, who were organizing against racial and sexual violence during the mid-twentieth century, laid the groundwork for feminist anti-violence organizing throughout the next two decades.

These movements addressed racial violence's sexualized nature and the racialized nature of sexual violence.[8] In 1974, a White jailer carrying an ice pick entered the jail cell of a young Black woman named Joan Little and tried to rape her. She killed him in self-defense. A massive campaign erupted for her defense and resulted in her acquittal.[9] The Free Joan Little Campaign and other anti-violence campaigns of the 1970s led to collectives and organizations of feminists of color who challenged gender-based violence, while also challenging the violence of the state.

Two critical forefronts of these efforts—naming the state's role in perpetuating violence and pushing to end violence against women (rather than only reacting to it)—became increasingly absent from feminist anti-violence work. Instead, anti-violence programs became more professionalized and institutionalized, resourced by federal funding and aligned with the criminal legal system.[10] As Mimi Kim explains, the 1994 Violence Against Women Act (VAWA), the first federal law to focus on violence against women, characterized this shift toward a more punitive approach:

> VAWA 1994 mandated a national domestic violence hotline and established the Office of Violence against Women, opening significant funding and advocacy opportunities for anti-violence programs. Advocates struggling many years for the passage of these provisions were finally able to get this Act passed as an attachment to the Violent Crime Control and Law Enforcement Act of 1994 (Crime Act) under the Clinton Administration, an example of pragmatism or opportun-

ism which took the breath away from many struck by the political and practical implications of this compromise.[11]

While the passage of VAWA represented decades of work to bring attention to the severity of violence against women and to provide much-needed resources for survivors, it also represented an increasing shift toward seeing the criminal legal apparatus and its expansion as the solution to gender-based violence.[12] This state approach has come to be known as "carceral feminism." Impacted by the changes VAWA wrought, women of color began calling for a return to the radical roots of anti-violence activism. They focused their activism on ending interpersonal *and* state violence by organizing for cultural and social change, not more "law and order" approaches. Their insights led to the formation of INCITE! Women of Color Against Violence, an organization that both gave expression to a movement already taking place and worked to advance the movement.[13]

INCITE! Women of Color Against Violence (now simply INCITE!) is described as a "network of radical feminists of color organizing to end state violence and violence in our homes and communities."[14] INCITE! emerged from conversations among women of color who were active within racial justice movements against mass incarceration and police brutality, and from feminist movements that were working against domestic and sexual violence. Through their shared convenings, experiences, and observations, they began to identify significant gaps and challenges in each movement's ability to work toward safety and justice.[15] Whereas movements against state violence (e.g., the prison abolition movement, anti-police brutality movement) focused almost exclusively on the violence that men of color experience, feminist movements to combat sexual and domestic violence centered the experiences of White women who were also heterosexual and middle class.[16] It became clear to many radical feminists of color that neither movement was addressing the needs and experiences of women of color.

Efforts to expand policing and criminalization in our communities place us at higher risk of being arrested and incarcerated, which then puts us at higher risk for experiencing sexual violence (from routine strip searches to rape).

INCITE!'s founders recognized that "women of color experience state and interpersonal violence disproportionately and simultaneously."[17] For example, when undocumented women have called the police to report domestic violence, they have been arrested and deported. Multiple survivors of gender-based violence have been incarcerated when the actions they took to survive were criminalized.[18] Efforts to expand policing and criminalization in our communities place us at higher risk of being arrested and incarcerated, which then puts us at higher risk for experiencing sexual violence (from routine strip searches to rape).

INCITE!'s founders saw a critical need for an anti-violence movement that centers women of color and addresses all forms of violence that women of color *and* our communities experience—whether the violence is caused by law enforcement officials, intimate partners, invading armies, or neighbors. INCITE! convened a conference for critical dialogue and action planning. Ana Clarissa Rojas Durazo, Alisa Bierria, and Mimi Kim, co-editors of a special issue of *Social Justice* on "Community Accountability," write, "The Color of Violence Conference, which took place on April 28 and 29, 2000, at the University of California, Santa Cruz, brought together over 1,200 people, mostly women of color, who were enlivened by a promise of something different."[19] With the formation of INCITE!, organizations and individuals already invested in this work connected with one another, and new collectives, political education projects, organizing campaigns, and collaborative initiatives were born. INCITE!'s founding members—including Mimi Kim, Andrea Smith, and Beth Richie—shared not only a collective analysis of the limitations of the anti-violence and prison abolitionist movements, but also a vision for how each movement's gifts and contributions could address the other's limitations and gaps.

In 2001, INCITE! members began circulating this analysis and vision through a groundbreaking statement that they developed and released in partnership with Critical Resistance (CR). The latter is a national organization that works to end the prison industrial complex by challenging the idea that putting people in cages makes us safer.[20] "The Incite!–Critical Resistance Statement on Gender Violence and the Prison Industrial Complex" explained that movements to end policing and prisons fail women of color, as well as many others, when they do not adequately address how we will end sexual and domestic violence. At the same time, because mainstream movements to challenge sexual and domestic violence have increasingly relied on policing and prisons as their main approach, they have placed women of color, poor women, lesbians, women with disabilities, and other marginalized people at risk of increased state violence. The joint statement explained that we need holistic anti-violence strategies that address both state violence and interpersonal gender-based violence.

Together, INCITE! and Critical Resistance called for social justice movements to develop community-based responses to violence—"strategies that do not rely on the criminal legal system and have mechanisms that ensure safety and accountability for survivors of sexual and domestic violence." Furthermore, "transformative practices emerging from communities should be documented and disseminated to promote collective responses to violence."[21] The call to action laid out ten additional steps critical to working for community safety, holistically. These steps ranged from working to challenge sexism and homophobia within communities to challenging legislation that would expand criminalization and incarceration within poor communities and communities of color—even if that legislation also provided resources for victims of interpersonal violence. This call to action catalyzed organizing for community safety on an unprecedented scale. INCITE! began a national campaign to address the law enforcement violence that women and transgender People of Color experience. It also initiated local campaigns to create strategies to address domestic violence, sexual violence, and child abuse that do not require any interaction with the criminal legal or social services systems.

Existing collectives of women of color around the country held activist institutes that provided a critical space for nurturing these strategies. INCITE! members Alisa Bierra, Mimi Kim, and Ana Clarissa Rojas Durazo recount an activist institute held in New York City:

> In October 2001, INCITE! convened an activist institute with Sista II Sista—a collective of young and adult working-class Latinas, Afro-Latinas, and black women in the Bushwick neighborhood of Brooklyn, New York. . . . A momentous innovation emerged at the New York Activist Institute. During a discussion of alternatives to the violence of criminality and potential organizing strategies, a 12-year-old sista stood with her hand in the air and exclaimed, "Why don't we make Bushwick a liberation zone for women?" . . .
>
> That question sparked our imaginations to think as a community and to imagine solutions and responses not offered by the mainstream anti-violence movement. Sista II Sista then began its campaign to make Bushwick a liberated zone, and INCITE! took steps to deepen its work concerning community accountability.[22]

As this example illustrates, grassroots movement-building for community safety has been characterized by intergenerational collaboration, intensive innovation, and a radical imagination.

In 2004, I attended a workshop led by members of the Washington, D.C.–area chapter of INCITE! The workshop focused on how to prevent and intervene to stop sexual harassment in public spaces, including unwanted sexual comments, gestures, and physical touching. The workshop was a part of a

. . . grassroots movement-building for community safety has been characterized by intergenerational collaboration, intensive innovation, and a radical imagination.

campaign to engage everyday people in the work of addressing violence within our communities. Soon after, I decided to join INCITE! D.C. and quickly became involved in the campaign. Like other members, I was directly affected by sexual harassment on the street in my day-to-day life. We saw sexual harassment in public spaces as part of a continuum of violence against women. In response, we educated members of our communities on how to recognize sexual harassment in public spaces, developed and shared strategies to nonviolently intervene in sexual harassment, and organized rallies and marches to challenge popular opinions and attitudes. We claimed our right to walk down the street without being whistled at, directed to smile, solicited, or touched, and we increased the capacity of the people around us to respect that right. By taking steps to engage ourselves and the people around us in intervening and responding to street-based harassment, we were also taking strategic steps to build our capacity to address other forms of gender violence in similar ways.

The next year, I traveled to New Orleans with other women in my INCITE! chapter to participate in INCITE!'s national gathering and organizing institute. While there, I heard from members of Sista II Sista about their work to create a violence-free zone in Bushwick; I participated in a popular education workshop based on the INCITE!-CR statement; and I learned the names of a vast array of organizations and groups committed to advancing a movement for community safety and liberatory responses to violence. Some of these organizations include Communities Against Rape and Abuse, the Boarding School Healing Project, the Young Women's Empowerment Project, Creative Interventions, Critical Resistance's Harm Free Zones, and many more.[23] Participating in the conference and in my local INCITE! chapter gave me a more critical analysis of violence. These experiences allowed me to understand the connections between intimate violence; the violence of imprisonment, detention centers, and deportation; and the violence inflicted by the US beyond its borders. They reshaped my understanding of organizing not only as knocking down that which we do not want, but also as building that which we desperately need. Most important, I gained an expanded imagination of what is possible rather than settling for accepted "solutions."

I brought this imagination and analysis into other areas of my social justice work. In 2006, I was organizing alongside youth and adults in Washington, D.C., to defeat the newest package of punitive policy proposals introduced to D.C. City Council as a response to "youth violence." We recognized that these policies would not make young people or their communities safer but would target them for further violence. Furthermore, the voices and visions of young people of color, demonized through the discourse of "youth violence," were left out of public conversations about safety and how to work toward it.

The following year, I founded the Visions to Peace Project—a short-term initiative to engage Black youth in efforts to develop and promote creative,

They reshaped my understanding of organizing not only as knocking down that which we do not want, but also as building that which we desperately need.

community-based strategies to challenge violence within their own communities. The first stage of this work was to learn what already existed. Over the next year, I traveled to visit and learn from organizations and groups in other cities. The people who generously agreed to meet with me welcomed me into a movement committed to envisioning and enacting safety outside of systems. The terms "transformative justice" and "community accountability" are most often used to describe this movement.

Growing a Movement for Safety and Liberation

What is the transformative justice and community accountability movement?

The contemporary transformative justice and community accountability movement has grown considerably over the last decade. It is now a network of numerous activists and organizations that generate strategies for healing and justice, challenge systems of oppression in all their forms, and work toward prison abolition.[24] People of Color, particularly women, trans, and queer People of Color, are this movement's lead architects and visionaries.[25] The terms "transformative justice" and "community accountability" also name the approaches, strategies, and frameworks birthed by this movement. While "transformative justice" and "community accountability" have no single definition, they do have defining contours.

Transformative justice works for safety, justice, and healing without relying on state systems.[26] According to community organizer Ejeris Dixon:

> Transformative justice and community accountability are terms that describe ways to address violence without relying upon police or prisons. These approaches often work to prevent violence, to intervene when harm is occurring, to hold people accountable, and to transform individuals and society to build safer communities. These strategies are some of the only options that marginalized communities have to address harm.[27]

Dixon's definition emphasizes non-state-based approaches for violence prevention, intervention, and response. According to Mia Mingus, a member of the Bay Area Transformative Justice Collective, transformative justice responses "actively work to cultivate the very things that we know will prevent violence, such as accountability, healing, trust, connection and safety."[28] Mainstream responses to violence rely on one-size-fits-all models and on a criminal legal system that is oppressive. In contrast, transformative justice offers diverse and alternative approaches to prevent, stop, and respond to interpersonal and societal harms, integrating personal and social transformation.

Transformative justice can also be understood as a political project for envisioning, creating, and sustaining safe and accountable communities. Yet, it is a project that recognizes how dynamics and patterns of domination are also replicated within our relationships. In the words of scholar and activist Andrea Smith,

> Developing community-based responses to violence cannot rely on a romanticized notion of "community" that is not sexist, homophobic, or otherwise problematic. We cannot assume that there is even an intact community to begin with. Our political task then becomes to create communities of accountability.[29]

As members of families and communities, we must learn how to recognize and challenge patterns of domination and oppression. We need education and training on how to intervene safely to stop violence that is happening and prevent more harm from occurring. Furthermore, we must learn how to address the societal factors and community dynamics that make interpersonal violence more likely. Each of these elements is key to transformative justice.

GenerationFIVE is an organization founded by survivors of child sexual abuse. Their vision is to end child sexual abuse in five generations by connecting efforts for individual justice with efforts for political/social change.[30] For generationFIVE, "transformative justice" designates a model for creating liberatory responses to intimate and community violence:

> The term "Transformative Justice" emerged directly out of generationFIVE's work on child sexual abuse as the term that best describes the dual process of securing individual justice while transforming structures of social injustice that perpetuate such abuse. While we developed this model as a response to child sexual abuse, we imagine Transformative Justice as an adaptable model that can and will be used to confront many other forms of violence and the systems of oppression they enable and require.[31]

We must learn how to address the societal factors and community dynamics that make interpersonal violence more likely.

GenerationFIVE defines transformative justice as an approach that emphasizes transformation and liberation in responding to and preventing intimate, interpersonal, and community violence.[32] Transformation refers to fundamental change within individuals, communities, and society; liberation refers to a commitment to end all forms of oppression as well as to actively build a society that affirms the dignity, value, and self-determination of every person. As Sarah Kershnar, a White practitioner in the harm-reduction movement and co-founder of generationFIVE, explains:

> Transformative justice invites us to ask: How do we build our personal and collective capacity to respond to trauma and support accountability in a transformational way? How do we shift power toward collective liberation? How do we build effective and sustainable movements that are grounded in resilience and life-affirming power?[33]

In this way and others, transformative justice functions as a conceptual framework that, again, joins work on interpersonal violence (e.g., sexual assault) with other political projects and concerns.[34]

An alternative term and concept, "community accountability" has been preferred and popularized by INCITE!, who define it as a process consisting of many intertwined practices:

Community accountability is a community-based strategy, rather than a police/prison-based strategy to address violence within our communities. Community accountability is a process in which a community—a group of friends, a family, a church, a workplace, an apartment complex, a neighborhood, etc.—work together to do the following things:

- Create and affirm values and practices that resist abuse and oppression and encourage safety, support, and accountability
- Develop sustainable strategies to address community members' abusive behavior, creating a process for them to account for their actions and transform their behavior
- Commit to ongoing development of all members of the community and the community itself, to transform the political conditions that reinforce oppression and violence
- Provide safety and support to community members who are violently targeted that respect their self-determination[35]

Like transformative justice, community accountability is also "about radical transformation of the conditions that create racial/gender/homophobic/economic violence. In this sense, community accountability is fundamentally an abolitionist strategy, one that creates the groundwork for the obsolescence of policing and prisons."[36]

While transformative justice offers an overall framework, community accountability refers to specific processes that proactively respond to and transform harm. These processes mobilize and engage those directly connected to and impacted by violence. However, the terms "transformative justice" and "community accountability" are also often used interchangeably.

Yet, not everyone uses those labels to describe their efforts to build safety without dependence on policing. Many organizers prefer to use words and concepts that their communities can easily understand and access. For example, Ejeris Dixon, the founding program director of the Audre Lorde Project's Safe OUTside the System (SOS) Collective, an anti-violence program led by and for Lesbian, Gay, Bisexual, Two Spirit, Trans, and Gender Non Conforming people of color, has used "community safety" to describe the collective's campaigns in challenging hate and police violence. Mimi Kim, oft credited as one of the movement's leading thinkers and organizers, uses the term "community-based interventions" to describe collective efforts to interrupt interpersonal violence. Still others use the terms "liberatory approaches to violence" or "liberatory anti-violence organizing." Each of these concepts is grounded in specific histories, communities, and needs. The concepts are also shaped by a set of shared commitments, goals, principles, values, and visions—ideas rooted in the experiences of groups and communities impacted by interpersonal and state-sponsored violence.

Liberatory movement-building for community safety shares the same guiding analysis, based on three key insights. First, the people closest to us provide our best hope for safety. Prisons and policing have failed to function as effective anti-violence strategies for communities and People of Color. People cannot turn to the state for help when their family or community is experiencing state-sanctioned violence.[37] Instead, when we experience harm, we are more likely to go to people within our networks, particularly people we trust, before we turn to the state or nonprofit social services.[38]

Second, interpersonal violence does not happen out of the blue but is encouraged by many of the conditions of our society. Interpersonal violence is rooted within systems of oppression, including white supremacy, capitalism, patriarchy, heterosexism, and adultism.[39] In fact, all forms of harm, abuse, and assault have their roots in oppression.[40] Therefore, we must transform

---

Interpersonal violence is rooted within systems of oppression, including white supremacy, capitalism, patriarchy, heterosexism, and adultism.

---

the conditions that lead to violence, including societal patterns of domination and injustice. Working toward transformation requires approaches that are fundamentally anti-racist, feminist, anti-capitalist, and anti-colonial. We need liberatory, holistic strategies and approaches that address the intersections of all forms of oppression.[41] In fact, this holism is one the critical features of this movement—a sustained emphasis on cultural transformation and liberation from oppressive systems as the way to end violence.[42]

Third, all of us can change and heal. Transformation and healing are possible for people who have experienced *and* committed gender violence as well as other kinds of violence. Trans activist and professor Dean Spade talked with activist and filmmaker Reina Gossett about this idea in a series of videos about how to build communities where no one is exiled: "One of the frames that we're using for this conversation is that no one is disposable," Spade explained, "which I think is one of the most radcal ideas I can imagine, because our culture's all about disposability, and who can be left behind, and left out, and thrown away, and left to die."[43]

One of the frames that we're using for this conversation is that no one is disposable," Spade explained, "which I think is one of the most radical ideas I can imagine, because our culture's all about disposability, and who can be left behind, and left out, and thrown away, and left to die.

In the same conversation, Gossett emphasized that the process we use to work for justice must be aligned with our goals.[44]

So, what are the goals and ultimate vision of transformative justice and community accountability efforts? For therapist, writer, and educator Nathaniel Shara, transformative justice is primarily defined and distinguished by its aims: "Transformative justice seeks to provide people who experience harm with immediate safety, long-term healing and reparations, while demanding that people who have done harm take accountability and mobilizing to shift oppressive social and systemic conditions."[45]

A first and primary goal is the safety and healing of people who have experienced violence. When this goal is met, as was explained during a Zehr Institute webinar on "Transformative Justice" that I hosted, survivors are believed and adequately supported by their communities when they come forward.[46] Ongoing harm is interrupted, and new incidences of violence are prevented.

A second important goal is "accountability and transformation for people who have abused and violated others."[47] Accountability means that if I have harmed someone, then I must recognize the harm, acknowledge its impacts, make reparations, and work toward personal development and transformation with the support of others, so I do not hurt others again.[48]

A third goal in creating community safety is "community response and accountability."[49] This goal means that networks of people become equipped to respond to harm in ways that do not cause more harm. They know how to work together to provide support for survivors and other impacted people, hold harm-doers accountable, and transform problematic norms, without needing or involving the state.[50] Mia Mingus envisions community safety systems that operate independently from police and government systems—"where we could get help from the people in our everyday lives."[51]

Finally, a fourth goal is to transform the community and shift the social conditions that create and perpetuate violence.[52] This goal pushes communities to engage in practices such as community organizing, which can transform institutions and norms that operate through "power-over" rather than "power-with" frameworks. In their place, communities begin to cultivate the everyday norms, practices, and relationships that lead to healthy and sustainable communities.[53]

Most obviously, community accountability and transformative justice are intimately connected to a broader vision of a world without prisons, jails, and detention centers—a vision that is both critical and generative.[54] Critical Resistance teaches that abolition involves not only dismantling and changing existing systems, but also building new, non-retributive forms that are liberatory and transformative.

INCITE! describes its ultimate vision as the creation of "a society based on radical freedom, accountability, and passionate reciprocity; where safety and security are not premised on violence or threat but a collective commitment to survival and care of all people."[55] While violence and oppression breed both fear and distrust, building meaningful and accountable relationships creates trust—and with it safety.[56] A commitment to people's survival and care means that no one is disposable; we can't throw anyone away.[57] Embracing the values of trust, respect, vulnerability, accountability, care, love, and healing are foundational to advancing this vision. [58]

Creating Safe and Accountable Communities—What It Looks Like

What practical steps can we take to prevent, respond to, and intervene in violence?

Centering the knowledge and power of everyday people, especially those directly impacted by violence, is a core value in building liberatory strategies for safety.[59] Projects working to cultivate community-based interventions thoroughly reflect this value, although in different ways. In 2004, for example, INCITE! co-founder Mimi Kim launched Creative Interventions in the California Bay Area, an initiative working to develop creative, community-based strategies for reducing intimate violence, particularly intimate partner violence. Creative Interventions partnered with local Asian immigrant anti-violence organizations as a resource for anyone who was in an abusive relationship but did not want to involve the police or leave their home. A member of the Creative Interventions team asked those who came to them for support to identify additional people who they believed could help in the situation. The team member then met with the entire group, including the person requesting support, to facilitate dialogue and action planning. They asked the group questions and provided them with tools to help figure out what was going on, what their goals were, how safety would be established, how accountability could be provided, who would follow up, and so on. Their organizing model involved getting people together to collectively identify objectives, create sustainable strategies, take collective action, and progressively assess the impact they were making, while offering support to one another. Creative Interventions facilitated cases over a three-year period. At the end of the three years, they compiled the tools and resources that they had developed together into a toolkit. The toolkit is 608 pages and can be found online at www.creative-interventions.org.[60]

Creative Interventions also developed a spin-off project, the Storytelling and Organizing Project. Recognizing that many communities have never been able to fully rely on the state for protection, the Creative Interventions team concluded that collective strategies for safety must already exist. The Storytelling and Organizing Project (STOP) created a methodology for collecting stories in which people had intervened to stop violence and to use this storytelling as a vehicle for ongoing action. Stories were collected in libraries, in grassroots organizations, and in living rooms, and were used in the same kinds of spaces. People listened to the stories and identified values, principles, and approaches they could use in their own communities.

Listening to and discussing STOP stories helped people learn about what works for preventing and intervening in interpersonal violence as well as what is not effective. The project now exists as an online archive of stories of everyday people ending violence in their own communities. The stories can be accessed online at www.stopviolenceeveryday.org alongside multiple examples of how groups have used the stories within their organizing.[61]

Creativity, imagination, and experimentation define contemporary organizing for community safety. With these resources, communities generate bold and radical experiments for achieving the healing and accountability they need. Most transformative justice projects address intimate violence—for example, intimate partner violence, which occurs among people with close relationships to one another. But sometimes, additional areas of focus have emerged in response to the felt needs of a given community.

Members of the Audre Lorde Project, a community organization in New

York City, found that they needed strategies to protect themselves from racist, homophobic, and transphobic violence, which they experienced from random strangers as well as police officers. The Audre Lorde Project is a community-organizing center for lesbian, gay, bisexual, two spirit, transgender, and gender non-conforming People of Color. In 2007, they created a new program, the Safe OUTside the System (SOS) Collective, which works to challenge hate and police violence against queer People of Color. The collective began by launching the Safe Neighborhood Campaign as a multi-year, multi-faceted approach to generate community-led strategies for safety.

Ejeris Dixon told me how she brought her background as an economic-justice organizer to the work of organizing to challenge violence:

> I had been organizing low-wage workers and low-income communities and folks who were receiving public benefits. That was my organizing history before that. . . . And that's why the work I did looked a particular way, was campaign-based, meta to micro. . . . I'm doing that kind of work of thinking about, all right, if we were going to build up a neighborhood or these couple blocks, or this specific area's capacity to address violence, what are the skills that we need to build, what other community-based connections do we need to build, and what type of analysis do we need?[62]

Dixon and other SOS members also began to ask themselves, "How do you un-stranger?"—how do you build relationships among people in neighborhoods using basic community organizing approaches, such as base-building, in conjunction with various community-building processes.

One of the collective's initial goals was to establish safe spaces in their neighborhoods. In solidarity with SOS, leaders of local businesses, community-based organizations, and faith institutions committed to establishing spaces where oppressive comments and behaviors would not be acceptable. For example, they requested that their patrons stop using homophobic language and asked them to leave when they did not stop. Many also agreed to allow their sites to become spots where community members could flee if they felt unsafe, were being chased, or were in danger of being attacked. Members of the SOS collective led political education within the various spaces, for instance, by teaching people about oppressive behaviors and their impacts. They also trained staff in bystander intervention skills, so they could safely intervene in situations of harassment or other harm.

More than ten years later, the SOS collective continues its work. Members lead community education activities, organize pride parades, and host cultural events. They learn and train others in skills for preventing and inter-

. . . in 2017, Dixon was asked what it really means to practice transformative justice. She responded: "Be brave enough to try something new. Be humble enough to change it—if it doesn't work—or refine it. Be smart enough to write it down and communicate it."

vening in violence. In addition, they develop and distribute resources, such as their Safe Party Toolkit—a guide for how to throw parties where safety is prioritized as well as how to intervene or prevent violence from happening. At a ten-year anniversary celebration of the SOS collective held in 2017, Dixon was asked what it really means to practice transformative justice. She responded: "Be brave enough to try something new. Be humble enough to change it—if it doesn't work—or refine it. Be smart enough to write it down and communicate it."[63]

Fortunately, many projects have reflected this wisdom. A wide range of groups have shared detailed accounts of various community-based interventions. Philly's Pissed and Philly Stands Up are two organizing collectives that grew out of mostly White punk/anarchist communities in West Philadelphia. They have documented their work over the last decade to support survivors of sexual violence and to work directly with perpetrators to transform their behavior.[64] Philly's Pissed and Philly Stands Up illustrate what community accountability processes often look like in the wake of sexual violence. In many such cases, the survivor receives dedicated support from a small group that is convened to focus on their healing, needs, and demands. Another small group is convened to work with the person who committed the assault, helping that person make amends and account for their behavior. Intensive education about sexual violence, systems of oppression, and consent is typically part of the accountability process. The separate and intensive work can last for twelve or fifteen months or more, and may or may not culminate in a facilitated process that brings the person harmed and the harm-doer together. People who are a part of the communities and networks in which the harm took place also engage in ongoing education, dialogue, and skill-building to prevent sexual violence and to develop a culture of "enthusiastic consent."

Mariame Kaba, a restorative and transformative justice practitioner who has led several community accountability processes, has stressed that community accountability processes are not for everyone. Rather, they are one way that survivors can express their agency if they would like to pursue healing and safety outside of state systems and institutions. It is critical that everyone who participates in such a process do so willingly, without coercion. Finally, most people leading transformative justice and community accountability processes do so as members of grassroots, volunteer-run collectives, not as paid staff members of organizations and institutions.

Connecting Restorative and Transformative Justice

How can transformative justice deepen the liberatory potential of restorative justice?

Restorative justice (RJ) is a philosophy that emphasizes healing and accountability to repair harm and wrongdoing, strengthen community, and build relationships. Both restorative and transformative justice approaches share the goals of providing those harmed with safety, healing, and repair, as well as holding people accountable for harm. However, conventional restorative justice approaches run the risk of sustaining, rather than challenging, systemic injustice.[65] In contrast, many approaches to restorative justice rooted in social justice movements are aligned with the transformative justice aims of individual and collective liberation. As Ejeris Dixon put it, "Particularly most people doing this work within communities of color, I think, have some analysis of state violence and intersecting forms of oppression at this point in the game."[66] Though practitioners who facilitate RJ processes as a social service may agree with social justice values, transforming social and systemic conditions is not typically the focus of their processes. Yet, according to Mariame Kaba, who has decades of expertise in leading and teaching about restorative justice, "Within radical spaces, RJ is employed as a strategy to try to respond to interpersonal violence while transforming conditions of power."[67]

Conventional restorative justice approaches run the risk of sustaining, rather than challenging, systemic injustice.[65] In contrast, many approaches to restorative justice rooted in social justice movements are aligned with the transformative justice aims of individual and collective liberation.

Conventional restorative justice approaches also differ from transformative justice in its relationship to the state. Outside of Indigenous communities, restorative justice has largely been co-opted by the state and other non-state actors.[68] Transformative justice activists point out that the state easily co-opts alternatives that lack a fundamental critique of the state.[69] Transformative justice, by contrast, critiques the state as a primary arbiter of violence, and seeks alternatives to containment and control. Many restorative justice practitioners of color share that critique and vision. For example, Jodie Geddes, a Black restorative justice practitioner, teaches young people about prison abolition as part of educating them about how to work for restorative justice in their communities. Similar to many transformative justice activists, Geddes links participatory community-based approaches to justice with grassroots organizing for long-term social change.

Finally, transformative justice has a very different relationship to sexual violence and domestic violence than conventional restorative justice approaches. While most transformative justice models were specifically created to address cases of intimate violence, restorative justice has not generally been applied to these cases. In fact, many anti-violence advocates distrust restorative justice due to the absence of adequate safety mechanisms and/or its weak power analysis.[70] Restorative justice practitioners have often paid insufficient attention to power relationships within the family and community, leading some practitioners to behave as if survivor needs and agency are not as important as restoring community.[71] Restorative justice has also been criticized for placing the burden to address violence on the survivor or person harmed, instead of developing community members who have the understanding and commitment to get involved, even if the survivor opts out.[72] Sonya Shah, a South Asian restorative justice practitioner, challenges this version of restorative justice practice.[73] Shah is the founder and director of the Ahimsa Collective, which works with sexual abuse survivors inside and outside of prisons through an approach that is intersectional and based on an anti-oppression framework.

Comparing and contrasting restorative and transformative justice in this way highlights differences. But more important, it shows how the transformative justice movement illuminates existing perspectives held by many restorative justice practitioners of color, particularly women of color. Because of this confluence, explanations of transformative justice can help us to articulate an analysis and vision that captures our concerns and hopes for restorative justice. I believe that people working for restorative and transformative justice, especially within communities of color, would benefit from more cross-fertilization and connection.

RJ Maccani, a White cisgender man, is the assistant director of Intervention for Common Justice in Brooklyn, New York. Common Justice is the first alternative-to-incarceration program and victim-service program in the United States to focus on violent felonies in adult courts. Maccani's combined experience of working both as a restorative justice practitioner and as someone with extensive experience with transformative justice offers insights in this area. "My first engagement with explicitly transformative justice work was in 2005 when I participated in a men's digital storytelling project with generationFIVE," Maccani shared.[74] He went on to explain:

> As a project focused on transformative justice responses to child sexual abuse, generationFIVE spoke to both my PIC (prison industrial complex) abolitionist commitments and to my own experiences

> of sexual abuse as a child and teenager.... In 2008, I cofounded the Challenging Male Supremacy Project, a collective based here in New York City of men working to end gender-based violence, build transformative justice, and contribute to broader social movements.... Through the Challenging Male Supremacy Project and generationFIVE, I've been involved in many grassroots responses to gender-based and sexual violence primarily in the form of accountability processes, group work to shift community norms and practices, and through the creation of cultural and educational tools.[75]

Outside of his graduate education in social work, the practical training and experience that Maccani draws on most heavily in his day-to-day work comes from his involvement in transformative justice practice for over a decade.

Maccani's job is to "support people who have caused harm through a twelve- to fifteen-month program rooted in restorative justice principles to make things as right as possible with the people they have harmed, to challenge violence and oppression, and to identify and move toward positive goals in their own lives."[76] There are many connections between his current work and the accountability processes he has led as a member of volunteer transformative justice collectives. However, one way of responding to violence operates almost entirely outside of the criminal legal and social services systems, while the other operates in ways that are directly linked to those systems. Into such a context, Maccani brings an ongoing awareness of the legacies of colonialism, slavery, and other forms of systemic violence. He names the importance of using different methods of intervention for different levels of change: "Put pointedly and flippantly," Maccani told me, "a million restorative justice Circles won't defeat the white-supremacist capitalist patriarchy. And all those Circles *do* have the potential to produce transformative individual, interpersonal, familial, and even community experiences, which are a valuable end in themselves."[77] Maccani's ongoing work to identify and address specific incidences of violence and their underlying structural conditions is a skill he first honed through transformative justice.

Dixon is now the founding director of Vision Change Win, a Black-led queer and trans social justice consulting team. Their work ranges from strategic planning and organizational restructuring to supporting organizations in deepening their skills around anti-violence programming and/or responding to violence within their own organizations. Dixon explained that from her vantage point, restorative justice and transformative justice tactics have significant overlaps, including facilitating Circles, identifying types of harm, setting goals, and holding people accountable to those goals.

Both Dixon and Maccani, whom I interviewed for this project, emphasized that the names, or banners, under which this work takes place is not the most important factor. As Dixon said, "I'm really like, who do you practice with, what does it look like, what can we learn from each other?"[78] She pointed out that people who work as restorative justice practitioners in schools often get a lot of practice in process facilitation because of their work in institutional settings. However, people who work with transformative justice projects have expertise in how to create and lead processes that do not have institutional support. "I'm working on a process because someone that I'm in community with asked me to be on their team," Dixon explained. "They were contacted by someone who named them as someone who sexually violated them. It's me, whatever team we create, whatever team they create, and we coordinate among ourselves, and we figure it out."[79]

How are people working for restorative and transformative justice connecting with and learning from each other? And, what are some ways to further ongoing connection and dialogue? People who work from one model or another come together within community-based organizations and movement spaces, particularly those working on issues of violence. Dixon named the Movement for Black Lives as one such movement space.[80] There are also a limited number of trainings, convenings, and conferences. Some of these gatherings are organized by bridge-builders, such as Mariame Kaba, who uses both restorative and transformative justice to describe her philosophy and practice. Increased spaces for training, practice, and dialogue—ongoing needs named by restorative and transformative justice leaders—can also serve as routes for further exchange and mutual learning. Because restorative justice has much more infrastructure and is more resourced than transformative justice, it may be more suitable to host such gatherings.[81]

Transformative Justice: Feeding Our Political Imaginations

Legal scholar Angela P. Harris has called transformative justice an ideal that resembles restorative justice but infused with the politics and principles of critical race feminism.[82] Transformative justice is wholly grounded in a politics of liberation. It acknowledges intersecting systems of oppression and seeks to transform them on multiple levels. In community accountability processes, people work together to address harm through strategies that lead to safety, healing, and accountability. They build the collective capacity to transform the political and social conditions at the root of violence and oppression. And they work outside of the criminal legal system and other government institutions because of the role these structures play in perpetuating violence and oppression. Transformative justice resonates with my lived experience and values as a Black woman, follower of Jesus, prison abolitionist, and sexual abuse survivor. It also captures my political imagination.

The underlying analysis of the transformative justice and community accountability movement illuminates the perspectives that many restorative justice practitioners of color hold—particularly women of color grounded in social justice organizing. Furthermore, transformative justice offers lenses and language that can support our articulation of a broader analysis and vision for restorative justice. It also informs practical steps and strategies. As an area of practice, community accountability also provides fresh tools to tackle existing questions. What can we do to create safety in our own communities? This question has engaged me the most.

Transformative justice resonates with my lived experience and values as a Black woman, follower of Jesus, prison abolitionist, and sexual abuse survivor. It also captures my political imagination.

Lessons from the transformative justice and community accountability movements continue to help me as I wrestle with how to teach and engage restorative justice as a liberatory practice that furthers racial and gender justice. I now give my students literature from the transformative justice and community accountability movements in order to feed their political imaginations. This literature challenges the limitations of mainstream expressions of restorative justice in academic and professional literature, which are the models most available to them. I have found that the transformative justice movement helps to address areas where restorative justice theory and practice are inadequate or insufficient. This includes limited attention to structural and systemic violence, as well as forms of intimate violence.

Most of all, transformative justice and community accountability give me hope that we can face the experiences of harm we have not allowed ourselves to name. The fear of the state's violent interventions into our lives and families keeps many of us silent about the abuses that take place within our homes, neighborhoods, social networks, and movement-building spaces. When I look back at my own experience of childhood sexual abuse, I see that the people with the greatest power to interrupt the violence were those in my immediate and extended families. But they lacked the know-how and skills to do so. There was no collective action.

Today, many of us will find ourselves in situations in which we dare to act but see no alternative to state intervention. Yet, we make a new road by walking. As we develop our collective capacity to challenge the patterns of violence that touch us most deeply, we can withdraw our investment in the institutions and systems that play a large role in sustaining violence. By reducing our dependence upon prisons and policing, we become more equipped to end the harms we experience in our day-to-day lives. Creating safety for ourselves activates our imaginations, strengthens our resilience, and cultivates joy and love.

DISCUSSION QUESTIONS

Transformative justice offers three key contributions that can be integrated within restorative justice philosophy and practice within communities of color and beyond. The following discussion questions provide guidance for individuals and organizations to assess their work in relation to each principle.

1. **A holistic analysis of violence.** It is critical to understand the linkages among state-sponsored violence, structural violence, and interpersonal violence.

   Violence: What do we mean by "violence"? How do we understand violence? What forms do state-sponsored violence, structural violence, and interpersonal violence take? How do these different forms of violence interact and intersect? What is our commitment to resisting each form of violence? What does addressing each form look like in practice?

2. **Transformation of the conditions that lead to violence and harm.** To address interpersonal violence, then, we need a sustained focus on the conditions (state-sponsored and structural) that lead to it and support it.

   Conditions: What political, economic, and interpersonal conditions and relationships do we recognize as creating and sustaining harm? What conditions can we work to transform, and what does this work look like in our practice? What is our relationship to other organizations and movements working to transform those underlying conditions?

3. **Community capacity-building through organizing, education, and long-term engagement.** Building the skills and capacity of people within our intimate and social networks to effectively respond to and prevent interpersonal violence requires sustained work: relationship-building, grassroots organizing, and political education and skills training. This approach to transformation involves long-term engagement. It calls for a commitment and ability to support collective learning and development over an extended period of time (e.g., multiple years). Building our communities' capacities also involves shifting material and financial resources from the state, so we can invest these resources in creating and sustaining alternative models led by People of Color.

   Engagement: What is the role of grassroots organizing and community education in preventing and responding to harm? How do we integrate community organizing, political education, and long-term engagement in our work, so that we continually build the capacity of communities to create their own safety and justice? How do we redirect resources from government institutions and programs to community-based institutions and organizations led by People of Color, who are invested in building alternative models?

ACTIVITIES

Re-imagining Safety Circle

Restorative justice invites us to redefine justice by centering our experiences and needs. It is important that we re-imagine safety in similar ways. Convening a Circle for "Re-imagining Safety" is one way to do this. Invite participants to tell stories of an occasion when they felt safe. Next, ask, "What makes us feel safe?" Then, invite people to reflect on what was shared and identify commonalities. List their responses on flipchart paper. Finally, in Circle, invite participants to share ways they can use this knowledge to create safer spaces for themselves and others. For example, how can you create spaces where you and others feel safer within your classroom, household, organization, or workplace?

StoryLab

This activity is designed for groups that have a high degree of trust and vulnerability; and a facilitator skilled in racial and gender justice praxis, as well as trauma sensitivity. Every day, people are taking small and large actions to interrupt interpersonal violence. Unearthing these stories and learning from them can help us to imagine what this looks like in practice. The Storytelling and Organizing Project (STOP) features audio stories of everyday people intervening to stop interpersonal violence. In your role as a facilitator or educator, listen to a few stories that catch your attention. Then, select a story that is likely to be especially relevant for your group. Provide participants with an overview of the content or issues the story addresses (e.g., sexual violence). Then, play the story, inviting people to listen deeply. After the story, provide five to ten minutes for personal reflection and journaling on the following questions:

- What happened?
- What parts of the story did you identify with?
- How do you feel about what happened?

After participants have an opportunity to share their personal responses to the story, invite group members to identify their own story using the following prompt:

- Think about a time when people who were connected to each other (for example, family members, neighbors, friends, co-workers) worked together to prevent or stop someone from being hurt.

You can invite participants to share their stories aloud, write them down accompanied by simple illustrations (as in a children's book), or compile them into a zine or other booklet. You can return to the new stories for ongoing discussion and learning.

> *Note:* Audio clips and transcripts of STOP stories can be accessed online at www.stopviolenceeveryday.org/stories/. Additional guidance on how to use STOP stories is at www.stopviolenceeveryday.org/stop-in-action/.

Mapping Your Pod

How do we create strategies for community safety if we cannot easily define who or what is our "community"? To address this challenge, the Bay Area Transformative Justice Collective created the concept of "pods" to refer to people in our lives whom we would turn to for support in abusive or violent situations. Read and discuss their web post entitled "Pods and Pod Mapping Worksheet" by Mia Mingus with others interested in exploring community safety. Next, complete their "pod mapping" worksheet to identify the people you could turn to for support, whether you are a survivor, bystander, or someone involved in harming others.

> *Note:* The pod mapping guide and worksheet are available at https://batjc.wordpress.com/pods-and-pod-mapping-worksheet/.

RESOURCES

Recommended Readings

*Creative Interventions Toolkit: A Practical Guide to Stop Interpersonal Violence***.** This toolkit offers more than 600 pages of tools, lessons, and stories for people working to respond to interpersonal violence collectively. Creative Interventions also details the community-based interventions model they developed and practiced over three years. The toolkit can be downloaded in part or in whole entirely free of charge at www.creative-interventions.org/tools/toolkit/.

Ending Child Sexual Abuse: A Transformative Justice Handbook **by generationFIVE.** GenerationFIVE is a collective of adult survivors of child sexual abuse with a vision for ending the sexual abuse of children in five generations. This handbook, which presents key insights from their last decade of learning and practice, is designed to be of practical use. This free handbook is available in three languages at www.generationfive.org/resources/transformative-justice-documents/.

Feminist Accountability: Disrupting Violence and Transforming Power by Ann Russo (New York University Press, 2018). This collection of essays explores accountability as a framework for building movements to transform systemic oppression and violence. It offers an intersectional analysis of transformative justice and community accountability, as well as anti-racist activism and US-based organizing around violence in the global south. Russo is a Women's and Gender Studies professor and the founder of the "Building Communities, Ending Violence" project at DePaul University.

The Revolution Starts at Home: Confronting Intimate Violence in Activist Communities edited by Ching-In Chen, Jai Dulani, and Leah Lakshmi Piepzna-Samarasinha (AK Press, 2016). In this visionary book, social justice activists share stories of their collective efforts to prevent and stop intimate violence without engaging the police or social services system. The editors and authors are People of Color, LGBTQ people, and survivors who testify to the power and practice of transformative justice and community accountability work.

Websites/Multimedia Resources

Chain Reaction: Alternatives to Calling the Police (a youth media project). A negative chain reaction is set off when police are called on young people, but we can set off a different chain reaction through alternative community interventions. The website *alternativestopolicing.com* features audio and video stories by youth about their encounters with police and a curriculum for groups who want to work toward alternatives to policing in their own communities. Chain Reaction was developed by Project NIA, a grassroots organization in Chicago working to end youth incarceration.

Six Steps for Responding to Racist Attacks (video). Violent attacks against Muslims, People of Color, LGBTQ people, and immigrants are on the rise. This video provides six clear steps to bystander intervention that do not rely on the police. It was created by the Barnard Center for Research on Women and members of Project NIA. The video can be accessed at https://bcrw.barnard.edu/videos/dont-be-a-bystander-6-tips-for-responding-to-racist-attacks/.

Transformative Justice (webinar). This ninety-minute webinar, hosted by the Zehr Institute for Restorative Justice at Eastern Mennonite University, provides an introduction to transformative justice targeted to restorative justice practitioners. The webinar is online at http://zehr-institute.org/webinars/transformative-justice/.

TransformHarm.org. This website is a digital resource hub on ending violence. Site resources are organized into six content areas: transformative justice, community accountability, restorative justice, abolition, healing justice, and carceral feminism. Each area includes a brief overview as well as articles, audiovisual media, curriculum, and other materials. The site was created by Mariame Kaba and designed by Joseph Lublink. You can access the resource hub at https://transformharm.org/.

NOTES

1. Special appreciation to Sarah Appelbaum who generously provided extensive research assistance for this project and contributed insightful questions that shaped its trajectory. I also extend great gratitude to Ejeris Dixon and RJ Maccani who

graciously participated in interviews with me for this project, and to Jodie Geddes and Sonya Shah who participated in previous interviews.

2. See INCITE! "The Critical Resistance–Incite! Statement on Gender Violence and the Prison-Industrial Complex," (2001), https://incite-national.org/incite-critical-resistance-statement/.
3. See Ejeris Dixon, "Building Community Safety: Practical Steps Toward Liberatory Transformation," *Truthout*, August 25, 2015, https://truthout.org/articles/building-community-safety-practical-steps-toward-liberatory-transformation/.
4. See, for example, Dixon, "Building Community Safety"; Ana Clarissa Rojas Durazo, Alisa Bierria, and Mimi Kim, "Editors' Introduction" to special issue: "Community Accountability: Emerging Movements to Transform Violence," *Social Justice: A Journal of Crime, Conflict & World Order* 37, no. 4 (2011–2012): 1–12, https://communityaccountability.wordpress.com/social-justice-journal-issue/article-downloads/; Mimi Kim, "Innovative Strategies to Address Domestic Violence in Asian and Pacific Islander Communities: Examining Themes, Models, and Interventions," Asian Pacific Islander Institute on Domestic Violence, July 2002; Walidah Imarisha, Alexis Gumbs, Leah Lakshmi Piepzna-Samarasinha, Adrienne Maree Brown, and Mia Mingus, "The Fictions and Futures of Transformative Justice: A Conversation with the Authors of Octavia's Brood," *The New Inquiry* (blog), April 20, 2017, https://thenewinquiry.com/the-fictions-and-futures-of-transformative-justice/.
5. Rachel Herzing and Isaac Ontiveros, directors, "Self Defense: Interview with Mariame Kaba," *Breaking Down the Prison Industrial Complex* (a video series). Critical Resistance, September 15, 2007,https://www.youtube.com/watch?v=TWx8NUk5-hA.
6. See Rojas Durazo et al., "Editors' Introduction" to "Community Accountability."
7. See Danielle McGuire, *At the Dark End of the Street: Black Women, Rape and Resistance—A New History of the Civil Rights Movement from Rosa Parks to the Rise of Black Power* (New York: Knopf, 2011).
8. Ibid.
9. See Rojas Durazo et al., "Editors' Introduction" to "Community Accountability." The case of Joan (pronounced "Jo-Anne") Little helped bring awareness to the sexual abuse of women in prison. In 1975, Ms. Little became the first woman acquitted of murder using a self-defense plea after she killed an abusive white prison guard who was attempting to rape her.
10. See Beth E. Richie, "Foreword" to Rojas Durazo et al., "Community Accountability," 12–13; Mimi Kim, "Alternative Interventions to Intimate Violence: Defining Political and Pragmatic Challenges," in *Restorative Justice and Violence Against Women*, ed. James Ptacek (Oxford University Press, 2009), 193–217, http://www.creative-interventions.org/wp-content/uploads/2012/06/Ptacek-ed-Restorative-Justice-book-Kim-Alternative-Interventions-article-PublicVersion1.pdf; Andrea Smith, "Preface" to *The Revolution Starts at Home: Confronting Intimate Violence within Activist Communities*, Ching-In Chen, Jai Dulani, and Leah Lakshmi Piepzna-Samarasinha, eds. (Chico, CA: AK Press, 2011), xiii–xvii.

11. Kim, "Alternative Interventions to Intimate Violence," 200–201.
12. Ibid.
13. Ibid.
14. INCITE! "Welcome!" INCITE!, https://incite-national.org.
15. See INCITE! "The Critical Resistance–Incite! Statement on Gender Violence and the Prison-Industrial Complex," Reflections, 2008, on the Original Statement, 2001, https://incite-national.org/wp-content/uploads/2018/08/CR-INCITE-statement-2008discussion.pdf.
16. See "Incite!–Critical Resistance Statement," 2001.
17. Ibid.
18. See "Survived and Punished: End the Criminalization of Survival." Online at survivedandpunished.org to learn about and support the campaigns of criminalized survivors and to take action to end the criminalization of survivors.
19. Rojas Durazo et al., "Editors' Introduction" to "Community Accountability."
20. See Critical Resistance: Mission and Vision at http://criticalresistance.org/about/.
21. "Incite!–Critical Resistance Statement," 2001.
22. Rojas Durazo et al., "Editors' Introduction" to "Community Accountability."
23. For more information about Sista II Sista and their work, see their article "Sistas Makin' Moves: Collective Leadership for Personal Transformation and Social Justice," https://collectiveliberation.org/wp-content/uploads/2013/01/Sista_II_Sista_Sistas_Makin_Moves.pdf.
24. See Imarisha et al., "The Fictions and Futures of Transformative Justice."
25. Ibid.
26. See Dixon, "Building Community Safety"; Imarisha et al., "The Fictions and Futures of Transformative Justice"; Project NIA, "Transformative Justice: A Curriculum Guide" (Project NIA, Fall 2013), https://niastories.files.wordpress.com/2013/08/tjcurriculum_design_small-finalrev.pdf.
27. Dixon, "Building Community Safety."
28. Imarisha et al., "The Fictions and Futures of Transformative Justice." See also Dixon, "Building Community Safety"; Nathaniel Shara with generationFIVE, *Ending Child Sexual Abuse: A Transformative Justice Handbook* (hereafter referred to as *A Transformative Justice Handbook*) (San Francisco: generation FIVE, June 2017), http://www.generationfive.org/wp-content/uploads/2017/06/Transformative-Justice-Handbook.pdf; Ching-In Chen, Jai Dulani, and Leah Lakshmi Piepzna-Samarasinha, eds., "Introduction" to *The Revolution Starts at Home*, xix–xxxvi; Sara Kershnar, Staci Haines, Gillian Harkins, Alan Greig, Cindy Wiesner, Mich Levy, Palak Shah, Mimi Kim, and Jesse Carr in connection with generationFIVE, *Toward Transformative Justice: A Liberatory Approach to Child Sexual Abuse and Other Forms of Intimate and Community Violence* (San Francisco: generationFIVE, 2007), http://www.generationfive.org/wp-content/uploads/2013/07/G5_Toward_Transformative_Justice-Document.pdf.
29. Andrea Smith, "Preface," *The Revolution Starts at Home.*
30. GenerationFIVE's conceptualization and use of the term "transformative justice" has no connection to the work of Ruth Morris, a Canadian Quaker who centers the term in her writing and work. In *Stories of Transformative Justice*, Morris de-

fines transformative justice as similar to restorative justice but with more emphasis on structural change and economic inequality (Toronto: Canadian Scholars Press, 2000). In his blog, Howard Zehr, a contemporary to Morris, referred to her elaboration of the term, not to the contemporary movement's understanding of it, and then said that he hoped restorative justice and transformative justice are "the same thing," though "in practice, this is often not the case." See Howard Zehr, "Restorative or Transformative Justice?" March 10, 2011, https://emu.edu/now/restorative-justice/2011/03/10/restorative-or-transformative-justice/.

31. Kershnar et al., "Toward Transformative Justice."
32. Ibid.
33. GenerationFIVE, "Transformative Justice," http://www.generationfive.org/the-issue/transformative-justice/.
34. See Esteban Lance Kelly, "Philly Stands Up: Inside the Politics and Poetics of Transformative Justice and Community Accountability in Sexual Assault Situations," in Rojas Durazo et al., "Community Accountability," 44–57. Also online PDF at https://communityaccountability.files.wordpress.com/2012/06/philly-stand-up.pdf.
35. Incite!, "Community Accountability," online at https://incite-national.org/community-accountability/.
36. Julia C. Oparah, "After the Juggernaut Crashes," "Afterword" in Rojas Durazo et al., "Community Accountability," 133–38.
37. See Rojas Durazo, et. al., "Editors' Introduction" to "Community Accountability."
38. See Mia Mingus, "Pods and Pod Mapping Worksheet," *Bay Area Transformative Justice Collective: Building Transformative Justice Responses to Child Sexual Abuse* (blog), June 2016, https://batjc.wordpress.com/pods-and-pod-mapping-worksheet/.
39. See Beth Richie, "Foreword" to "Community Accountability: Emerging Movements to Transform Violence," *Social Justice: A Journal of Crime, Conflict and World Order* 37, no. 4 (2011–2012): 12–13.
40. See Project NIA, "Transformative Justice."
41. See Bonnie Chan, "An Interview with Mia Mingus, Oakland Champion of Change, on Transformative Justice," online publication, *Oakland Local*, 27 May 2013, http://oaklandlocal.com/2013/05/an-interview-with-mia-mingus-oakland-champion-of-change-on-transformative-justice/; Mingus, "Pods and Pod Mapping Worksheet"; Richie, "Foreword" to "Community Accountability"; INCITE!, "INCITE! Critical Resistance Statement," 2001
42. See Shara with generationFIVE, *A Transformative Justice Handbook.*
43. Reina Gossett and Dean Spade, "No One Is Disposable: Everyday Practices of Prison Abolition," a series of four online videos, Barnard Center for Research on Women, February 7, 2014, http://bcrw.barnard.edu/event/no-one-is-disposable-everyday-practices-of-prison-abolition/ also at https://www.youtube.com/watch?v=Dexpp5oJoh4; Imarisha et al., "The Fictions and Futures of Transformative Justice."
44. See ibid.
45. The Zehr Institute, webinar: "Transformative Justice," hosted by Johonna Turner

with guests Nathan Shara, RJ Maccani, and Ejeris Dixon, February 15, 2017, http://zehr-institute.org/webinars/transformative-justice/.

46. Ibid. See also California Coalition for Women Prisoners et al., "#SURVIVEDAND PUNISHED: Analysis & Vision," #SURVIVEDANDPUNISHED: End the Criminalization of Survivors of Domestic & Sexual Violence, accessed December 13, 2017, https://survivedandpunished.org/analysis/.
47. Ibid. See also Kelly, "Philly Stands Up"; Project NIA, "Transformative Justice."
48. See Shara with generationFIVE, *A Transformative Justice Handbook*, 40–41.
49. Zehr Institute, "Transformative Justice."
50. See California Coalition for Women Prisoners et al., "#SURVIVEDAND PUNISHED: Analysis & Vision"; Oparah, "After the Juggernaut Crashes"; Kelly, "Philly Stands Up"; Mingus, "Pods and Pod Mapping Worksheet."
51. Imarisha et al., "The Fictions and Futures of Transformative Justice."
52. Zehr Institute, "Transformative Justice." See also Shara with generationFIVE, *A Transformative Justice Handbook*.
53. See Kim, "Alternative Interventions to Intimate Violence"; Dixon, "Building Community Safety"; Imarisha et al., "The Fictions and Futures of Transformative Justice."
54. See Imarisha et al., "The Fictions and Futures of Transformative Justice."
55. INCITE!, "INCITE! Critical Resistance Statement," 2008.
56. See Dixon, "Building Community Safety"; Mingus, "Pods and Pod Mapping Worksheet."
57. See Gossett and Spade, "No One is Disposable"; Imarisha et al., "The Fictions and Futures of Transformative Justice."
58. See Kim, "Alternative Interventions to Intimate Violence"; Imarisha et al., "The Fictions and Futures of Transformative Justice."
59. Ibid.
60. See Creative Interventions, *Creative Interventions Toolkit: A Practical Guide to Stop Interpersonal Violence*, http://www.creative-interventions.org/tools/toolkit/.
61. For some of the stories, see http://www.stopviolenceeveryday.org/stories/.
62. Author's online video interview with Ejeris Dixon, November 3, 2017.
63. Crystal Waterton, "The Audre Lorde Project SOS 10 Yr. Anniversary Celebration," https://alp.org/media/sos-collective-10-yr-anniversary-celebration.
64. For example, see Kelly, "Philly Stands Up." Also Timothy Coleman, Esteban Kelly, and Em Squires, "Philly's Pissed & Philly Stands Up—Collected Materials," In the Middle of a Whirlwind, https://inthemiddleofthewhirlwind.wordpress.com/philly%E2%80%99s-pissed-philly-stands-up-collected-materials/; and Esteban Lance Kelly and Jenna Peters-Golden, "Philly Stands Up Portrait of Praxis: An Anatomy of Accountability," https://www.transformativejustice.eu/wp-content/uploads/2010/02/portrait-of-praxis.pdf
65. See Mariame Kaba, "Restorative Justice as Liberatory Praxis," conference session abstract, 2018 Soros Justice Fellowships Conference, New Orleans, LA. Author received abstract through email correspondence, July 12, 2018.
66. Author's online video interview with Ejeris Dixon, November 3, 2017.
67. Mariame Kaba, "Restorative Justice as Liberatory Praxis" conference session ab-

stract. 2018 Soros Justice Fellowships Conference. New Orleans, LA. [E-mail correspondence. 12 July 2018].

68. See Kershnar et al., "Toward Transformative Justice."
69. See Rojas Durazo et al., "Editors' Introduction" to "Community Accountability."
70. See Smith, "Preface" to *The Revolution Starts at Home*; Kershnar et al., "Toward Transformative Justice"; Kim, "Alternative Interventions to Intimate Violence."
71. See Kershnar et al., "Toward Transformative Justice."
72. See Gossett and Spade, "No One Is Disposable."
73. See Carl Stauffer and Johonna Turner, "The New Generation of Restorative Justice," in Theo Gavrielides, ed., *The Routledge International Handbook of Restorative Justice* (London: Routledge, 2018).
74. Author e-mail interview with RJ Maccani, May 27, 2018.
75. Ibid.
76. Ibid.
77. Ibid.
78. Author's online video interview with Ejeris Dixon, November 3, 2017.
79. Ibid.
80. Ibid.
81. Ibid.
82. See Angela P. Harris, "Book Review: Beyond the Monster Factory: Gender Violence, Race, and the Liberatory Potential of Restorative Justice," in *Berkeley Journal of Gender, Law and Justice*, May 21, 2010: 199–225.

PART V

A Call to Settlers in RJ

Alice Walker, African American, novelist, poet, and activist, writes, "Healing begins where the wound was made."[1] Restorative justice is about healing, but how can this healing happen or be real until those of us who are in the RJ movement attend to healing "where the wound was made"? The unhealed wound? The world knows, as Indigenous Peoples all do, that the US was birthed with genocide and slavery, and that the legacies of these massive harms remain in force today. Every place the foot of a person whose people are not indigenous to this hemisphere lands is a place of fraud, theft, and murder. And the wealth that White settlers have extracted from indigenous lands, both personally and institutionally, has been gained through enslavement and then concentrated in White hands through theft, injustice, terrorism, murder, and exclusion.

As long as the restorative justice movement confines its focus to harms done by individuals today, the work will prove superficial in effect. If RJ remains silent about these twin wounds, its ability to transform society remains compromised. The mindset that believes in doing harm to gain benefits will continue unchallenged, justified even. Hence, the transformative impact on individuals will be limited, imbalanced, and unsatisfactory, because the far greater harms that do far greater structural damage hang all around us. The restorative effect will stop with "just us," violating from the get-go the core RJ principle of inclusion. Moreover, unrepaired harms make all settlers complicit in their perpetuation. Part 5 colorizes restorative justice by taking us back to "where the wound was made." Repairing these harms heals trauma on all sides, so that children, especially the children of settlers, can learn the ways of self-transformation—personally and as people.

Chapter 18

Undoing The First Harm: Settlers in Restorative Justice

Edward C Valandra, Waŋbli Wapȟáha Hokšíla

A Space for Our Realities

When Living Justice Press (LJP) decided to publish *Colorizing Restorative Justice* (*CRJ*), restorative justice (RJ) experienced a nuanced, but profound shift in its color. This shift will become more pronounced in the United States (herein the States) when no particular racial group numerically dominates. However, even a minority racial group can wield political, economic, and social power over others when it controls a state's apparatus, as happened in apartheid South Africa, British-colonized India, and pre–Civil War South Carolina. For example, the US national legislature and its fifty state legislatures are disproportionally males who are White and settlers. These governing bodies are sites of power in which White settlers have turned their fictions and fantasies of racial entitlement into social realities for People of Color (POC). The school-to-prison pipeline and the disproportionate number of non-Whites incarcerated, many of whom are on either probation or parole, reveal how Whites racially criminalize non-White bodies. Hence, the Black Lives Matter (BLM) movement contests White subjectivities about Black Peoples.

Similarly, Whites' pushback on the Deferred Action for Childhood Arrivals (DACA) program primarily impacts non-Whites south of the "US border." Whites perceive these People of Color as uncivilized "hordes" (rapists, drug dealers, etc.), which instills in Whites unwarranted fears of becoming the hordes' victims. These fears have made politically popular the call for Whites—and People of Color who drink White-settler Kool-Aid—to chant "Build the Wall" at rallies where White settlers predominate.

But as much as unfounded fantasies, especially settlers' fantasy of entitlement, drive Whites' pushback against any actions that benefit POC and Indigenous Peoples, POC's and Indigenous Peoples' resistance—often by simply asserting basic human rights—unsettle Whites and their fantasies. The

Očhéthi Šakówiŋ Oyáte's resistance to the Dakota Access Pipeline (DAPL) and the Native Hawaiians' Sovereignty Movement demonstrate this unsettling effect. With respect to Native Peoples, settlers' fantasies position Whites as being the "true" North American landowners, when in reality they continue to illegally occupy lands they stole from us. For these reasons, dedicating a book to communities of color is historically transformative, not only for POC but for settlers as well. Most settlers and their apologists struggle with either authentically engaging or intimately knowing non-White communities.

Of course, *CRJ* concerns community transformation, but it is also about restoring community. The RJ literature is clear: those harmed must have a space to tell their story, and *CRJ* is one such space. Hearing from and listening to those who are suffering or have suffered harm, whether individually or through structural marginalization, is RJ's core value—is it not? In this space, I want to talk about settler colonialism and its structure from the perspective of someone whose people, the Očhéthi Šakówiŋ Oyáte, is subject to its ongoing harms.

The RJ literature is clear: those harmed must have a space to tell their story, and CRJ is one such space.

Why structural marginalization? In discussing structural marginalization and its harms to Indigenous Peoples, I want RJ's rank and file to know that these harms are being done in their names, which means they cannot ignore it. Without this awareness, RJ's core values and principles, which theorists and practitioners pride themselves in, become little more than tools in the service of settler colonialism. Because settler colonialism (a structure that harms) and RJ (a framework that addresses harms) intersect in settler states, I challenge RJ theorists and practitioners alike to address this intersection with another fundamental RJ principle: *the mandate to undo harm caused by wrongdoing*. This challenge to settlers and others in RJ is what I call "Undoing The First Harm."

Understanding this challenge that I, as an Indigenous person, lay before the RJ movement requires establishing a nomenclature or common understandings, some of which would be familiar to RJ, some not. Structural marginalization, for example, includes recognizable themes, such as institutional racism (e.g., disproportionate disparities between races, such as incarceration), a stained-glass ceiling (e.g., economic inequity between racialized gender), American nativism (targeted versus favored immigrants), and other core concepts of critical thinking. *CRJ*'s call for abstracts assumed a level of critical awareness equal to my challenge.

Communities of color have historical and contemporary experiences that differ from White communities, as recent actions led by Indigenous Peoples and People of Color show. Both systemic racism and colonization account for these disparities in experiences. The most disconcerting dispar-

Though the field makes repairing harm from wrongdoing a fundamental tenet, acknowledging RJ's Indigenous antecedents (e.g., Circles) is not the same as addressing or undoing settler colonialism's First Harm.

ity is the sanctioned, structural violence ubiquitous throughout communities of color.[1]

Yet the RJ movement, while doing some good in many areas, has not produced a critical awareness about race, as these *CRJ* chapters attest. When Indigenous Peoples become involved with RJ, what has seemed obvious—a commitment to repairing harms—becomes less so. Though the field makes repairing harm from wrongdoing a fundamental tenet, acknowledging RJ's Indigenous antecedents (e.g., Circles) is not the same as addressing or undoing settler colonialism's First Harm.

Settler colonialism's literature provides disturbing insights as to why RJ sidesteps this harm in particular. Most notably, RJ counts settlers among its numbers, some of whom are considered its leaders. Yet, almost all Whites neither think of nor see themselves as settlers on a daily basis. Whites attending a 2018 restorative practices conference, for example, were unsettled when I used the term "settler" to describe them and to discuss what their settler identities mean for my people. My allies who attended breakout sessions or talked with the attendees at this conference related to me that White men were angry, White women cried. Their anger indicates to me that even fewer Whites in RJ comprehend what settler identity means for Indigenous Peoples—not only in the past but now and going into the future.

In "Beyond White Privilege: Geographies of White Supremacy and Settler Colonialism," Anne Bonds and Joshua Inwood, both White professors, explain why settlers become unhinged when Indigenous voices deconstruct their settler identity:

> Settler colonialism focuses on the *permanent* occupation of a territory and removal of indigenous peoples with the express purpose of building an ethnically distinct national community [e.g., Americans, Canadians, Australians, New Zealanders]. Because of the permanence of settler societies, *settler colonization is theorized not as an event or moment in history, but as an enduring structure requiring constant maintenance in an effort to disappear indigenous populations.* Settler colonialism is therefore premised on "logics of extermination" as the building of new settlements necessitates the eradication of indigenous populations, the seizure and privatization of their lands, and

the exploitation of marginalized peoples in a system of capitalism established by and reinforced through racism.[2]

Here, Bonds and Inwood refer to a foundational understanding that has become decolonization literature's baseline since the 1990s: settler colonialism is "a structure, not an event." This structure secures settler "permanence" by disappearing Indigenous populations, which is discussed later in this chapter. Because settler colonialism is how settlers live on Indigenous lands every day, the structure through which it makes invasion and land theft "permanent" requires constant maintenance, something settlers perceive as necessary to secure a feeling of certainty. Settler identities are a prime vehicle for doing this.

Does settler colonialism's structural genocide fit with restorative (or any) justice? Among settlers in RJ, what commitment is there to interrupting this pattern of harm and repairing it? The issue is ever-present. For instance, not only does our physical presence remind settlers of their theft of—and illegal occupation in—our homelands, but it also raises challenging questions about the fundamental relationship of settlers within RJ to restorative justice's philosophy, core values, and principles. Trevor Noah, Black South African and host of *The Daily Show*, noted this disconnect around racial relationships when he observed that the Second Amendment is a "Whites Only" right.[3] Similarly, does RJ apply to White settlers only and not to us? Whose harms matter and warrant repair? From Indigenous Peoples, then, comes a decentering question for RJ: "Other than adopting Circles or paying token homage to Indigenous Peoples' influence on RJ, what is RJ doing to undo The First Harm perpetrated against Indigenous Peoples?" No doubt, such an honest Native question will rattle settlers in RJ, as it should. If you have read this far, and you are truly a believer in justice, I encourage you to continue reading.

Among settlers in RJ, what commitment is there to interrupting this pattern of harm and repairing it? The issue is ever-present.

Contextualizing The First Harm

A few years ago, I visited the Highland Park area in St. Paul, Minnesota. While there, I read a realtor's advertisement in a community paper that unmasks settler colonialism's unmarked, yet normative structure. The real estate agent asked a colleague, "Do you know when the first land claim was in Mendota [MN]?" The colleague answered, "I believe that would be Constant Le May's farm in 1849." To the uninitiated who reads the advertisement, the question poses little more than local community trivia, an interesting ad gimmick, and not worth the effort to retain it—or so it seems. However, deconstructing settler subjectivities—i.e., settler attitudes, assumptions, personal feelings, tastes, and opinions—reveals that these subjectivities are thoroughly embedded in millions of such ostensibly innocuous exchanges that, in reality, maintain settler colonialism and its structure. And through these exchanges, settler identities are formed and reinforced.

"The first land claim" narrative is a typical, i.e., unmarked, yet normative subjectivity. It suggests to contemporary settlers that their progenitors possessed a land claim superior to all others, including Indigenous Peoples. Moreover, this narrative invokes commonsense understandings that only settlers self-identify with. Le May, a White immigrant who worked for a fur trading company located on the "frontier's fringes," was one of several settlers who, at the US' discretion, lived within a US military reservation or outpost illegally established in my homeland.[4] Like all settler land claims in the states, Le May's Mendota land claim is not as innocent as the advertisement would like us to believe. With US acquiescence, not only did he steal land—The First Harm—that rightfully belongs to the Očhéthi Šakówiŋ Oyáte, but also his land claim, one of hundreds of thousands in Minnesota (as well as in the other forty-nine states), eventually resulted in my people's forced, physical removal from Minnesota.[5]

Of course, stealing land that rightfully belongs to someone else and then framing the theft as a legitimate land claim requires settlers to rationalize the harm(s) they commit. Constructing fictional or fantasy entitlements does the job. One such fictional entitlement is the Discovery Doctrine (as in "Columbus Discovered America"). Infamous as this fiction is, the Discovery Doctrine is seldom thoroughly, much less critically, discussed in White society. Only in rarified circles such as in colonizer courts, or in certain academic courses such as property law, "Federal Indian law," or in academic fields such as Native Studies is it discussed. Settler states founded on this doctrine normalize the idea that settlers are the true owners of Native lands. In *American Indians*, Jack Utter, federal Indian law historian, writes:

Stealing land that rightfully belongs to someone else and then framing the theft as a legitimate land claim requires settlers to rationalize the harm(s) they commit.

> National celebrations of European arrival in the Western Hemisphere cause resentment among many American Indians who are aware of the so-called "doctrine of discovery." *This doctrine is the European-invented legal theory upon which all claim to, and acquisition of, Indian lands in North America is ultimately founded.*[6]

This particular settler narrative is not about "discovery" but is about Whites rationalizing their theft of Indigenous Peoples' land.

This widely celebrated idea flies in the face of factual reality: Indigenous Peoples, by virtue of our physically being in our respective territories before White invasion, remain the rightful, permanent landowners. Structural colonialism, then, keeps the lie going. It invokes the settlers' Discovery Doctrine in a variety of ways that justify their privatizing or nationalizing land they continually steal from Indigenous Peoples. Hence, this particular settler narrative is not about "discovery" but is about Whites rationalizing their theft of Indigenous Peoples' land.

Not surprisingly, the US Supreme Court's Chief Justice John Marshall—a White male settler who also owned slaves and speculated in selling stolen Indigenous land—first employed this doctrine in an 1823 court case. That case rid settlers of ever having to confront the reality that Indigenous Peoples possess absolute title to their homelands.[7] Ironically, the court case did not directly involve a land dispute between Indigenous Peoples and White settlers; instead, the dispute involved two White settlers, both of whom claimed ownership of the same Indigenous land.[8] One settler, Johnson, acquired land by purchasing it directly from Indigenous Peoples; the other, McIntosh, acquired it from the United States. Though we still own absolute title to the North American continent since time immemorial, with a pen's stroke, Chief Justice Marshall ignored this reality. His ruling in favor of McIntosh meant that, as far as US settler law is concerned, Indigenous Peoples do not own any land outright in the continent, and Indigenous Peoples cannot do what we want with our land.

> Thus, all the nations of Europe, who have acquired territory on this [North American] continent, *have asserted in themselves*, and recognized in others, the exclusive right of the discoverer to appropriate lands occupied by the Indians. Have the American States rejected or adopted this principle?[9]

Of course, White Justice Marshall answered his own question in the affirmative. When the White settlers defeated their British cousins and negotiated a subsequent peace treaty with them, the (now self-identified) White American settlers presumed to have acquired from the British the lands the British stole with no justification but the Discovery Doctrine. Hence, Marshall's contrived legal fiction elaborates how White settlers stole Indigenous lands.

> By this treaty [of Paris 1783], the powers of government, and the right to the soil, which had previously been in Great Britain, passed definitely to these states. . . .
>
> They [White American settlers] hold, and assert in themselves, the title by which it was acquired. . . . [T]hat discovery gave an exclusive right to extinguish the Indian title of occupancy; . . . and gave also a right to such a degree of sovereignty [over Indians and their land], as the circumstances of the people [of the US] would allow them to exercise.[10]

Although the Discovery Doctrine is widely discredited for its extreme racist and colonizing assumptions, its legacy of land theft remains in force. Steven T. Newcomb, Indigenous law scholar and author of *Pagans in the Promised Land*, decodes a Christian character embedded in the doctrine, which explains why its structural perseverance is so bone-deep and enjoys uncontested popularity amongst present-day settlers:

> When forms of reasoning found in the Old Testament narrative are used to reason about American Indian lands, the result is that Indian lands metaphorically become conceptualized—from the viewpoint of the United States—as the "promised land" of the "chosen people" of the United States. . . .
>
> There is ample evidence to show that prominent leaders of the United States have applied the Chosen People–Promised Land cognitive model as a way of thinking about and experiencing the identity of the United States, both in relation to the lands of the North American continent and, by means of words such as *pagan*, *heathen*, and *infidel*, in relation to American Indians. Once one begins looking for evidence of the Chosen People–Promised Land model in the historical record, it seems ubiquitous.[11]

Without the tremendous cultural energy expended in sustaining this fictitious Chosen People–Promised Land narrative—or as Newcomb labels it, the Doctrine of *Christian* Discovery—the settler society that I am so familiar with could not maintain itself. Indeed, our mere presence in North America pierces through the settlers' discovery facade and its derivatives.

However, whenever Indigenous Peoples intentionally expose settlers' illegal presence in North America, we do so at great risk. For example, our 1973 Wounded Knee II stand against our colonization and the Spirit and Sacred Stone Camps' 2016 actions against the Dakota Access Pipe Line (DAPL) show that we can expect settler retaliation in the form of structural violence.

Our settlers do not disappoint either. They militarize law enforcement and utilize private security to protect their ill-gotten property against the rightful owners. Settler legislators have since proposed post-NO2DAPL punitive measures that target future Indigenous decolonization actions.[12] And the settlers' sitting president approved executive actions (the Discovery Doctrine's descendants) to proceed with illegal pipeline development within occupied, treaty-recognized Indigenous land.[13] These actions underscore how settler colonialism takes, as Newcomb argues, ubiquitous form within settler structures. Certainly, twenty-first-century settlers—those who benefit from either private property or public lands—cannot deny that they remain the Discovery Doctrine's primary, if not sole, beneficiary.

Certainly, twenty-first-century settlers—those who benefit from either private property or public lands—cannot deny that they remain the Discovery Doctrine's primary, if not sole, beneficiary.

The structures supporting settler colonialism, while simultaneously colonizing Indigenous Peoples into oblivion, are evident in settler states. For most settlers and their apologists, being a settler has a positive subjectivity, especially in settler states such as Canada, Australia, New Zealand, and particularly the United States—or CANZUS for short. In other words, the structures that socially, politically, economically, and "legally" give settlers their "permanence" are not only external; integral to settler colonialism's persistence is the settlers' subjectivity or "structure of feeling."[14] First among these internalized structures of feeling among settlers is unexamined entitlement to Indigenous land. This unexamined entitlement and other settler fantasies have no basis in fact, let alone reality, yet their social consequences are lethal.

To ensure that new generations of settlers embrace these fiction-based subjectivities, like the Discovery Doctrine, settlers socialize their people from cradle to grave to believe that they are entitled to this continent, even though they clearly are not. For example, in February 2018, while passing through a South Dakota White border town, I purchased a children's coloring book, "Taming the Prairie: Pioneers of the Great Plains."[15] Other than the three less-than-gratuitous but generic mentions of "Native Americans," *the* settler experience is central. Homesteading, for example, is portrayed positively. The narrative introduces the *1862 Homestead Act* that enjoins settlers to come to the Great Plains and establish themselves as private property owners:

> Under this Act a person over 21 years of age could have 160 acres of undeveloped land for only an $18.00 fee. He had to live on the land for 5 years, build a home and make improvements before he could own it.[16]

This narrative is quintessential settler poppycock. Undeveloped land? Establishing a five-year residency? Build a home? Make improvements? These last three criteria are prerequisites for a settler to convert stolen, Indigenous homeland into private property after the US settler state "nationalized" our territory—all-out land theft. Not surprisingly, this settler narrative never mentions Indigenous Peoples as *the* permanent, original landowners, except to say in the first mention—and a conditional one at that—that the first people in the Great Plains "were likely Native Americans" and then to associate us with "untamed" land. The settler narrative does not teach settler children that we Indigenous Peoples have lived here for many thousands of years, built our homes here since time immemorial, maintained the buffalo commons and a thriving, diverse, ecosystem, and never turned the Great Plains into a dust bowl within a few decades and a national sacrifice zone due to radiation and other toxic poisoning within a century.

Of course, settler subjectivity becomes meaningless without mentioning hardship and labor, and, true to form, the settler children's book drives home this point. It depicts White settlers overcoming hardships with their labor. Presumably, this settler experience singularly justifies settler actions of expropriating land from its rightful owners, Indigenous Peoples. In her work about settler colonization, Eva Mackey, a settler Canadian professor, explains why repeating this generic settler narrative is crucial for settlers: it clothes their lies and myths as certain facts.

> When I began my interviews with members of CKCN [Chatham-Kent Community Network], people often introduced themselves by telling me stories of how long their families had been in the area and what kind of hard work they had done to settle the land and build their homesteads; . . . Each person provided me what I think of as a personalized settler genealogy of land possession and labor.[17]

For settlers (historic, contemporary, and future), their stories provide an emotional base of attachment or belonging to the land in the form of private or state—never as Indigenous—property. This land-possession narrative, bolstered by a labor genealogy, prompts settlers' irrational reaction of anger whenever Indigenous Peoples assert either a land claim (settler's angry response: "Go back to where you came from!") or treaty-based rights, such

Settler literature inculcates a fictional and fantasy entitlement that not only is undeserved but also has deadly consequences for Indigenous people.

as fishing (settler's angry response: "Spear a pregnant Native woman, save two fish") or both. Again, settler literature inculcates a fictional and fantasy entitlement that not only is undeserved but also has deadly consequences for Indigenous people.

Mackey accounts for settlers' reactive anxiety toward Indigenous Peoples. Contrary to their benign depiction of us in their literature, settlers know settlement's unspoken, ultimate function—the disappearing of Indigenous Peoples:

> Yet, this sense of belonging and attachment to home, to the land, can also be mobilized to defend expectations of entitlement and certainty in settler possession of land and *contribute to legitimizing Indigenous dispossession*. Again, it is labour, in Locke's view, which turns wilderness into private property. By stressing the long years of labour that it took to make the land into their home, they implicitly make a claim of possession through labour.[18]

The connections between the settler children's coloring book and Mackey's analyses of settler subjectivities merge in settler daily life. For example, in South Dakota, a state internationally known for its Native-hating, the personal story of Dennis Daugaard, the state's former White governor, follows this settler narrative and, as we shall see, repeats its deadly consequences for Indigenous Peoples.

> Dennis Daugaard grew up . . . on his family's dairy farm, which his grandfather purchased in 1911 after they emigrated from Denmark. . . . Daugaard moved back to South Dakota in 1981 to marry his high school girlfriend. . . . Two years later, they purchased the Daugaard family farm site where, over the next year, they built their own home.[19]

The Daugaard narrative contains settler colonialism's structural elements, starting with a European emigrant (White) settler genealogy that omits Indigenous Peoples. Serving to normalize land theft, the narrative justifies with labor a settler's illegal occupation of Indigenous land. Of course, Daugaard's narrative exemplifies what Emma Battell Lowman and Adam Barker describe as one of settler colonialism's three pillars: transcending colonialism.[20]

Serving to normalize land theft, the narrative justifies with labor a settler's illegal occupation of Indigenous land.

> That is, Indigenous peoples are eliminated and the presence of this new people—the settler society—becomes so deeply established that it is naturalized, normalized, unquestioned and unchallenged. As Jodi Byrd has shown, settler colonialism is a type of colonialism that "succeeds" not by preserving a given colonial order, but by superseding it. In order to obscure the violence of persistent invasion and dispossession, the histories of the new people are whitewashed. Sanitized emphasis on practises of benevolent or philanthropic colonialism . . . is used to overwrite the realities of how the new nation was formed through warfare, terrorism, subjugation, and theft.[21]

Moreover, as with so many Whites' settler narratives, Daugaard's is not benign but structurally harmful, especially when he acts on or evokes his settler identity. As the South Dakota governor, Daugaard introduced and eventually signed into law a state bill that only settlers would, of course, appreciate. To those untutored in settler-speak, the law's interpretation comes across clinically.

> SB 176 prohibits individuals from blocking highways and interfering with traffic and allows the South Dakota Department of Transportation to temporarily establish no parking zones. The new law also gives the [SD] Chief Justice authority to temporarily license outside attorneys to assist counties with an increase in criminal cases.[22]

Daugaard invokes the settler spin when he says that the law is "to protect those who want to peacefully exercise their First Amendment rights, as well as the people who reside in and travel through our state."[23] The law imposes a settler understanding of what constitutes "public safety," all the while promoting harms against Indigenous Peoples.

First, when settlers employ their laws, like SB 176, their fictional subjectivities—as in Oh! My! God! Indians!—come out. A SD governor can establish public safety zones (read: pipelines and other development infrastructure rights-of-way) that limit frontline actions to not more than twenty people without subjecting them to arrest. Second, this state law is aimed at Indigenous Peoples who dare defy settler colonialism's lethal excesses, such as the Keystone XL (KXL) pipeline (figure 1). Recall that, based on treaty, the KXL pipeline is a criminal trespass, since my nation has *never given its consent* for settlers to build a pipeline across our homeland to transport toxic tar sands from Canada, let alone allow them to become "permanent" residents.

In short, the egregious harm that my people suffer at the hands of settlers is that of being a national sacrifice peoples. The Indigenous Question for the

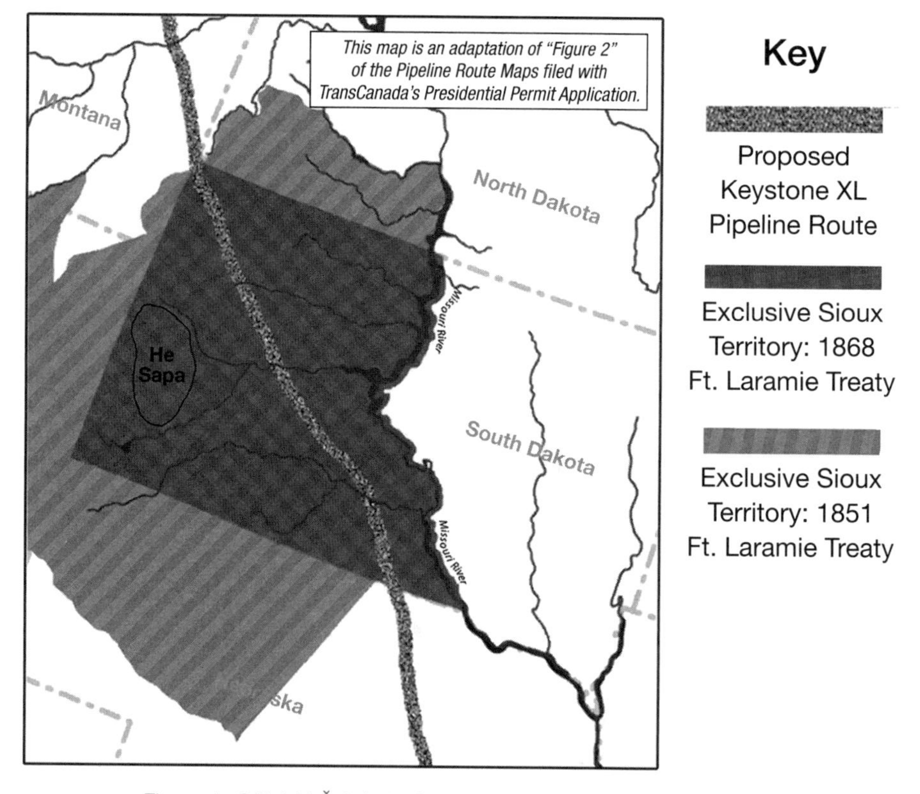

Figure 1. Očhéthi Šakówiŋ Oyáte Homeland and KXL Pipeline.

RJ community becomes, "Why is restorative justice silent with respect to settler colonialism's harms against Indigenous Peoples?" Could it be that RJ has settlers within its rank and file who not only benefit from stealing Indigenous land but also condone the genocide that goes with such theft? If they do not condone settler colonialism's genocide, then where are their actions to stop and undo it?

The First Harm: Mandates the Logic of Elimination

From its inception, settler colonialism's agenda has been not only to displace existing Indigenous societies with a settler one but also to maintain the outcome. This agenda is what makes settler colonialism so distinctly lethal for Indigenous Peoples from other forms of colonialism, such as extractive colonialism. The settler narrative socializes and reinforces settlers' raison d'être: they have come to stay in Turtle Island.

Now settler descendants, i.e., US and Canadian citizens—many of whom are engaged in RJ and other social justice organizations—continue to maintain that purpose. But that purpose carries a price—racially, politically, and morally too. The late Patrick Wolfe, Euro-Australian anthropologist and ethnographer, is the one who first stated the now-famous axiom that "invasion is a structure, not an event" and linked it with "the logic of elimination." He explains how constructing race socially serves settlers and their colonization:

> As opposed to enslaved people, whose reproduction [i.e., the one-drop rule] augmented their owners' wealth, Indigenous people[s] obstructed settlers' access to land, so their increase was counterproductive. In this way, the restrictive racial classification [i.e., use of blood quanta] of Indians straightforwardly furthered the logic of elimination.[24]

His observation gives yet another example of how settler colonialism operates as a structure. Blood quantum—"how much 'Indian' are you?"—becomes core to how white supremacy mediates settler–non-settler relationships. Without white supremacy, racial conventions could not be organized to harm communities of color in the ways that they do.

As Wolfe makes clear, Indigenous Peoples face the multitude of racial harms that the logic of elimination generates, and it is an ongoing project. Settlers employ this logic first to obtain and then to maintain 100 percent of Indigenous-owned territory: Indigenous land becomes "theirs" in the form of either private property or state ownership. As the children's book about pioneers illustrates, this logic is inherent in settler nations' identity. Wolfe explains that settlers employ a variety of methods to justify and maintain their outright theft of Native territory:

> The logic of elimination not only refers to the summary liquidation of Indigenous people[s], though it includes that. In common with genocide as Raphael Lemkin characterized it, settler colonialism has both negative and positive dimensions. Negatively, it strives for the dissolution of native societies. Positively, it erects a new colonial society on the expropriated land base—as I put it, settler colonizers come to stay: *invasion is a structure not an event.* In its positive aspect, elimination is an organizing principle of settler-colonial society rather than a one-off (and superseded) occurrence.
>
> The positive outcomes of the logic of elimination can include officially encouraged miscegenation [increasing a Native person's "White" blood quantum], the breaking-down of commonly-held native title into alienable individual freeholds [fabricating the Discovery Doctrine and its derivative of allotting Native land to individuals to establish private property], native citizenship [forcibly incorporating Native people into the US without our consent], child abduction [forcing Native children into adoptions and foster care, including sex trafficking], religious conversion [church and state joining forces to achieve

> assimilation], resocialization in total institutions such as mission or boarding schools, and a whole range of cognate bicultural assimilations [imposing a westernized education model]. All these strategies, including frontier homicide, are characteristic of settler colonialism.[25]

Settler structures and white supremacy are, of course, the head and tail of settler colonialism's coin, which means Indigenous Peoples will always lose this coin toss when we call for justice from settlers. Bonds and Inwood reveal how this coin's initial manufacture ensures that Indigenous Peoples *can never obtain justice from settlers.* For instance, as mentioned earlier, settler colonialism is different from other forms of colonization because (1) settlers come to stay, not leave; and, as a result, (2) they expressly build their own distinct, national community, i.e., white supremacy or nationalism, to replace Indigenous national communities and to exploit non-White, non-Indigenous communities. Bonds and Inwood name this pattern of colonization, which is in force and every bit as virulent today:

> Colonization, from the settler colonial perspective, is a kind of permanent occupation that is always in a state of becoming. This unfolding project involves the interplay between the removal of First Peoples from the land *and* the creation of labor systems and infrastructures that make the land productive. These two processes are interconnected and necessary: land must be cleared of indigenous populations, privatized, and then cultivated and made profitable. This ongoing project requires the continued displacement of indigenous and other marginalized peoples who are impediment to capitalist development, as well as particular forms of labor exploitation that extract value from appropriated land.[26]

The logic of elimination, then, requires that settlers *must* displace and replace already existing Indigenous societies with their own structure (e.g., the illegal establishment of the United States of America and Canada). Because restorative justice counts settlers among its numbers, RJ's moral quandary is plain: if the movement ignores The First Harm, RJ's legitimacy within settler states becomes untenable. This predicament became painfully evident in September 2007 when the US was one of four settler states to vote against the

---

RJ's moral quandary is plain: if the movement ignores The First Harm, RJ's legitimacy within settler states becomes untenable.

United Nations Declaration on the Rights of Indigenous Peoples (UNDRIP).[27] The First Harm against Indigenous Peoples continues as long as settlers continue to ignore The First Harm, all the while benefitting from it.

Native Permanence: A Settler Trigger

From birth to death, our settler friends, our settler colleagues, our settler lovers and spouses, our settler allies, our settler apologists, our settler opponents, etc., are socialized to believe that, however unfortunate, stealing Native homelands and killing Native Peoples—the hallmarks of settler colonialism's structure—are acceptable actions. For example, settlers' civic behavior (e.g., Independence Day) celebrates the Marshall Trilogy (*Johnson v. McIntosh*, 1823,[28] *Cherokee Nation v. Georgia*, 1831,[29] and *Worcester v. Georgia*, 1832[30]) as determinative decisions that, among others, define settlers' ongoing structural relationship with Native Peoples. Unlike the *Johnson* decision, both the *Cherokee Nation* and *Worcester* decisions came immediately after a May 1830 settler law—the Indian Removal Act—which called for Indigenous Peoples' physical removal from their homelands east of the Mississippi River.[31] Indeed, seven months after removal became law and eight years before the infamous Cherokee Trail of Tears death march, Whites' settler President Andrew Jackson cloaked Indigenous Peoples' ethnic cleansing in settler fantasy:

> Doubtless it will be painful [for Indigenous Peoples] to leave the graves of their fathers; but what do they more than our [White, European] ancestors did or than our [White American] children are now doing? To better their condition in an unknown land our forefathers left all that was dear in earthly objects. . . . Does Humanity weep at these painful separations from everything, animate and inanimate. . . ? Far from it. It is rather a source of joy that our country affords scope where our young population may range unconstrained in body or in mind. . . . These remove hundreds and almost thousands of miles at their own expense, purchase the land they occupy, and support themselves at their new homes from the moment of their arrival.[32]

For any settler of any era to compare Indigenous Peoples' removal as even remotely akin to the settler experience defies reality.

The Cherokee people, quite naturally, resisted the settlers' removal law for reasons not foreign to today's settlers, who scream "**Unfair!**" when confronted with the idea, let alone the reality, of returning stolen Indigenous land. When Mackey interviewed settlers about Indigenous land claims in Canada, they, much like their settler cousins in the States, invoked cherished tropes. Appealing to their frontier narrative, they both cast themselves as the innocent victims-to-be and portrayed Indigenous Peoples as perpetrators who were unjustly disrupting their fantasy-of-entitlement regime:

> These [settler] stories are told in a manner that implicitly communicates a kind of "evidence" demonstrating not only their emotional attachments to place, but also their sense of legitimate and rightful possession of the land. It is not only about purchasing land, but it also about making it one's own through years of labour. As one person said, "This isn't just about a farm, it's our *home*," which shows the deep attachments people have to specific pieces of land, and the pride they have in the work done to build their farms and lives.[33]

Prior to the Cherokee People's forced removal from their homeland in the late 1830s, the Cherokees also presented settlers with "it-is-not-just-about-a-farm, it-is-our-home" narrative. As past- and present-day settlers are wont to do, Cherokees also claimed a significant investment of labor in their homesteads. For example, on the material side of the ledger, an 1828 Cherokee census reveals that they possessed significant farm property (table 1) and farm-related infrastructure.

Table 1: Cherokee Farm Property (livestock)

District	Cattle	Horses	Swine	Sheep	Goats
Coosewaytee	2944	1207	4965	369	91
Tahquoa	1506	554	2419	323	
Chickamauga	1505	1175	8900	397	111
Hickory Log	1733	520	3178	187	24
Aquohee	1799	1191	5544	765	37
Ahmohee	1730	845	6080	243	93
Chattooga	7018	1318	4654	335	15
Hightower	3170	818	3777	298	67
Total	21405	7628	39517	2917	438

Source: http://www.cherokee.org/About-The-Nation/History/Facts/1828-Cherokee-Census-Information

Indeed, three years prior to the census, Thomas L. McKenney, a settler appointed to be the Indian Affairs first superintendent, issued an 1825 report about the Cherokee to the War Department that the census corroborated (table 2). No doubt both the 1828 Cherokee census and McKenney's observations depict a thriving Indigenous society amidst settlers:

Table 2. Cherokee Farm-related Infrastructure

District	Looms	Spinning Wheel	Wagon	Plough	Saw Mill	Black-smith	School	Grist Mill	Cotton Gin	Ferry	Store	Turn Pike	Roads	Threshing Machine
Coosewaytee	113	397	33	461	5	10	2							
Tahquoa	53	211		308		1		1						
Chickamauga	121	368	18	354	2	11	4	1	1	5	4			
Hickory Log	76	232	32		1	5			1		2			
Aquohee	145	346	7	446	1	5	1							
Ahmohee	70	327	29	372	3	7	5	6	2	5	1	1	6	1
Chattooga	124	307		446	1	11	6	5	2		2			
Hightower	67	240	7	65		5	1	2						
Total	769	2428	126	2452	13	55	19	15	6	10	9	1	6	1

Source: http://www.cherokee.org/About-The-Nation/History/Facts/1828-Cherokee-Census-Information

The northern part is hilly and mountainous; in the southern and western parts there are extensive and fertile plains. . . . These plains furnish immense pasturage, and numberless herds of cattle are dispersed over them; horses are plenty; numerous flocks of sheep, goats, and swine cover the valleys and hills. . . . In the plains and valleys the soil is generally rich, producing Indian-corn, cotton, tobacco, wheat, oats, indigo, and sweet and Irish potatoes. The natives carry on considerable trade with the adjoining States; some of them export cotton in boats down the Tennessee [River] to the Mississippi [River], and down that river to New Orleans.

Apple and peach orchards are quite common, and gardens are cultivated, and much attention paid to them. Butter and cheese are seen on Cherokee tables. There are public roads in the nation, and houses of entertainment kept by natives.

Numerous and flourishing villages are seen in every section of the country. Cotton and woolen cloths are manufactured: blankets of various dimensions, manufactured by Cherokee hands, are very common. Almost every family in the nation grows cotton for its own consumption. Industry and commercial enterprise are extending themselves in every part. Nearly all merchants in the nation are native Cherokees. Agricultural pursuits engage the chief attention of the people.[34]

Ironically, McKenney's report about the Cherokee describes in detail various accomplishments that present-day settlers also cite to convince themselves they are the "legitimate or rightful" landowners. No doubt, the Cherokee belonging to the land is authentic and inalienable, and they did not need these settler-type achievements to justify their existence on the land. However, knowing that settler society views Indigenous and other non-White peoples as occupying a very low rung on a human evolutionary scale, the Cherokee people rightly anticipated that only bad faith would come from settlers, as the 1830 Indian Removal Act eventually proved.

Owing to their national resilience, the Cherokee flipped the Whites' evolutionary scale and, in doing so, unsettled settlers' fantasies of entitlement. In addition to the Cherokee's stunning prosperity, which both the 1828 Cherokee census and McKenney document, the Cherokee took two other self-determining acts: they adopted a constitutional government in 1827, and they built their literacy rate until it exceeded that of all the states, thanks to Se-

---

The Cherokee flipped the Whites' evolutionary scale and, in doing so, unsettled settlers' fantasies of entitlement.

---

quoyah, a Cherokee citizen who developed a Cherokee syllabary. The Cherokee people's dramatic transition, without ever having to relocate west of the Mississippi River, so stunned White settlers that, through their westernized lens, they took to labeling them a "Civilized Tribe."[35]

Being a Civilized Tribe also indicates that settlers grudgingly viewed the Cherokee as having *the* attribute commonly associated with settler identity, namely, having fulfilled the Lockean requirement for possessing land: privatizing it (turning it into private property).[36] John Locke, seventeenth-century English philosopher, argued that humans—European capitalist ones, that is—have a natural right, first, to acquire land and then to privatize it by imbuing "the Earth" with their labor:

> Though the Earth, and all inferior Creatures be common to Men, yet every Man has a Property in his own Person. . . . . The Labour of his Body, and the Work of his Hands, we may say are properly his. Whatsoever then removes out of the State that Nature hath provided, and left in it, he hath mixed his Labour with, and joined to it something that is his own, and thereby makes it [the acquired land] his Property. It being by him removed from the common state nature placed it, it hath by his labour something annexed to it, that excludes the common right of other Men.[37]

From the Lockean perspective, then, a person's labor is solely his or her "property." It follows, in his view, that when a person works the land (the pioneer/homesteader/settler story), they infuse, somehow, the land with their labor. Through this act, the soil becomes their private property. Based on all available evidence, the Cherokee easily met Locke's requirements for establishing private property. They assumed that their private property (and rights thereof that go with it) would shield them against The First Harm.

Settlers in restorative justice and other allied fields (e.g., community justice, transformational justice, reparative justice, social justice, or environmental justice) must be especially cognizant of the context in which settlers perpetrate The First Harm. In this case, Cherokee people (as other Indigenous Peoples also did) virtually remade themselves in their colonizer's image (even privatizing land into property in the manner of settlers), yet this did not shield them from settlers' violent dispossession. The Cherokee case study reveals a fundamental reality about settler colonialism: *Settlers are deaf to humane calls not to perpetrate harms against Indigenous Peoples.*

Settlers are deaf to humane calls not to perpetrate harms against Indigenous Peoples.

Institutional oppression (e.g., the 1924 Indian Citizenship Act and the

Indian Reorganization Act), social marginalization (e.g., racism, claiming Indigenous land as private and state property), and trivializing Indigenous cultures (e.g., sports mascots, attaching Native nations' names to military hardware) all contribute to normalizing settler violence against Indigenous communities, and all these harms need to be addressed. However, the outright theft of Native lands—*our homelands—remains the outstanding First Harm that leads to all the other harms.* This settler violence is the harm that settlers in restorative justice deliberately ignore, though at an extremely high moral price.

Studying colonialism by researching not the Indigenous Peoples impacted but the behavior of the invader-settlers, Wolfe deconstructs for settlers why they, in the main, are fine with perpetuating this harm and living with its outcome: structural genocide. Wolfe's deconstruction challenges settlers in restorative justice to act. Absent reparative actions, restorative justice's credibility among Indigenous Peoples and People of Color will continue to implode, as the existing gaps between settler praxis and RJ's principles become wider and more indefensible.

Absent reparative actions, restorative justice's credibility among Indigenous Peoples and People of Color will continue to implode . . .

These gaps are where restorative justice and settler colonialism intersect with painful truth and reality, which go to the core of who settlers are. Settler colonialism differs from colonialism's other forms because of the settler identity that this system creates and requires to keep its structures going. Wolfe observes that a settler society does not eliminate Indigenous Peoples because of where the latter just happen to live or who they just happen to be, but because of the threat we represent to settlers' identity:

> So far as Indigenous people[s] are concerned, *where they are is who they are*, and not only by their own reckoning. As Deborah Bird Rose has pointed out, to get in the way of settler colonization, all the native[s have] to do is stay at home. Whatever settlers may say—and generally they have a lot to say—the primary motive for elimination . . . is access to territory. Territoriality is settler colonialism's specific, irreducible element.[38]

In the Cherokee's case, Wolfe clarifies the root of settler society's stance toward Indigenous Peoples—what drives its genocide-structured behavior:

> But if the natives [Cherokee] are already agriculturalists, then why not simply incorporate their productivity into the colonial economy? At this point, we begin to get closer to the question of just who it is (or, more to the point, who they are) that settler colonialism strives to eliminate—and, accordingly, closer to an understanding of the relationship between settler colonialism and genocide. To stay with the Cherokee removal: when it came to it, the factor that most antagonized the [White] Georgia state government . . . was not actually the recalcitrant savagery of which Indians were routinely accused, but the Cherokee's unmistakable aptitude for civilization. . . . They had become successful agriculturalists on the White model, with a number of them owning substantial holdings of Black slaves, and they had introduced a written national constitution that bore more than a passing resemblance to the US one. Why should genteel [White] Georgians wish to rid themselves of such cultivated neighbours? *The reason why the Cherokee's constitution and their agricultural prowess stood out as such singular provocations to the [White settler] officials and [White settler] legislators of the state of Georgia—and this attested over and over again in their public statements and correspondence—is the Cherokee's farms, plantations, slaves and written constitution all signified permanence.*[39]

For settler societies (e.g., Canada and the United States) to feel secure in their private or state property, any Indigenous signifier that recognizes permanence (treaties and the rights stated in them, homelands, sovereignty, Traditional Ecological Knowledge [TEK], etc.) must be eradicated. Consequently, to secure the very land that they falsely claim as either private or state property, settlers have to collectively reinforce a fantasy—one that crumbles at the mere presence of Indigenous Peoples. In North America, knowing how they came by the land, settlers experience primal uncertainty about their very legitimacy. This uncertainty drives them deeper into their fantasies of entitlement and fuels their resolve, by any means necessary, to eliminate Indigenous Peoples.

In North America, knowing how they came by the land, settlers experience primal uncertainty about their very legitimacy. This uncertainty drives them deeper into their fantasies of entitlement and fuels their resolve, by any means necessary, to eliminate Indigenous Peoples.

Red Earth, Black Lives, and White-Created Dilemmas

Wolfe and others identify the one Indigenous theme—that we are the land's original title and therefore its rightful owners—that settlers acknowledge but find so disquieting to their settler identity. To implement the fantasy of settler entitlement to Indigenous land, CANZUS states have fashioned racial regimes that target Indigenous Peoples. While a fuller treatment of racial constructions in the states merits a thorough discussion, this chapter can provide only a quick tour of how the settler structure and its concomitant racism have harmed—and continue to harm—Indigenous Peoples.

One settler racial regime involves forcing Indigenous Peoples to emigrate from Africa. In the antebellum US, settlers constitutionally sanctioned Indigenous Africans and their descendants as three-fifths of a person until 1868. Until 1865, the states designated them as personal property, i.e., slaves, which socially "constituted their blackness."[40] These regimes continue to inform settler society's perceptions of race, and those of us on the receiving end are not always aware of how the logic of elimination impacts us personally.

For example, President Obama had a racial option to exercise, which in his case shows how far the social construction of race has come from its original, narrow definition. After all, prior to 2000, the US census did not provide options for an individual to self-identify with one of several races as we do today or as a blend of different races. Hence, Barack Hussein Obama II self-identifies as Black, and settlers and others identify him as the first Black US president.

But from an Indigenous worldview, Obama is arguably the first Indigenous US president. Unlike many Blacks in the states who, because of slavery, are several generations removed from their Indigenous roots in Africa, Obama is only one generation removed. His biological father is Luo, the East African Indigenous Peoples of Kenya and the upper Nile valley, and his father came to the states voluntarily. That Obama chose a non-Luo identity is a familiar but complicated story for Indigenous people in settler states. Exercising this choice comes at a high cost: it is, in fact, a choice that aligns with the logic of elimination. Obama surely felt this cost of not fully embracing his indigeneity when Alice Matthew, a Malaysian citizen, confronted him in September 2016 about his ambivalent responses to the Očhéthi Šakówiŋ Oyáte's resistance to the Dakota Access Pipe Line (DAPL) at a town hall gathering.[41]

We know that the settlers' racial regime adopts new forms when white supremacy is threatened.[42] It morphed in response to slavery's abolition on one hand and Indigenous Peoples' national character on the other.[43] Almost five decades ago, Vine Deloria Jr., Húŋkpapȟa Thitȟuŋwaŋ/Očhéthi Šakówiŋ Oyáte citizen (1933–2005), mapped how settlers racially manage our Indigenous African and Indigenous North American identities and what it has meant for each:

> The white man adopted two basic approaches in handling blacks and Indians. He systematically excluded blacks from all programs, policies, social events, and economic schemes. He could not allow blacks to rise from their position because it would mean that the evolutionary scheme had superseded the Christian scheme that man[kind] perhaps truly descended from the ape.
>
> With the Indian the process was simply reversed. The white man had been forced to deal with the Indians in treaties and agreements. It was difficult, therefore, to completely overlook the historical antecedents such as . . . the desperate straits from which various Indian tribes had often rescued the whites. Indians were therefore subjected to the most intense pressure to become white.[44]

Faced with these two approaches, Blacks (whose descendants suffer the outstanding debt incurred by the theft of their ancestors' labor) and Indigenous Peoples (whose descendants suffer the outstanding debt incurred by the theft of their Indigenous lands) rarely compared their distinct experiences with settler colonization. However, in the space that colorizing restorative justice creates, we conflate almost fifty-three decades of our experiences with settlers and find that, although People of Color and Indigenous Peoples are unique, we share common ground.

Without question, Black cultural expressions in the states have deep Indigenous African roots. It is not surprising that Blacks' oral tradition is replete with stories about Indigenous African "slaves"—and later their descendants—escaping from White settlers either to join other established Indigenous communities or to forge their own communities based on Indigenous African worldviews. From an Indigenous perspective, Red and Black Power movements are not about fighting for a settler-defined space at the settlers' table, i.e., equality; instead, such power is about self-determination as Indigenous Peoples.

From an Indigenous perspective, Red and Black Power movements are not about fighting for a settler-defined space at the settlers' table, i.e., equality; instead, such power is about self-determination as Indigenous Peoples.

The disconcerting reality is that, as long as we internalize the settlers' racial regime(s), we participate not only in sustaining The First Harm but also in undermining how People of Color interact or relate with each other. By contrast, whenever Indigenous North America's descendants recognize that African descendants are Indigenous or have Indigenous roots, this recognition disrupts the settler's racial framework. Rather than staying racially siloed as "American Indians/Alaskan Natives" and "Blacks/African Americans" and building race-based coalitions only within our own racial groups, as we are

For Indigenous Peoples and People of Color, constitutional incorporation is the answer neither to the settlers' political dilemma nor to the Whites' racial dilemma. Such incorporation will not lead to our decolonization, nor will it absolve settlers of their wrongdoing: stealing Indigenous North America's land and stealing Indigenous Africa's labor. The First Harm and The Second Harm stand unrepaired.

conditioned to do, we work collaboratively on our relationships as descendants of Indigenous Peoples. The result? Not only are we more effective at building coalitions across race but also our collaborations expose how the logic of elimination lies at the root of the settlers' racial setup.

For example, "American Indian/Alaskan Native" as a definition collapses the hundreds of existing Indigenous Nations into a single race; the term "Native American" has a similar effect. This racial positioning of Indigenous Peoples furthers the settlers' project of elimination, because it imposes a racial status that obscures our political status as self-determining peoples.

Another way settlers promote our elimination as distinct peoples is with their assumption that assimilation or some other Americanization program addresses the wrongs done to us. In the settlers' mind, racial groups (Blacks, Asian Americans, Latinxs, etc.) simply want equality: they desire to be free from discrimination; they want White social acceptance; or they want a chance at "equal opportunity" within a settler state. Rarely, if ever, does our *political status* as self-determining, Indigenous Peoples break through the settlers' racial regime. As far as settlers are concerned, simply carving out greater constitutional space (e.g., the Thirteenth, Fourteenth, and Fifteenth Amendments, civil rights laws, and court decisions) for Indigenous North American and Indigenous African Peoples will do the trick.

Yet for Indigenous Peoples and People of Color, constitutional incorporation is the answer *neither* to the settlers' political dilemma *nor* to the Whites' racial dilemma. Such incorporation will not lead to our decolonization, nor will it absolve settlers of their wrongdoing: stealing Indigenous North America's land and stealing Indigenous Africa's labor. The First Harm and The Second Harm stand unrepaired. To think that guaranteeing constitutional space might be equivalent to or a form of restorative justice is simply wrongheaded. Equity—constitutional, racial, or otherwise—will never be the answer to undoing these harms: equity not only leaves the settler structure unchallenged but also reinforces it with the mountainous benefits that come with leaving harms unrepaired. Failure to grasp the magnitude and nature of these harms, settlers continue to perpetuate them, both structurally and individually.

Perhaps Deloria did not foresee colorizing restorative justice. Nonetheless, he called it right when he predicted the challenge for late twentieth- and twenty-first-century settlers: "Between these two basic attitudes [toward Natives and Blacks] . . . the white man was impaled on the horns of a dilemma *he had created within himself*."[45] Settlers, who benefit from racial construction, as do their apologists of color, wince at the racial regime they have constructed: as of this writing, racial politics is playing out as the regime unravels. The post-9/11 cultural wars in the states expose the racial animus between White settlers and Indigenous Peoples and Communities of Color. Settlers do indeed find themselves impaled on the horns of a racial-political dilemma that is of their making.

It never had to be this way. Coexistence was the option that Indigenous Peoples always sought—and invaders-settlers-Whites continue to reject. Hence, this rejection, no doubt, reflects the racial disparities and socio-political inequities that plague Indigenous Peoples and other communities of color but do not affect White settlers to the same degree or in the same way.

"The Talk": What a Community Equal to It Requires

I speak from an Indigenous experience. More specifically, I speak with an Očhéthi Šakówiŋ Oyáte voice. Although what I say may resonate with Indigenous Peoples and perhaps other communities of color, I speak neither on behalf of all Indigenous Peoples nor for my own nation. Moreover, this chapter is not the first time that I and other Indigenous Peoples have raised our printed voices against settler injustices, which include genocide. Settlers can be assured that this chapter will not be the last, either.

So, turning my thoughts to our settlers, I do not see it as my job to come up with a "solution" for you, including those of you who are in restorative justice. I am willing, though, to engage "The Talk" about this dilemma your ancestors created for you and which you sustain. Restorative justice has promise, but I do not see how restorative justice can fulfill its promise as long as you turn a blind eye to the one massive harm that predicates all the rest and that has made you as a group believe that wrongdoing can stand as your society's foundation.

Turning my thoughts to our settlers, I do not see it as my job to come up with a "solution" for you, . . . I am willing, though, to engage "The Talk" about this dilemma your ancestors created for you and which you sustain.

Restorative justice literature recognizes the role of community in addressing and undoing harms as a result of wrongdoing; yet this role remains problematic between Indigenous Peoples and settlers. To repair The First Harm, you first need some way to come together among yourselves that carries the community or relationship muscle equal to addressing a harm of this magnitude—one whose repair will and must be deeply transformative. I know many of you believe it is not in your interests to repair The First Harm; otherwise, you would have done so. I believe it is, but that is another discussion. Here, I want to explore how to create a space that builds the community-muscle equal to the task—that keeps the harm of stolen Indigenous land central in the minds of settlers in restorative justice.

To repair The First Harm, you first need some way to come together among yourselves that carries the community or relationship muscle equal to addressing a harm of this magnitude—one whose repair will and must be deeply transformative.

To start, Indigenous Peoples and settlers experience community very differently. Acknowledging this difference is critical, because forming community relations is core to the RJ process. I would say settlers experience community in ways that are alien, if not antithetical, to Indigenous communities. While considering this difference is also not within the scope of this chapter, I can point to how settlers have thought about and struggled with the notion of community.

Daniel Kemmis, a White male attorney-settler, for example, explains community in a way that is likely to be familiar to his White compatriots, namely, as a procedural republic. He recognizes that local or regional community development schemes, public works, or other shared interests may bring people or communities together. However, the public discourse surrounding community development often reveals more disconnection than common ground. In short, people break into factions and fight.

Kemmis attributes this disconnection to the nature of these forums. In them, people speak "the first language of individualism," as he puts it. In a structured, public discourse, individual rights dominate, which frames the exchange with defensiveness, opposition, and conflicts; connections and trust are unlikely to develop. He writes:

> People in this situation [e.g., public hearings] do not speak of what they have in common, or how the common good might be guarded and enhanced. What they speak of is how a proposed initiative (in this case the land use plan) either enhances or threatens their individual lives. They speak in terms of the ideologies most conducive to their particular [individual] rights.[46]

However, according to Kemmis, individuals also possess "second languages of cooperation, tradition, and commitment" that must be invoked in order to achieve a higher common ground or good. For Kemmis and others who share his view—and there are many—the politics of place reveals an "unencumbered space" where these second languages reside and where settlers are likely to express their common structure of feelings. In this space, people are likely to tell stories about their lives and share a sense of meaning.

To illustrate the characteristics of community, Kemmis invokes a well-known settler trope: barn raising. Whenever a ranch or farm family or individual decided to build a barn, every able-bodied person within horse-riding (now a pickup-driving) radius arrived. Their help was unsolicited, because raising a barn represented a higher common ground or good. It opened an unencumbered space where cooperation and other values subordinated individual rights and tolerated a wider range of contrasting or conflicting values. Whether we agree with Kemmis on his notion of a higher common ground, we can agree that community-based relationships are decidedly pragmatic. Among farm families, having a barn is a matter of survival. For Kemmis and others who desire a seamless web between the procedural (re)public space and the unencumbered community space, *the challenge is twofold: it is relational, and it involves real-world concerns.*

To go deeper into these notions of community, Kemmis' observations about how diverse groups engage one another differently in formal spaces than in informal spaces (and visa versa) are instructive. To link these two spaces, Kemmis borrows from Hannah Arendt, a German-Jewish philosopher and political theorist, who argued that we enter public spaces (publica) in a concrete (res) way (in Latin "res publica" means "the (or a) public thing"):

> Hannah Arendt offers this perspective on the relationship of the public and the *res*. "To live together in the world means essentially that a world of things is between those who have it in common, as a table located between those who sit around it; the world, like every in-between, relates and separates men [and women] at the same time. . . . The public realm, as the common world, gathers us together and yet prevents our falling over each other, so to speak. What makes mass society so difficult to bear is not the number of people involved, or at least not primarily, *but the fact that the world between them has lost its power to gather them together, to relate and to separate them.*"[47]

Kemmis finds in Arendt a clue for why people in a community space have so much trouble with relationality. Arendt reflects on how a table—a concrete thing perceptible to our senses, something tangible—seemingly disappears for the people sitting around it and what this disappearance entails.

> The weirdness of this [common world-of-things] situation resembles a spiritualistic séance where a number of people gather around a table might suddenly, through some magic trick, see the table vanish from their midst, so the two persons sitting across from each other were no longer separated but also would be entirely unrelated by anything tangible.[48]

For Kemmis, Arendt's simile of the "world as vanishing table" appeals to his settler sensibilities. He argues that without such tangibility to draw people together, the world between us loses its power to gather us together.

How do these ideas relate to The Talk and the call for settlers in restorative justice to address The First Harm? Whatever other dynamics may be in play, settler fantasies—the magic trick Arendt alludes to—impair or even eclipse our capacity to track the world between us. These fantasies disconnect you from me and hold more power over you than realities. Settlers' fantasies of entitlement have made the "table"—the land's first and only owners—"vanish from your midst." This dilemma is why settlers construct their fantasies in the first place: to disappear inconvenient realities.

But choosing to believe in the magic trick is costly, and not only for Indigenous Peoples. I observe among you that, as White settlers, you lose the capacity to come together, not only with others but also among yourselves. The single most important thing "settling" has done to make your existence on this continent possible—stealing a continent of land through structured colonialism—vanishes like Arendt's table in your public spaces. With it goes an ability to let the world gather you. Hence, the consequences of fantasy-disconnection appear today when any fantasy substitutes for socio-political reality, and facts have no power to pull factions together in problem-solving.

For "The Talk" to happen, then, settler fantasies must be exposed as the magic trick, and the realities of how you came here and how you exist today must stand at the center of public discourse. Nothing is more real for your existence. For those of you in restorative justice who are prepared to release yourselves of settler fantasies—a lifelong endeavor, to be sure—I am prepared to take a step further and suggest a way for you to keep "the real world between us" front and center—visible, so as not to vanish from your midst—during your dialogues.

Settlers' fantasies of entitlement have made the "table"— the land's first and only owners—"vanish from your midst." This dilemma is why settlers construct their fantasies in the first place: to disappear inconvenient realities.

Settler Structures of Feeling: Unlikely to Budge

Before I go further, though, I want to pause and acknowledge the challenge before you. As I said earlier, the settler structure is not only external. Its roots lie in settler subjectivities, the structures of feeling that perpetuate The First Harm's continuation. The challenge to dismantle these internal structures demands disrupting lifetimes of experiences as White settlers. Will the settler identity prove too strong for restorative justice to win out?

Well-meaning settlers in RJ can ill afford to underestimate the strength of your identities as White settlers. Kemmis discusses how inhabitation of place brings tangible elements associated with forming relationships. Of course, bond formation among settlers reinforces their self-perpetuation:

> But it [genuine public life] is also concrete in the actual, specific places within which those practices and that cooperation take place. Clearly, the practices which shaped the behavior and the character of frontier families did not appear out of thin air; they grew out of the one thing those people had most fundamentally in common: the effort to survive in a hard country. And when the effort to survive comes to rely upon shared and repeated practices like barn raising, survival is transformed; it becomes inhabitation. To *inhabit* a place is to dwell there in a practiced way, in a way that relies upon certain, trusted habits of behavior.[49]

Kemmis makes clear that for each person inhabiting a place, relationships blossom out of necessity from a community born out of shared inhabitation. His narrative communicates settlers' formative experience about survival in a hard country or, more accurately, Native Country. Just as survival constitutes the one thing that all settlers have in common, so, too, has stealing Indigenous Peoples' land proven a common community practice—one that has shaped not only settlers' behavior and character but also their structures of feeling. With bonding-for-survival as settlers' glue, Kemmis' concept shows that the classic settler narrative excludes Indigenous Peoples from the settler narrative, let alone community. This peculiar and ongoing way of establishing community is where settler colonialism violently intersects with restorative justice. It is where settlers find themselves today: impaled on the horn of The First Harm's dilemma.

I have experienced settlers' structure of feeling often: pointing out settler fantasies is enough to trigger settlers' rage. Given how little it takes to trigger settlers' anger and defensiveness, it is not clear to me how you will dismantle your settler structures enough to be able to dialogue about The First Harm, much less to undo it. Granted, my naming of settler behavior comes with an edge born of seeing the human and natural world costs of settler colonialism every time I set foot out my door in my nation's homeland.

Restorative Justice Requires Self-Change

So, again, will settlers in restorative justice choose RJ principles that call for repairing harms, or will settler identities, reinforced for more than five centuries, prove too strong for your group? To put it another way, can restorative justice support settlers in holding yourselves accountable for the massive harms your settler identities perpetrate? If so, can settlers in RJ engage the reparative process as a group and effect your collective self-transformation? You may think I am asking a lot, but you ask a lot of us: Indigenous Peoples and Peoples of Color keep paying the consequences of your refusal to hold yourselves accountable—your determination to keep living at our expense—as if you can ignore both the crimes in the history and the injustices in the present that your settler structure maintains for its futurity.

The restorative justice literature takes much satisfaction from its community uniqueness. This claim to uniqueness is not unlike Kemmis' call for community to mean something more relationally genuine. So let us start with considering restorative justice principles. Johannes Wheeldon, criminologist, frames at least three restorative justice principles that differ from the westernized, state-run, punishment-based model.

> First is a focus on harms. Harms refer here to those suffered by the victim of a particular incident, by an offender, and even those suffered within communities. . . . The second is a desire to root processes in the communities where the harm occurred. . . . The third principle is related to the moral potential for restorative justice. Often tied to spiritual or religious traditions, there is a tradition of humanism described as rooting morality in attending to the real needs of actual individuals through processes which are consistent with and reflect community values.[50]

These principles are promising, no doubt, but it is also discouraging for me to read them. As much as these principles make intellectual space for repairing The First Harm and as many decades as the Western iteration of

You may think I am asking a lot, but you ask a lot of us: Indigenous Peoples and Peoples of Color keep paying the consequences of your refusal to hold yourselves accountable—your determination to keep living at our expense . . .

restorative practices has been gaining momentum, undoing The First Harm cannot be found on RJ's agenda. Reflecting the experiences of non-Whites and non-White communities, multiple chapters in *Colorizing Restorative Justice* question whether restorative justice—as a movement, as a field—is morally up to the task of addressing, let alone solving, two of modern, Western communities' most vexing moral challenges: decolonization (putting right the theft of Indigenous homelands) and reparations (putting right the theft of Indigenous African labor).

Admittedly, I share their skepticism that restorative justice's charge to undo harms that result from wrongdoing holds any real meaning for us, Indigenous Peoples, particularly when the movement is thoroughly peppered with settlers, many of whom are "leaders" in this field. No doubt, settlers and perhaps some non-settlers will find this critique harsh. And I suppose it is, but the following structural reasons inform my skepticism.

The fundamental relation between Indigenous Peoples and settlers is an extremely structured one, far more than Kemmis could even imagine for a "democratized," procedural republic. Consider the context from which this hyper-structure formed. Up until 1871, both settlers and Indigenous people signed treaties to resolve conflicts over land, jurisdiction, and relational rights to the natural world. That means settlers—past, present, and future—are, like Indigenous Peoples, treaty people, so much so that the settlers' venerated "Founding Fathers" recognized treaties as settlers' supreme law.[51] Treaties are, therefore, prima facie a hyper-structured relationship between Indigenous Peoples and settlers. Yet, though both parties signed treaties to secure peaceful relations, settlers violate these treaties daily. Honoring treaties is an obvious place to start, and yet it is what settlers refuse to do.

Though both parties signed treaties to secure peaceful relations, settlers violate these treaties daily. Honoring treaties is an obvious place to start, and yet it is what settlers refuse to do.

What is the result of generations of this settler behavior—namely, multigenerational contempt for agreements designed to establish relations between our peoples? Indigenous Peoples in the fifty states today represent less than one percent (1%) of the US population, and we *conditionally*, thanks to the settlers' 1823 *Johnson v. McIntosh* ruling, "retain" about two percent (2%) of our homeland within the US. Comparatively, prior to October 1492, Indigenous Peoples constituted one hundred percent (100%) of the population and held unconditionally one hundred percent (100%) of the land that the fifty states now occupy. In the 527 intervening years (and counting), what happened? Settler colonialism happened. Eliminating Indigenous populations and outright stealing our lands from us are the *sine qua non* of settler identity.

No wonder our relation(ship) with our colonizers is fraught with deep distrust, and the likelihood of having an authentic conversation is slim. A most telling statement (and personal favorite) about settler trustworthiness comes from Harold Fey, a White settler, who, in 1955, wrote for *The Christian Century*. He sarcastically self-observed then what I find to be much more true about settlers today:

> Why don't the Indians trust us? We mean well toward them. We want them to succeed. Indeed, we would be glad if the Indians were just like ourselves, and what more could they desire than that? We are not like some nations we could mention—deceivers, slave-drivers, treaty-breakers. We are upright people, and it irritates us a little to have to say so. Some of us are in the habit of referring to the United States as a Christian nation. So if the Indian does not trust us, it must be because he [or she] has some unfortunate defect in his [or her] own character, such as innate suspicion. If so, that is something we should help overcome. . . . These things we [settlers] say to ourselves to calm the uneasiness which clings to the fact that we are not trusted by the original Americans, *who have known us longer than anybody else.*[52]

As Kemmis observed, structured, formal relations amongst settlers lead to arguments over rights, especially around private property, which many of them own or idealize. If restorative justice depends on people coming together in "unencumbered" spaces to share their stories, speak from the heart, and have their words count toward working out solutions that are good for everyone, then what are the chances for the kind of authentic conversation that RJ requires in the hyper-structured, therefore hyper-contentious, context that surrounds Indigenous and White-settler relations?

Hence, when we talk about the possibility of having the authentic conversations necessary to undo The First Harm, we are asking restorative justice to find and thread a needle in a land strewn with blunt instruments—a crime scene, an open wound with blood and pain everywhere. Settlers, especially those of you who have either internalized or are on the path to internalizing restorative justice principles, have always known of The First Harm, the subsequent harms against Indigenous Peoples, and your culpability in all of this. You know that The First Harm exists and continues on behalf of your descendants, your futurity.

So, even if that needle is miraculously found and somehow threaded, stitching together an extremely damaged and one-sided relationship between settlers and Indigenous Peoples into a relationship that is less damaged and reciprocal will require that Whites disavow their core settler identity. This transformation includes disavowing Settler Structures of Feelings (settler attitudes or emotional qualities that rationalize or justify your land theft);[53] Settler Expectations (legal, institutional, and cultural processes supporting your idea that you are entitled to Indigenous territory);[54] and Fantasies of Settler Entitlement (socially internalized privilege without any factual basis in reality).[55] Settlers in restorative justice must be committed to doing this work. Is restorative justice up to providing the muscle that supports a commitment to repairing The First Harm?

An Unencumbered Container Equal to Undoing The First Harm

In "Passing the Cup of Vulnerability," *CRJ* contributor Gilbert Salazar uses the image of a container to describe the intentional spaces we create to hold different kinds of dialogue for different purposes. What container can we create to hold dialogue for undoing The First Harm?

Some nations, like South Africa and Canada, have created Truth and Reconciliation Commissions (TRCs) that are more formal, drawing upon court and panel-inquiry models. Some TRCs focus on hearing the stories of those harmed and those who did harm, but repairing or undoing harm is not part of the process. Others TRCs, like the one in Canada, have involved reparations as well. In Canada's case, though, the reparations for boarding-school harms were state determined by a fixed algorithm and came with the condition that, upon paying victims, Canada viewed that chapter in its settler history closed. The takeaway from these examples was not about building relationships and community between settlers and Indigenous Peoples. The outcome was formal and procedural, absolving settlers, as in the White Canadians' case, of further responsibility for the harm.

What container can we create to hold dialogue for undoing The First Harm?

Restorative justice critiques formal institutional processes precisely for their failure to use the harm to build the very relationships and community that prove transformative and sustainable going forward. Even if formal processes start with good intentions, as is the case with these TRCs, formal processes do not build relationships, which, when one reads the RJ literature or hear RJ practitioners extoll RJ virtues, are the might and muscle of RJ. No relationships, no real RJ process, hence no authentic or transformative outcomes with which to build a new future.

Yet it is hard to escape formal processes, since Western-based societies impose them in every direction. For example, much like the public proceedings or hearings Kemmis witnessed, court hearings, public school hearings, and other institutionalized hearings prioritize individual rights above community and elicit the disconnect that Kemmis observed among community members when they participated in formal, structured procedures.

RJ practitioners find themselves negotiating formal systems regularly, if not mostly. They struggle to insert restorative processes into institutional spaces that operate at cross-purposes, since most institutions function in hierarchical, adversarial ways (the procedural republic). The chapters in this book testify to the magnitude of the struggle, since People of Color are keenly aware of how White-run settler institutions not only fail communities of color but also co-opt restorative processes to protect the status quo and keep system change at bay.

To unencumber structured procedures and explore space for deeper, more "second language" dialogue, restorative practices turn to—more like, resort to—Circles as an alternative to institutional processes. Can Circles provide a container strong enough to undo The First Harm? Perhaps—but if and only if they do not reinforce settler fantasies or cause them to invoke white fragility.[56] I suspect Kemmis would nod approvingly at White settler and Circle trainer Kay Pranis' description of Circles as an unencumbered space:

Can Circles provide a container strong enough to undo The First Harm? Perhaps—but if and only if they do not reinforce settler fantasies or cause them to invoke white fragility.

> Our ancestors gathered in a circle. Families gather around the kitchen table in a circle. Now we are learning to gather in a circle as community to solve problems, support one another, and connect to one another.
>
> A new way of bringing people together to understand one another, strengthen bonds, and solve community problems is blossoming in *modern Western communities*. . . .
>
> Peacemaking circles are providing a space in which people from widely divergent perspectives can come together to speak candidly about conflict, pain, and anger and leave those conversations feeling good about themselves and about others.[57]

Echoing Kemmis' concern about the absence of informal relations—"second languages of cooperation"—in formal spaces, settlers who are in restorative justice also emphasize relational space being a priori essential to reparative work. In settler restorative justice, for instance, a Circle is designed to facilitate this relational space—at least ideally or in theory.

> The rituals of circle affirm a social order based on inclusiveness, equality, and respect for all participants. In circle, everyone is an equal part

> of the whole; a circle has no head and no hierarchy, each person has his or her individual place, and no place is outside the circle. A circle has no table to hide behind or back of the room to retreat. Each person faces others as a human being, leaving titles that signify position outside, using first names only. Everyone is given an equal chance to participate and is encouraged to speak from his or her heart or experience. The rituals of the circles are a way of practicing new ways of relating to one another.[58]

This description of a Circle's structure by Carolyn Boyes-Watson, a White settler in restorative justice, provides another way for groups to relate to one another. To those new to Circles, it is novel and appealing. However, as we will see, these factors do not alone make Circles subversive to the settler status quo.

Circle trainers emphasize that any table in the middle must be removed precisely so that there is "no table to hide behind" or to separate participants. But what "world in between" fills that function of gathering groups together in a Circle? What invisible worlds come into the room with the participants? What "world in between" frames the Circle, gathers groups together, separates them as well, and shapes the experiences of those who sit in it?

To address the "vanishing table"—the question of what draws groups together as well as separates them—Circle practitioners use various devices. One device Circle keepers use to build common ground—a world in between—are intentional discussions about values and guidelines. Check-in rounds and learning about each other always precedes raising hard issues. Hence, settlers in restorative justice believe, or at least assume, that establishing Circle guidelines will transform a Circle into a "space safe to speak in their authentic voices."[59] Really? The "world in between" is not so handily stitched. Sitting in a restorative justice Circle amid settlers and their apologists is treacherous space, should you be Indigenous. I know personally from being in restorative justice that Circles neither alter settler colonialism's structured violence nor curb its systemic excesses, such as the logic of elimination. The reality, after all, is that, despite settler proclamations or protestations to the contrary, we live, work, and play in *your* colonizer society where Indigenous Peoples and so many other People of Color have never collectively experienced inclusiveness, equality (let alone equity), or respect from settlers.

... what I want from settlers—especially those who are in restorative, social, community, transformational, and other fields of justice—is for you to undo The First Harm.

Not surprisingly, what I want from settlers—especially those who are in restorative, social, community, transformational, and other fields of justice—is for you to undo The First Harm. The initial harm we continue to experience has everything to do with the outright theft of our land, and therefore its rightful return to its Indigenous owners can undo the ravages we endure from The First Harm. To help move forward with returning stolen Indigenous land, I have a simple yet elegant Indigenous proposal for settlers and others when you gather in Circles either within or without restorative justice's framework.

Earth as The Talking Piece

My proposal concerns the talking piece(s) used in restorative justice Circles or their derivatives. *Circle Forward*, a restorative justice field manual popular among settlers and others, has a "How Circles Work" section that explains a talking piece's importance:

> The talking piece is a powerful equalizer. It gives every participant an equal opportunity to speak and carries an implicit assumption that every participant has something important to offer the group. As it passes physically from hand to hand, the talking piece weaves a connecting thread among the members of the Circle. . . . *Whenever possible, the talking piece represents something important to the group. The more meaning the talking piece as (consistent with the values of Circle), the more powerful it is for engendering respect for the process and aligning speakers with the core self. The meaning or story of the talking piece is shared with the group when it is introduced.*[60]

This field manual does not specify a talking piece's shape, color, material, size, texture, or other tangible qualities that would identify it as extraordinary. Yet this statement indicates that its intangible qualities make it quite remarkable: it is an equalizer, it weaves a connecting thread, it represents something important, it helps align a person's core self from within, and so forth.

I propose to restorative justice a talking piece (herein The Talking Piece) designed to match a metaphysic that,[61] in any Circle or gathering concerned

---

The Talking Piece I have in mind would necessarily contain a handful of Earth from North America and, inscribed on its surface, would read: "The land on which you stand rightfully belongs to [insert name of Indigenous People(s)]."

---

with justice, mindfully centers The First Harm. For a talking piece to do such society-wide heavy lifting is not as unimaginable as others might (have us) think. The Talking Piece I have in mind would necessarily contain a handful of Earth from North America and, inscribed on its surface, would read: "The land on which you stand rightfully belongs to [insert name of Indigenous People(s)]."

An initial reaction to this proposal might be similar to how restorative justice literature perceives things Indigenous—the medicine wheel or the four directions—as lending gravitas to restorative justice. But what would The Talking Piece contribute to Circles, to restorative justice, or to settlers' and others' core self? Or to undoing The First Harm? The field manual's "Circle for Making a Talking Piece" section speaks to these questions:

> You know from our previous Circles that the talking piece is a very important part of how the Circle works. . . . A symbol is an object that can stand for more than one thing—it can have many meanings. . . . *Your talking piece can symbolize something about who you are as an individual. We can talk about who we are by telling the story of our talking piece, and what the parts mean.*[62]

Hence, The Talking Piece I want to see adopted throughout restorative justice or in every Circle would certainly address Indigenous Peoples' First Harm stories, much as I have done here or as Harold Fey hinted at over six decades ago from self-reflecting on White settler behavior. Land dispossession stories tell the many faces of The First Harm.

Land dispossession stories tell the many faces of The First Harm.

The subsequent reactions from settlers and their apologists to my proposal—outrage, anger, denial, dismissal—should emerge about now, which is not the least bit surprising to Indigenous Peoples and People of Color. For one, settlers become extremely reactionary whenever Indigenous Peoples broach the subject of returning stolen land—and more than land ownership is being triggered. Lorenzo Veracini, like Wolfe, Bonds, and Inwood, is one of a growing number of non-Indigenous people in the academy who critically examine settler colonialism. Veracini sheds light on settlers' intense reactions to land return, which is really quite disturbing. As he frames settler colonialism's theoretical evolution, Veracini shows why this visceral reaction has everything to do with Indigenous permanence and its challenge to your settler identity, not only your illegal occupation of our homelands but also who you are now and in future generations.

> The [Bowman] essay identified who was a "pioneer": "a young man bent upon winning from the wilderness with strong hands and the hope of youth a homestead for himself and *an inheritance for his children*." This definition encapsulated many of the long-lasting traits of settler colonial political traditions: a gendered order, a focus on *mononuclear familial relations and reproduction, and the production of assets transferable across generations.* Its author did not mention it, but it went without saying: this young man had a white wife, his children were white and, if he had non-white neighbors, it was understood that they would be gone by the time his children were to inherit.[63]

Of course, as far as settlers are concerned, inheritance (or in this case "pioneer birthright"), familial reproduction (increasing settler population and therefore land acquisition), and transferable assets (private or other tangible property) are all ephemeral so long as their non-White neighbors, i.e., Indigenous Peoples, exist. So far, this settler understanding—the logic of elimination, i.e., that I should not exist here today, let alone be writing this paper or editing this book—remains unrealized, thankfully, yet simultaneously our very presence activates a bone-deep angst within settlers. How could it not, right?

The Talking Piece can help work through this impasse. Though hand-size, then, The Talking Piece is quite extraordinary in its message.

And yet The Talking Piece can help work through this impasse. Though hand-size, then, The Talking Piece is quite extraordinary in its message. If we take at face value how settlers perceive a talking piece and Circles—a major assumption given settler history—this perception could prove helpful in making space both for you to gather yourselves together around addressing The First Harm and for us to voice our realities.

> The talking piece is an object that is passed from person to person around the Circle. As its name implies, the holder of the talking piece has the opportunity to talk while all other participants have the opportunity to listen without thinking about a response.... *The talking piece is a critical element of creating a space in which participants can speak from a deep place of truth.*[64]

Imagine Indigenous people sitting in a Circle with our perpetrators. While holding The Talking Piece, we speak to them about how we come to *experi-*

ence reality, compared to how they *construct* reality. Such a Circle becomes a deep place of truth. The First Nations Sculpture Garden (FNSG), a project that memorializes four Očhéthi Šakówiŋ Oyáte citizens, perhaps opened a window on the question of truth, which I acknowledged at the FNSG's dedication ceremony.

> Because the FNSG's story is an indigenous one, certain challenges arise. The challenges are not just project related, such as funding or getting Rapid City [SD] whites' buy-in. They are about how two different societies understand and interpret their place in the same space; one being endogenous, the other exogenous; one being about uniqueness, the other being about universalism; one being about authenticity, the other about appearances; and the comparisons go on. These differing narratives push us to confront the difference between *what has always been true and what others wish to be true*. This sculpture garden shows us that difference.[65]

The Earth contained in The Talking Piece with the inscription connects settlers to The First Harm as no other convention has done. Moreover, The Talking Piece, given its magnitude of importance in Circles, unsettles the space where settler colonialism intersects with restorative justice. It disrupts restorative justice's complicity in not undoing—hence perpetuating—The First Harm. I ask settlers—all settlers—who want more than to just live but to live justly or who struggle with living justly: Is not addressing harms resulting from wrongdoing and undoing them restorative justice's raison d'être? How do settlers tell their offspring that stealing is wrong, when the entire relationship between settlers and Indigenous Peoples is a story about theft and the failure to put it right?

How do settlers tell their offspring that stealing is wrong, when the entire relationship between settlers and Indigenous Peoples is a story about theft and the failure to put it right?

As I have found need to write before, stealing others' property is a crime, a criminal act, yet settlers embrace a fantasy of innocence around it.[66] Genocide, like stealing other's property, remains a crime, which the world community recognizes, yet North America's settler states refuse to hold themselves accountable for the crime and repair it. And, after more than five centuries, settler colonization constitutes a crime and is finally named as such, yet this awareness remains remote from mainstream White consciousness. Being Indigenous, I dare settlers to prove Harold Fey wrong. I now pass The Talking Piece.

DISCUSSION QUESTIONS

1. What role and responsibility do settlers in RJ have for perpetuating The First Harm and for undoing it? What obstacles (outer and inner) block settlers from owning their complicity in The First Harm and holding themselves as a people accountable—all the way to undoing it?
2. How does the logic of elimination operate as a structure today? That is, how is the logic of elimination institutionalized?
3. How does settler identity serve settler colonialism? Related to this, what might it mean to dismantle internalized settler structures? What does that look and feel like? How might it move settlers toward undoing The First Harm and working toward coexistence as peoples?

Note: The following questions are from Emma Battell Lowman and Adam Barker, Wolfe, Patrick, Global Social Theory, https://globalsocialtheory.org/thinkers/patrick-wolfe-2/.

4. How is "elimination" pursued through both state violence and also legal and political—as well as educational and economic—mechanisms? (Quotation marks added.)
5. What are the common stories and cultural narratives that justify settler colonial invasion and dispossession of indigenous peoples?
6. Wolfe has argued that settler colonial societies are exceptionally "resistant to regime change." Why is this?
7. Describe the differences between racialisation for elimination, as in settler colonization, and racialization for exploitation, as in imperial enslavement.
8. What is the end goal of settler colonialism? Has it ever been achieved?

ACTIVITIES

1. "Playing" with Cowboys and Indians. This activity involves obtaining a "Cowboy and Indian" figurines play set. This play set is commonly sold in toy stores or can be purchased online. It is important for Circle participants to have an equal chance of being selected as a volunteer for this activity. I recommend participants' names randomly number themselves off. This activity should prompt participants to understand the game's connection with settler colonialism's logic of elimination (structural genocide).
    a. In Circle, place the container with cowboy and Indian figurines in the center. Have a randomly selected volunteer spill them out in the center. This action will result in a random placement of the figurines.

   b. Have another randomly selected volunteer arrange them as children are taught to play cowboys and Indians.
   c. After the cowboys and Indians are so arranged, look at the arrangement, and pose the following questions:
      i. Why are the cowboys and Indians arranged as such?
      ii. What does the technology depicted imply about each group?
      iii. Examine the respective postures of each group: e.g., Which group minimizes its exposure to harm? What do their postures imply about each group?
      iv. Why are Indigenous children and women not included?
      v. Why is a set of "how to play" instructions not included?
      vi. Why is this game still being manufactured?
      vii. How do we respond to the charge, "It's only a game!"?
      viii. Why is there no "Slaves and Slave owners" figurine game set?
2. Talking Piece or Peace? Building on activity 1 and this chapter's content, this activity involves the construction of The Talking Piece for Circle use on a specific landbase. This activity should prompt Circle participants to act on an understanding that, without returning stolen Native land—The First Harm—restorative justice cannot be transformative.
   a. Prior to constructing The Talking Piece, research where the land's Indigenous owners are today. How does the loss of Native landownership continue to benefit settlers?
   b. However The Talking Piece is constructed, at a minimum it should be transparent, so the Earth contained within it is visible, its dimensions fit comfortably in the hand, and the inscription—"The land on which you stand rightfully belongs to [insert name of Indigenous People(s)]"—should be visible.
   c. As a settler or recent immigrant, determine what concrete actions you can take to undo The First Harm.

RESOURCES

DiAngelo, Robin. *White Fragility: Why It's So Hard for White Peoples to Talk about Racism*. Boston: Beacon Press, 2018.

Lowman, Emma Battel, and Adam J. Barker. *Settler: Identity and Colonialism in 21st Century Canada*. Halifax and Winnipeg: Fernwood Publishing, 2015.

Mackey, Eva. *Unsettled Expectations: Uncertainty, Land and Settler Decolonization*. Halifax and Winnipeg: Fernwood Publishing, 2016.

Picoult, Jodie. *Small Great Things*. New York: Ballantine Books, 2018.

Regan, Paulette. *Unsettling the Settler Within: Indian Residential Schools, Truth Telling, and Reconciliation in Canada.* Vancouver: UBC Press, 2010.
Veracini, Lorenzo. "'Settler Colonialism': Career of a Concept." *Journal of Imperial and Commonwealth History* 41, no. 2 (2013): 313–33.
Wolfe, Patrick. "Land, Labor, and Difference: Elementary Structures of Race." *American Historical Review*, June 2001: 866–905.
Wolfe, Patrick. "Settler Colonialism and the Elimination of the Native." *Journal of Genocide Research* 8 no. 4 (December 2006): 387–409.

NOTES

1. See *Coloring Restorative Justice*'s "Call for Contributors: Living Justice Press (LJP) invites abstract submissions" in the appendix.
2. Anne Bonds and Joshua Inwood, "Beyond White Privilege: Geographies of White Supremacy and Settler Colonialism," *Progress in Human Geography*, 40, no. 6 (2016): 716. Emphasis added. In-text citations omitted.
3. Trevor Noah, "Emantic Bradford Jr.'s Death & Why the Second Amendment Doesn't Apply to Black Men," *The Daily Show*, November 28, 2018, https://www.youtube.com/watch?v= wWwQjH7T1bE.
4. Fort Snelling is the military reservation in question. From November 1862 to May 1863, White settlers interned at least 1,700 Dakȟóta, mostly elders, children, and women, for no reason other than that they were defending themselves against settler-sanctioned genocide. At this fort, White settlers' descendants continue with celebratory reenactments of their settlement from the time period.
5. See Waziyatawin Angela Wilson's *In the Footsteps of Our Ancestors* (St. Paul, MN: Living Justice Press, 2006) and *What Does Justice Look Like? The Struggle for Liberation in Dakota Homeland* (St. Paul, MN: Living Justice Press, 2008). See also Edward C Valandra's, "'Forgive Everyone Everything'—For What? 1862 Dakota–US War Sesquicentennial, A Case Study," Community for the Advancement of Native Studies, 2015 (unpublished), Academia.edu.
6. Jack Utter, *American Indians: Answers to Today's Questions,* 2nd ed. (Norman: University of Oklahoma Press, 2001), 10. Emphasis mine.
7. *Johnson v. McIntosh* 21 US (8 Wheat.) 543, 5 L.Ed. 681 (1823).
8. See Steven T. Newcomb's *Pagans in the Promised Land: Decoding the Doctrine of Christian Discovery* (Golden CO: Fulcrum, 2008). Newcomb questions whether the dispute was genuine or instead fabricated in order to assert the Discovery Doctrine.
9. *Johnson v. McIntosh.* Emphasis mine.
10. Utter, *American Indians*, 12.
11. Newcomb, *Pagans*, 52–53.
12. Several North and South Dakota settlers introduced legislative bills targeting Indigenous decolonizing actions. On January 9, 2017, seven North Dakota settlers introduced a legislative bill (House Bill 1203) that would provide protection from liability for a driver who "unintentionally" hits a person protesting on a public highway. A close vote in committee (41 YES, 50 NO, 3 Not Voting) stopped HB

1203. Dennis Daugaard, a White settler and South Dakota governor, introduced legislation and, on March 13, 2017, signed Senate Bill 176 into law. This settler law establishes "public safety zones" limited to twenty people. The settler law anticipates Indigenous decolonizing actions to stop the Keystone XL Pipeline's development.

13. On January 24, 2017, President Trump issued a series of memoranda and executive orders to push pipeline construction forward, including a Construction of the Dakota Access Pipeline Memorandum; a Construction of the Keystone XL Pipeline; an Executive Order Expediting Environmental Reviews and Approvals for High Priority Infrastructure Projects; and a Construction of American Pipelines Memorandum.
14. See Eva Mackey, *Unsettled Expectations: Uncertainty, Land, and Settler Decolonization* (Halifax and Winnipeg: Fernwood Publishing, 2016), 76–77.
15. Ken Alvine, n.d.
16. Ibid., 5.
17. Mackey, *Unsettled Expectations*, 83–84. The CKCN is a settler organization whose purpose was to derail an Indigenous land claim.
18. Ibid., 84. Emphasis mine.
19. South Dakota Career and Technical Education Summer Conference. July 31–August 1, 2017, Brookings, SD, 9.
20. Emma Battell Lowman and Adam J. Barker in *Settler: Identity and Colonialism in 21st Century Canada* (Halifax and Winnipeg: Fernwood Publishing, 2015) outline settler colonialism's three pillars. The other two pillars are settler colonialism's invasion is a structure not an event; and settlers came/come to stay (permanence), 25–26.
21. Ibid., 26. Footnote references omitted. *See* also Edward C Valandra's "South Dakota Board on Geographical Names (SDBGN): Testimony Regarding The 'Renaming' of Harney Peak." Community for the Advancement of Native Studies, submitted to South Dakota Board on Geographical Names, April 2015.
22. "Governor Daugaard Signs Senate Bill 176 'Public Safety Bill' to Suppress Protest" March 14, 2017, https:// www.thesiouxempire.com/gov-daugaard-senate-bill-176/.
23. "South Dakota Legislature—Senate Bill 176—2017," the Free Speech Project, Georgetown University, http://freespeechproject.georgetown. domains/state-and-local-government/south-dakota-legislature-senate-bill-176-2017/.
24. Patrick Wolfe, "Settler Colonialism and the Elimination of the Native," *Journal of Genocide Research* 8, no. 4 (2006): 388. Emphasis mine.
25. Ibid.
26. Bonds and Inwood, "Beyond White Privilege," 721. In-text citations omitted.
27. The UN General Assembly September 2007 vote was 144 Yes, 4 No, 11 Abstentions.
28. This decision upheld a White settler's claim, McIntosh, against another White settler, Johnson. In that decision, the settlers' government (US) did (and still does) not recognize any property title as valid if it was purchased directly from a Native nation, which Johnson did. Using this decision, the settler court (US Supreme Court) articulated the Discovery Doctrine, which fictionally—i.e., arbitrarily and unilaterally—determined that settlers, and not Native Peoples, are the "true" landowners of North America. They alone possess absolute title over the North

American continent, including the sole right to decide what happens to the land. This settler-court decision did assert that Native Peoples possess a diminutive land right of use and occupancy only, *which is a subordinate right to the settlers' fictional ownership.*

29. The settler court determined that it had no power to hear the case. The Cherokee were neither a foreign nation nor a state of the United States. They constituted a "domestic dependent nation." This settler-court interpretation excluded the use of US courts to resolve disputes involving Native nations as independent sovereigns. Today this subordinate condition is called "Tribal Sovereignty."
30. This settler decision held that Georgia law does not apply within the Cherokee Nation's exterior boundaries. This case involved a White male missionary's refusal to obey Georgia's law that required him to have a license to legally reside within the Cherokee Nation.
31. 1830 *Indian Removal Act*, 21st Congress, Session I, Chapter 148: An act to provide for an exchange of lands with the Indians residing in any of the states or territories, and for their removal west of the Mississippi River.
32. Andrew Jackson's speech to Congress on Indian removal, https://www.nps.gov/museum/tmc/MANZ/handouts/Andrew_Jackson_Annual_Message.pdf, accessed July 4, 2018. See also President Jackson's message to Congress "On Indian Removal," December 6, 1830; Records of the United States Senate, 1789–1990; Record Group 46; National Archives and Records Administration.
33. Mackey, *Unsettled Expectations*, 84.
34. Helen Hunt Jackson, *A Century of Dishonor: The Classic Exposé of the Plight of the Native Americans* (Mineola, NY: Dover Publications, 2003), 275.
35. Faced with physical removal, a significant number of Choctaw citizens, another "Civilized Tribe," opted to invoke a clause in their removal treaty, much to settler dismay, if not chagrin. This clause allowed a Choctaw citizen to remain rather than to relocate; however, Wolfe points out that the trade-off requires invoking the logic of elimination.
36. Prior to possessing property, however, Locke argues that there exists a natural right to acquire land.
37. https://www.libertarianism.org/columns/john-locke-justification-private-property.
38. Wolfe, "Settler Colonialism," 388. Emphasis mine. Footnote reference omitted.
39. Ibid., 396. Emphasis and underline mine.
40. Wolfe, "Settler colonialism," 388.
41. See "President Barack Obama on #NoDAPL and Dakota Access Pipeline," https://www. youtube.com/watch?v=gIMlc-iaxsk.
42. For example, states' stricter voter identification laws negatively impact non-White voter turnout more than they do White voters. See North Dakota voter ID law, H.B. 1369. It requires a North Dakota or other valid ID card to have physical street address. In North Dakota, many Indigenous Peoples who reside in Native Country often use a P.O. box for their mailing address.
43. The Thirteenth Amendment's language carves out an exception for slavery. A person who is duly convicted of crime (i.e., a felon) can, as punishment, be enslaved. Indeed, US twenty-first century incarceration rates exceed that of other countries,

and non-Whites are disproportionately or overly represented in prisons, jails, and other forms of detention. A felony limits other rights or privileges, such as voting as well as housing, employment, and educational opportunities. In 1871, our colonizers passed a law (16 Statute 566) that unilaterally declared they would not acknowledge or recognize Indigenous Peoples as sovereign, independent nations, hence "the United States will no longer contract by treaty" with them.

44. Vine Deloria Jr., *Custer Died for Your Sins* (Norman: University of Oklahoma, [1970] 1988), 172.
45. Ibid., 172. Emphasis mine.
46. Daniel Kemmis, *Community and the Politics of Place* (Norman: University of Oklahoma Press, 1990), 66–67. Kemmis notes that public hearings "would be part of an honest conversation which the public holds [with] itself. But that almost never happens" (p. 53).
47. Ibid., 5–6. Emphasis mine.
48. Ibid., 6. See also Deloria's *Custer Died for Your Sins* and *We Talk You Listen: New Tribes, New Turf* (New York: Dell Publishing Company, 1970). These are only two of hundreds of books that reveal that the magic trick alluded to is the Western worldview and its derivatives, such as white supremacy.
49. Ibid., 79.
50. Johannes Wheeldon, "Finding Common Ground: Restorative Justice and Its Theoretical Constructions," *Contemporary Justice Review* 12, no. 1 (March 2009): 93.
51. See Article VI, second clause: "This Constitution . . . and all Treaties made, or which shall be made, under the Authority of the United States, shall be the supreme Law of the Land."
52. Harold E. Fey, "Our National Indian Policy," *The Christian Century* 72, no. 13 (March 30, 1955): 395. Emphasis mine.
53. See Mackey *Unsettled Expectations*, 7–8.
54. Ibid., 8–9.
55. Ibid., 9–12.
56. In Robin DiAngelo's *White Fragility: Why It's So Hard for White People to Talk about Racism* (Boston: Beacon Press, 2018), Michael Eric Dyson describes white fragility in his foreword: "It is an idea that registers the hurting feelings, shattered egos, fraught spirits, vexed bodies, and taxed emotions of white folk. In truth, their suffering comes from recognizing that they are white—that their whiteness has given them a big leg up in life while crushing others' dreams, that their whiteness is the clearest example of the identity politics they claim is harmful to the nation, and that their whiteness has shielded them growing up quickly as they might have done had they not so heavily leaned on it to make it through life" (xi–xii). On the notion of Circles as containers, see also Kay Pranis, *The Little Book of Circle Processes: A New/Old Approach to Peacemaking, The Little Books of Justice and Peacebuilding* (Intercourse, PA: Good Books, 2005), 9.
57. Kay Pranis, *The Little Book of Circle Process: A New/Old Approach to Peacemaking* (Intercourse, PA: Good Books, 2005), 3, 6. Emphasis mine.
58. Carolyn Boyes-Watson, "Seeds of Change: Using Peacemaking Circles to Build a Village for Every Child," *Child Welfare* 84, no. 2 (March/April): 196.

59. Pranis, *Little Book of Circle Processes,* 34.

60. Carolyn Boyes-Watson and Kay Pranis, *Circle Forward: Building a Restorative School Community* (St. Paul: Living Justice Press; Boston: Institute for Restorative Initiatives, 2015), 30–31. Emphasis mine.

61. Ibid. Indeed, the two authors devote three sections to a talking piece: "Introducing the Talking Piece," "Circle for Making a Talking Piece," and "Practicing the Use of the Talking Piece Circle." Emphasis mine.

62. Ibid., 52.

63. Lorenzo Veracini, "'Settler Colonialism': Career of a Concept," *Journal of Imperial and Commonwealth History* 41, no. 2 (2013): 315. The essay Veracini references is Isaiah Bowman's "The Pioneer Fringe," *Foreign Affairs: An American Quarterly Review* 6, nos. 1–4 (1927–28): 49–66. Emphasis mine.

64. Pranis, *Little Book of Circle Processes,* 35.

65. Edward Valandra, "Why a First Nation Sculpture Garden?" November 16, 2017, delivered at Rapid City, SD.

66. Edward Valandra, "Stolen Native Land," 2014, http://themedes.org/articles/stolen-native-land/; or see Academia.edu.

Acknowledgments

From this book's inception to its final form, my experience can best be described as a Circle journey in community—fitting for a restorative justice subject. Such a book needs a community to make it a reality, a community that listens to all voices. Of course, forming meaningful relationships is basic to restorative justice and its practices, and that is what has happened while working on this book.

I am grateful to the board of directors and staff at Living Justice Press (LJP) who stepped forward to support this project financially and professionally. But more importantly, the LJP family is acutely aware that, as the book title implies, People of Color and Indigenous Peoples are transforming restorative justice in ways unanticipated thirty years ago.

For all those courageous people who answered the call when it came out, I am deeply moved. The number of abstracts submitted and the content of each showed the restorative justice world that communities of color and Indigenous communities have much to contribute to restorative justice. I am grateful to Denise Breton, LJP's executive director; Stephanie Autumn, Indigenous restorative practices trainer; Alexis Goffe, associate editor; and Rita Renjitham Alfred, who is also an RJ trainer, for the various roles they assumed in making this book. We read through the abstracts and deliberated over each one. Knowing that every abstract submitted deserved publication made our collective decisions difficult ones. While each contributor to this book is a restorative justice and restorative practices practitioner, what stands out is what these individuals bring to restorative justice: racial justice, social justice, and decolonization. Their words and thoughts make it clear that they—and thousands like them—are the frontline practitioners colorizing restorative justice.

My dear friend and colleague Alexis Goffe made the making of this book a complete joy. He managed to bring the contributors together periodically to share our trials and tribulations about the writing process, as well as our struggles with work, family, and being a community member. We would be less of a community without Alexis's belief in us and the book. I look forward to how he will continue to expand the circle of those engaged in colorizing restorative justice.

I am also indebted to Denise Breton, Dave Spohn, Loretta Draths, Cathy Broberg and Wendy Holdman. Denise's experience as a writer and publisher proved invaluable to this book. She brought another critical lens to the content, which sharpened the book's edge about restorative justice's role in marginalizing People of Color and Indigenous Peoples. Dave, the designer of the book's cover, and Loretta, who designed other promotional material related to the book, took up the challenge of creating graphic art befitting the ideas and essential understandings between the book's covers. Though finding just the right image was a challenge that spanned a year's search and experimentation, they created a beautiful and meaningful cover. A master of copyediting, Cathy Broberg helped us shape the articles into a fluid whole. And Wendy Holdman not only made the text beautiful and a pleasure to read but also contributed her time and expertise as her gift to the project.

The index was a team effort by Deb Feeny, Denise Breton, Kully Vance, and myself. It is extensive, because the more we worked on it, the more we came to see it as a context-sensitive analysis of the issues that these twenty authors of color explore. We hope you find it of use.

I also want to thank Justice Robert Yazzie, Diné citizen, for writing the book's foreword. His work in restorative justice is well-known and foundational, and, as the National Association for Community and Restorative Justice's 2019 conference attests, he is well-received among restorative justice and restorative practices practitioners. It is fitting that a person of his standing contributed his Indigenous voice to a book whose contributors appreciate restorative justice's Indigenous influences.

Living Justice Press and I are deeply grateful for the grant that the Life Comes From It Advisory Council awarded LJP to support the contributors in generating community dialogue around *Colorizing Restorative Justice.* The LJP family is especially grateful to Christianne Paras and Belinda Dulin for writing the grant and to Alexis Goffe for his role in coordinating it on behalf of LJP.

Finally, I want to thank you, the reader, for your time and openness in considering these ideas. If you are a Person of Color or Indigenous person, I hope you will experience a deep resonance, even a sense of coming home, while reading these pages. If you are White, I hope that reading these chapters will unsettle both your understanding of and your practice within restorative justice and restorative practices. Whatever your positionality, I hope this book helps us make a stronger restorative justice movement—one that is more self-aware, more honest, more just, and hence more capable of being truly transformative in a society desperately needing systemic reconstruction.

Appendix

***Colorizing Restorative Justice*: Call for Contributors (2017)**
Living Justice Press (LJP) invites abstract submissions

Communities of color have historical and contemporary experiences that differ from White communities, as recent actions led by Indigenous Peoples and Peoples of Color (POC) show. Examples include the No to the Dakota Access Pipeline action (or #NODAPL) in Indigenous homelands, the Black Lives Matter (BLM) movement, and the anti-xenophobia actions that challenge Build-the-Wall and Islamophobia. Both systemic racism and colonization account for these disparities in experiences. The most disconcerting disparity is the sanctioned, structural violence ubiquitous throughout communities of color—the school-to-prison pipeline being a prime example.

Restorative justice (RJ) and restorative practices (RP) have emerged over the past generation to address the harms that result from systemic disparities and violence. In addressing root cause(s), RJ/RP hold relationships to be core. However, an ongoing concern among communities of color is how restorative justice is being structurally or institutionally co-opted. Racially and colonially based, co-opting patterns prevent restorative justice/restorative practices from being truly transformational. Restorative justice literature is only beginning to address these racial and colonizing dynamics.

Colorizing Restorative Justice is a book project that privileges restorative justice practitioners, trainers, or generalists of color to write about what they believe will make restorative justice and restorative practices relevant and effective in their communities. We envision this book as one that practitioners can use in trainings, their work, and their communities. So we are looking not only for insights and experiences but also for ways to apply and work with them, such as discussion questions, sample Circles, activities, models or approaches. Acceptable manuscript formats for the book include articles, essays, or transcribed and edited interviews or dialogues. The word length is 3,000–8,000.

Abstract submission guidelines:

1. Between 300–500 words
2. A PDF labeled: CRJ_Last Name_First Name

3. Deadline date for abstract submission: 31 October 2017
4. A short biography including contact information
5. Send to LJPress@aol.com

Themes: The following questions are offered only as samples to get the dialogue going:

- In the restorative justice/restorative practices spectrum, where are you as a practitioner, i.e., are you at the center or the margin?
- As a person involved in the restorative work, what does RJ/RP look like on the ground, institutionally, or in your experience?
- What does "colorizing RJ/RP" mean to you, and what challenges do you see in colorizing the RJ movement?
- How do race and economics play out in RJ/RP? What do equity and inequity look like in your RJ/RP experience?
- What do people need to know about RJ/RP with respect to race? For example, how does race or colonization impact RJ and vice versa? What harm comes from not addressing race in RJ/RP?
- What is the structural nature of the RJ/RP movement with respect to race?
- What are the dangers of RJ/RP being co-opted along racial and institutional lines?
- What disparities have you observed between what is professed and what is experienced in RJ/RP?
- What structural dimensions within the movement prevent communities of color from achieving justice through RJ/RP work? For example, are qualifications or credentials necessary to do work in RJ/RP?
- What processes marginalize People of Color's voice within the RJ movement?
- What are the consequences for challenging either Whites or White institutions in RJ/RP?
- What experiences have communities of color had with Whites when engaged in RJ practices?
- Have you been concerned about losing RJ/RP work if you spoke about racial inequities in the practice? What experiences have you had?
- How much of your RJ/RP work involves negotiating "White fragility?"
- How can RJ/RP become more meaningful in communities of color?
- What cultural competencies are important in developing RJ/RP protocols?

- What skills sets do RJ/RP practitioners and others who work in RJ/RP need to have with respect to race?
- What do curricula developers and program designers need to know about race and colonization?
- How are RJ/RP leaders accountable to local communities of color?
- In communities of color, what makes for an effective RJ/RP process?
- Where do you see the RJ/RP movement in the middle of this century and beyond?
- What are your expectations of RJ/RP? What do you want to see in RJ/RP?
- How do we bring racial equity and decolonization into RJ/RP?
- What is at stake with colorizing RJ/RP? What are the consequences as long as RJ/RP is not colorized? Who pays? And what are positive potentials and outcomes of colorizing RJ/RP?
- Do issues of race in RJ affect only people and communities of color, or do they affect everyone in the movement and beyond? Who stands to gain by addressing issues of race in RJ/RP and how?

Please share this call with your friends, colleagues, organizations, and communities of color involved in the work. This is an open invitation.

Thank you for considering being part of it.

About the Authors

Desirée Anderson

Dr. Desirée Anderson (she/her/hers) was born in San Diego, California. She earned her B.A. and Master's from the University of Louisville and her Ph.D. from the University of New Orleans studying the use of campus-based restorative justice approaches as a response to racially motivated bias incidents. Before becoming the Associate Dean of Diversity and Student Affairs at the University of New Orleans, she held positions at Saint Mary's College of California, Tulane University, and Texas State University. Desirée occasionally serves as an adjunct instructor and an RJ Trainer and Facilitator. In her free time, she watches an unnecessary amount of TV, especially kdramas.

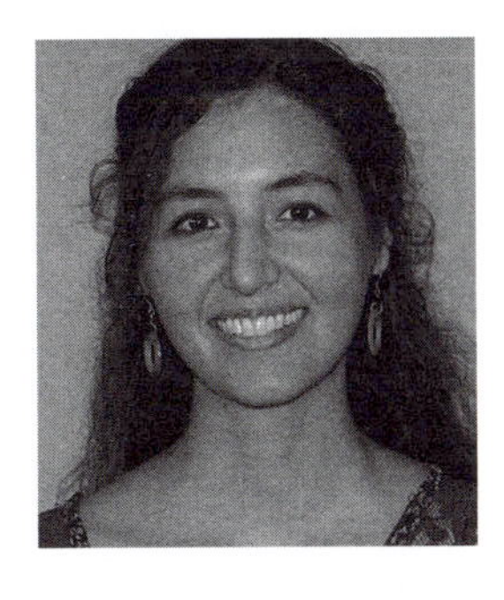

Rochelle Arms Almengor

Rochelle Arms Almengor is a professor, mediator and restorative justice practitioner. She is currently Assistant Professor in the Peace and Social Justice Studies Department of Berea College. Before joining Berea, she was Assistant Professor in the Dispute Resolution Program of John Jay College of Criminal Justice (CUNY). She received her Ph.D. in 2018 from the School for Conflict Analysis and Resolution at George Mason University (now the Carter School). Her research focuses on critical reflective practice, restorative justice, participatory action research and epistemologies of conflict practitioners. Before entering academia, she managed mediation and restorative justice initiatives in Brooklyn and Manhattan as Restorative Justice Coordinator of New York Peace Institute. Since 2000, she has worked in the U.S. and abroad in collaborative processes and restorative justice projects with a variety of groups, including civil society organizations in India, indigenous peoples in Argentina, immigrants and refugees, and homicide offenders and victim survivors in Kentucky. Dr. Arms

Almengor has a B.A. in Religion and Peace Studies from Swarthmore College, and an M.A. in International Relations through a Rotary Peace Fellowship at Universidad del Salvador in Argentina. She lives with her multigenerational family in Kentucky. Email: armsalmengorr@berea.edu

Michelle Armster

Michelle Armster is African American. She is also the executive director for the Mennonite Central Committee (MCC) Central States in North Newton, KS. She worked for MCC in the US Peace and Justice program in urban peacemaking as the director of Conciliation Services and co-director for the Office on Justice and Peacebuilding. She attended Lancaster Theological Seminary, where she received a master of divinity. Michelle is a trainer, teacher, and practitioner in the areas of conflict transformation, mediation, anti-racism/anti-oppression, offender-victim mediation (OVM), restorative justice/practices, and crimes of severe violence.

Belinda Dulin

Belinda Dulin is the executive director of the Dispute Resolution Center in Ann Arbor, Michigan. She has been involved with mediation and restorative practice programs for fifteen years. She has trained students and adults to be mediators and restorative practice facilitators in schools and in the community. She has a BS in business administration and an MA in dispute resolution, both from Wayne State University.

Leon Dundas

Leon is passionate about social justice issues and has wide-ranging (including senior-level) experience in the public sector, community-conflict resolution, prison systems, and health care organizations. His career spans both international and multicultural contexts in Guyana, Trinidad, and Tobago, Jamaica, the US, and now in the UK.

Sharon Goens-Bradley

Sharon is a queer black woman from rural Michigan and is a spouse, daughter, mother, friend and racial justice advocate. She is also a huge believer in the power of transformation through healing and restoration. Sharon values restorative justice because it offers a compassionate approach to harm that humanizes those who cause harm while also holding them accountable.

Sharon is the Regional Director for the American Friends Service Committee's Midwest region. She is passionate about undoing racism through education, the utilization of decolonization practices, and the facilitation of healing from historical trauma. Sharon is a Circle Keeper, has facilitated and participated in restorative justice conferencing, and has been trained as a mediator. She holds a BA in Russian language and literature, and an MA in Counseling Psychology. Sharon loves to travel, walk, read and cook and lives with her wife and kid in Minneapolis.

Janice Jerome

As a young girl, Janice grew up in the Pitsburgh neighborhood in Atlanta. After several years living in Pitsburgh, her parents bought a home and moved the family to East Atlanta. She is the former Assistant Director for the University of Texas at Austin, Steve Hicks School of Social Work, the Institute of Restorative Justice and Restorative Dialogue (IRJRD). She is a doctoral student at Saybrook University for her Ph.D. in Transformative and Social Change. She received her master's degree in public administration and her bachelor's degree in computer science from Troy University, Troy, Alabama.

Janice has worked for the United States Department of Justice (USDOJ), Executive Office for Immigration Review (EOIR), Immigration Court in Miami, Florida, and Atlanta, Georgia. She is the former Supervisor of Diversion / Intake for the Juvenile Court of Clayton County, Georgia. Janice is co-author of a family genealogy book titled *Blessed from the Beginning* and authored *A Dust of Flour and Without the White Man, The 1914 Ledger of Alonzo Talmadge*. Ms. Jerome envisioned and hosted a forum that discussed the idea of genealogy as a form of reparation, which contributed to the website *RestorativeTree.com*. Janice is the recipient of many awards, including the 2015 Community and Leadership Restorative Justice Award from the National Association of

Community and Restorative Justice (NACRJ), the Romae Powell Award, and the Director's Award from the Juvenile Courts Association of Georgia. Ms. Jerome is a Certified Anger Management Specialist by the National Anger Management Association (NAMA), and she is a member of the Association for Professional Genealogists (APG). Ms. Jerome is the Founder and Director of the Restorative Justice Institute of Atlanta, LLC (RJIA); the website is *JusticeMovingToday.com*. She received her first training in restorative justice from Kay Pranis and Gwen Rivers Jones in 2004. She is a professional genealogist, mediator, anger management specialist, numismatics, restorative practitioner, and paralegal.

Gaye Lang

After serving as the senior advisor to the Texas commissioner of education, Dr. Gaye Lang was appointed to her current position as the director for restorative practices for the Texas Education Agency. Before that, she was the acting secretary regional representative and the deputy secretary regional representative for the US Department of Education, Region VI, where she managed the rollout of the No Child Left Behind Act for five southern states. Dr. Lang has also served as project manager for the Houston Independent School District Virtual School, where she developed courseware for middle school students (grades 6–8) in four subject areas—the first of its kind created by a public school.

Her career in education—a classroom teacher in elementary and middle schools, a secondary assistant principal and elementary principal, a regional service center field service specialist, and a university adjunct professor—has earned her the respect of her colleagues. She holds a BA in elementary education from Dillard University, an MA in teaching and administration from Pepperdine University, and a doctorate of education in Cultural Studies from the University of Houston. In addition, she has certifications in science and superintendency from Texas A & M University and has taken a graduate course on restorative justice at the University of Texas. She has served as adjunct professor for Texas Southern University and the University of Texas at Austin.

Dr. Lang has presented numerous workshops and trainings on restorative discipline practices across Texas. Her dynamic trainings equip thousands of educators to transform their schools and classrooms into restorative places of learning and community. These presentations were a result of her leadership as the point person for the Restorative Discipline Program for the State of Texas.

Dr. Lang is the author of several books on education, including *Restorative Discipline Practices* (2017), *This Is How We Do It! The School Turnaround Challenge* (2009), and *Administering a Virtual School* (2004). In 2021, Dr. Lang published *Seven: A Sorority Story,* a book of historical fiction about seven African American women who stood up against racism and violence during the 1920s. She has also written numerous articles for collected volumes and journals.

Erica Littlewolf

Erica Littlewolf is from the Northern Cheyenne and works for the Mennonite Central Committee Central States with the Indigenous Visioning Circle. She is committed to the work of decolonization, authentic relationship, and healing. With her BS in psychology and American Indian Studies, she applies her education to social justice issues and how they impact Indigenous people.

Shameeka Mattis

Shameeka is a holistic practitioner focused on equity, justice and healing. Since 2003 she has served in social welfare and criminal justice reform, particularly through organizational development and implementation, clinical engagement, building partnerships, designing and facilitating strategic planning initiatives, and writing and teaching curricula. Shameeka is a founding member of Common Justice, an innovative national restorative justice and anti-violence model. Before leaving the program in 2017, she helped Common Justice earn the Professional Innovation in Victim Services Award from the Department of Justice's Office of Victims of Crime (OVS) and led its replication in the Bronx Supreme Court after solidifying its success in Brooklyn, NY. Early in her career, Shameeka served communities in Philadelphia's prisons in addition to reentry and child welfare initiatives. When she is not championing for social justice, Shameeka is a writer, motivational speaker, and skillful trainer and facilitator.

Shameeka received her Bachelor's (BA) in English and Sociology from SUNY Binghamton and Master of Social Work (MSW) from the University of Pennsylvania. She is a licensed clinical social worker and has received several honors, including the K2 REACH Second Chance Award and NASW-NYC Emerging Leader Award. Shameeka is currently an educator, consultant, and psychotherapist serving predominantly queer and trans people of color.

Abdul-Malik Muhammad

Dr. Abdul-Malik Muhammad has been a grassroots organizer and activist for marginalized communities for nearly twenty-five years. As a student organizer in high school and college, he led protests, helped found and build student organizations, and was committed to fulfilling his role as a youth organizer. As an educator, Dr. Muhammad has more than twenty years of experience serving both youth and adults as a teacher, principal, campus president, executive and state director, and vice president of organizations. Always working with the underserved in urban and rural areas, he has focused on the development of Black boys to men, establishing a progressive pedagogy for oppressed youth and building progressive organizations. He is currently the vice president of several educational, mental health, and human services operations in seven states across the US. Additionally, he has founded two organizations, Akoben LLC and Transforming Lives Inc., as vehicles to "transform lives, one community at a time." He is also actively involved in several national and international organizations, championing an emphasis on leadership, relationships, and social justice.

Dr. Muhammad holds a BA in international affairs from Franklin & Marshall College, an MA in educational leadership from the College of Notre Dame of Maryland, and an EdD in educational leadership from the University of Delaware.

Christianne Paras

Christianne Paras is Iluko from her mother's side and Kapampangan from her father's side. She is originally from the Ilocos region of the Philippines (by its colonized name), now residing in British Columbia (BC), Canada. She is a co-founder of ROOTS—Reclaiming Our Truths & Stories, an organization that provides training, consultation, and dialogue events on decolonization, anti-oppression/anti-racism, and relational and healing practices. With over 20 years' experience in the restorative justice field, she is an accomplished facilitator with expertise in a variety of practice models including victim offender dialogue, family group conferencing, and peacemaking circles. She is also a long-time anti-oppression and anti-racism facilitator providing training in schools and organizations.

Christianne holds a Bachelor of Arts Degree (with Recognition) in Criminology from Simon Fraser University, and a Diploma in Criminology from Douglas College. She is a published researcher and author, and has been involved in a wide variety of research projects on topics such as safety in seniors' living spaces, online gambling, race and the criminal justice system, and restorative justice. She is known as a passionate, reflective, and ethically grounded practitioner who brings authentic presence and insight into her practice and training.

Christina Parker

Christina Parker is an Associate Professor in Social Development Studies at Renison University College at the University of Waterloo. She holds a Ph.D. and Master's from the Ontario Institute for Studies in Education at the University of Toronto and is an Ontario Certified Teacher. Christina's research on peacebuilding and restorative justice education with historically marginalized children and youth show how dialogic pedagogies facilitate inclusive spaces where all students can participate and have their voices heard.

Gilbert Salazar

Gilbert Salazar's work lies in the intersection of community, culture building and leadership, storytelling and story development, and ritual and theater for healing and liberation. Gilbert has worked with young people in school re-entry and violence prevention work, and has worked in Restorative Justice training and coaching school leadership teams for community and culture development and implementation of Restorative Practices. Gilbert was among an initial cohort of Restorative Justice Coordinators within LAUSD schools and was trained and coached by the California Conference for Equality and Justice. His work includes integrating applied theater modalities and techniques into training curriculums and bridging play into the work of Community Building Circles, Restorative Dialogue and trauma informed care. He produced a podcast about Restorative Justice practitioners and the topics of culture, community, and justice, called "Whatchu Know about RJ: Sharing Stories and Skills of Restorative Justice."

Gilbert is also a playwright and is producing his first short film, *Sippin'*, based on the excerpts of the play in his chapter for *Colorizing Restorative*

Justice. His former studies include interdisciplinary studies with focuses on social justice education and ritual at California State University, Monterey Bay and USC's Applied Theater Arts program. He is currently enrolled in a doctoral program in Depth Psychology.

Victor Jose Santana

Victor Jose Santana is an international restorative justice practitioner, facilitator, trainer, mentor, and leader. Victor Jose has worked with local, national, and international organizations that serve young people and families exposed to violence and poverty. Over the past 20 years, the core of his work centers on youth development, racial equity, trauma neurology, and the peacemaking Circle process.

Victor Jose has a BA in science communication and a music minor degree from Salem State University. He currently holds a Master of Arts from Lesley University specializing in restorative justice through youth leadership development and trauma neurology. Victor Jose has been trained in the peacemaking Circle process by Mark Wedge, Elder/leader from the Tagish Tlingit Nation; Judge Barry Stuart, first chief judge of the Yukon Territory, now retired; and Kay Pranis, former restorative justice planner for the Minnesota Department of Corrections (author of the article "Empathy Development in Youth through Restorative Practices").

Victor Jose collaboratively developed, wrote, designed, and implemented training institutes for the City of Boston for anyone working with children exposed to violence. Through his leadership and community partnership, he and his team were able to train approximately thousands of people using the peacemaking Circle process.

Additionally, Victor Jose has launched restorative justice and racial equity training institutes across the country which currently includes the Boston Public School system and the Massachusetts Transgender Political Coalition where his work integrates healing education and policy change. He also works with an international Indigenous women's network that brings people together through cultural revitalization and social justice movements globally. Victor Jose is currently working on several projects and growing his business VJS Consulting.

Barbara Sherrod

Barbara A. Sherrod, M.S. once an at-risk youth is dedicated to improving the quality of school life and community building for children of Baltimore through Restorative Practices. Through advocacy and whole school approach, Barbara educates school communities on discipline disparities, relationship building and achievement gaps among children based on race, gender and socioeconomic status. Barbara is currently researching how restorative practices can reverse the negative impact of social expectations placed on African American, Indigenous and Latina girls specifically. Through social platforms such as blogging in conjunction with dialogue circles, Barbara facilitates conversations around motherhood and what it means for Black and Brown millennial women like herself who became a mother at a young age. Barbara works at the Community Conferencing Center of Baltimore located in Baltimore City as Restorative Practices Specialist and is Co-Director of HollaBack! Baltimore, a non-profit committed to anti-street harassment. Baltimore born and raised, Barbara holds a Bachelor of Arts in English and a Master's of Science in Negotiations and Conflict Management both from the University of Baltimore.

Johonna McCants-Turner

Dr. Johonna McCants-Turner (she/her) is Associate Professor of Peace and Conflict Studies at Conrad Grebel University College at the University of Waterloo in Ontario, Canada. Her areas of scholarship and teaching include restorative and transformative justice, contemporary anti-violence movements, and narrative approaches to social change. She is interested in the ways contemporary Black women and youth define and organize against multiple forms of violence, and the ways liberatory Christian theologies nourish resistance to violence and injustice. Her first book, *In the Wake of Wounding: Black Womanist Ethics and Reparative Justice,* is in progress. As a trainer, scholar, board member, convenor, and co-learner, she has contributed to numerous social justice and community development organizations, and to collaborations, delegations, and multi-disciplinary projects around the world. She formerly served as the founding director of the Visions to Peace Project, a special education teacher with the District of Columbia Public Schools, and an adjunct professor at the University of Maryland, where she earned her PhD. She also holds a graduate certificate in Women's Studies from the University of Maryland and another graduate certificate from Fuller Theological Seminary. Dr. McCants-Turner serves on the advisory board of Life Comes From It, a U.S.-based grantmaking circle supporting restorative justice, transformative justice, and Indigenous peacemaking initiatives led by Black, Indigenous, People of Color.

Edward C Valandra, Waŋbli Wapháha Hokšíla (Eagle Bonnet Boy)

Edward Valandra is Sičáŋǧu Thitȟuŋwaŋ, born and raised on the Rosebud Sioux Reservation. He received a BA in chemistry from Mankato State University, an MA in political science (public policy) from the University of Colorado-Boulder, and a PhD in American Studies (Native Studies concentration) from SUNY-Buffalo. Both Vine Deloria, Jr., Húŋkpapȟa Thitȟuŋwaŋ, and John Mohawk, Seneca, were his committee chairs, respectively.

Edward has served his nation, the Sičáŋǧu Thitȟuŋwaŋ Oyáte, in various capacities. He served on the Rosebud Sioux Tribal Council (1985–89) and as a representative on the Inter-Tribal Bison Cooperative (ITBC) Board of Directors (1996–2000). He also served on his nation's seven-member Constitutional Task Force (2004–2006).

Dr. Valandra has taught at both Native and non-Native colleges and universities: Oglála Lakȟóta College, Siŋté Gleška University, Metropolitan State University (St. Paul, Minnesota), the University of California at Davis, and the University of South Dakota in Vermillion. His research focuses on the national revitalization of the Očhéthi Šakówiŋ Oyáte (People of the Seven Fires, commonly called the D/L/Nakȟóta People) and the development of Native Studies. In February, 2010, he was elected president of the American Indian Studies Association.

He has had numerous articles published. In 2006, the University of Illinois Press published his book on the "Termination Era" in the US and South Dakota, *Not Without Our Consent: Lakota Resistance to Termination, 1950–59*.

Edward is the founder and research fellow for the Community for the Advancement of Native Studies (CANS), a Native-government-chartered, research-based, reservation-rooted organization. Since 2003, he has served as an advisor to Living Justice Press on Native understandings of justice and on how to apply restorative justice to repairing longstanding, historical, and current harms between Peoples. In 2011, he became officially LJP's Senior Editor for Native Studies.

Anita Wadhwa

A native Houstonian, Anita Wadhwa has taught for 15 years and has been a restorative justice coordinator for nine years. Her book, *Restorative Justice in Urban Schools: Disrupting the School to Prison Pipeline,* outlines how the use of peace circles engages students emotionally and academically. Last year she co-authored *The Little Book of Youth Engagement in Restorative Justice,* which offers case studies of intergenerational work around liberation and restorative justice. She received her Ed.D from the Harvard Graduate School of Education and is available to consult at anitawadhwa.com. She owes everything to her parents, husband, and two lovely girls.

Sheryl R. Wilson

Sheryl R. Wilson holds a BS in mediation and Communication Studies and a restorative justice-based master of Liberal Studies from the University of Minnesota, Twin Cities. She is a resourceful facilitator and mediator, consistently recognized for building effective relationships.

Sheryl has been a practitioner, trainer, and educator in restorative justice for more than fifteen years. Beginning her restorative justice career as a trainer and research associate at the Center for Restorative Justice and Peacemaking in the School of Social Work at the University of Minnesota, Sheryl developed and facilitated "Victims, Offenders, Community: A Restorative Experience" (VOCARE) dialogues in Minnesota's correctional facilities. She also worked as a community mediator with the Victim Offender Conferencing program in Washington County, Minnesota. As a researcher, she was actively involved in the evaluation of the VOCARE prison-based program.

She has served as a special projects coordinator for the Georgia Council for Restorative Justice (GCRJ), a program of Georgia State University. As executive director of Southern Truth and Reconciliation (STAR of Atlanta, GA), she was able to work with communities affected by historical harm.

In the summer of 2008, Sheryl coordinated a group of victim-offender facilitators to serve as support people for witnesses who gave testimony to the Liberian Truth and Reconciliation Commission (TRC) during hearings for the United States Diaspora held at Hamline University in St. Paul, Minnesota. She continued working with a contingent of the Liberian TRC residing in the Atlanta area through her work as executive director of STAR.

Since 2017, Sheryl has been the director of KIPCOR, the Kansas Institute for Peace and Conflict Resolution, located in Newton, Kansas. Sheryl also serves as the president of the National Association of Community and Restorative Justice (NACRJ)

Robert G. Yazzie

Robert Yazzie is a citizen of and Chief Justice Emeritus of the Navajo Nation. He served as Chief Justice from 1992 through 2003. He practiced law in the Navajo Nation for sixteen years and was a district judge for eight years. He was formerly the director of the Diné Policy Institute of Diné College (Navajo Nation) developing policy using authentic Navajo thinking. He is a visiting professor at the University of New Mexico School of Law, an adjunct professor of the Department of Criminal Justice of Northern Arizona University, and a visiting member of the faculty of the National Judicial College. He recently taught Navajo law at the Crownpoint Institute of Technology.

Justice Yazzie earned a Bachelor of Arts degree from Oberlin College of Ohio, and a Juris Doctor degree from the University of New Mexico School of Law. He is a member of the Navajo Nation Bar Association. He is the author of articles and book chapters on many subjects, Navajo peacemaking, traditional Indian law, and international human rights law. His seminal article, "Life Comes From It," is a classic in restorative justice literature. Yazzie continues a career devoted to education in formal participation in faculties, lectures, and discussions of traditional Indigenous law at various venues throughout the world. He has a global audience and has frequently visited foreign lands to share his wisdom about traditional Indigenous justice and governance.

Index

E

F

G

H

I

J

K

L

M

N

O

P

Q

R

S

T

U

V

W

Y

Z

Books from Living Justice Press

Based on Dakȟóta homeland, now called Minnesota, Living Justice Press publishes books on restorative justice (RJ), focusing on the Circle process and its uses, on Indigenous restorative ways, and on applying restorative justice to addressing harms between Peoples.

On the Circle Process and Its Uses

Circle Forward: Building a Restorative School Community by Carolyn Boyes-Watson and Kay Pranis. By far LJP's bestseller to schools, *Circle Forward* provides Circle formats, models, and flows that bring Circles into every aspect of school life.

Creating Restorative Schools: Setting Schools Up to Succeed, by Martha Brown, offers an honest picture of what "doing restorative school" looks like, based on the experiences of two Oakland middle schools. A perfect companion to *Circle Forward.*

Circle in the Square: Building Community and Repairing Harm in School by Nancy Riestenberg. Another high seller to schools, *Circle in the Square* helps a school's adults understand what doing school restoratively means and looks like day to day.

Heart of Hope: A Guide for Using Peacemaking Circles to Develop Emotional Literacy, Promote Healing and Build Healthy Relationships by Carolyn Boyes-Watson and Kay Pranis. Like *Circle Forward, Heart of Hope* offers Circle plans designed to help students and adults develop social and emotional awareness and skills.

Peacemaking Circles: From Conflict to Community by Kay Pranis, Barry Stuart, and Mark Wedge. Often referred to as "the bible of Circles" for non-Indigenous people, *Peacemaking Circles* explores the inner and outer practice of Circles for those of us not raised in Circle-based cultures.

Peacemaking Circles and Urban Youth: Bringing Justice Home, by Carolyn Boyes-Watson, tells the story of how an innovative youth center used Circles not only with youth but also with families and communities as well as throughout the organization.

Doing Democracy with Circles: Engaging Communities in Public Planning by Jennifer Ball, Wayne Caldwell, and Kay Pranis. This book offers communities a means to arrive at good and often transformative resolutions when conflicts in planning arise.

Building a Home for the Heart: Using Metaphors in Value-Centered Circles by Patricia Thalhuber and Susan Thompson. Discussing values is the foundation of Circles and restorative practices; this book shows how to use metaphors to deepen that discussion.

On Indigenous Understandings of Justice

Justice As Healing: Indigenous Ways, edited by Wanda D. McCaslin. Drawing on a decade of writings on justice and community-based, healing responses to conflicts and crimes, this substantive book features forty-five articles from community members, scholars, judges, lawyers, and Elders, most of whom are Indigenous.

On Addressing Harms between Peoples

Colorizing Restorative Justice: Voicing Our Realities, edited by Edward C Valandra. Twenty authors of color turn the lens of critical racial awareness on how the RJ movement operates in funding, training, decision-making, doing the work, and choosing the harms that need repairing.

What Does Justice Look Like? The Struggle for Liberation in Dakota Homeland by Waziyatawin tells Minnesota's long-untold history of harms and what it has meant for the Dakȟóta People. The book explores how we can reverse the patterns of genocide, colonization, and oppression and instead do justice.

Indigenous Community: Rekindling the Teachings of the Seventh Fire by Greg Cajete "answers the most important education question today: What kind of pedagogy can maintain and revitalize the Indigenous peoples in the 21st century? Twofold: Comprehend Indigenous peoples' historical trauma and reclaim Indigenous ways," says Marie Battiste, Mi'kmaq First Nation, author and educator.

Indigenous Nations' Rights in the Balance: An Analysis of the Declaration on the Rights of Indigenous Peoples by Charmaine White Face. Nowhere else are the three versions of the UN Declaration on the Rights of Indigenous Peoples documented and the changes made analyzed for their impact on Indigenous Nations—their sovereignty and survival.

In the Footsteps of Our Ancestors: The Dakota Commemorative Marches of the 21st Century, edited by Waziyatawin Angela Wilson. "May this book be recognized as a part of the healing process that restorative justice champions and as bringing some understanding to the atrocities still inflicted on Dakȟóta people, for only with understanding can healing come," writes Harley Eagle, Dakȟóta, one who stands with restorative and peacemaking Indigenous ways.

He Sapa Woihanble: Black Hills Dream, edited by Craig Howe, Lydia Whirlwind Soldier, and Lanniko L. Lee. Twenty-three Očhéthi Šakówiŋ writers speak of the beauty and power of Ȟesápa, known as the Black Hills of South Dakota, as well as of the painful history of its appropriation by the United States.

From the River's Edge, by Elizabeth Cook-Lynn. "Seeing the Missouri River country of the Sioux is like seeing where the earth first recognized humanity...." Yet the White man's humanity is forcing wrenching change upon the land. Based on an actual trial, this novel offers an introspective appeal for Indigenous Peoples to retain their culture.

Harm-Dependent No More: Who Are We—Winners and Losers or Relatives? by Denise C. Breton (available in-progress on LJP's website). This book explores win-lose thinking, which claims that doing harm is the way to "win." In contrast, Indigenous philosophies center us on moral and scientific truth: We are all related. By calling for harms' repair, RJ embodies a paradigm shift: How can we move away from the win-lose model, and how can we move toward being good relatives to each other and all that is?

Please visit LJP's website for more information about these and other books, free downloads of Circle graphics, Circle practitioners and trainers, interviews with authors and practitioners, and the training schedules of LJP authors. Thank you for your support and for the restorative and Circle work you do.

www.livingjusticepress.org